The Intelligent LifeCycle Theory

By Thomas O. Mitchell

ILC Theory, LLC  Houston, TX

Copyright © 2012 by ILC Theory, LLC

All rights reserved. This book, or any portion thereof,
may not be reproduced in any form without
express written permission of ILC Theory, LLC,
except for use in quotations for book review purposes.

For information on quantity sales and member discounts,
please contact:

ILC Theory

P.O. Box 19584
Houston, TX 77224
www.ILCTheory.com

First Printing, 2012
Library of Congress Catalog Number 2012945240
ISBN-13: 978-0615673783

Printed in the United States of America

DEDICATION

Writing *The ILC Theory* was an arduous and seemingly infinite process at best, describing and defining the evolution, continuity and perpetuation of Intelligent Life in the Universe, for all eternity.

Therefore, *The Intelligent LifeCycle Theory* is dedicated to all Sapiens who are currently experiencing their individual LiveTimes during LifeCycles on Earth, and other Intelligent Planets around the Universe. For all those difficult situations in life that each of us face individually, as we progress through our LC journeys, *The Theory* gives logic and reasoning to an otherwise seemingly chaotic existence.

The Theory is also dedicated to all Sapiens currently in RestTimes in their respective subHalos, awaiting their next LifeCycles. It is the hope of this author that all Sapiens, in LiveTime and RestTime, may find a renewed sense of life and self worth in these words.

Forward
By Thomas Jordan

Since I worked on research for the ILC project with Tom Mitchell, I have been asked to write the forward to *The Intelligent LifeCycle Theory*. I was told I could take any approach I wanted. I chose to use the forward section of this book to offer a personal perspective on Mitchell, a brief summary and some observations about the current and future direction of *The Theory*.

Let me start by saying, I believe in *The Theory*, which is obvious, or I wouldn't be writing this forward. I have known Tom for many years. I respect his abilities and his judgment in most cases, within limits. On a couple of occasions, I disagreed with Tom's business direction as he evolved in his business ventures and his quest to write. And I told him so, but like he says, that's the road he took with his LifeCycle (LC), this time.

I have studied *The ILC Theory*, and agree with most of its observations and conclusions. I would like to offer some personal opinions about *The Theory* from an Earthling's perspective.

I thought I had a pretty good handle on the concept of infinity prior to *The Theory*, wrong. To understand infinity, you must first admit that it exists. But if you do that, are you not also saying it is definable, which means it is finite?

As stated in the book, "Intelligent life had no beginning and has no end." Well, I can get behind the idea that there is no end, but to think there was never a beginning, that is tough. I guess you just have to get past that, to see the big picture, as infinite as it is. As they say in religious circles, you just have to have faith. It had to have started somewhere. We are here, we are the proof.

And besides, however it all began, it was trillions and trillions of years ago, and does not really have any impact on *The Theory* except for historical reference. Intelligent life exists in the universe, and we are part of it, which postulates the very basis of the *The Theory's* axiom.

So, if intelligent life exists in an infinite capacity throughout the universe, how does that work? According to *The Theory*, it all starts with the Sapien (Intelligent Energy Field or soul), and its process of being recycled to experience LiveTimes on Intelligent Planets (IPs), specifically like Earth.

An innate trait of intelligent life is that it seems to prefer good to bad, virtue over evil and progress over regress. It is the natural order of intelligent things in the universe. So with a majority of Sapiens on Earth preferring good over bad, that infers that most of us do want to improve our Individual Character Traits (ICTs) and our Intelligence Module (IM), during our LiveTimes. Sapiens innately wish to improve their beings and the world around them during their LCs. Coincidentally, that is the underlying reasoning that makes *The Intelligent LifeCycle Theory* actually work.

So we have identified the infinite scope of intelligent life in the universe, and its attempt to improve itself through recurring Sapien LifeCycles on Earth and other IPs. These are truths that would seem to be self-evident in their creation, and are indigenous to *The Theory*.

The basic premise of *The ILC Theory* is that your Sapien has had multiple LifeCycles (multiple lives) over a period of many thousands, if not millions of years. If you have not had a number of previous lives, you probably would not be reading this book. During each LC, your ICTs and IM adapt to and learn from the specific environment and applicable sociopolitical forces in place during your LiveTimes.

For most of us, as we progressed through our previous lives, our ICTs and IMs have steadily improved with each LifeCycle. Every LC we get helps enhance our qualities as intelligent beings, always striving to be better. Not necessarily getting better, but always desirous of becoming better.

Well, that is the Sapien side of my comments. Now for some thoughts on Earth's LifeCycle. Since the Sapien's Intelligent LifeCycle is totally dependent on the IP's LifeCycle, there are some interesting things to consider about our planet's past and future, in reference to *The Theory*.

As a typical intelligent planet, Earth has gone through its own IP LifeCycle of being a barren planet, to life-supporting, to one that supports intelligent life, more than once. According to *The ILC Theory*, Earth has supported intelligent life before, way before.

Earth was considered a thriving and prospering intelligent planet maybe a few hundred million years or even a billion years ago, classified an Active IP. This is not Earth's first time to the rodeo folks.

There are several factors that can change a planet's ability to support intelligent life. They include atmospheric changes, orbital changes in the Earth-Moon-Sun dynamic, shifts in Earth's continental shelf, variations in our Sun's solar output and large meteorite collisions.

If Earth gets closer to the Sun, we burn up. If it drifts further away from the Sun, we get another Ice Age, which has already occurred in our planet's history, at least once that we know of. During any of these scenarios, Earth ceases to have the capacity to support intelligent life.

When this happens, the subHalo reclassifies Earth as an Inactive IP. That's the downside of the IP LifeCycle, until it cycles back to become an Active IP once again.

The disappearance of dinosaurs was an important factor in Earth's LifeCycle adding further understanding to *The Theory*. Dinosaurs were the dominant species on the planet for over 100 million years until their extinction some 65 million years ago.

According to Wikipedia, "The Cretaceous–Paleogene Extinction Event, often referred to as the Cretaceous–Tertiary Extinction Event, occurred approximately 65.5 million years ago." This "led to the extinction of most dinosaur groups. It was a large-scale mass extinction of animal and plant species."

Even though dinosaurs were the dominant terrestrial vertebrates, they did not have physical dexterity, agility or intelligence to constructively improve life. Consequently dinosaurs were not intelligent beings, so Earth was not on the radar screen in the subHalo as a Sapien source nor Sapien destination planet. During the dinosaur era, Earth was classified as an In-Active IP.

We have been an 'Active IP' this time for at least the last few million years or so, since the prehistoric caveman era. Our planet has progressed from those early days as a C1 IP to the C4 IP we are today. Earth only has three more C-levels (C5-C7) it can progress to as an intelligent planet. That is of course, if our planet continues with its current IP LifeCycle long enough for that amount of Sapien maturation to accrue.

Considering Earth's current C4 IP status, it is expected that we still have a long way to go before advancing to the C5 IP level. It may take another hundred or so years for Earth to make the jump to C5. We can only imagine what Earth will be like as it advances to that level, possibly within the next couple of Sapien LifeCycle generations.

Future Sapien LifeCycles may enjoy all kinds of new technologies that will create their own brand of ICT events for Sapiens to experience. Undoubtedly transportation and communications will be drastically different than today. They will be faster and more readily available, of course.

Will this provide for more Sapien free-time to interact with other Sapiens? Or, will it make it easier for Sapiens to avoid physical contact with others? And if the latter is the case, what will that do to the reproductive rates among Sapiens?

Reduced birth rates on C5 IPs are a natural side effect, as the Sapien populations enjoy an expanded base of interests and leisure, without regard to having babies. Some countries on Earth are already experiencing a semblance of population implosions.

Imagine a world where there is no cancer, most everything is solar powered, star travel is not yet common but not uncommon either, and the average Sapien lifespan is over one hundred years. We may see some of those things as a C5 planet. We may not see star travel until we progress to C6 or C7 IP status.

The ILC Theory is definitely all about the future. Past LCs are just that, they are in the past. *The Theory* gives us the opportunity to understand a little bit better how our current LifeCycle actually fits with our individual futures. It can provide a roadmap to understanding our strengths and weaknesses as Sapiens. It might also increase our understanding of the impact our LCs have on our overall development as intelligent beings.

As we enjoy our LiveTimes on Earth, we all face many obstacles and challenges during our LCs provided of course that Earth is still here next year. I agree with *The ILC Theory* that the 2012 doomsday theories are unfounded. When the upcoming new year comes and goes, and we are still here, we will know. I am sure someone will soon set a new doomsday date. And if the 2012 doomsday prediction is right, like Tom says, "Then never mind."

As I look at what appears to be a fairly standard IP LifeCycle, it seems that certain eras and periods of growth are necessary in a planet's evolution. We had the ice age, the dinosaurs and the caveman. When it looked like Earth might be developing its Sapien population in the wrong direction, god and religion were introduced to get it back on track.

As we evolved as an intelligent planet over the last few thousand years, since the introduction of formalized religion, our average ICT and IM levels have continued to increase. As we Sapiens evolve, our belief systems also evolve.

Perhaps now is the time in Earth's life cycle for *The ILC Theory* to be introduced. Maybe it is the normal evolution of an IP to expand its understanding of intelligent life at this time in its historical development as an IP. I hope you enjoy *The Theory*.

Good luck with your current and future LifeCycles,
                                                              TJ

Contents

#	Chapter	Page
1	Introduction	1
2	ILC Theory Basics	9
3	Sapien & Intelligent Energy Field	31
4	Sapien CORE	91
5	Individual Character Traits (ICTs)	107
6	HALO & subHalos	171
7	Universal Energy Network	207
8	Sapien LifeCycle	225
9	Intelligent Planets & the Universe	281
10	Body & Sapien	309
11	The Theory & Religion	337
12	Individual Sapien Analysis Testing	347
13	ILC Theory Summation	371
14	About the Author	391
15	Appendix	399

The Intelligent LifeCycle Theory

Introduction

If you have ever thought about what happens to you when you die, you are certainly not alone. There are many religions, theories and beliefs with far-reaching implications and many diverse theoretical consequences. All are unproven and all are just that, theories and beliefs. Not to minimize theories and beliefs, to the contrary, these two components are vital to intelligent life, and indeed, one of the primary tests in defining intelligent life.

So in order to answer this age-old question, "What happens when you die?", we must first answer some basic questions. "What is your Soul or Spirit? Where did it come from? When did it arrive? Why did you get the soul you have? Is your soul unique? And, where does it go, when you die?" *The Intelligent Life Cycle (ILC) Theory* provides answers to these questions, and much more.

People (Earth humans) have been trying to find answers to these questions for a very long time. There have been reports that bodies have been weighed directly before and directly after death, with claims that the body weighs approximately .025 mg less after death, theoretically after the soul/spirit has left the body.

Reports also indicate that the Spirit has been photographed leaving the body upon death, through infrared spectrometry. Even before photographic technology, before there were cameras, centuries ago, artists painted graveyard settings showing the spirit as it rises from the dead body in the grave, portraying 'Ghosts' rising from the graves.

Thoughts of the afterlife have been around since the beginning of mankind, this time as we know it. Most mainstream religions, such as Christianity, Judaism and Islam do not espouse reincarnation, but do tout life after death in a variety of scenarios, whether it be Heaven, Hell, Limbo, Paradise, or somewhere in between. There are a number of other religions around the globe that do include some version of reincarnation in their belief structure.

The ILC Theory goes way beyond traditional reincarnation theory and incorporates the how's and why's of the entire life cycle process. Integral components of *The Theory* have some resemblance to components of current religions, including heaven, hell, limbo, souls, sin, good, evil, birth, death, the Ten Commandments, and of course gods and angels.

The ILC Theory is not intended to be any form of a new religion. Please do not try to make it one. It is just as the name says, it is *The*

Intelligent Life Cycle Theory. It is a comprehensive theory explaining the evolution, perpetuation and continuity of Intelligent Life in the universe and beyond, based on scientific concepts and precepts.

It is often quoted that 85 percent of this world's population believes in a god, a supreme higher power that controls the evolutionary process of man on Earth. What about evolution for the rest of the universe? What about the other worlds in the universe that support intelligent life forms, some even more advanced than ours?

In preparation for writing this book, a significant amount of research was done to provide authenticated proof of concept, utilizing existing scientific and philosophical methodologies. In addition, no other theory could be found that specifically describes how the evolution of Intelligent Life in the universe actually functions. No theories found among faith-based religions, non-religious after-life concepts, nor scientific theorem even hinted at how a phenomenon such as life after death would work.

Therefore, the consensus of opinion is that *The Intelligent LifeCycle Theory* is a first. *The ILC Theory* is the first and only theory that specifically addresses how LifeCycles work. *The Theory* also answers in detail the who, when, where and why questions that surround this infinitely important topic.

What Are The Odds?

You have to remember there are trillions and trillions of star systems in the universe. Current scientific knowledge indicates the universe, as we know it, is thought to be comprised of ten Sextillion (10^{22}) star systems, which equates to one million trillion stars. That is just an estimate of course. To understand the source of intelligent life, its development, evolution, perpetuation and eternal maintenance, we must first attempt to understand the requirements for, and the probabilities of, Intelligent Life in the universe.

If we conservatively assume that only $1/100^{th}$ of one percent of all star systems (99.99 percent do not) have planets that can support life. And we then assume only $1/100^{th}$ of one percent of those planets (99.99 percent do not) support Intelligent Life, by our calculations, there are 100 trillion worlds capable of supporting intelligent life, just in our universe.

If Earth is in the top $1/100^{th}$ of one percent of those planets that have intelligent life, there are ten billion planets with intelligent life equal to or surpassing that of Earth. These highly conservative numbers, according to most statisticians, theorists and scientists, would arguably be a safe assumption, if there is such a thing in astrophysics.

And this is assuming there is only one universe. What if there are multiple universes, or even multiple universes that co-exist in the same spatial void in different time dimensions?

To comprehend the premise of these theories, you need to think in terms of *infinity*. Current scientific theory of the universe attempts, both in space and time dimensions, to rationalize infinity, which may sound like an oxymoron. However, mankind continues to probe, expand and measure space, as if it were a finite entity of infinite proportions.

So, if life in the universe is in fact infinite, how can we measure its existence and the requirements needed to sustain its evolution? The answer is, we don't have to. The physical universe is constantly nurture the Sapien from birth to death, if you only get one shot at life, one life to live, never to be re-lived again. And, as a result of only that one life, however short it may be, you either get it right, or you do not get it right. You either go to heaven or hell, one or the other, and as a not-so-fully developed spirit after only one lifetime.

If there are no second chances, re-takes or do-overs, that just cannot be right. Since Intelligent Life is energy, and energy cannot be created nor destroyed, only reallocated between hosts, the Sapien (soul) must go somewhere, when you die. And it must come from somewhere, when you are born.

Wouldn't it be nice to get a do-over, a second chance at life, or a third, or fourth, or tenth? *The ILC Theory* shows you how that's possible, and why it's probable. *The Theory* illustrates why the perpetuation of Intelligent Life is absolutely critical to the existence of mankind on Earth, and indeed crucial to the very survival of Intelligence throughout the universe.

The Intelligent LifeCycle Theory

② ILC Theory Basics

The evolution of Intelligent Life in the universe has been occurring for millions, billions, even trillions of years. So the question of how it all began is a moot point to say the least. There may not be a 'Supreme Being' that actually invented mankind with Adam and Eve, but yet there has to be a controlling force that operates the functionality of Intelligent Life in the universe.

Is there one, final being, that controls everything? Yes and no, but probably not in reference to the physical evolution of the universe, which has been evolving for eternity. *The ILC Theory* only deals with the evolution of Intelligent Life in the universe, not the physical evolution of the universe itself.

It has been reported that approximately eighty-five percent of the world's population believe in a god. *The Theory* incorporates a number of components with functionality similar to those of traditional religions, components that are indeed vital to *The Theory*.

There are three primary scientific theories that explain the evolution of mankind on Earth, and to some degree, the physical expansion of the universe; (1) Determinism, (2) Randomness and (3) Free Will. Each of these three theories has its own inherent deficiency, in that it precludes the other two.

Determinism says that everything is connected by way of everything else in the cycle of life. It states there is a cause-and-effect relationship for everything that happens. Everything has an order to it. Everything is determined.

Randomness promotes the idea that every event that happens is a result of a random set of occurrences, that, when combined, produces an unpredictable and unrelated result. There is no plan, no purpose, everything just happens coincidentally. Even in the scientific community, there are those who subscribe to the theory that everything just happens, without rhyme or reason, without logic or predictability. Everything that happens in the universe is just coincidence.

Free Will takes the position that free will and determinism are logically incompatible, and that, free will and randomness are mutually exclusive. If everything is pre-determined, free will cannot exist, and if everything is random, free will has no impact on the outcome. *See Determinism, Randomness and Free Will in Appendix.*

Movie Quote: "*Knowing*", 2009, Nicolas Cage, an Astrophysics Professor at MIT, succinctly described his belief on the subject to his class, "I think...., shit just happens...., but that's me."

If *The ILC Theory* became the fourth scientific theory of man's evolution, it could be called *Intergyism* (Intelligent energy-ism), or just *Intelligent Life*, which has components of all the other three theories of evolution. The evolutionary cycle of Intelligent Life is based on determinism. The growth of Intelligent Life is influenced by free will. And random events positively and negatively affect the growth of intelligence, including the SH (Sh*t Happens) Factor.

Because of the miraculous nature of life and intelligence throughout the universe, there has to be a controlling entity or group of controlling entities to perpetuate the *Intelligent LifeCycle*. Such a complex and fully integrated cycle of life, by definition, has to have some semblance of control and order to its existence and thereby its successful evolution.

The name, *Intelligent LifeCycle (ILC)*, connotates a journey taken by 'intelligent life entities' throughout the universe and indeed throughout time itself. *The Intelligent LifeCycle Theory* provides scientific and mathematical logic to the LifeCycle (LC) process that does in fact go way beyond traditional reincarnation beliefs. *The ILC Theory* is comprised of a number of components, all integrated into a system that is critical to the perpetuation of Intelligent Life.

These components validate answers as to the 'how, what, when, where and why' questions surrounding Intelligent Life. It encompasses the entire LifeCycle of the Sapien, the Intelligent Energy Field (IEF). *The Theory* addresses Sapien evolution from pre-birth, to birth, to life, to death, and re-birth again. *The Theory* applies to humans on Earth and other intelligent beings on other Intelligent Planets (IPs) in the Milky Way and in other Galaxies around the universe.

The Theory was developed during the Technology Age (latter twentieth and early twenty-first centuries) and the resultant Age of Acronyms. Since this is a statistical and scientific theory, not a religious one, it makes more sense to refer to the ILC components with descriptive acronyms, rather than one or two-word cutesy names fabricated for

The Intelligent LifeCycle Theory

better market acceptance, such as Google, no offense. So, please be patient with our sometimes seemingly overuse of acronyms in describing *The Intelligent LifeCycle Theory*.

Intelligent LifeCycle components provide functionality and reason to concepts, precepts and theorem that exist in current scientific and religious beliefs. Initially, the comparison chart below should help in understanding some of ILC's unique terminology.

ILC Terminology Comparisons

ILC Component	Current Equivalency
ILC Theory	Evolution of Mankind
Sapien	Soul/Spirit
ICTs	Individual Character Traits, Personality, Mind, Psyche
Halo/subHalos	Heaven
LifeCycle (LC)	Reincarnation
Sapien L10s	Perfection, God
Sapien L9s	Near perfect, Angels
Positive Sapiens	Good Souls/Spirits
Negative Sapiens	Evil Souls/Spirits
Positive ICTs	Spiritual Fulfillment
Negative ICTs	Sin
10 Rules of Intelligent Life	4 of 10 Commandments
StarSpeed	Trillion x speed of light
TetraCell	1 trillionth of a cell

(See ILC Terminology in Appendix)

The above chart illustrates ILC terminology as it relates to current concepts, ideologies and their equivalent translations.

The Intelligent LifeCycle Theory

The table below identifies new terminology used during discussions and mathematical calculations in *The ILC Theory*.

ILC Terminology – New Terms

ILC Component	Current Equivalency
Dark TetraMatter	none (trillion x density of dark matter)
ICT Event	live, experiential situation during LC
Sapien/IEF Level Ratings	none
Star Speed	none (1 trillion x Speed of Light)
TetraCell	none (1 trillionth of a cell)
Tetricity	none (trillion x load capacity of electricity)
Tetrical Ionic Charge	none (trillion x density of electricity)
Tetronic Charge	none (unique per IEF)
Universal Energy Network	none (UENet)

Three Levels of Life

In order to understand intelligent life, we must also understand the other forms of life that support and coexist with intelligent life. Life, in its purest form, connotes the growth of a living thing with an expected evolutionary cycle. More specifically, life is an animate being in an organismic state, characterized by a capacity for metabolism, growth, reaction to stimuli, and reproduction. This precludes inanimate objects such as rocks.

Dirt cannot be included as an inanimate object, since there are millions of microscopic life forms resident in dirt. Otherwise, dirt and rocks are considered non-life forms.

The Intelligent LifeCycle Theory

Life is a self-evolving cycle of events and experiences that guide a living thing from birth to death, from conception to expiration, from beginning to end. Life, as we know it, consists of three primary groups. Not to minimize the categorization systems that are used to inventory all life, for purposes of *The Theory*, the following are the three primary groups of life that affect the evolution of intelligent life.

The *first group*, which is the vast majority of living things in the universe, is comprised of vegetative and low-level biological organisms that exist to provide support for other living things or beings in the form of food and shelter. This group functions as a primary food source for mobile life forms and is consistent with the 'balance of nature' syndrome, while providing the aesthetic benefit of the beauty of nature.

Group two in the 'chain of life' is the animal kingdom, which feed on the first group, but also exist as food sources for bigger, stronger animals. Animals, unlike vegetative life forms, have the advantage of mobility, giving them some semblance of control over their nourishment and growth potential as living beings.

The vast majority of beings classified as animals use their physical capabilities and movement skills primarily to gather sustenance for survival on a daily basis. No thought processes are needed at the animal level, other than getting food and shelter to continue their growth and existence.

The small brain capacity at the animal level is primarily dominated by pure survival instincts for the animal and their young. Smaller animals also maintain their position as a food source for species higher up the chain of life. And of course, some of the larger animals and fish, such as Lions, Tigers and Sharks will feed on smaller species higher up the evolutionary chain, such as mammals, if given the opportunity.

The *ILC Theory* only deals with intelligent life evolution, and does not deal with the lower species of life, that are used to support the intelligent species. In that regard, the energy fields of animals, fish, fowl and insects are static and non-evolving. The criteria for a being to possess its own intelligence is simple. Is that 'being' capable of thought? And can that being use that process of thought to evolve basic Individual Character Traits (ICTs)? This thought process, not memory, separates humanoids from other animals. All animals that have a brain have memory capabilities, to varying degrees, but only intelligent beings have the ability to reason and think in the abstract.

The *third group* of living things is referred to as *Intelligent Life*. In defining intelligent life, the distinction between physical and mental capabilities of a species is certainly the place to start. Can a life-form think, theorize in abstract terms and create something non-material that can then be materially communicated to others in the species?

Intelligent life requires logic and reasoning that is separate from the physical prowess of the species. In the case of mankind on Earth, we began theorizing and communicating with each other thousands, if not millions of years ago. We have developed as a species to the point of communicating on a very sophisticated level, or so we think, with such mediums as print, sound and visual. Someday mental telepathy or some other derivative may be added to our communications skills, as a result of our scientific and technological advancements.

If a species exhibits such mental and communications abilities, then that species is capable of and requires Intelligent Life to evolve, such as *homo sapiens* on Earth. Given that mankind is an intelligent species, whose actions sometimes indicate otherwise, what is the possibility that other intelligent beings exist in the universe? Can Earth be the only intelligent planet? Are we alone?

Intelligent Life Quantified

Is Earth a unique intelligent planet? Yes, and no. Are we more advanced than other planets in the universe? Yes and no, The table below illustrates how we can quantify Intelligent Life in the universe.

SIZE OF THE UNIVERSE
Basic Scientific Assumptions
A. More than one hundred billion (10^{11}) galaxies contain hundreds of billions of stars each.
B. With 10^{11} galaxies and 10^{11} stars/galaxy, there are 10^{22} stars in the Universe.

Conservative ILC Assumptions	
Stars in Universe: 10 Sextillion (10^{22})	10,000,000,000,000,000,000,000
99.99% of Star Systems Cannot Support Life	0.01%
Stars with min.1 Planet Supporting Life	1,000,000,000,000,000,000
	1 quintillion (10^{18}) Planets
99.99% of those Cannot Support Intelligent Life	0.01%
Planets Supporting Intelligent Life	100,000,000,000,000
	100 trillion (10^{12}) Planets
99.99% of those with Less Intelligence than Earth	0.01%
Intelligent Planets equal to or greater than Earth	10,000,000,000
	10 billion (10^9) Planets
00.01% of those with more Intelligence than Earth	0.01%
Intelligent Planets more advanced than Earth	1,000,000

If Earth is more advanced than 99.999999% of all IPs in the Universe, there are 1 million planets more advanced than earth. If Earth is more advanced than only 99% of all Intelligent Planets, there would be more than 1 trillion planets more intelligent than Earth.

"WE ARE DEFINITELY NOT ALONE!"

Copyright 2012 © ILC Theory, LLC. Printed in the USA. All rights reserved.

The Intelligent LifeCycle Theory

Yes, Earth is unique, because the composition, planet structure and evolution of every planet is different than the others to some degree. However, Earth is not unique, because it is an intelligent planet. And yes, Earth is more advanced than some planets, but less advanced than others.

The previous chart provides estimates for the number of intelligent planets (IPs) in the universe, based on current scientific knowledge, and highly conservative ILC assumptions. Even with such conservative estimates as these, *The ILC Theory* projects there are at least one million intelligent planets more advanced than Earth.

Over the last few years, scientists have increased their estimates of the number of stars in our universe, from one hundred sextillion to three hundred sextillion stars. Consistent with its conservative approach to data, *The ILC Theory* uses the more conservative number of only one hundred sextillion stars.

Consider this: The highly conservative estimate of one million planets, more advanced than us, assumes there is only one universe. What is outside our universe, nothing? Wrong, there are more universes, resulting in what *The Theory* refers to as a 'SuperVerse', which is a universe of universes.

Using the same 10^{11} theory as scientists have used to extrapolate the size of our universe, a superverse would be comprised of 10^{11} universes. We are way past infinity here, even though 10^{11} universes is a finite number. As shown in the previous Size of the Universe chart, *"We are definitely not alone!"*

So as we analyze intelligence in the universe, we can only use our own existence as a standard, from which to evaluate. *The ILC Theory*, therefore, focuses entirely on humanoid-type beings, who have a brain, two legs, two arms and mobility. Humanoids walk upright, breathe air/oxygen, require food and water to live, possess communication skills, and require a Sapien with intelligence to function, regardless of their intelligent planet of origin.

Other species such as four-legged animals, fish and fowl do not have the capacity nor the need for an intelligence component. They merely exist as a food source, recreation and/or entertainment purposes for humans.

And of course, the perpetuation of such non-Intelligent life forms on a planet such as Earth is necessary to maintain the planet's ecosystem. Such a delicate balance in nature is required to support the physical and mental needs of intelligent beings, during growth stages of *The Intelligent LifeCycle*.

The basic assumption of intelligent life is that all intelligent entities are individual and unique from others in the same species. The actual intelligence component requires a living, physical body from which to function and develop through the entire LifeCycle from conception to death. The term for this entity, in today's religious parlance, is the soul, which operates the physical host it occupies.

Such an entity, as invisible as it may be, exists in each person as 'pure energy' for the purpose of not only growing the body and operating the brain, but also to further develop the capabilities of its own unique energy field. The soul, in ILC vernacular, is called the Sapien. Every person has a Sapien, and every person's Sapien is unique.

Intelligent LifeCycle Logic

The LifeCycle for a Sapien begins after conception and before birth. On Earth, when a woman gets pregnant, she can sustain the growth of the embryo with her own energy field up to a certain point. And at that time, near the beginning of the second trimester, the new little fetus requires its own energy field to continue to grow. The mother cannot give up any more of her own energy field, or she will die.

This creates a void in the womb for a new source of energy. This void can only be filled by a newly acquired Intelligent Energy Field (IEF), or Sapien, from the *Universal Energy Field* (UEF), which religions call heaven. As The Theory evolved, UEF was replaced by HALO (Holistically Ascending Life Cycle Oasis) to encompass a broader range of attributes. *See Halo/subHalo chapter.*

As in all Sapien transfers, timing is critical. If the soon-to-be newborn does not receive this energy infusion in time, via the *Universal Energy Network* (UENet), the fetus will die, unless the mother gives up her own energy field.

Example: A mother dies during birth or in the last trimester, and the baby lives. Because the mother's fetus did not receive the Sapien infusion in time, the mother, unknowingly of course, gives up her own energy field to the child. When this infrequent tragedy occurs, it is expected that the child will have more of a predominance of the mother's character traits than normal.

Example: The mother lives, but the baby is still born. Much of the time, but not always, this tragedy also occurs because the baby's Sapien didn't arrive in time.

The Intelligent LifeCycle Theory

This focuses on the fact that for all its technology and advanced intelligence, the Halo, subHalos and UENet are not infallible. Timing discrepancies can and do occur during the Sapien selection and delivery processes. However, of the millions of Sapiens being distributed to newborns every year, chances for a Sapien timing discrepancy is extremely low.

In a normal LifeCycle on Earth, when the body of a human dies, its Sapien (soul) remains intact. And since it is pure energy, it cannot be destroyed, nor created, only relocated between hosts.

Because of its unique *tetronic charge* (tetrical ionic charge), the Sapien is pulled up to the subHalo for rejuvenation and inventory processing to await recycling to the next life. When a Sapien is recycled, it is drawn down into a pregnant woman's womb to populate the fetus.

The newborn will have some mental characteristics and mannerisms of both parents, but will also have many of its own character traits from its previous lives. The combinations of these traits in a Sapien are the deciding factors as to his or her normalcy, or more specifically, the Sapien's level of acceptable behavior as viewed by society. And of course, societal standards change as Sapien LifeCycles evolve.

Example: A serial killer, by today's standards, would be considered significantly below normal. However, in the 'caveman era', violence and killing were considered strengths.

As a Sapien progresses through its LifeCycles, it adapts to new social environments, customs and behavior. During each LC, the Sapien's *Individual Character Traits* (ICTs) are enhanced or diminished based on experiences gained during that LCs LiveTime. The cumulative tetronic charge of the Sapien's ICT Set greatly influences the overall development of the Sapien as an intelligent entity.

As its ICT Set improves, a Sapien can expect more favorable conditions during future LCs, because as the Sapien progresses to higher levels, its advancements are irrevocable and permanent. The goal of the Halo and its UENet is to continually enhance and develop all Sapiens toward perfection, which of course will never be reached.

During LifeCycles, as Sapiens improve, their value in future LCs increases, especially as it relates to the increased development of technology on Intelligent Planets (IPs). As Sapiens develop, through their LCs, they are able to continually improve the lifestyle of the worlds they inhabit, which in turn positively affects the entire Intelligent LifeCycle of the universe.

Technology development cycles on IPs provide better quality worlds, from which to foster higher-level Sapiens. More advanced worlds also offer better living conditions and more unique ICT-building events, as destination planets, from which lower-level Sapiens can evolve.

Sapien Rating System

As a Sapien progresses through its LifeCycles and continues to enhance its ICT Set, it develops a unique tetronic charge, which represents its level of development as an Intelligent Energy Field. This tetronic charge is unique to each Sapien and constantly changes during LiveTime as a result of experiences gained during an LC. The Sapien's tetronic charge emits its unique signal measured to the centillion decimals (10^{-303}), which directly correlates to its Sapien development rating.

The Intelligent LifeCycle Theory

The following chart identifies the Sapien's natural order of evolution, from origination as an L0 to perfection as an L10.

SAPIEN DEVELOPMENT RATING SCALE			
LEVEL	**% Completion**	**IEF Rating**	**Evolution Status**
L0	0%	0.00	New, uncirculated
L1	1% - 9%	1.0 to 1.99	Lowest, except for new
L2	10% - 29%	2.0 to 2.99	Low
L3	30% - 39%	3.0 to 3.99	Below average
L4	40% - 49%	4.0 to 4.99	Average
L5	50% - 59%	5.0 to 5.99	Above average
L6	60% - 69%	6.0 to 6.99	Very developed
L7	70% - 79%	7.0 to 7.99	Highly developed
L8	80% - 89%	8.0 to 8.99	Wisdom, little future growth
L9	90% - 99%	9.0 to 9.99	Near Perfect, little future growth
L10	100%	10.00	Perfect, no future growth

The ILC Theory specifically addresses humanoid–type intelligent beings only, and uses technology and mathematical progressions to tell the story of Mankind's evolution. The above unique rating scale is used to describe the various levels of development, for all Sapiens.

Example: A Sapien with a percentage completion of 53 percent of all its ICTs would have an overall ICT Rating of 5.3. Combining its ICT scores with its Intelligence Module (IM) and Parental Overlay Module (POM) ratings, that Sapien may have an overall L5.5 rating.

Of course, for each Sapien to be unique in its own development cycle and uniquely addressable in the UENet, these ratings are carried out to the centillionth decimal place. The above L5.5 rating might actually be $5.51912038420123 \times 10^{-289}$.

Example: A Sapien, with a cumulative tetronic charge of 5.69403939931120 x 10^{-289}, is approximately 57 percent complete as an Intelligent Energy Field. It is referred to as an L five dot seven (L5.7) Sapien and considered above average by Earth comparisons.

When a Sapien's LC is terminated (death), the Sapien becomes available for pick up by the UENet, which is constantly polling the intelligent planets in the universe. The Sapien, by its unique tetronic charge (L rating), is pulled up to the UENet and transported to the nearest subHalo, servicing that particular galaxy. Keep in mind, this automatically happens within seconds after death.

Upon arrival to the subHalo, the Sapien is inventoried, rejuvenated and stored in the L section most appropriate to its rating. While awaiting the next LC, the Sapien enjoys much needed 'RestTime'.

Earth is serviced by the MilkyWay subHalo, which resides at the center of the galaxy, referred to as the Milky Way's Black Hole. Current scientific knowledge leads us to think all galaxies are thought to have a black hole at their center.

ILC Confirmation: All galaxies do have a 'black hole' at their center. This is the obvious location for the subHalo in each galaxy. The concentration of super dark TetraMatter in the so-called black hole provides maximum protection for the subHalo, its operations and the trillions of resident Sapiens.

These black holes at the center of each galaxy are essential. Without this protection, Intelligent Life in the universe would be subject to any and all external forces of the universe for its survival.

Sapien Transfer Process

Back on Earth, when a fetus reaches the second trimester, it requires its own energy field. A temporary energy field is resident in the fetus, provided by both parents, and lives off of the mother's energy source. This results in a temporary physical deterioration of the mother, known as 'morning sickness', which is her body protecting the fetus from toxins ingested in food, while the fetus builds its own immune system.

As the fetus grows and its gender becomes identifiable, the little baby begins to require more energy than the mother can afford to give up. At that point, the fetus' energy field sends out a signal to the UENet, with its minimum Sapien requirements, based on gender, ICT and IM ratings of both parents. This is called the *Parental Overlay*, which becomes part of the Sapien.

Based on the unique tetronic void in the womb, the subHalo selects and transmits an available Sapien to fill the void. The match between the fetus request and the available Sapien is generally a good fit with similar intelligence levels and ICT development percentages to those of the Parental Overlay.

This coincides with the time that a mother stops having her morning sickness. Her own Sapien is freed up from doubling as the Sapien to the fetus, which by now has developed its own immune system to ward off toxins from the food the mother eats. The entire evolutionary cycle of intelligence in the universe is all about timing, even though time itself may seem infinitely inconsequential. Why should the beginning of LiveTime in an LC be any different?

Example: At the moment when the little fetus needs its own energy field (second trimester), it sends out a signal requesting a Sapien to match as closely as possible its parents' attributes. The gender of the fetus is the first prerequisite that needs to be fulfilled. The parents, both of whom have had a number of LCs themselves, have Sapien ratings of L4.5 and L4.8. The UENet selects an L4.7 Sapien with similar ratings to those of the parents and the same gender as the fetus. The match is good, and a healthy baby is born with intelligence and character traits approximating those of the parents.

Example: The same scenario as above, except that the UENet, based on time constraints and Sapien inventory availability, sends down an L5.9 Sapien. Such dissimilarities are not that uncommon and are acceptable. However as the little baby grows up and continues to enhance its already advanced ICT Set, he or she may have certain characteristics that are unlike the parents. Regardless, the Sapien offspring generally has a fondness and respect for both current parents during an LC, more so than with any other relationship between two Sapiens, primarily due to the Parental Overlay component.

However, as we have shown, the Halo and UENet are not infallible in the process of completing a successful Sapien transfer. Because of the sheer volume of Sapien traffic and other time constraints, the transfer must take place in a matter of seconds. Occasionally, time delays and differences in scheduling negatively affect Sapien transfer timings and result in mismatched Sapiens.

Example: A child's musical ability progresses at an early rapid rate. The child becomes a concert pianist prodigy at the age of five, with very little characteristics in common with its mortal parents. This exceptional ability deviated dramatically from the less-developed Parental Overlay in the original Sapien request.

Such a child that significantly excels in one area may have significant deficiencies in other ICTs that need work. However, a person growing up with this kind of special talent may not have time for experiences in other areas that will develop the deficient ICTs.

Example: At the far end of the spectrum, there are individuals we refer to as 'savants', who lack any semblance of social or communications skills, but have one unexplainable unique expert skill, usually in the area of mathematics, music or art. Such Sapiens may be L1.0s in all other areas except for the one area of proficiency. In such a child, most of the Sapien's focus is on that one trait, since the other traits are not yet very developed.

When a Sapien is absorbed into a little baby fetus, it adapts to the ICTs of the Parental Overlay already in the fetus, as the temporary energy life force. If its ICTs are less developed than the parents, then the Sapien might get some free development enhancements to more closely match those ICTs of the Parental Overlay. It will indirectly benefit from the parents' experiences gained from their current and past LCs. This Sapien will grow up with more reverence and respect for its parents, and may look up to the parents more as role models.

However, the Sapien that comes in with equal or higher ICTs than the parents may not be as reliant on the parents and may have less parental interaction growing up. Such a Sapien may begin to show outward appearances as an independent thinker, or maybe even a rebel.

ICT Events

During each LC, during each life, we understand, learn and practice things to do, and things not to do. This learning curve provides many developmental possibilities for enhancements to specific sets of ICTs.

A LiveTime experience that affects an ICT is referred to as an *ICT Event*. During the course of an LC, a Sapien will have many thousands of ICT events that will continue to shape the overall development of its ICT Set.

As a LifeCycle progresses, the Sapien may experience up-and-down spikes in its ICT development. Hopefully, at the end of each LC, the Sapien's development cycle moves upward, slowly but surely, as the completion percentages of its character traits improve. It's important to remember, all Sapiens are being recycled for their own individual development needs. All LC assignments are gender specific, race neutral and generally within the same species.

Example: During an LC, a Sapien improves its rating from an L4.9 to an L5.4, a very significant half-point improvement. When the Sapien is returned to the subHalo, it goes back as an L5.4 and is then available for more high-end L5 searches. Prior to the LC, the Sapien was only available for L4 selections, unless of course a mismatch occurred.

As a Sapien progresses at its own overall development rate, attributes of its energy field change (hopefully positively) and may make it more attractive to the next level of Sapiens. Thus, it will migrate toward that group in the subHalo. It is the old adage of 'likes attract'. It is an automatic grouping phenomenon that increases the efficiency of the subHalo and UENet.

The same concept also seems to apply to Sapiens during their LC LiveTimes. In most major metropolitan areas in the United States, there is a China town, where a large percentage of the Chinese population in that city live, work and play. Other racially-aligned communities exist to accommodate their populations as well.

Whites, blacks, and Hispanics seem to congregate in certain parts of a metroplex, even though these three races have begun to integrate within current society over the last few decades. Of course, as the Sapien levels improve in a society, this built-in and self-fulfilling segregation of Sapiens becomes less important, even though it is the natural evolution of a species and races within a species to voluntarily segregate themselves.

The overall assumption of *The Theory* is that the Halo, UENet and Intelligent LifeCycles in the universe function primarily to enhance and expand the capabilities of the Sapien population in the eternal quest for seemingly unattainable perfection. Ultimately however, it is up to the individual Sapien and the exercise of its free-will component during LCs to actively pursue activities that will enhance its ICT ratings and improve its overall Sapien rating. As you may have surmised by now, the Sapien is the most important component to *The ILC Theory*. Its evolution is the sole reason for everything else in the metaphysical universe.

Think of your ILC journey during this and future LifeCycles as working toward your retirement, over many lifetimes. Each time, you get to be young, grow up and become old all over again, if you are lucky. Then, when you reach L8 Sapien status or above, you have really earned a full retirement. And the beauty of this system of intelligence in the universe is that it lets you keep doing it over and over again, until you get it right, so to speak. So just sit back and enjoy the ride.

Movie Quote: "18 Again", 1988, Charles Schlatter and George Burns. At his 81st birthday party, Burns was told to make a wish, he smiles and says, "I wish I were eighteen again." Then he actually does swap spirits and bodies with his eighteen year old grandson, and gets his wish.

According to *The Theory*, if you live a relatively decent life, try to improve and do not hurt too many other Sapiens, you will progress to your next LC, your next life, in better shape. So in reality, you will actually be eighteen again, and again, and again.

Once you understand and appreciate *The ILC Theory* in its entirety, it should give you some semblance of solace in your life, so you can get on with more important things, like enhancing those ICTs that you can improve. And by doing so, it should improve this LifeCycle and enhance your ICT and overall Sapien ratings for better positioning in the selection process for your next LC. Chances are, you will have an equal or better life the next time. When you know this, it may allow you some inner peace in this life, something we all could use a little of.

The *Intelligent LifeCycle Theory* is not a static theory. It is highly dynamic in its own evolution. And that is the beauty of Intelligent Life, it builds upon itself through a cycle of natural evolution. So, enjoy your LiveTime during this and all your future LC journeys.

The Intelligent LifeCycle Theory

Sapien & Intelligent Energy Field

In 1999, during the initial development stages of *The ILC Theory*, the overriding question became, "What is the soul?" This is assuming, of course, that the soul is separate from the physical body, a premise with which most religions, theorists and scientists today agree.

As *The Theory* began to materialize, a new name for soul was needed that more comprehensively described the entity. The Intelligent Energy Field or IEF was initially used, which seemed to accurately describe a living intelligent entity.

As the IEF became the central focal point, *The Theory* also became acronym-intensive very quickly. So a new name was designed that was recognizable with a significantly more intrinsic meaning, consistent with life and intelligence. IEF was upgraded to SAPIEN, which is an acronym in itself, meaning 'Standard Astrologically Perpetual Intelligent Energy Nucleoid'.

The word *Sapien* is not listed in Webster's Dictionary, except for its use as the plural noun *Homo sapiens* (first known use in 1802), meaning the human race. *Sapient* is listed as an adjective, meaning wise and intellectual through reflection and experience. *Neosapien* is a Wikipedia entry, referencing the genetically engineered humanoid race of automatons featured in the animated TV series, *"Exosquad"*, but is not listed in Webster's as a word.

Being surrounded by words like *intelligent, wise, experience, individual and humankind,* the new word *Sapien* was the logical choice for the Intelligent Energy Field.

To complete the acronym, *nucleoid*, meaning the DNA-containing area of a prokaryotic cell, was selected as the noun in the name. The origination of the word nucleoid adds more credibility to the name, where *oid* represents an entity, and *nuclei* represents the center/heart of the entity. Perfect.

So, the word Sapien was born (first known use in 2011 in *The ILC Theory*), loosely translated as soul or spirit. It is certainly befitting to have SAPIEN (Standard Astrologically Perpetual Intelligent Energy Nucleoid) as the crucial, central component of *The Intelligent LifeCycle Theory.*

Sapien also seems to be less technical than IEF, and easier to say, use and remember. And, since Sapien replaces soul and spirit, a couple of inconsequential but interesting observations were made.

Soul has one syllable, *spirit* has two syllables and *Sapien* has three syllables. Syllabically speaking, 1 (soul) +2 (spirit) = 3 (Sapien) indicates the Sapien encompasses both soul and spirit. Alphabetically, Sapien would be listed first, followed by soul and then spirit.

Of course, that's in English. In other languages, these observations would be even more inconsequential.

Sapien Basics

To understand the ILC theory, we need to fully understand the Sapien, the Intelligent Energy Field (IEF), commonly referred to as the soul, spirit or mind, in pre-ILC days. The Sapien is the mental, or metaphysical component to the living being, not to be confused with the brain, which is one of the physical components of the Sapien's host body.

The Sapien is comprised of multiple NanoCells that provide intelligence to the functioning of the physical body. This NanoCell configuration is not yet detectable using current available technology, even though there are a few scientists today that are beginning to study, what they have named, *Nano Science and Nano Technology.*

The Sapien is attached, or fused, to the brain through the Sapien-Brain Bridge (SBB). The proximity of the Sapien to the brain is important, so as to maximize response capabilities to the physical body, covering all five senses: smell, touch, taste, hearing and sight, as well as a sixth called the 'sense of movement'. Current scientific theory refers to the this sixth sense as proprioception. In layman's terms, it is the sense of knowing where your body and its various parts are in space, relative to your other body parts or even to surrounding objects, without looking.

For example: Reaching for a glass of soda while reading, and picking it up without looking, is proprioception, or sense of movement. Although the six senses are brain functions, physical responses to their usage are controlled by the appropriate NanoCells in the Sapien.

The Intelligent LifeCycle Theory

This brings us to the all-important question, "Where is the Sapien?" Is it an aura around the body, is it in actual residence somewhere in the brain or is it an extraordinary fluid throughout the brain?

Since the Sapien is neither visible nor detectable yet, you might want to think of it as an aura covering or surrounding the brain, so thin as to be invisible, but fused with the brain. In current computer terms, the Sapien functions as the operating system to the body. The Sapien monitors and manages brain functions, which in turn controls the host body's physical movements and responses to external physical and mental stimuli.

The Sapien communicates with the brain via *tetricity*, using signal transmissions that are a trillion times faster and have a trillion times the capacity of electricity. Tetrical transmissions between the Sapien and its brain are instantaneous, handling massive TetraCell transfers of data and knowledge, 24/7.

Example: Think of it in terms of today's technology. The Sapien is the operating system. The brain is the computer with RAM and memory storage. The six senses and bodily responses function as the input/output devices, all communicating at a trillion times the speed of light.

And like all forms of energy, the Sapien cannot be created nor destroyed, just relocated between hosts. True to this natural law of the universe, the Sapien continues to get recycled, via different host bodies, during a continual progression of individual LifeCycles.

The Sapien is the central focal figure in *The Intelligent LifeCycle Theory*. So how does it work? Where does the Sapien come from, when you are born? And where does it go, when you die?

To answer these questions, as with all theories, we must first agree on certain assumptions in *The ILC Theory* that are considered basic and incontrovertible. Every Sapien (mind/spirit/soul) is unique, an assumption that is currently accepted within today's religious and societal ideologies.

So if we make the assumption that every Sapien is unique, how does that work? Individual Character Traits (ICTs) in a Sapien are common to all humanoid Sapiens (referred to as humans on Earth), such as good/evil, love/hate, honesty/deceit, happy/sad, leader/follower, creative/mundane, quantitative/abstract, loyalty/traitorous, right/wrong, corrupt/honor and so on.

Every Sapien has the exact same set of Individual Character Traits. However, ICT development percentages is what makes each Sapien totally unique. *See ICT Lists in Appendix.*

The Sapien is gender specific and race/species neutral. The physical body, regardless of species, race within a species, ethnicity or worldly location, is the host for the Sapien's LiveTime during an LC.

Similar to current-day religious beliefs, the Sapien (soul/spirit) does go on to a better life, theoretically. Since ICT development normally does not digress, Sapiens either remain the same or progress. So in theory, your next LC should be equal to or better than this one, assuming there are no significantly negative events incurred during LiveTime.

For purposes of *The ILC Theory*, the Sapien is the entity that allows the body to live and function in its societal surroundings. All Sapiens have the same finite set of character traits, but with individually unique development percentages. Each and every Sapien is totally unique from all other Sapiens in the universe.

ILC Discovery: The thing that makes every Sapien unique is the level of development of its set of character traits. The infinite number of combinations that can be derived from different development levels of character traits within a Sapien, by definition, makes each Sapien unique in substance and uniquely addressable by the UENet.

In addition to the Individual Character Traits (ICTs), other vital components of the Sapien are the Intelligence and Conscience modules. Both of these Sapien components have specific developmental levels, that in combination with the development levels of all ICTs, pretty much guarantee that each Sapien is totally unique.

Sapien Functionality

At the center of the Sapien is the Sapien CORE (Concentric Octahedral Residual Energy). The Core's controller is the Central NanoCell Control (CNCC) module. The CNCC controls all activity between the Host Interface, the ICT Set and other components, such as the Parental Overlay, Intelligence and Conscience modules. *See IEF octagonal illustration below.*

Basically, the Sapien is a living entity and lives in perpetuity, from life to life. Through each lifetime, referred to as a LifeCycle (LC), the Sapien's set of ICTs, Intelligence and Conscience modules are further developed, as a result of experiences incurred during the LiveTime of each LC. *The Theory* quantifies and measures the Sapien's development status as an intelligent being, based on such LiveTime experiences during the Sapien's LCs.

The Intelligent LifeCycle Theory

As shown below, the CNCC is in constant communication with all ICTs and other modules. This allows the body to respond to external stimuli. The way in which the Sapien responds to external stimuli is the defining characteristic that makes up the person, also known as the 'body and soul', or in ILC parlance, the 'Body and Sapien'.

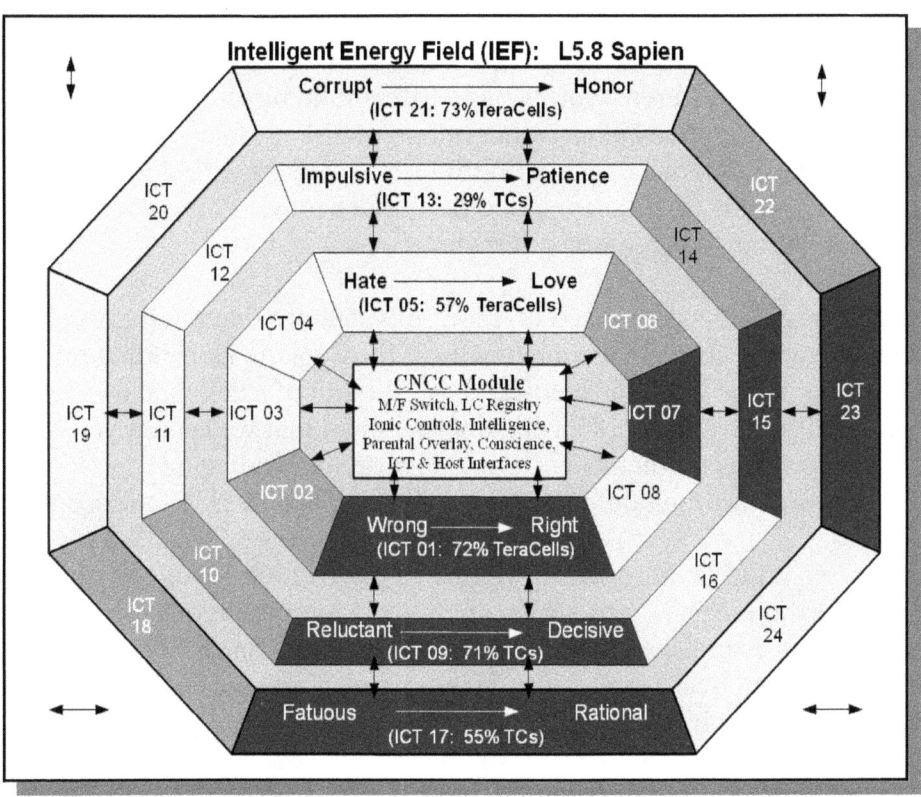

As shown above, the ICTs emanate from the CNCC with constant two-way communications. For purposes of space, we only show a portion of the ICT Set. Most interactions between ICTs and the Core include consultative input from the Intelligence, Parental Overlay and Conscience modules, through the CNCC module.

The Sapien does not have much of a memory. Such a tetracell configuration would require too much overhead and storage capacity. During a LifeCycle, the memory function is serviced by the brain.

Since Sapiens travel between LCs in different cultures, and in some cases between different worlds with different humanoid host forms, memories of previous lives would not be useful. In fact, they would actually be a hindrance and inhibit future Sapien growth. Individual Character Traits (ICTs) developed from those previous lives are more important than the memories of them.

Each NanoCell is comprised of TetraCells that provide intelligence, reasoning and emotional components of the Sapien. Depending on how you define a cell, a NanoCell is a billionth of a cell, and a TetraCell is a trillionth of a cell, sizes so small that we cannot yet detect nor measure them. The Sapien is way beyond being microscopic, with modules that are truly Nanoscopic and Tetroscopic.

Since mankind on Earth has developed a civilization based on numerical representations and mathematical interpretations, *The ILC Theory* has established a rating system to measure Sapien growth. The Sapien Rating Scale gauges the developmental progress of Sapiens and their respective ICTs throughout their LC journeys.

Generally a Sapien will begin its first LifeCycle on a C1 Intelligent Planet as an L1.0. As it gains more LiveTimes through recurring LCs, the overall development of a Sapien increases as it is exposed to many different experiential events.

The following chart illustrates the different levels of attainment a Sapien achieves throughout its LC journeys.

SAPIEN DEVELOPMENT RATING SCALE			
LEVEL	**% Completion**	**IEF Rating**	**Evolution Status**
L0	0%	0.00	New, uncirculated
L1	1% - 9%	1.0 to 1.99	Lowest, except for new
L2	10% - 29%	2.0 to 2.99	Low
L3	30% - 39%	3.0 to 3.99	Below average
L4	40% - 49%	4.0 to 4.99	Average
L5	50% - 59%	5.0 to 5.99	Above average
L6	60% - 69%	6.0 to 6.99	Very developed
L7	70% - 79%	7.0 to 7.99	Highly developed
L8	80% - 89%	8.0 to 8.99	Wisdom, little future growth
L9	90% - 99%	9.0 to 9.99	Near Perfect, little future growth
L10	100%	10.00	Perfect, no future growth

The Sapien rating system is based on elementary mathematics, physics and the natural laws of the universe, which reflect the overall percentage development of the Sapien on a scale of 1 to 10.

In determining the aggregate overall level of achievement of a Sapien, the Sapien score is referred to as a single number with one decimal, such as 4.8, 5.4 or 6.2. It is a number representing the accumulated development of all ICT's, as well as the accumulated development of all CNCC components.

Consistent with today's usage of acronyms and mathematics to describe human conditions, The Theory provides one single number that is representative of a Sapien's development level in conjunction with the IEF Ratings. Similar to calculating the IQ (Intelligence Quotient) of a person, the SQ (Sapien Quotient) is calculated by multiplying the IEF Score by 100.

Example: If a Sapien has an L5.8 IEF, then that Sapien has a 580 SQ.

The Intelligent LifeCycle Theory

To further define the Sapien's progress, if the Sapien has had 10 LCs, then that Sapien's identifying name would be 'Sapien 10-580', commonly referred to as a 1058.

Sapien Development Levels (L0-L10)

L0: 0% Completion
L0.0s are brand new energy fields having zero LC LiveTime, and are referred to as 'NBLs', Never Before Lived. These Sapiens are considered a part of the subHalo's Sapien reserve inventory. Generally, L0s are attracted/pulled to very primitive planets at the beginning of civilization development, such as Earth a million years ago, during the evolution of the caveman.
Est. Earth Pop: 0.0%   *LCs: (none)*   *IP Ratings: L1-L2*

L1: 1% to 9% Completion
The first level of a Sapien, as a semi-functioning member of a primeval society, is the L1.0 level. This Sapien has a core that's semi-functional and significantly incomplete. The Sapien enters its first LC as an L1.0, and may develop a few ICTs to a 1.5 level, but has very little prospects of ICTs above that. Most ICTs are barely formed at the L1 completion level. L1s are generally attracted to or pulled by planets with primitive cultures. In today's world on Earth, when an L1 Sapien inadvertently arrives on Earth, the populace deems this Sapien a moron or idiot, because its ICTs are so low. A savant may fall into this group with one or two low developed (1 percent or less) ICTs. L1s have few functioning characteristics needed to assimilate into a structured society.
Est. Earth Pop: 0.0%   *LCs: 1-2*   *IP Ratings: L1-L2*

L2: 10% to 29% Completion
When an L1 reaches an average 10 percent completion rate of all its ICT configurations, this Sapien progresses to L2 status, with significant work remaining for the majority of ICTs with tetronic charges less than 10 percent. A low-end L2 Sapien, such as 10.2 percent, may also be seen by others as a moron or idiot. A high-end L2 Sapien, such as 28 percent may have a few L3/L4 ICTs at varying stages of development, but is unlikely to have accumulated enough LC LiveTime to possess any ICTs greater than L4.
Est. Earth Pop: 15%　　　*LCs: 3-4*　　　*IP Ratings: L1-L3*

L3: 30% to 39% Completion
On L4 IPs such as Earth, L3 seems to be the average evolutionary status of many nations that Earth classifies as third world countries. L3s as a group still have remaining L1 and L2 ICTs, which require more LCs for improvement, and may have some L4 and L5 ICTs. L3s are not thought to have any ICTs developed beyond L5.
Est. Earth Pop: 30%　　　*LCs: 5-6*　　　*IP Ratings: L2-L4*

L4: 40% to 49% Completion
Low L4s are slightly below the Earth average of L4.4, while Sapiens with higher L4 ratings are slightly above the average. A Sapien's advancement from L3 to L4 may evolve within only a few LCs, while future improvements may develop at a slower pace.
Est. Earth Pop: 50%　　　*LCs: 7-9*　　　*IP Ratings: L2-L5*

L5: 50% to 59% Completion
Advanced L5 Sapiens possess a majority of ICTs in the 50 percent completion range, including some L4 and L6 ICTs. L5s on a planet tend to group together, due to the strength of their overall ionic rating and attractions between Sapiens of the same class. L5 Sapiens are

considered well developed, only three levels shy of Wisdom status, which may only require another few thousand LifeCycles.
Est. Earth Pop: 4.9%   ***LCs: 10-14***   ***IP Ratings: L3-L6***

L6: 60% to 69% Completion
L6 Sapiens have a majority of ICTs above 6.0, with some L3 to L5 ICTs, but most ICTs are around two-thirds developed. These Sapiens may be the 'movers and shakers' of an intelligent society in areas of business, education and research on L4 and L5 IPs. However, not all L6s are movers and shakers and not all movers and shakers are L6s.
Est. Earth Pop: 0.1%   ***LCs: 15-100***   ***IP Ratings: L4-L7***

L7: 70% to 79% Completion
Sub-wisdom levels are achieved at this stage, with the development of all ICT categories above 70 percent, through LCs in more advanced L7 planetary systems. Occasionally, an L7 might get mismatched and sent to a lower L4 IP, such as Earth. At any point in time, there may be a few L7s on Earth, but they are a significantly small group, compared to Earth's total population.
Est. Earth Pop: 0.0%   ***LCs: 101-∞***   ***IP Ratings: L5-L7***

L8: 80% to 89% Completion
L8 Sapiens are considered to have reached wisdom, with 80 percent or higher development of all ICTs, and are permanent members of the Halo. In addition to extraordinary ICT development, L8 Sapiens also have IM ratings above 99.5 percent and a fully developed and populated core. L8s have little need for, nor attraction to, future LC requests, even on the more advanced planets. They are in effect 'out of the loop' in the subHalo LC inventory database that services each galaxy.

The L8's tetronic charge is so strong, it cannot easily be pulled from the Halo pool. For an L8 to take an additional LC, it would need to be instigated by the L9 In Charge (L9IC) of a specific galaxy, for a specific IP intervention assignment.

Retired L8s reside in the Halo and are once removed from daily subHalo traffic. Some of the more ambitious L8s function as controllers of the subUENets for each galaxy and provide support functions in the subHalos, and may be bucking for promotions to L9 status. There have been a few L8s in Earth's history.

If an L8 Sapien is offered another LC, that Sapien's 'Fairness ICT', which is obviously well developed to this point, might prohibit it from accepting, since it might deprive another more needy Sapien at a lower level of their next LC. However, if an intelligent planet needs assistance in evolving into a positive breeding ground for Sapien development, L8s and L9s are sometimes called upon to accept another LC to get such planets back on track with their moral characteristics that benefit continued Sapien development.

Est. Earth Pop: 0.0%   LCs: ∞   IP Ratings: All planets

L9: 90% to 99% Completion
This Sapien level is affectionately referred to as the angel level. L9s are permanent members of the Halo, and require no more LCs at this level. There are five groups of L9s.

L9 Retirees: The largest group of L9s consists of retirees, who have decided to spend the rest of their eternity in peace, and tranquility, and enjoy a total void of negative thought, forever. These Sapiens have already paid the price and have said, "OK, it's been fun, but I've had enough." These Sapiens have more than earned the right to say, "I

The Intelligent LifeCycle Theory

quit.", and retire to the Halo in total bliss for all eternity.

L9 Advisers: Another group of L9s, not ready to retire, assist the Halo L10 Board in engineering and monitoring duties for the *Intelligent LifeCycles* of the universe. These Sapiens may gain additional enhancements to their IMs and ICTs for their duties as advisers.

L9 subHalo Angels: Another select group of L9s individually have responsibility for the IPs in assigned Galaxies and the continued Sapien recycling operations supporting those assigned territories. These L9s have responsibility for the subHalo in each galaxy. They report to their respective L10 in the Halo, responsible for their galaxy's universe quadrant. Similar to the L9 Advisers, Sapiens in this L9 group will continue to develop their IMs and ICTs through their operational experiences gained in running the subHalo activities.

Rotating L9s: These Sapiens periodically relieve the subHalo L9s for time off and provide them with a hiatus from the daily business of managing the subHalos, every few hundred years or so, for a couple of years at a time. Keep in mind, time is irrelevant, when you consider infinity. L9s provide continual 24/7 reporting to the L10 Board in the Halo, tracking Sapien inventory and Sapien development percentages in their respective regions of the universe

Roving L9s: These Sapiens are IP troubleshooters, referred to as Roving L9s. This select group of L9s accept one-time LC assignments to early growth stage worlds that need help in developing their standards of morality, so as to foster a more positive Sapien growth environment. There is one known instance of a Roving L9 on Earth, dating back a couple of thousand years.

Est. Earth Pop: 0.0%   LCs: ∞ IP Ratings: All planets

L10: 100% Completion

This is the Sapien that has reached perfection in its development, in all areas of evolution, over trillions of years. This intelligent entity is most commonly referred to, in today's religions, as God. It is thought that there has never been an instance in history, when an L10 physically visited an IP in life form. With all the sophistication of the Halo and UENet management systems in place, there is no reason for an L10 to experience another LC. L10 Sapiens are permanent members of the Halo, and exist in three groups.

L10 Retirees: As in L9s, this is the largest group of L10s, albeit a substantially smaller group than the L9s. They have definitely earned the right to eternal bliss.

L10 Halo Board Members: An elite group of L10s are designated as permanent board members of the Halo. Similar to the U.S. Supreme Court, there are an odd number of permanent members of the Halo L10 Board, to prevent stalemate decisions. However, unlike the U.S. 'Supremes', there are eleven L10 Halo Board Members, and they cannot recuse themselves from decisions.

L10 Quadrant Directors: These L10 Sapiens are responsible for subHalo operations in their respective quadrants of the universe, each quadrant consisting of multiple subHalos in multiple galaxies. L9s from subHalo operations report to this group of L10s, who in turn interface with the L10 Halo board members. These L10 Sapiens are ultimately responsible for the overall Intelligent Life Cycles of trillions of Sapiens in the universe.

Est. Earth Pop: 0.0%   LCs: ∞ IP Ratings: All planets

If you consider the possibility of multiple universes, and possibly even multiple time dimensions, each universe would be expected to have its own L10 Halo Board, comprised of select L10s that have evolved throughout their respective universes. If such a superverse exists, it would have an L10 Superverse Board of Controllers, who represent their respective universes. Superverse L10s, called Supers, would be responsible for intelligence development across multiple universes.

Sapien Populations (L0-L10)

Sapien population estimates indicate Earth is a little more developed at some levels and a little less developed at others, compared to the galaxy percentages. Estimated Sapien populations for the Milky Way Galaxy and Earth are included in the table below.

	subHALO: Milky Way Galaxy		Intelligent Planet: Earth		
IEF Levels	**Sapien Reserve Count X $10^{'}$** **Sapiens in 'Rest Time'**			**Sapien Population Count X 10^9** **'Live Time' Sapiens**	
L 1.0 – 1.9	0.38493284958	12.80%	L1s	0.000000000	0.00%
L 2.0 – 2.9	0.39383024984	13.09%	L2s	1.057622058	15.00%
L 3.0 – 3.9	0.65483994329	21.77%	L3s	2.115244116	30.00%
L 4.0 – 4.9	1.26783837564	42.15%	L4s	3.525406860	50.00%
L 5.0 – 5.9	0.27067399830	9.00%	L5s	0.345489872	4.90%
L 6.0 – 6.9	0.03109284031	1.03%	L6s	0.007050814	0.10%
L 7.0 – 7.9	0.00483370261	0.16%	L7s	0.000000000	0.00%
Total	**3.00804195958**	**100.00%**	**Total**	**7.050813720**	**100.00%**
Sapien Reserves	**3,008,041,959,576**		**Tot Sapiens**	**7,050,813,720**	
Intelligent Planets	100,000		Daily Traffic %	0.003%	
Sapiens/IP	30,080,420		Net Daily Sapiens	212,876	
MilkyWay Galaxy: **705,081,372,028,430** total Sapiens on all IPs in MilkyWay subHalo					

Accordingly, Earth is comprised of approximately 95 percent L2s, L3s and L4s, with an estimated average Sapien level of L4.4. This means that Earth is about 44 percent developed as an intelligent planet.

By comparison, the average Sapien rating for all IPs in the Milky Way is approximately L4.2. And that includes a 12.8 percent overhead in our subHalo of L0s and L1s to accommodate lesser developed planets that are nearer to their 'Intelligence Big Bang' beginnings.

The MilkyWay subHalo's reserve of three trillion Sapiens is more than enough to handle any natural disaster many times over the existing population growth rates in the galaxy. Using Earth as the average populated planet, estimates of the Sapien population of the galaxy is possible. The net population growth (births minus deaths) for the planet Earth during 2011 was estimated to be 212,876 per day.

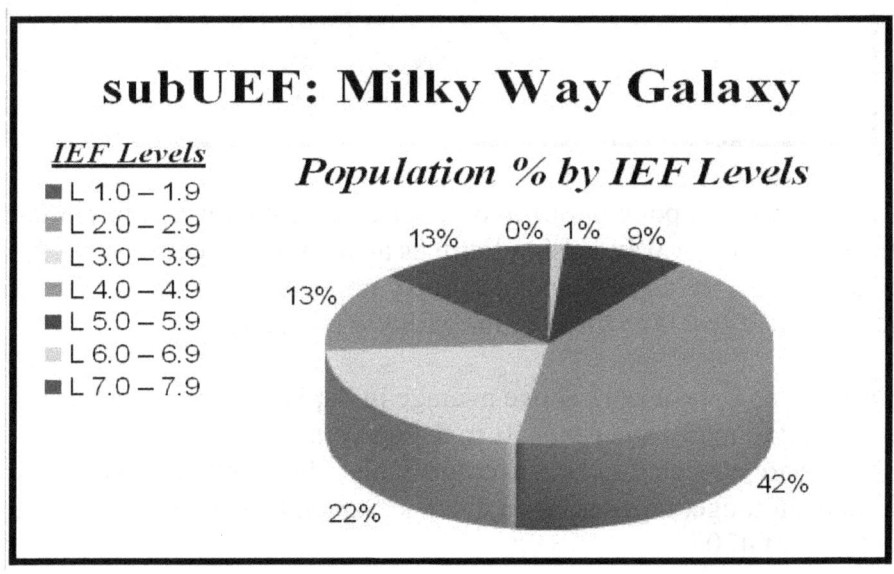

Estimates of Sapien Levels in the Milky Way, Earth's galaxy, indicate approximately 77 percent of all Sapiens in the galaxy are L2s, L3s and L4s. However, over 10 percent of the galaxy's Sapien population is

L5s and L6s, as compared to Earth's 5 percent.

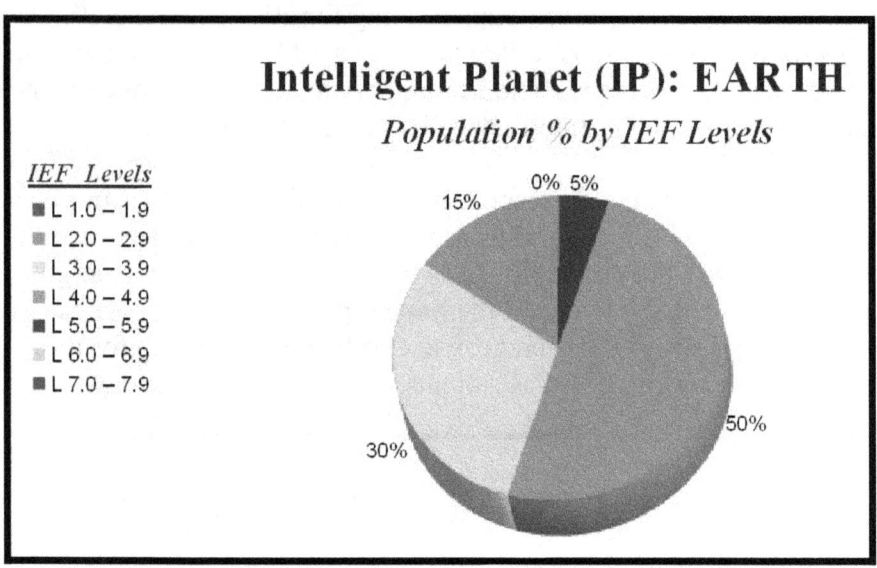

Levels of Sapien populations in other galaxies are expected to replicate those of the MilkyWay. Using Earth as an average IP with the same methodology, we can extrapolate galaxy populations of similar Sapien development levels as those of the MilkyWay galaxy.

Earth seems to be a little above average in Sapien development as compared to many other planets in the universe. Other IPs in other galaxies are expected to host average Sapien development levels in the 42 percent range, registering an average Sapien level of L4.2 with an IP Index of 420.

However, according to extremely conservative ILC estimates, there are still one million intelligent planets in the universe more advanced than Earth. This certainly indicates, "We are definitely not alone."

Using such data, we can make estimates of Earth's Sapien populace by country and region. Sapien estimates below are influenced to a large degree by the societal and political structures in different countries.

Global Sapien Ratings		*ILC Theory*	
Country/Region	**Avg. Sapien**	**Country/Reg.**	**Avg. Sapien**
USA	5.1	Italy	4.7
Canada	5.1	Spain	4.7
Great Britain	5.1	Japan	4.7
Mexico, Central Am.	4.1	Indonesia	4.3
South America	4.1	Russia	4.5
Australia	5.0	China	3.9
Scandinavia	5.0	Africa	3.8
France	4.9	Middle East	3.2
		Other	3.3
AVG Sapien Currently on EARTH			**4.4**

The type of living environment that exists in a country directly affects the level of Sapiens that live there and the level of Sapiens that are drawn to it. The majority of Sapiens, in a given country, represents the average Sapien development levels of its populace, and consequently influence current and future Sapien selections.

Example: A fetus in the womb has a father with an L5.2 Sapien and a mother with an L5.4 Sapien. After the first trimester, the fetus attracts a Sapien with similar characteristics and Sapien levels to those of the parents. With these parents, Sapien probabilities for this fetus range from L4 to L6, and will most probably be in the L5 range, to more closely approximate that of the parents.

In rare instances, the Sapien delivered to the fetus might deviate dramatically from the parents because of transmission timing errors or inventory availability. In the above case, if the incoming Sapien was an L3.3 or an L6.6 for example, the Sapien would theoretically have less characteristics in common with the parents.

It is expected that lesser developed Sapiens are attracted to countries with more repressive regimes, and a lack of free will that is available to its population. This occurs because average parents in those countries are generally at lower levels of Sapien development themselves. Such countries with lower average Sapiens tend to attract similarly developed Sapiens during their population growth phase.

Example: Parents, in a third world country with an average Sapien population base of L3.2, will produce Sapien requests for their offspring, unknowingly of course, that are near their own levels. Such Sapien requests, during pregnancies, would be influenced significantly by the L3.2 Sapien parents. Sapien requests during pregnancy are predominantly skewed toward the parental overlays of the embryo.

Of course, there are citizens in these countries that have more advanced Sapien levels than the populace, an L4.8 for example. These citizens have a tendency to become part of the ruling class in these types of societies and attempt to control their lower Sapien populations through fear and violence. In such repressive socioeconomic conditions, high-end L4s rule a significantly deficient, uneducated and subordinated Sapien population of L2s and L3s.

The primary ICTs that are deficient in this type of regime-oriented country are Sanctity of Life, Respect for Others, Tolerance and Understanding. If there were any L5 Sapiens or higher in these countries, they most likely migrated to other countries with more freedoms and less violence, in pursuit of their inalienable right to live. Even though citizens with slightly higher Sapien levels may live in these under developed countries, they are definitely in the minority.

However, not all immigrants leaving these oppressive third world countries do so to escape such oppression. To the contrary, there are some extreme Muslim countries that, as this book goes to print, are attempting to take over certain other countries through a massive migration of their loyal populace to those countries. France seems to be such a target state for Muslims. Currently, approximately two-thirds of France's total immigration is from Muslim countries.

This strategy seems to be the method of choice for some extremist Muslim nations. They are attempting to spread their backward cultures to other countries, so that they might someday be able to control those countries from within. For such repressive countries, world domination is the goal of their under-developed leaders. This is not to be confused with true world leadership, as shown by the United States, Great Britain and others, that fight to protect personal freedoms, wherever they are threatened.

It has been noted on more than a few occasions, that Middle Eastern culture seems to be some five hundred years behind Western culture. That means that the Sapien infrastructure in that part of the world has not yet evolved to levels acceptable for modern civilization. As a result, their newborns, whether they are in their home country or transplanted abroad, continue to receive low Sapien levels, which fuels their expansive plans to dominate the masses.

However, as these Sapiens become more exposed to Western culture, they will progress in their development and begin raising their Sapien levels, and thereby raise the Sapien requests for their newborns over time. Currently, Sapien requests from these third world, Middle Eastern countries are probably averaging L3.2 or below.

As the populations of these backward countries increase, they have an increased requirement for lower-developed Sapiens. To enter this environment as babies, Sapiens would have low IEFs with low sanctity of life ICTs and a higher propensity for violence than peace.

In this environment, negatively developed Sapiens can more easily be recycled. On the other hand, there may not be that many negative Sapiens available. As these populations get more educated, begin to enjoy some semblance of personal freedoms and have more exposure to real world experiences, their average Sapien requirements improve, outside their radical Muslim ideologies.

The good news is that the more these backward cultures gain exposure to Western values, the more their Sapien levels will increase. As the populace develops more toward free will in their expectations, the parents will begin to request higher Sapiens in their offspring, unknowingly of course. Thus, as third world cultures evolve, the radical element of these groups is reduced over time.

However, as it stands right now, many third world countries have predominantly low Sapien populations. Such countries have leaders that are not much more developed, who preach violence and hatred to their followers.

So, you can see how such radical Muslim leaders could think this approach of controlling through fear and violence might work. Reports have shown that Muslims inside and outside Muslim countries reproduce at significantly higher rates compared to the reproductive rates for other races and religions. This indicates the Muslim approach to world domination is to out-populate the free world.

The minimum reproductive rate for a race or species to survive over time is 2.1 children per couple. Over the next few hundred years or so, the reproductive rates of these Muslim countries should begin to fall, with higher Sapien requests in the range of L3s and L4s.

This seems to be the normal evolution of races within an intelligent species. In the early period of a race's development, the Sapien birth rate is high, partly because the Sapien populace is uneducated and has not yet developed their culture sufficiently, and partly because they just don't have alot of ways to spend their time otherwise.

As a race within a species develops, and the populace begins to enjoy more freedoms in their LiveTimes, they begin having fewer babies, choosing instead to have fun, travel and advance their own Sapien development. Personal freedoms become more important than the hindrances and obligations inherent in having lots of babies.

At this point in our IP's LifeCycle, lower level Sapiens on Earth produce many babies. Higher level Sapiens have fewer babies. As lower level Sapiens improve their SQs, the populace begins to start living a better life. In doing so, they begin to reduce their procreation frequencies, as well. It is a self-perpetuating societal life cycle.

With the average Sapien on Earth in the low to mid L4 range, we have a long way to go. As Earth Sapiens approach L5.0 as an average, there should be noticeable improvements in living conditions and personal freedoms in some of these underdeveloped countries.

In the United States, the average Sapien SQ is currently estimated to be 510. As this country continues to develop its Sapien population, which is currently about halfway to full development, future Sapien advancements are expected to take longer periods of time to accomplish smaller gains in average Sapien levels.

Example: A Sapien with an SQ of 310 could possibly progress from an L3.1 to an L4.0 in a single LifeCycle. However, for a Sapien with an SQ of 580, it is expected that it might require multiple LCs to grow from an L5.8 to an L6.3.

The closer a Sapien gets to wisdom (L8), the longer it takes to gain smaller incremental enhancements to the Sapien's ICT Set and IM (Intelligence Module). Once a Sapien reaches L7, smaller incremental improvements require an inordinate number of LCs to accomplish. On Class C7 IPs, with an average population base of L7.0 or higher, LCs become much more enjoyable and productive for their Sapien populace. Mixing today's vernacular with ILC parlance, a C7 IP might be thought of as "Halo on earth."

Basically, Earth is a little ahead of the curve in Sapien development, as compared to our galaxy. If the Milky Way Galaxy is indicative of the other 10^{11} galaxies, then Earth is a little above average in comparison to all other Intelligent Planets (IPs) in the universe.

Even though there are a million IPs in the universe that are more advanced than Earth, populations of the various C-level IP groups indicate the universe is approximately 42 percent developed in its Sapien evolution. So as a universe, intelligent life is less than 50 percent developed today. This development level of the universe has taken trillions of years, in billions of galaxies and on billions of planets. This is where you really need to start believing in infinity.

SAPIEN Addressing Protocol

Because there are trillions of unique Sapiens in the universe, each Sapien must have a unique address used by the UENet and the subHalo. The Sapien addressing scheme below is similar to Internet Protocol addressing. This is Basic Inventory Management 101.

SAPIEN ADDRESSING SCHEME	
HALO[1]	1.
subHalo - Milky Way[2]	042764874923.
Star System - Sun[3]	032985.
Planet - Earth[4]	03.
Country - USA[5]	003.
LifeCycles[6]	10.
Current SQ Rating[7]	530
Sample Sapien Address: 1.042764874923.032985.03.003.10.530	

(1) Halo: The 1st number of a Sapien's address, indicates this universe's Halo. All Sapiens in the universe begin with the same descriptor of 1. If there are multiple universes, those addresses would begin with 2., 3., 4. and so on. (2) subHalo Galaxy: This Sapien's first LC in the Milky Way Galaxy, its originating or home galaxy, indicated by the galaxy's unique 12 digit descriptor. (3) Star System: Our Sun, one of 10^5 intelligent star systems in the Milky Way Galaxy, indicated by the star's unique 6 digit descriptor. (4) Planet: Earth is designated with a 03. descriptor, indicating the 3rd closest planet to the Sun. (5) Country location: Of the 204 recognized countries in the world, the USA descriptor is 003., indicating the third most populated country. (6) LifeCycles: This descriptor shows the number of LCs for this Sapien, including the present one, as indicated with a 10. entry. (7) Current SQ Rating: This descriptor, the most important and most dynamic field in the address, reflects the Sapien's current development level as an intelligent life entity. It is updated by the controlling subHalo periodically in real time, so as to have an accurate count for inventory purposes.

The Intelligent LifeCycle Theory

The unique Sapien addressing scheme (as shown above) is located in the Sapiens' CNCC. It is used in the tracking, distribution and inventory management of every Sapien in the universe in perpetuity. As long as the Sapien continues to be recycled to and from Earth, the first four descriptors remain the same for future LCs.

The last three descriptors change as the Sapien goes through its LifeCycles. These indicate the current country location, number of lives and its SQ Rating, which is actually the Sapien tetronic charge, extended to 100 decimals. This unique tetronic charge, representing its development level, combined with the first five descriptors, guarantees each and every Sapien in the universe is indeed unique.

When a Sapien advances to L7.0 status or above, the Sapien may be assigned to a more advanced planet in another galaxy during future LCs for continued development. When this infrequent transition occurs, the Sapien address is amended to show the new galaxy, star and planet locations, while maintaining its originating subHalo address.

Sapiens who are transplanted between galaxies have a longer address than ones that stay within the same galaxy. The Sapien addressing scheme becomes even more important, once intergalactic travel is accomplished by LiveTime Sapiens in real time.

Even though it has a unique address, the Sapien in the above example would be more easily known by its number of LCs and its Sapien Rating. The last two fields of data in the address identify the Sapien's 10 LCs and current SQ Rating of 530, which is an L5.3 IEF rating. So this Sapien would be known as a '1053' for short. Just as there are many John's in the world, there are probably many 1053's as well.

Since each Sapien is unique in its character trait development and intelligence level, the unique addressing system is necessary to monitor and locate all Sapiens in the universe. The addressing scheme allows the Sapien to be uniquely inventoried regardless of subHalo location and transported via the UENet, without any duplications and redundancies from other Sapiens.

Example: The 1053 Sapien, in the above example, migrates to another galaxy, which does occur, albeit infrequently. After the current LC is terminated, its new Sapien address would reflect the new galaxy, sun and planet locations.

The Sapien's new address auto-populates for subHalo inventory purposes. The ending digits would be updated to indicate the number of LCs and a beginning L5.7 Sapien, which was gained from its 10th LC above. This Sapien's new address includes the originating subHalo's 12-digit number, the new galaxy, star, planet and Sapien information: 1.042764874923.073324195309.061374.007.47.11.570

When we begin traveling to other star systems and galaxies during an LC, the Sapien's home subHalo must maintain inventory integrity. So the originating subHalo always maintains control of its Sapien inventory, regardless of any current deviation in its IP location.

Sapien Order Fulfillment

The unique tetronic charge of each Sapien requested and transmitted over the UENet is based on its own Sapien development level. Sapien Request Orders (SROs) sent to the subHalo for newborn Sapiens are based on Sapien requirements from the Parental Overlays. Similar to

The Intelligent LifeCycle Theory

FM radio stations, 98.5, 98.6, and so on, where every tenth is a new radio station, Sapien signals are also unique to the trillions of digits.

Initial requirements, included in the Sapien Request Order (SRO) to the subHalo, encompass the parental overlay's IM and ICT Set development levels. The gender of the fetus, which is a critical component of the SRO, is predetermined by the time the Sapien selection occurs (after the first trimester of pregnancy). Sapien matches to these initial criteria are viewed as high compatibility priorities during the subHalo selection process, which takes a few tetraseconds of Earth time to complete.

Example: A female fetus has a parental overlay from parents with SQs of 540 and 560 and IMs of 7.1 and 7.3, respectively, with dominate Creativity ICTs in their ICT sets. The fetus receives its Sapien during its 12th week of pregnancy, with an SQ of 570, an IM of 7.2 and above average Creativity ICTs. Physical attributes of the baby are passed on from the parents genetically. Sapien attributes are chosen during the Sapien selection process in the subHalo to closely approximate those of the parents.

Sapien orders are fulfilled after the first trimester to avoid any unpleasant and needless Sapien transfers, in case the fetus dies during the first twelve weeks of pregnancy. And to further protect the Sapien from wasted transfers, the Sapien is not fused with the fetus until the fetus has sufficiently built up its own immune system.

The fetus' immunities are generally developed sufficiently during this period. As the new Sapien takes control, the mother's morning sickness begins to dissipate rapidly. Since the mother's body no longer needs to protect the physical fetus from toxins ingested by the mother during its initial development phase, the mother regains her health, well-being and happiness. Her little baby Sapien begins to nurture its physical growth to term, to begin its next LifeCycle.

The vast majority of Sapien requests from fetuses is for positive Sapiens from most L levels. But occasionally, the subHalo gets requests for negative Sapiens, usually from parental overlays, who are highly negative in certain ICTs and have relatively low SQs.

Regardless, the Sapien arrives at the beginning of the second trimester of pregnancy, not the third trimester, which was originally thought to be the case. Biologically, the Sapien should arrive after the first twelve weeks of pregnancy. At that time, the Sapien can begin protecting itself from toxin impurities, which also halts the mother's morning sickness. *The ILC Theory* actually corrected itself here.

ILC Discovery: This answers the abortion debate, as to when the fetus actually becomes a living being. It is twelve weeks. Before that, the fetus has not received its Sapien, so it would not be defined as an intelligent life yet.

Researchers and other medical professionals have conducted studies as to the viability of the fetus. In this vein, viability refers to a point in fetal development, where the fetus can survive outside the womb, with medical assistance of course. The lower limit of viability is thought to be approximately five months, or twenty weeks for the host body, even though Sapien transfer usually occurs after twelve weeks.

Data accumulated from 2003 to 2005 studies indicate that only 20 to 35 percent of babies born at twenty-three weeks survive. They further report that 50 to 70 percent of babies born at twenty-four to twenty-five weeks, and more than 90 percent born at twenty-six to twenty-seven weeks, survive. Basically, preterm births (or preemies as they are called) account for nearly 30 percent of all neonatal deaths.

Incidentally, a fetus is currently defined as a developing mammal after the embryonic stage and before birth. Medical research and studies on the topic help elevate our Sapien population to higher levels, as a matter of course. The viability potential of the fetus is certainly important, but not the primary issue. Sapien viability is key.

According to Rule No.1 of the *Ten Rules of Intelligent Life*, an abortion after the twelfth week would be prematurely and willfully terminating a Sapien's LifeCycle, and thus would be an infraction. Since the fetus is populated with its own Sapien at twelve weeks, it is by definition a living intelligent being.

However, before the twelfth week, abortion would not violate this rule. In addition, if an abortion is done after 12 weeks, it may be construed as a judgment call, since the Sapien's LiveTime had not yet actually begun.

Assuming you have a healthy pregnancy during the first three months and are expected to carry full term, the Sapien transfer occurs, and in a sense breathes life into the fetus. This is the point in which the accuracy of the SRO program is assessed. Is it a match between the fetus' parental overlay or not? Fortunately, the vast majority of Sapien transfers successfully meet the parental requirements inherent in the temporary energy field of the fetus. This accounts for the vast majority of babies that have mental resemblance to their parents.

However, a Sapien will not normally be recycled to a fetus, who's parental overlay is more than one development level higher than that achieved by the Sapien to date. And conversely, a Sapien will not generally be sent to a fetus, who's parental overlay is more than one development level lower than that of the Sapien. However, as shown before, mismatches do occur during the Sapien order fulfillment phase, as infrequent as they may be.

Multiple Births

So far, we have only talked about single births, requiring only one Sapien. For multiple births, each fetus requires its own Intelligent Energy Field (IEF), its own Sapien.

Multiple births occur, when more than one fetus is carried to term in a single pregnancy. The most common multiples are twins and triplets. Multiple pregnancies in humans are usually born earlier than the average length of pregnancy. Twins average thirty-six weeks, triplets thirty-two weeks and quadruplets thirty weeks.

These and other multiple births occur to varying degrees in most animal species. Many non-Sapien species give birth to multiples as a matter of course, with the resulting group called a litter.

Multiple-birth siblings are either identical or fraternal. Identical multiples result from a single fertilized egg splitting into two or more embryos, each carrying the same genes (genetic material). Siblings created from one egg are referred to as identical, since their physical resemblance is extremely similar.

When an egg splits into multiple eggs, indicating multiple Sapiens will be required, the Sapien Request Order (SRO) would include a more specific match of ICT sets and Intelligence for the siblings-to-be. When multiple eggs result from the split, the original parental overlay is automatically replicated to each new egg prior to transmitting the

The Intelligent LifeCycle Theory

SRO to the subHalo.

As the physical maturation of the fetuses occur, their bodily attributes develop so similarly, they are called identical, and rightfully so, since they came from the same fertilized egg. Even though multiples are considered identical in body and mind, they will exhibit some differences in their character traits, since they are all separate Sapiens.

Such differences in character traits in multiples become more recognizable in some sets than others, but the differences are nonetheless there. When egg splits occur, the SROs not only include matches to the parental overlays, but would then include more exact matches of character traits and intelligence for each multiple fetus, to match the near identical physical characteristics of each sibling.

The physical attributes of each fetus evolve identically, since they come from the same egg. In the vast majority of multiple birth situations, the sex of the multiples is the same. However, when they are different, it just adds another dimension to SRO fulfillment.

The order fulfillment process at the subHalo level for multiples does require more time to complete, maybe a few thousand tetraseconds more than normal. Then of course, there may be some timing issues to deal with in the Sapien transfer scheduling at the subUENet.

Sapiens for multiples do not necessarily have to arrive in the womb at the same time, but such Sapien downloads do need to be coordinated for transmission at approximately the same time window in the network. Remember, after the Sapien arrives in the fetus, it still has six months for further development before its original birth date.

The other type of multiples is called fraternal births. Instead of the egg splitting, as with identical multiples, the ovary releases multiple eggs during the same menstrual cycle in the woman. When multiple eggs are fertilized, the physical appearances of fraternal fetuses develop similarly, but with some differences.

And the Sapien levels for multiple fraternals are not as specific, during the ICT development and intelligence searches. Thus, fraternal multiples may exhibit surprisingly different character traits and intelligence to each other, more so than identical multiples, because of their different Sapien matches.

Multiples births with three or more offspring may also result in a combination of fraternal (physically, genetically different) and identical (genetically identical) siblings.

Example: A set of triplets may be composed of identical twins from one egg and a third sibling from a second egg. The identicals may have more Sapien traits in common with each other than with the third sibling, even though they are all extremely similar as triplets.

Rare occurrences of quadruplets can result in several ways. Four eggs are released and fertilized at once, one egg splits into four, one egg splits into three with the fourth one fertilized individually, two eggs split into two, or one egg splits and two are fertilized separately.

The Sapien search criteria and time required to fulfill SROs for multiples increases significantly. Although manageable by the subHalo, time required to fulfill such SROs may be considerably longer than the few tetraseconds normally required.

Example: A set of quadruplets may consist of two sets of identical twins. In this instance, each child will have one identical and two fraternal siblings. Each set of twins would require specific Sapien searches to more exactly match the other's ICT set and IM. This could possibly produce two sets of very different twins, since search criteria for both sets would be slightly different, even though their physical characteristics are very similar.

Although extremely rare, natural multiple live births of as many as eight babies have occurred. The first set of octuplets on record occurred in Texas in 1998; one died and seven survived. In 2009, a second set of octuplets was born in California, and to date, all eight have survived. With that many Sapiens required for one birthing session, the chance for mistakes and errors during subHalo selection and UENet transmissions increases exponentially.

There have been a few sets of nonuplets (nine) in which a few babies were born alive, though none lived longer than a few days. There have even been cases of human pregnancies with ten, eleven, twelve and fifteen fetuses, but no instances of live births have occurred.

If a fetus dies after the twelfth week, after being populated with its own Sapien, that Sapien probably experiences the shortest LC in its history. However brief the Sapien transfer may have been, it does get an entry into the Sapien's LC Registry, as another LifeCycle.

Sapien Gender

The gender of a Sapien is hard-wired, so to speak, into the Sapien core. The gender/sex component of the Sapien is constantly accessed, but cannot be altered. The differences, and similarities, between Sapien genders, that make them compatible as well as combative, are considered integral ingredients to a successful and perpetual

The Intelligent LifeCycle Theory

procreation cycle to ensure longevity of the species, or race within a species.

Depending upon the country, the heterosexual population accounts for 95 to 96 percent of the total population, resulting in gays, lesbians and bi-sexuals comprising 4 to 5 percent. In the United States, that is approximately ten to twelve million Americans. *The ILC Theory* explains why this happens.

With a database management system as sophisticated and intricate as the one used by the subHalo to fulfill SROs, errors are uncommon but expected in some Sapien matches. When the subHalo commits a gender error with the SRO, which does happen occasionally, it might send a female Sapien to occupy a male fetus, for example.

When this happens, the Sapien's dominant ICT set, from it's previous LCs as a female, will conflict with the male gender of the host body. Conversely, the same applies in reverse, if a male Sapien is sent to a female fetus.

This type of Sapien selection error results in gays and lesbians. The Sapien may attempt to live as he or she had in previous LCs. If a male Sapien is wrongly sent to a female fetus, then that female growing up may exhibit male ICT tendencies, and vice versa, if a female Sapien is wrongly sent to a male fetus.

Accordingly, a male homosexual, which is a misplaced female Sapien in a male body, may exhibit ICTs that are consistent with her Sapien's actual gender characteristics. If she was normally a very feminine Sapien in her previous LCs, her male host body might exhibit mannerisms that are consistent with female characteristics.

However, if her characteristics are masculine leaning, then the female sapien in the male body may exhibit more macho traits in gay relationships, labeled by society as butch, or dyke. Regardless of which sex is mismatched, gender errors in Sapien selection occur relatively infrequently, approximately 5 percent of the time. This indicates that 95 percent of all SROs are correct gender matches.

In some cases, because of the availability of compatible Key ICTs and IM requirements, a Sapien may not be available in the same sex within the required time frame. When this occurs, the Sapien may be gay, but with have similar ICTs and IM to the parents.

ILC Discovery: Homosexuals are gender-misplaced Sapiens. It is an error in the SRO fulfillment process, beyond the control of the Sapien.

Not to sound condescending, but if you are gay, it is not your fault. It is a gender misplacement error during the subHalo Sapien selection process. Remember, the gender integrity of your Sapien cannot be altered only compromised by an SRO misplacement.

ILC Discovery: There are more gays than lesbians, because the female Sapien population is larger than the male Sapien populace in the subHalo. So, gender-misplaced Sapiens occur more with female Sapiens sent to male fetuses.

If you are heterosexual, your Sapien is, and will be for all time, your current LC's gender. If you are homosexual in your current LC, your Sapien is actually the opposite gender, but do not worry, the odds are in your favor of getting the right body in your next LifeCycle.

Example: Here is an interesting twist. A female Sapien goes into a little male fetus. He grows up and falls in love with another guy. who is straight. The straight guy likes the male Sapien (who is actually a gender-misplaced female), but rejects the relationship, unaware his suitor is actually a female.

Think of all the ICT development that was missed between these two Sapiens, because the subHalo and/or the UENet screwed up. Then again, that's life.

Since the UENet is known to have a high accuracy rate, in excess of 99 percent, the primary reasons for 5 percent mismatched Sapiens comes from the subHalo database query and retrieval program. As you can imagine, it is quite old.

As a note of comfort to all us heterosexuals and all misplaced genders, it has been reported that the Halo has been testing a newly developed database management system that equals the UENet accuracy rate. It is projected to improve the accuracy rate in all SRO gender matches to 99 percent, reducing the misplaced gender matches to less than 1 percent. This new and improved subHalo application to be used for future SRO fulfillments with superior hierarchical protocols, is expected to be rolled out real soon.

ILC Discovery: Regardless of whether you are heterosexual or homosexual this time, there is better than a 99 percent chance you will get the right gender body for your next LifeCycle, as soon as the new database management system is rolled out to all subHalos!

Keep in mind, procreation between males and females of an intelligent species is critical to its continuity. Therefore, it would seem appropriate to say that, sex is great. It is the perfect method designed to guarantee procreation rates to sustain a species' evolution. It provides immense pleasure, so that a species will desire the activity and automatically reproduce, as a matter of course.

Since sex is such a powerful force in our LifeCycles, it is no wonder it has several ICTs related to its use. Regardless of gender, each of us have plenty of ICTs to work on, during our current LifeCycles. And hopefully, if we can improve certain ICTs this time around, our next LiveTimes will be better.

Sapien Evolution

All Sapien's are born and recycled with the same rights and privileges afforded to intelligent life. All Sapiens have the same core and the same ICT sets, even L10s. Sapien evolution is as a result of trillions of years of development from gases and Dark TetraMatter throughout the universe. All Sapiens are created equal in the beginning, as L0s, before entering as an L1.0 in their first LC.

Beginning with that first LifeCycle, Sapiens develop their character traits differently through different LiveTime experiences, known as ICT events, during different LCs. These events affect the degree to which ICTs and IMs (Intelligence Modules) are developed. As we evolve through our LCs, our Sapiens evolve at different rates because of the very different experiences we individually face in life.

New Sapiens, never before experiencing any LiveTime in an LC, have a tendency to be attracted or drawn to early growth stage planets, primarily C1 and C2 planets, that reproduce L1s and submit L1-L2 SROs. This would be the environment most analogous to Earth, in the early days of humankind's evolution, millions of years ago, before civilized man evolved. Earth's caveman era was the perfect breeding ground for early growth stage Sapiens.

The Intelligent LifeCycle Theory

In the grand scheme of things, nobody is superior and nobody is inferior, even though all Sapiens are unique, by definition. Our uniqueness comes from the cumulative impact of the many ICT events, we've experienced, through many LC trips.

The success of your current LC is not contingent upon nor measured by financial rewards or social acclamations. The success of your LiveTime is directly related to your ability to enhance and improve your ICTs, which indirectly enhances your Intelligence Module.

During this LC, you might want to identify a few ICTs that obviously need help. We all have them. If you didn't, you would already be an L8 or L9 in the Halo.

So as occasions arise, it may be time well spent, if you consciously try to improve those ICTs that could use some work. It can only benefit you in your current and future LifeCycles.

To a large degree, the level of development of a Sapien is directly proportional to the number of LCs experienced. The more LiveTimes a Sapien has, the more developed their ICT Sets and IMs will be, with the exception of the evil Sapien.

Evil is unfortunately a fact of life and is inferior to normal Sapiens. As a Sapien digresses in its development, over a period of LCs, its frequency of LiveTime trips will be reduced, commensurate with its lack of ICT development, in relation to its number of LCs.

Example: A Sapien who has had 12 LCs and is only an L2 with deficiencies in its ICT set, is considered significantly below expected levels and may qualify as evil. This Sapien, because of its deficient energized TetraCells in key character traits, will not get as many SROs. And the ones it does get will probably be to C1 or C2 planets in early stages of intelligent life, similar to the caveman days on Earth.

In a sense, this might be construed as a form of hell. As a side note, this Sapien could possibly be recycled to countries in developed worlds that request deficiently developed Sapiens, like certain Middle Eastern countries on Earth.

At the other end of the spectrum, the highly advanced Sapien with an IEF of L7.8 for example, will have developed a keen sense of tolerance, acceptance and nurturing of lower-developed Sapiens. These ICTs, including Understanding, Compassion, Tolerance, Acceptance and Humility, are critical for Sapien progression to higher levels and to higher level IPs.

This, however, is not to be confused with certain Sapiens among us today who feign tolerance, compassion and acceptance, because they actually think of themselves as superior to other Sapiens. Such elitist attitudes are only detrimental to overall Sapien development.

If there is such a thing as a normal growth curve for Sapiens, it might evolve through a steady and methodical progression as the Sapien ages. This normal development results as the Sapien engages a variety of very different ICT events during its maturation process.

As Sapiens negotiate their ICT events during growth years of a their LCs, they respond differently based on their individual Sapien development percentages. Depending on the chronological age of the Sapien, reactions to external stimuli may include certain ICTs and preclude others. Remember, all Sapiens are unique.

The Intelligent LifeCycle Theory

The following chart illustrates a fairly standard Sapien growth curve.

Positive Sapien Growth During SLC Trip			
Child	**Teen**	**Adult**	**Retired**
Born, an L4.7 with 8 SLCs, the child developed a couple of ICTs	The teen yrs didn't allow much time for character development	Had a few loves, married, 2 children, some success as Architect, lots of experiences, no tragedies	Retirement was good, a few more ICTs developed, played some golf
IEF L4.8	IEF L4.9	IEF L5.2	IEF L5.4

This Sapien advanced from an IEF Level 4 to a Level 5 as an adult, gaining almost a full point through retirement, and will enter the next SLC as an L5.4 IEF. When This IEF reaches L6.0, future advances in L ratings will slow and require more time.

This Sapien's life began after eight previous LCs and an accumulated L4.7 IEF rating. As a child, this 847 Sapien was able to develop its Honesty and Acceptance ICTs, ending its childhood years as an L4.8.

As it grew through its teen years, 847 had little time to further develop other ICTs. Through its adult years, 847 had a few relationships, got married, had two children and experienced some success as an Architect, while developing some ICTs. After retirement, 847 enhanced a few more ICTs and ended as an L5.4 Of course, there are many Sapiens today who have similar growth stages and growth rates as referred to in the above chart.

The Intelligent LifeCycle Theory

For most of us, a normal development cycle is the natural order of things, during our current LCs. Most of us are L4s, L5s and L6s during this LC. We were born on Earth and have pursued our own dreams in our own way, whatever those dreams are. We have had some successes and some failures, and have been able to improve some of our Individual Character Traits.

Many of us deal with a variety of difficulties and hardships in our lives that are inherent in each phase of our growth as human beings. The key to our growth as intelligent beings is not the magnitude, or lack of magnitude, of events affecting our LiveTime. Rather, it is the way in which we handle such adversities that build our character, enhance our Individual Character Traits and elevate our Intelligence Module.

LiveTimes for all Sapiens are as different as there are different Sapiens in the universe. Even so, there is a normal progression to a Sapien's existence, which begins with its first LifeCycle as an L1.

As it progresses through many LCs, the Sapien enhances its capabilities as an intelligent being. Sapiens continue to advance in L levels toward the elusive L8 IEF, which is considered 'Wisdom'. L8s are promoted from their respective subHalos to permanent member status in the Halo.

When a Sapien reaches L8 IEF status after a millennium of LCs, it doesn't require anymore LiveTime assignments. Even so, an L8 might request an additional LC, so as to further develop its Sapien and ICT set, with the possibility of progressing to the L9 Angel level.

However, advanced L8 Sapiens understand that if they take an LC slot in the SRO process, they might be denying a more needy Sapien another trip to further its own IEF development. And, such an L8 would, by definition, already have a near fully developed ICT set, which includes Fairness, Compassion and others.

It is expected that the majority of L8s, by the time they get to that level, acquiesce and accept their position as a permanent member of the Halo. In doing so, such L8s will enjoy much needed serenity and live out their eternity of tranquility and sublime happiness, without a physical body.

A percentage of L8s, however, may elect to continue their Sapien development through support and administrative functions in the Halo, subHalos and their respective subUENet operations. An 800+ Sapien might do this in an effort to continue to grow as an intelligent being, in hopes of someday becoming an L9 with angel status.

The goal of the Halo is certainly commensurate with the importance of the evolution of Intelligent Life in the universe. It is to continually enhance and improve the intelligence level of all Sapiens throughout the universe, through an infinite number of experiences gained from an infinite number of LifeCycles.

As you progress through time and space, your Sapien enrichment will certainly benefit your own personal LiveTimes, as well as those of other Sapiens affected by your presence in their LCs. And ultimately, your Sapien and ICT improvements gained from this life will benefit you personally in future LifeCycles.

If you see adversity as an ally that helps build your character traits, and you live a relatively descent life, you will have many more LiveTimes to look forward to. And, unless you screw up big-time in this life, your next LifeCycle should be equal to or better than this one. That's the Sapien evolutionary process. That's life.

Individual Sapien Analysis Testing (ISAT)

As you will see, our self-analysis program is to a large degree dependent upon your own subjective input. Therefore, it is important to approach this phase of self-awareness with deliberate thought and caution, so as not to unduly inflate your score. Your final analysis should reflect your actual Sapien development, as closely as possible.

As you rate your own character sets, please keep in mind that a Sapien with an L8 IEF is considered to have reached pure wisdom, and is generally no longer in circulation. And of course, an L9 Sapien is considered angel status.

You have two options for developing your own ISAT Score (not to be confused with higher education SAT or LSAT testing). You can go to our website, *www.ILCTheory.com* and use our interactive application. The website app auto-calculates your scores, after you provide your analysis and creates your own SQ Certificate, suitable for framing. Or, you can manually use the SQ Self-Analysis in the ISAT chapter.

Before you do either, it would be a good idea to spend a couple of days informally observing the people around you. Be cognizant of their actions toward you, your feelings about those actions, and their reactions to you. This might help you during your self-analysis.

We have found that Sapiens taking this self-analysis have a tendency to overestimate their actual character traits, intelligence and parental Sapien levels. The analysis will only benefit you, if you try to be as fair with yourself as possible, both positively and negatively. *See chapter on Individual Sapien Analysis Testing.*

Movie Quote: "Burlesque", 2010, Cher, Christina Aguilera. Cher telling her ex-husband about a business issue with her nightclub, "Look. You've got some fine qualities, and then you have some iffy qualities. But you've never been a phony."

Even though this is a subjective evaluation, be as objective as you possibly can with yourself. And have fun, it's cool. When you do your Sapien self-analysis, and understand who you really are, consider this.

Movie Quote: "Dance With Me", 1998, Kris Kristofferson, Vanessa Williams, Chayanne. Kristofferson owns a dance studio in Houston. After dance classes, he walks back to his office for the class schedule, spots his secretary and quickly observes, "There you are." She smiles and replies rhetorically, "Yeah, I was wondering where I was."

Sapien Quotient (SQ)

The Sapien Quotient, or SQ, is your Sapien's IEF developmental rating in relation to your ICTs, Intelligent Module and parental overlay. Similar to calculations used in developing the IQ of a person, your SQ is your IEF Level Score times 100. If your IEF score is an L4.8, then your SQ is 480, which should be easier to remember and compare as you evolve.

Sleep and the Sapien Dream State

The physical body, to run at peak performance, needs a significant portion of the twenty-four hour day to rest. According to doctors and human biologists, the right mixture of sleep and wake times should be about a third for sleep, or eight hours a night. Sleep is a recurring physical and mental state that includes unconsciousness, suspended senses and the cessation of most muscle activity. Sleep is necessary for the growth and rejuvenation of the immune, nervous, skeletal and muscular systems, which includes the brain.

Sleep is also thought to conserve energy and is divided into two types: rapid eye movement (REM) and non-rapid eye movement (NREM or non-REM) sleep. REM sleep accounts for 20 to 25 percent of total sleep time in most human adults. The majority of memorable and vivid dreams occur in the REM stage of sleep.

An individual's dream state is generally used to describe a person who is asleep and experiencing mental, life-like images of situations, ideas, emotions and sensations. Studies have shown that people all over the world dream about similar topics and subject matter, with a variety of explanations as to why dreams are so similar.

The commonalities of dreams indicate all people (regardless of sex, race, religion, knowledge, intelligence, ethnic background and country of origin) have similar components to their dreams. And that is because everyone, all beings, all Sapiens, have the same ICT set and the same character traits that come through in dreams.

ILC Discovery: The subject matter of dreams is similar for all Sapiens, because all Sapiens have the same set of ICTs, on which dreams are based. It is expected that most, if not all, intelligent beings in the universe share the same set of character traits.

The earliest recorded dreams, acquired from materials dating back approximately five thousand years in Mesopotamia, were documented on clay tablets. During ancient Greek and Roman periods, people believed that dreams were direct messages from the gods, or from the dead, and that they predicted the future. Some cultures practiced dream incubation, with the intent of cultivating dreams to prophesize the future.

However, events in dreams are generally outside the control of the Sapien doing the dreaming. Dreams can last for as little as a few seconds, or as long as twenty minutes. During an average lifespan, a person will spend an estimated total of about six years dreaming, or about two hours each night. Dreams are thought by some to be the portal to the subconscious, where you are alive mentally, but not physically.

The most vivid dreams occur during the last hour of sleep. Dream analysts say that people are more likely to remember their dreams, if they are awakened during the REM phase of sleep.

In reality however, most people have a hard time remembering very much detail about their dreams after they awaken. The logical reason for this is that dreams exist in temporary memory in the brain, similar to RAM in computers. And when the brain awakens, it instantly becomes flooded with new images and sensations of the surrounding environment.

These new images rapidly overwrite any remnants of dreams in RAM, so specifics of dreams are hard to remember when you awake. To compensate, try keeping a handheld voice recorder next to your bed. When you awake, while your eyes are still closed, you can use your sixth sense to pickup the hand recorder with your eyes still closed, and record your dream thoughts, before they're erased or overwritten.

Dream images are very temporary. When you lose consciousness and fall asleep, your temporary brain memory gets zeroed out, leaving room for your dreams. When you awake, your temp memory is reset back to zero, leaving room for real life. Research tells us that at least 95 percent of all dreams are not remembered. Certain brain chemistry necessary for converting short-term memories into long-term ones is suppressed during REM sleep.

People like Austrian neurologist Sigmund Freud, who developed the discipline of psychoanalysis, wrote extensively about dream theories and interpretations. Freud explained dreams as manifestations of our deepest desires and anxieties, often relating to repressed childhood memories or obsessions.

The visuals of a dream generally reflect a person's memories and experiences. The most common emotion experienced in dreams is anxiety. Other emotions include abandonment, anger, fear, joy and happiness. Negative emotions are more common than positive ones.

Further dream analysis indicates that sexual dreams occur about 10 percent of the time. Dreams with sexual themes are more prevalent in adolescents to mid-teens. In some instances, sexual dreams may result in orgasms or nocturnal emissions, which are commonly known as wet dreams, and are more common among males.

Even with extensive research, scientific breakthroughs over the years, and state-of-the-art technology we have today, it is still unknown, as to where dreams originate. Is there a single origin for dreams? And what portions of the brain are responsible for the dream cycle? And finally, what is the purpose of dreams? Current scientific knowledge cannot provide answers to any of these questions.

Alright, so that is what learned Sapiens say about dreams. Here is the real story about sleep and dreams. It is quite simple. Sleep is for the physical host body to rejuvenate. Dreams are for the Sapien's mental stability. Unlike the physical brain and body, the Sapien does not need rest. It lives eternal, 24/7, all waking and non-waking moments. So when you sleep, your Sapien fills the activity void with dreams.

ILC Discovery: Dreams are the result of the Sapien getting bored in the sleep mode, with nothing to do. So the Sapien creates fantasies about ICT events in a person's life. It plays 'what if' games in the brain's temporary memory. Dreams are the way the Sapien amuses itself, until the body awakens from its much needed rest.

That is what happens, when you are alive. In between LifeCycles, the Sapien is in a seemingly constant dream state without a body, while in the subHalo, awaiting the next LC assignment. In such a dream state, Sapiens are thought to be able to communicate with other Sapiens in the subHalo, who are also awaiting their next LC.

It is expected that this mental communication between Sapiens, while in the subHalo, does not provide any experiential occurrences that affect a Sapien's evolution in any way. But it does indicate that a Sapien's time in the subHalo would not be boring.

Good & Evil Sapiens

Fortunately, the vast majority of Sapiens in the universe are considered good Sapiens. This means most Sapiens have a relatively balanced Conscience, the ability to intuitively know what is right and what is wrong. And as important, good Sapiens generally follow their conscience and/or let it lead them in their actions and decisions. Sapiens that are considered good have generally had a number of LCs, while developing their ICTs in a positive direction.

However, as in the Yin-Yang theory, there are also evil Sapiens in the universe. The Yin-Yang philosophy believes there are two complementary forces in the universe. One is Yang, which represents everything positive. The other is Yin, which is described as negative. This ancient Chinese theory states that neither is better than the other, and that they are both necessary for the equilibrium of the universe.

Fortunately for The ILC Theory, the Yin negative component is quite small compared to the Yang's presence . Yin's negative impact on our LiveTimes continues to decline, as Earth Sapiens progress toward more positive development. Nonetheless, there is definitely an evil force in the universe that attempts to prevail over good.

And yes, there are evil Sapiens in this world of ours. Much of the time, an evil Sapien is easily recognizable. However, in today's age of mass communications, evil can be positioned, so as not to be associated with negative actions and characters. These evil Sapiens attempt to carry out their agendas and theories of world domination seemingly without detection and with impunity.

Consider an evil civilization in a world far more advanced than ours, where sanctity of life has no meaning, and violence is a way of life. Good versus evil is unfortunately a fact of life in the universe. Evil exists on Earth in many forms: killers, rapists, terrorists and some political leaders in a number of countries.

When an evil Sapien is recycled, it may be so evil that it cannot develop any positive attributes. As this occurs, evil Sapiens are aggregated in a small portion of the subHalo between lives, because of their negatively ionized energy fields, consistent with the theory that likes attract.

Example: A Sapien with an IEF rating of L2.3 after ten LCs would be considered evil and incorrigible. This Sapien will most likely experience less LCs, since SROs that require such evil traits are not that common on Earth, except maybe in some middle eastern countries that have a significantly deficient Sapien population.

Such negative Sapiens become irrelevant in more advanced or cultured societies. As worlds advance in their Sapien level requirements, evil Sapiens are less needed, since those worlds have already developed beyond a violent and/or deceptive approach to life.

If Earth is a microcosm of all intelligent planets in the universe, the assumption that good and evil do in fact co-exist is intuitively obvious to the most casual observer. There will always be good guys and bad guys, with the latter reducing in populace as Earth attempts to progress toward perfection with its Sapien population.

Roving L8 and L9 Sapiens

As previously mentioned, when a Sapien reaches L8 status, wisdom, it may retire to the Halo. Or, it may become an administrative L8 in the Halo and subHalos in support of operational L9s.

The other option for L8s and L9s is to become a Roving L8 or a Roving L9. Earth, during its current IP LifeCycle, may have had a couple of interventions by L8s and one by an L9. These advanced specialty Sapiens may accept assignments to worlds that seem to be headed in the wrong direction in their Sapien development with regard to the *Ten Rules of Intelligent Life*.

Jesus Christ was thought to be a Roving L9. He was sent to Earth about fifteen hundred years after Moses (an L8) came down from the mountain top with the Ten Commandment tablets in an attempt to get Earth back on track. Jesus is thought to be the only L9 to visit Earth. Gandhi may have been another L8, sent to Earth to correct the natural evolution of Sapiens on the planet.

Sapien Recap

SAPIEN is the acronym for Standard Astrologically Perpetual Intelligent Energy Nucleoid. The Sapien is the ILC equivalent to the soul or spirit. Given that there are a number of assumptions necessary for *The ILC Theory* to work, including the Halo, subHalos and UENet, the primary assumptions involve the Sapien.

And those assumptions, with which we should all agree, state that the Sapien (soul) is the intelligent entity that controls the body (including the brain). And the Sapien is a separate entity from the body. Most importantly, it is assumed that each Sapien is unique from the other trillions of Sapiens in the universe.

The Sapien is the Intelligent Energy Field (IEF), comprised of many NanoCells. At the heart of the Sapien is the Sapien core, which functions as the nucleus of the entity's configuration. It is surrounded by hundreds of Individual Character Traits (ICTs), consisting of one or two NanoCells each, depending on complexity.

The Central NanoCell Control (CNCC) Module is the resident communications component in the core. As their CNCC and ICT components develop, Sapiens are rated according to their individual

IEF development levels on a scale from 1 to 10. Sapiens enter their first LifeCycle as an L1. As they progress through multiple LCs, Sapiens enhance their ICT and IM ratings through experiences gained from their unique LiveTimes, resulting in improved Sapien ratings with each Cycle.

The Sapien core includes the CNCC, Parental Overlay, Intelligence and Conscience modules, LC Registry, Ionic Controls, ICT Interface, Host Body Interface and the Male/Female Switch.

The Parental Overlay Module (POM) represents a temporary energy field for the fetus to use, while awaiting its own Sapien and IEF. This temporary energy field includes IM and ICT development levels that are representative of the parents.

The Intelligence Module (IM) represents the logic, reasoning and analytical components of the Sapien's intelligence. IM enhancements are slower, more gradual improvements gained over many LCs

A Sapien's Conscience Module is either on or off. You either have one or you don't. Since the vast majority of all Sapiens do have a conscience, at varying degrees of development, it plays an important role in the Sapien's decision making.

The LC Registry is a permanent log of Sapien previous lives. It contains dates, places, names and occupations of the Sapien during previous LCs. For LCs that involved significant ICT development, an image attachment may be included in those LC entries.

Ionic Controls are present in the CNCC to assist in connecting all parts of the Sapien during its 24/7 operations. These controls ensure proper ICT and IM responses to LiveTime events during an LC.

ICT and host body interfaces are just that. They are the components that connect the Sapien to its ICT Set, and the Sapien to the host body via the Sapien-BrainBridge. These interfaces transmit critical Tetronic information about an event from the Sapien to the body, resulting in physical and mental responses to external stimuli encountered outside the body and mental images encountered within the Sapien.

The Male/Female Switch identifies the Sapien's gender. It is the one component of the Sapien that is permanent, unchanging and irreversible. Even though the M/F switch represents a physical characteristic, it also affects certain ICTs that are more prone to gender slant and interpretation.

The reason the gender switch is permanent is because it is the basic component that allows for a species to reproduce, which provides for continued Sapien LCs. Imagine a world that relied on sexual reproduction of the intelligent species between a male and female, in which gender was a variable, from LC to LC. There could be no accountability for Sapien inventory in the subHalos, nor any semblance of expected Sapien growth rates on IPs, without clear lines of gender among the species' populace.

All Sapiens have the same identical set of 512 Individual Character Traits (ICTs), some more important than others. The thing that makes the Sapien unique from other Sapiens is the fact that a Sapien's ICT and IM development percentages exist in infinite combinations, thereby creating a totally unique Sapien.

Each ICT is comprised of one to two NanoCells populated with energized TetraCells (TCs) equivalent to its percentage completion. An ICT NanoCell that has 43 percent of its TetraCells energized is rated as a 4.3 ICT, one with 52 percent energized TCs represents a 5.2 ICT, and so on.

During LiveTime, ICTs are developed toward 100 percent completion, which indicates perfection. In reality, a 10.0 ICT is not practical, nor achievable in most cases, however, there are certainly exceptions. After all, *The Theory* embraces the concept of infinity, and with infinity, anything is possible.

A Sapien's overall rating is calculated according to its IM, POM and ICT percentage developments. The Intelligence Module represents 20 percent of the total Sapien score. The parental overlay accounts for another 20 percent of the score, leaving 60 percent for ICTs. Sapien ICTs are divided into two groups; Critical ICT sets representing another 20 percent and supporting ICT sets accounting for the remaining 40 percent of a Sapien's IEF Score.

Keep in mind, when you are doing your own Sapien self-analysis, extremely high scores are not probable, nor practical. Remember, a Sapien with an L8.0+ is considered to have achieved wisdom, an L9.0+ is considered near perfect, with angel status, and an L10.0 is considered perfection, with god status, none of which currently exist in our world today.

And do not forget that Earth, as a slightly above average intelligent planet (IP) in the universe, aggregately has an average Sapien level of L4.4 globally, which includes the United States average of L5.1. Soyaseetimmy, if there are in fact no L8s to L10s on Earth, your Sapien self-analysis scoring is in reality between 1.00 and 7.99.

If your Sapien score is an L5.8 for example, which correlates to an SQ of 580, you are probably more advanced than 90 percent of all Sapiens on Earth. However, as always, since we are dealing with the concept of infinity, anything is possible.

Movie Quote & ILC Discovery: "Speechless", 1994, starring Michael Keaton, an ex-TV sitcom writer, and Geena Davis, both political speech writers. Keaton is explaining how he usually ends a sitcom episode. "I always end with a 'soyaseetimmy' to give a little back to the audience." The father tells his 11 year old boy named Timmy, about the facts of life, beginning with "So ya see Timmy." An ILC Discovery is a 'soyaseetimmy' about Intelligent Life in the universe.

The unique tetronic charge emitted by the Sapien represents its overall Sapien score and developmental level as an intelligent entity. Such a unique signal measured to the trillions of decimals is included in the Sapien's addressing scheme. This tetronic charge in combination with other pieces of information identifying the number of LCs and physical location data are used to provide a specific and totally unique Sapien address. This lengthy Sapien address is used by the subHalo for inventory purposes and SRO fulfillment, such as the following: 1.042764874923.073324195309.061374.007.47.11.570

All Sapiens are created equal initially, but depending on where they are in their development cycles, during a specific LiveTime, they are not equal. That's a fact of life, no way around it. The Sapien has to develop through experiential events during LiveTimes. All Sapien's are created equal, initially as an L1.0, and they all have opportunities to evolve through many LCs.

Movie Quote: "Forces of Nature", 1999, Ben Affleck, Sandra Bullock. Affleck writes attention-getting phrases on book covers, mostly fiction, some non-fiction. He tells Bullock, "I'm a jacket copywriter." She responds, "Oh, so you write blurbs, you're a blurbologist". "No," he says, "I'm a jacket copywriter."

As an Earth Sapien, you are interpreted in two ways. You are who you think you are. But you are also who others think you are. It just depends on your perspective, and where you are in your own LC development schedule. It seems to be a natural instinct for a Sapien to want recognition and/or approval from others for his or her accomplishments during an LC, since LifeCycles are so very hard.

You just don't end one life as an L1.0, and come back as an L6.5 in the next. During any LC, Sapien development levels and mental capabilities progress differently, and are not necessarily equal. But as for Sapien rights, all Sapiens are equal, intelligent beings on intelligent planets, as they pursue their own individual LifeCycles.

After an LC is terminated, the Sapien retains all previous character traits and intelligence, when drawn up to the subHalo for rejuvenation and RestTime. However, the Sapien does not have the capacity to retain full memories from LC to LC. The Sapien, during these RestTime periods in the subHalo, does retain all applicable personality traits from the previous LC, without a physical body.

It is expected that most intelligent societies and civilizations on different planets have similar interactions between intelligent beings and similar goals of the intellect. Some Sapiens exceed, some are mediocre and some are deficient. Some Sapiens receive praise, some commit crimes, some are egotistical, some are introverted. These qualities generally exist in all Sapiens in the universe to some degree, regardless of the physical body of the intelligent being, and regardless of the planet or galaxy in which the Sapien resides.

As a Sapien develops and ascends to higher group levels, it may require more LifeCycles to achieve smaller gains in its development. Whereas, a lesser developed Sapien could improve its overall Sapien score fairly significantly in just one LC.

Example: An Earth Sapien, with an L6.3 IEF rating for an SQ of 630, might require multiple LCs to improve to an L6.5 with an SQ of 650. However, an Earth Sapien, with an L3.3 IEF rating for an SQ of 330, might be able to progress to an L4.0 with a 400 SQ, in one LC.

As the average Sapien levels of a species or a race within a species improve, the rate of procreation subsides. This happens because higher level Sapiens tend to concentrate on individual fulfillment and personal Sapien improvements during LCs, instead of having babies.

The problem with this self-fulfilling prophecy is the fact that if the reproduction rates drop low enough, the population of a species or race begins to deteriorate, and ultimately will become extinct. Reports have shown that this seems to be happening with white Americans, who currently reproduce at the rate of 2.4 children per couple, when the minimum average to sustain a race is 2.2 births per couple.

This trend applies to all races over time, as black Americans, who previously posted high reproductive rates, now produce 2.8 children per couple, and hispanic Americans, also previously high, have subsided to 3.4 births per couple. This is in stark contrast to Muslim families around the world that are currently reproducing at the rate of 8.8 children per couple.

Regardless of the actual numbers, the trend is unmistakable and as it continues, Sapien matches for such a group may not align with existing gene pools from a dwindling Sapien group. This could account for an increasing number of developed Sapiens recycling to

China and third world countries, for example. This will eventually change those countries to more mature, peaceful nations.

As a species becomes more extinct on certain planets, the excess Sapien count for those planets will be transplanted to other planets in need of developed Sapiens, usually within the same galaxy. Cross-universe travel between galaxies may not be that common for Sapien's, if it even occur at all.

As the world advances in technology, and becomes more of a breeding ground for advanced Sapiens, it is important that the technology that fosters higher level Sapiens is controlled by positive Sapiens, not negative or evil ones. This becomes more important, as major technology advances occur, while the Earth's Sapien population is still deficiently low.

Just as Sapiens go through their LifeCycles, so do intelligent planets. After so many millions of years, some IPs will become extinct, as life-supporting planets. Life Extinction Level Events (LELEs) generally result from geophysical disruptions, or interference with their orbital paths around their Suns, or from interstellar collisions with meteors, or possibly even from unexpected solar flares. It is inevitable over time.

When a civilization or even a planet ceases to exist, the Sapien population of that planet exits en masse to the nearest subHalo. As the number of Sapiens being recycled from massive prematurely terminated LCs, instantly increases by millions or even billions, there may be a slight periodic impact on the UENet. However, the UENet and all respective subUENets servicing individual galaxies can easily accommodate such excessive amounts of Sapiens going in and out of subHalos through the normal channels simultaneously.

ILC Discovery: There is a high probability that there are thousands if not millions of planets going in and out of existence annually.

Such magnitudes of Sapien population transfers are, however, miniscule by comparison to the birth and death rates of all intelligent societies in the billions of other star systems in the universe. The total number of available Sapiens to service the universe from all available Sapien groups could easily be in the trillions of trillions at any given time.

In addition, there is a large population of L0.0 Sapiens in all subHalo reserves, which are virginal, uncirculated Sapiens. And, if there are multiple universes and possibly multiple time dimensions within universes, from which Sapiens can live and develop, there does not seem to be any shortage of Sapiens in the universe. The continuity of intelligent life in the universe would seem to be safe for another few billion years or so. There's that infinity deal again.

If Earth is a slightly above average IP with an average SQ of 440, and the universe is thought to be slightly lower, that would indicate that intelligent life in the universe is approximately 40 percent developed. And if that is the case, then the natural development cycle of the entire pool of Sapiens in the universe is less than half complete, which has only taken a few trillion years or so to accomplish.

The master plan of the HALO (Holistically Ascending Lifecycle Oasis) is to progress all Sapiens to Level 8 status or higher with highly positive ionic charges. Of course to attain this, it has required and will continue to require billions of years of evolution with the trillions and trillions of Sapiens (souls) in the universe.

Sapien CORE

The Concentric Octahedral Residual Energy (CORE) module is considered to be the nucleus of the Sapien. The Core is pure energy, residual energy that is. Webster's Dictionary defines *residual* as something that has "an internal aftereffect of experience or activity that influences later behavior". That definition succinctly encapsulates *The ILC Theory,* and the natural evolution of Sapiens in the universe.

The Sapien Core consists of eight operational components, including Sapien gender, survival instinct, conscience, intelligence, parental overlay, ICT interface and log, Sapien-BrainBridge interface and the LC Registry. The eight Core modules and all ICTs are octahedrally connected tetronic residual energy fields.

The Core has three components that cannot be altered: the male/female gender switch, the survival instinct and the conscience module. In today's techno-speak, they would be considered 'hard-wired' to the Sapien, since its first LC.

Existing in a very fluid and dynamic environment, the Core adapts to constant daily exposure to the Sapien's LiveTime experiences, which affect the intelligence and conscience modules and especially ICTs. All such activities and tetronic transfers function under the Central NanoCell Controller (CNCC), which coordinates and enables communications between the Core and the Sapien-BrainBridge.

The following chart illustrates the eight operational components of the Sapien core. They are all inter-connected with all ICTs, and they all interface with applicable outside stimuli, through the CNCC.

The Sapien CORE

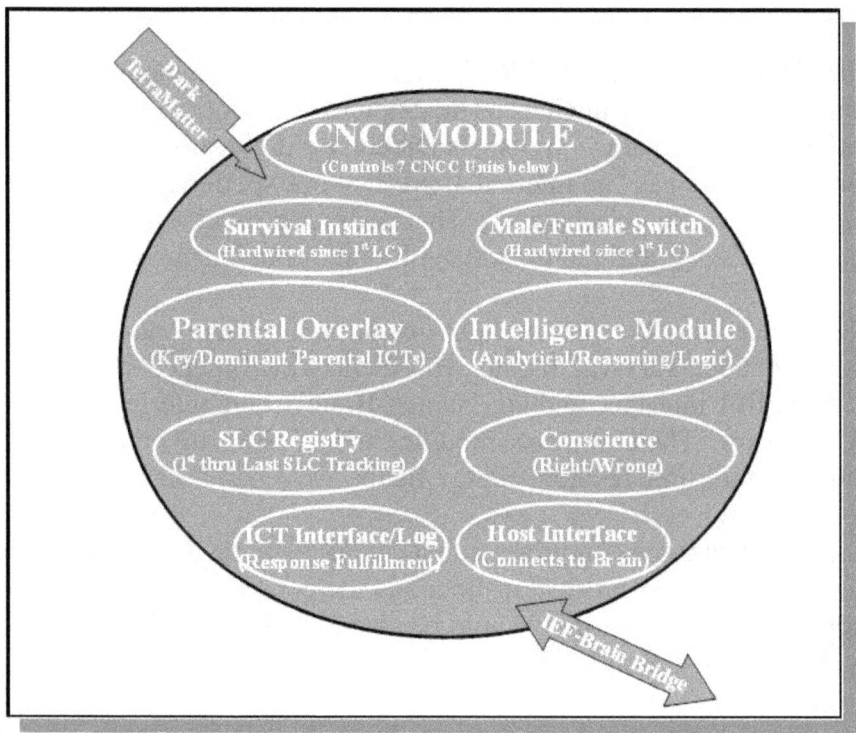

Central NanoCell Controller (CNCC)

The CNCC functions as the interface manager, responsible for coordinating communications traffic between other components of the Core, all ICTs and the Sapien-BrainBridge. The CNCC has perpetual access to the disposition and development status of all Sapien components at all times. It regulates all ICT responses to external stimuli between the Sapien and the host body.

The chart below illustrates interactions between core components.

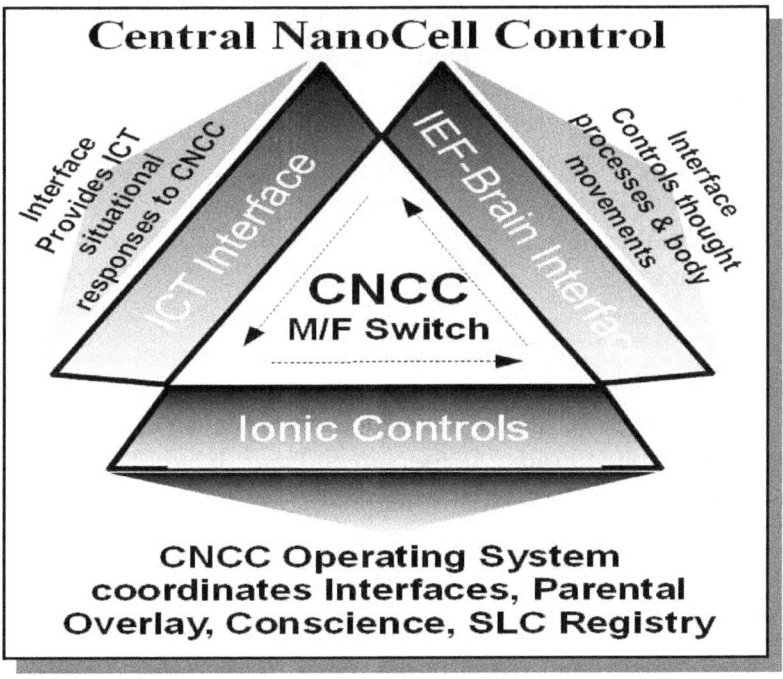

The CNCC is analogous to a resident operating system running in the background of a computer. All daily activities of the host are recorded in the CNCC's temporary storage area, equivalent to RAM (Random Access Memory) in today's computer terms.

As an ICT event is resolved with the core's appropriate responses to external stimuli, the appropriate ICTs are auto-updated, reflecting any change in development status, as a result of the event. Once a day, during a Sapien's dream state (sleep), key components of the day's ICT events, that are still in the CNCC's temporary memory, are transferred to the Sapien's short term memory.

After this brief transfer of only the key memories of the day, the core is cleared. This daily purging of data from the CNCC is best done during sleep time, since the Sapien is void of any external stimuli that might interfere with the purge.

After nightly ICT and IM updates and transfers are completed during sleep, the Sapien's core RAM is reset to zero, ready to start a new day all over again. A fresh, unpopulated core memory is essential to the daily CNCC management of Sapien components and LiveTime ICT Event resolutions.

With its resident operating system that connects and cross-connects ICTs with other core Modules, the CNCC transmits ICT responses to outside stimuli, to the brain, via the Sapien Brain-Bridge, during and after all ICT events. The CNCC module, has no short or long term memory storage, only activity-based temporary TetraCell storage.

Male/Female Switch

The M/F switch, is in a permanent and incontrovertible position, either male or female, always and forever. The gender of a Sapien never changes throughout all its LifeCycles. It is accessed constantly during most ICT events, providing the appropriate M/F slant to the Sapien's response to a situation. The subHalo, as with all good database systems, fulfills each Sapien request, matching all applicable Sapien and ICT minimums as closely as possible, including the gender match with the intended fetus.

However, the subHalo and UENet interface sometimes make mistakes with gender misplacement and delivery timings. These infrequent occurrences illustrate how the subHalo and the UENet are not infallible in their executions.

Survival Instinct

All animals, and even some plant life, have a built-in survival instinct, whether they have a brain or not, whether they have a Sapien or not. There exists an innate sense of protection for themselves and their offspring. The survival instinct module inherent in Sapiens is also considered hardwired into the Sapien core. The survival instinct generally kicks in when the entity's life is in jeopardy, and supersedes most other ICT/IM commands.

Intelligence Module (IM)

There are a number of factors that are generally considered to be responsible for the intelligence level of a Sapien. They include: verbal comprehension, word fluency, mathematical and analytical aptitude (number sense), spatial visualization, associative memory, movement/speed perception, reasoning, induction and attention span.

Most of these are attributes measured in current IQ tests. They are all equally important for a well-rounded Intelligence Module. The IM communicates with the parental overlay, conscience, ICT and host interfaces to perform continual actions and thought processes required of a Sapien on a second-by-second basis during LiveTime. *See Intelligence Module in Appendix.*

Parental Overlay

The Parental Overlay component is what we generally refer to as the personality of the Sapien. The parental overlay replicates ICT and intelligence levels from both parents during fetal growth, prior to Sapien arrival. This provides a basis for the Sapien selection process to match as closely as possible certain dominant traits of the parents with those of the requested Sapien.

Much of the ICT levels from the parents are skewed favoring the parent with the same sex as the fetus. Some ICTs of the incoming Sapien may be upgraded to match those of the parents, while others with more advanced ratings than the parental units will retain the higher ICT Ratings of the Sapien. So in some cases, the incoming Sapien may benefit from its parental units' previous LCs.

Other than certain dominant ICTs, the parents are primarily responsible for inherited physicals traits. These traits are passed on to the fetus, in the form of DNA strands from the parents' gene pool.

Physical attributes are likely to include race, body strength and type, height, weight, eye and hair color, athletic ability and physical coordination. ICTs passed on are generally referred to as personality traits, sometimes consistent with the parents, sometimes not.

The Sapien's Intelligence Module will usually override any intelligence component of the parental overlay. This is generally not a problem, since the Sapien fulfillment process from the subHalo traditionally provides a Sapien that closely approximates the Intelligence level of the parents, +/- a quarter point in the IM Rating.

Example: The incoming Sapien has a Patience ICT Rating of 5.3, while the effective parental overlay registers a Patience ICT Rating of 8.7, which is one of the reasons the father has become a successful psychotherapist. In this instance, the new Sapien's Patience ICT may be automatically increased to more closely approximate that of the parent, thereby allowing the incoming Sapien to benefit from the parental units' character traits.

When the Sapien's LC is terminated, the parental overlay module, like the CNCC memory, is reset to zero, to accommodate a new parental overlay in the next Cycle. A Sapien begins each new LC with a new parental overlay, which is contributed by the new fetus' parents.

Conscience

The Sapien's conscience component is predominantly inherited from both parents. It provides a basis for the scrupulous nature of actions and thoughts. The conscience becomes the Sapien's barometer to gauge what is right and what is wrong.

Although there may be degrees of conscience, it is similar to the M/F switch. It is either on or it is off. For the vast majority of Sapiens, the conscience is alive and well. Most Sapiens would prefer right over wrong, and good over bad, if possible. The Sapien conscience helps guide the rest of the Sapien core to do what's right, most of the time.

How the ICTs use the conscience to carry out tasks may vary, depending upon the combination of ICTs involved and the complexity of the action or thought. There are, in extreme cases, instances where a Sapien's conscience switch is turned off.

This gives rise to the retort from one person to another after observing that person's actions, "You have no conscience." Fortunately, most Sapiens in the free world do have a conscience. I suspect a large percentage of the suppressed, subordinated masses in third world countries also have a conscience, even though the dictates of their unscrupulous leaders indicate otherwise.

The conscience is an integral component of the Sapien core. The successful development of a number of ICTs, both positive and negative, can be directly related to the Sapien's conscience level. The conscience is influenced not only by the parents, but also by the environment, surroundings and beliefs of current and previous LCs.

The conscience sets the standard for determining the rights and wrongs of daily activities during an LC. It interfaces with certain ICTs such as pride, honesty, loyalty, humility, deceit, guilt, remorse and others, depending upon the situation.

Example: A young attorney began his legal career with great enthusiasm, a strong desire to make a difference and a goal of helping people. Because of his Christian upbringing, he felt he had a strong, positive conscience to do the right thing, as he began his career with an 8.4 conscience ICT rating. As his career continued through several decades, he found himself acquiescing on moral points out of necessity. It became easier and easier for him to make decisions and implement actions that were not based on any moral fiber whatsoever, but did in fact comply with current laws and regulations. His conscience rating suffered, as did some of his other ICTs, and dropped significantly by the time he retired. When he died a few years later, his ending conscience rating had dropped to 5.1, which would become the starting point for his next LC. This shows that an ICT's rating can actually be lowered based on the events of one LC.

The conscience is the engine that fuels the body's reaction to an event that involves right and wrong. It is the component that cannot fool a polygraph test. If a Sapien takes the wrong approach and attempts to lie, the conscience makes the body exhibit symptoms consistent with lying, such as nervousness, sweating, increased blood pressure and eye movement. All the while, the Sapien is hoping not to get caught.

Since a lie-detector actually measures such abrupt bodily functions, the Sapien exposes its leanings as a positive or negative entity. This is not to say, however, that anyone who lies is absolutely bad. That is not the point. We all agree lying is bad, and it is an integral part of *Rule No.3*.

However, for the most part, we have all lied to a small degree during our LC, usually for selfish reasons. But your conscience will usually tell the truth, if you listen. It could just be a temporary error in judgment, during a stressful time. And whatever the reason for submitting to a polygraph, it is certainly a stressful situation. When in doubt, tell the truth.

An untrained sociopath can pass a polygraph without any problem. A sociopath is a Sapien whose conscience switch is turned off, and who has the innate ability to pass a polygraph, while lying.

ICT Interface/Log

The ICT Interface is the controlling module that polls applicable ICTs during an event (actions and/or thoughts). It relays results to the Sapien-BrainBridge, which in turn instructs the brain as to the body's appropriate response and disposition relating to the event.

The ICT Log tracks the ICT Ratings of all ICTs, and is kept current and updated after each event, which directly affects the overall Sapien Rating. Even so, the ICT interface still polls applicable ICTs before communicating with the host interface, to ensure its recommendations are the most current for the Sapien at the time of the event.

Other than actual events occurring that require live polling of the ICTs, the Central NanoCell Controller polls, at frequently scheduled times, all ICT NanoCells. This is done to maintain current individual development levels and TetraCell completion percentages, which continually updates the ICT Log.

As an individual ICT NanoCell evolves, reaching a higher percentage of completion, the CNCC's polling of that specific ICT may reduce in frequency. This requires less communications power that can be focused on more needy NanoCells, during LifeCycles.

Example: A level 2 ICT NanoCell at 23 percent completion, may require more CNCC communications time than a level 7 ICT NanoCell at 78 percent completion, since the L2 ICT is subject to more rapid change than the L7. The object of each LC is to enhance the completion rates of all ICT NanoCells, which inherently and indirectly enhances the Sapien's Intelligence Module.

The Intelligent LifeCycle Theory

Host Interface

The Host Interface is the connection point between the Sapien core and the Sapien-BrainBridge (SBB). It interacts with the IM, ICTs, conscience and parental overlay components.

To ensure the accurate execution of physical, biological and mental duties are commensurate with the dictates of the Sapien, the host interface connection to the Sapien-BrainBridge is paramount for a successful LC. And as such, in today's terminology, the host interface represents a single point of failure for the Sapien.

The chart below shows key components and their integral relationships necessary to function as the controlling unit of the Sapien.

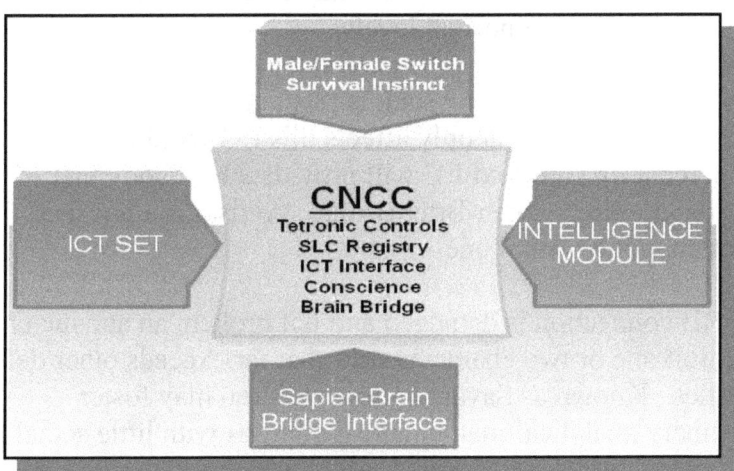

If the connection between the Sapien-BrainBridge (SBB) and the host interface is damaged or broken, it has a dramatic impact on the physical and mental functions of the host body. Without a solid connection to the body, proper ICT responses and IM input/feedback to the brain are greatly diminished. This results in a significant lack of awareness of surroundings and a severe inability to communicate with others, even in the most familiar of surroundings.

Example: A child with autism could be the result of such a faulty connection between the Sapien and the host brain. In severe cases, the majority, if not all, of the Sapien's ICTs cannot get through to the brain to guide the person's physical and mental responses to outside stimuli. In more moderate cases of autism, the SBB may be able to coordinate some tasks with thought and social interaction.

Please remember, the Sapien in an autistic person is alive and well, and undoubtedly frustrated, because of the physical malfunction of the SBB. An autistic person must live with the deficiencies of not being able to communicate at normal levels.

The good news, if that can be said, is that autism is a temporary setback for the Sapien that only affects this LC. And chances are close to 100 percent that the next LC will provide a host body that will have a solid, functioning Sapien-BrainBridge. Autism is a physical impairment, not a mental one.

If the SBB connection is damaged and not broken, an autistic child may exhibit one or two characteristics that far exceeds other deficient capabilities. Known as Savants, these children may foster extraordinary analytical/mathematical abilities with little social skills.

On the other hand, the tetronic connection between the core's host interface and the host brain far surpasses any state-of-the-art technology we have today. This tetrical connection has proven itself over millions of years with extremely high stability and reliability factors, with very few exceptions, one in a million. Fortunately, Sapiens with such an SBB malfunction will have another shot at a full life with real LiveTime in future LCs.

LC Registry

The LC Registry is the permanent record of a Sapien's LC journeys. It logs each LifeCycle occurrence according to dates, locations, vocations and Sapien Ratings, preserved strictly for posterity purposes. This is the only module within the Sapien that has any permanent memory of previous lives, albeit on a cursory basis.

Each line item entry also has a short multimedia file attachment, which is indicative of that LC's LiveTime. Such files are not normally addressable by the Sapien, except by external regression procedures. Because the LC Registry only contains brief stats and short multimedia files indicative of each LC entry, memories gained from regression sessions will generally depend on these attachments.

--- Beginning ---					-------- Ending ----------		
LC	Date	Sapien	Galaxy/Star/Planet/Loc.	Occupation	Date	Live Time	Sapien
01	1mil BC	1.0	MW/Sun/Earth/mountains	Caveman	999,974 BC	26yrs	1.9
09	1345	3.6	MW/Sun/Earth/England	Gypsy	1392	47yrs	4.2
14	1891	5.1	MW/Sun/Earth/USA	Singer	1945	54yrs	5.7
15	1947	5.7	MW/Sun/Earth/USA	Entrepreneur	open	open	6.3

The LC Registry is not accessible to other modules, so as not to create ICT conflicts between current lives and past LCs. The above table illustrates an example of a few LC Registry entries of one Sapien, over the course of 1,000,2011 years of LC occurrences, beginning as a Caveman a million years ago.

During all LifeCycles, the CNCC Module is the controlling entity for the Sapien and directly interfaces with the Sapien-BrainBridge to maximize its LiveTime experiences. The intricate interaction between the components of the core is critical. Fortunately, the Sapien Core and all its components have an extremely high reliability rate.

As the core components progress in their development, the overall Sapien rating should enjoy enhancements with each ensuing LC. Theoretically, most ICT Ratings will also improve as the Sapien continues through its series of LifeCycles. This is the normal progression, unless a significantly negative experience during LiveTime occurs that inordinately affects an ICT, or group of ICTs.

When such a severe ICT Event occurs, resulting in negative ICT impact on specific ICTs, Sapien development may be reduced. Given the severity of such events, and the severity of ICT impact, a number of future LCs for could conceivably be required for the affected ICTs to repair themselves.

Example: A male Sapien with an L6.1 IEF, circa 2011, is conscientiously providing for his family of four as a chemical engineer. Through hard work and late hours working as he put himself through college, he had enhanced much of his ICT Set, well on his way to an L6.2. While away for the weekend at a business conference, his wife and two children were murdered during a home invasion. Needless to say, his hatred and violence ICTs among others were inflamed. His compassion and forgiveness ICTs suffered greatly. He was able to control his violent response to such a senseless act, which resulted in a few ICTs actually improving because of the tragedy.

However, the man in this example no longer had the same beliefs in humanity that he once had. Even though he wanted to, had he taken the law into his own hands, searched for and killed the murderer of his family, his Sanctity of Life ICT would have suffered drastically, as would other ICTs that were affected by this tragic incident.

In this situation, the man did show restraint, and mentally survived the tragedy. This man is expected to finish his current LC with some degree of improvement in his SQ and a number of ICT enhancements. His next LC should be much better.

Sapien Core Recap

All eight components of the Sapien Core are crucial to the successful evolution of the Sapien. The Central NanoCell Control module, which directs the flow of information between all other core components, effectively manages the most efficient method of satisfying and/or disposing of ICT events successfully.

As the eight core components work in unison with the Sapien's ICT sets, the Sapien develops a stable platform for future performance levels. Effective CNCC communications, working in concert with all core components, assist in maximizing event outcomes that are consistent with core attributes. Optimal core functionality provides for overall improvements in ICT development during any given LC.

The Sapien core has a high reliability factor. It's functionality and efficiency in the physical realm, however, are sometimes beyond the control of the Sapien. External stimuli may sometimes dictate core responses and eventual outcomes of ICT events.

The Intelligent LifeCycle Theory

5 Individual Character Traits

The Individual Character Trait (ICT) is the basis of evolution within all intelligent life in the universe. The full spectrum of character traits is common to all people (Sapiens). The overall ICT set, inherent in each of us and used in *The Theory,* is described with thousands of words in the English language representing attributes, emotions and character traits in humans. Some words may seem the same, but have different meanings in relation to character traits.

Example: The loving ICT is very different than the loveable ICT. trusting is different than trustful' and so on. But that's why new words were created in the first place, to describe something a little differently than existing words can.

For purposes of *The ILC Theory*, we have used 512 different ICTs to measure the development of the Sapien. However, when you evaluate your own ICTs, do not get caught up in strict definitions of words used to describe ICT sets. Sometimes words may mean something different to different people. Just consider what the words mean to you.

The development, of ICTs during LiveTimes, dramatically affects the evolution of the Sapien itself. According to the Individual Sapien Analysis Testing (*ISAT*) rating system, ICTs represent about eighty

The Intelligent LifeCycle Theory

percent of the overall Sapien level ratings. The only component in the ratings not related to ICTs is intelligence.

Although intelligence does not specifically involve ICTs, it directly interfaces with ICTs in response to live experiential situations, referred to as ICT events. On any given day, a Sapien may encounter many ICT events, some small and some big, some important and some nominal. An ICT event is a mental or physical activity that requires the Sapien to respond with experience and thoughts relating to specific character traits, instead of mere physical reactions.

All character traits are considered equal, just as all Sapiens are considered equal in *The Theory*. The only difference in character traits between Sapiens is their individual development percentages. As a Sapien experiences ICT events throughout its LC journeys, its Set of ICTs evolve, hopefully in the positive direction. All ICTs are equal, but they all develop differently. Depending upon the situation, however, certain ICTs may be more valuable than others.

Example: If you are suddenly trapped in a lion's cage, timidity and patience might be your most valuable ICTs. Confidence and dominance might not be good here, but they might be valuable ICTs in a back alley mugging. Both scenarios would be considered significant ICT events in an LC. Both would require different development levels of ICTs to survive.

As a Sapien progresses through its LC cycle, ICT events during those LiveTimes shape and formulate its Individual Character Traits. The development level of a person's character traits ensures that all Sapiens are indeed unique. It is nearly a mathematical impossibility for two people to have the exact same combination of ICTs with the exact same development percentages.

Sapiens experience different ICT events every day that continually add to or detract from the development of a person's overall character traits. Even though all Sapiens have the same ICT Set, all Sapiens have different levels of development for those same ICTs, thus making all Sapiens unique.

ICT Basics

An Individual Character Trait is pure intelligent energy with a unique tetronic charge equal to the percentage of its TetraCells that are energized. The more developed an ICT becomes, the greater its tetronic charge, both positively and negatively.

Each ICT is comprised of nanocells, containing energized tetracells and dark tetramatter. Positive ICT nanocells emit a tetrical charge, the strength of which indicates the percentage of positive ICT development, whereas, the negative ICT nanocells emit a negative tetrical charge. Inactive tetracells in an ICT nanocell are energized by a signal transmitted from the Sapien core to the ICT, during and after every ICT event throughout the LiveTime of an LC.

ICTs are politically and religiously neutral, but may have a gender slant that affects a Sapien's response. They are not value based. They are statistically based, with regard to specific reactions to incidents that require ICT involvement. Political and religious preferences are learned beliefs, not innate character traits.

As a Sapien develops its ICTs through many LCs, it's overall development percentages are tracked and monitored by its core module. Sapiens with more LCs to their credit are more advanced and have higher ICT development percentages than Sapiens with less LiveTimes. This is considered one of the basics of ICT evolution.

Each ICT NanoCell has either a positive or negative ionic charge, based on its individual development history. Each ICT is also included in the core's ICT Development Registry. This registry is used as the summary table of ICT development for each Sapien, so as to facilitate subHalo searches for Sapien matches and SRO fulfillment.

ICT NanoCells have a finite weight and volume, even though we cannot measure them with our current technology. Each ICT NanoCell has one thousand Intergy (Intelligent Energy) TetraCells available to be energized and developed to full potential at 100 percent.

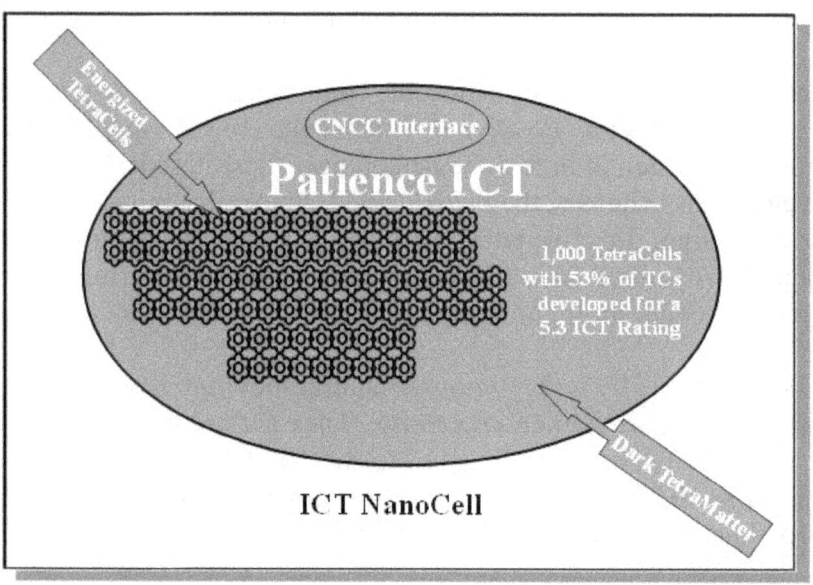

The patience ICT, as illustrated above, has attained a 53 percent completion of its energized tetracells, over a number of LCs. This ICT would receive a 5.3 rating, meaning it is a little over halfway developed as a character trait.

You may have noticed that I have used the patience ICT more than once to describe the ICT development process. Apparently I used patience as one of the first examples I created, since it is one of my own ICTs that I am currently trying to improve. Incidentally, I estimate my own patience ICT at 3.8, but I'm working on it.

There are two basic types of ICT sets: Key ICTs and Supporting ICTs. Key ICT sets, furnished by the parental overlay during conception, are predominantly used during the selection process to obtain a suitable Sapien match for the parental units. Other than that, all ICTs are of equal value.

ICT Development

A Sapien's ICTs develop primarily through LiveTimes, during real live ICT events. ICT Development begins at birth, which other than death, is the most significant ICT event in any LC.

Even though the Sapien is fused with the fetus after the first trimester of pregnancy, the child does not generally begin exhibiting signs of its ICT set (personality) until twelve to eighteen months of age. This seems to be commensurate with the time in which the little baby begins to show actual awareness of its surroundings and activities occurring that are external stimuli to its own existence.

A child generally does not start showing any semblance of a personality until its physical host body can support coordinated movement, represented by the interpretation of a Sapien's ICT commands. When the host body develops to that point, the Sapien will begin to have an impact on its own growth and can then express itself through bodily movements and sounds.

At that moment, a Sapien's ICT Set begins to respond to outside stimuli and continues to develop throughout the LifeCycle. The overall development level a Sapien achieves with its ICTs, reflects on how well its ICTs react to each other in addressing LiveTime ICT events.

Murder, which is a malicious premature termination of a Sapien's LC, is not covered by the disclaimer in *Rule No.1* of the *Ten Rules of Intelligent Life*. It involves the violence ICT, as well as sanctity of life, remorse, compassion, respect, shame, regret and a few other ICTs.

If these other supporting ICTs show positive signs of Sapien redemption, then the violence ICT may be reduced in its intensity. However, with such an infraction of Rule No.1, even with genuine remorse and shame, it may still take a Sapien a number of future LCs to correct itself.

Conversely, if the supporting ICTs do not provide positive ionic responses, which means they are likewise deficient ICTs, then the violence ICT may become more violent and digress even further, becoming more negative. If the Sapien does not genuinely show its remorse and shame for such a traumatic ICT event, then the Sapien may be recycled in future LCs, as a negative or evil Sapien.

Such an evil Sapien would not be expected to receive many future LC assignments, since parental overlay requests usually prefer non-violent Sapiens. This is generally the case, except maybe in the Middle East, where it is obvious that sanctity of life is not as revered as it should be,

The Intelligent LifeCycle Theory

given our current level of development as a society.

Example: A person commits a murder and shows true remorse, during their lifetime. The tetronic charge of their violence ICT might improve from a -8.1 to a -6.2 rating. However, if a person fakes remorse, just to get a lighter sentence or to get a better deal from prosecutors, such an ingenuous action could in fact hurt the ICT's development, lowering it even further from a -8.1 to -9.3.

If a Sapien continues to progress with negative ICT development, such a Sapien will carry those negative tetronic charges into the next LC, which could result in its conscience switch being turned off. If not corrected, this individual evildoer might perpetuate its violence, through its misleading convictions that there's nothing wrong with violence and murder.

If nothing changes to reverse the violent trend, this Sapien will continue its negative ways through less frequent LCs . There needs to be a fundamental change in philosophy, that has not yet been learned. Until the Sapien learns it is not okay to kill, and violence is not the answer, the evil Sapien will only continue to digress.

At some point, the high negativity of the Sapien will become irreversible. At that point, the Sapien may be segregated to the lower-level Sapien section of its home-base subHalo, while awaiting fewer and fewer LCs.

When the Sapien becomes so evil and nonredeemable, this could be construed as some semblance of hell with permanent seclusion to the lower levels of the subHalo and no chance for future LiveTimes. No more LCs for this guy.

LiveTime ICT events are the only venue for ICT development. Without them, a Sapien cannot progress nor digress any further ICT development. LifeCycles are the lifeblood of a Sapien's evolution.

When looking at the overall Sapien development percentages, you have to consider the options of the Sapien during a LiveTime Event. If you have a developed ICT, to whatever degree that addresses the event, you use it. If not, you learn from the event and the affected ICT gains enhancement.

If you do neither, you lose the opportunity to improve your ICT. This in itself means that you may be destined to repeat the event in the future. Remember, the primary goal of all Sapiens is to develop and enhance all positive ICTs and minimize or neutralize all negative ICTs during all LCs.

When you evaluate the development of your own ICT sets, you can usually spot specific ICTs that are already developed and/or those ICTs that need additional work. Ideally, during your current LC, it would be good to capitalize on those positive ICTs already developed and enhance those that need help.

A Sapien may have a highly developed ICT, like creativity for example. That Sapien might become a music composer, an artist, a writer, or even an entrepreneur. And it may seem natural for a Sapien to use that ICT as the primary reason for its existence in life, without regard to enhancing other ICTs. Motivation, discipline, patience and other related ICTs are prerequisites for this type of Sapien.

If a Sapien doesn't have any prominent ICTs that consume its thought processes, that Sapien has the luxury of developing other ICTs that may not be available to the more focused Sapien. Basically, it's a match between the physical capabilities (including the brain) of the host body and the Sapien's ICT sets required to capitalize on those inherent physical attributes.

As the Sapien develops, its IEF level is generally irreversible, unless some significant negative ICT event occurs. As a rule, a Sapien will continue to progress in its development through its LCs. More often than not, a Sapien's IEF Level at the beginning of the next LC will be no lower, overall, than the beginning of the current life, with some exceptions of course, since we are dealing with infinity.

ICTs however, may experience reductions in development from one LC to another, as a result of LiveTime experiences negatively impacting an ICT. Negative ICT events can be significant ICT enhancers and/or detractors. The ultimate effect an event has on an ICT depends on how the Sapien responds to the event. The same negative event could 'build character' or tear it down.

Movie Storyline: In *"Turk 182"*, 1985, Timothy Hutton, Robert Urich. Off duty firemen were drinking at their local fireman's watering hole, when a child runs into the bar screaming about a fire, begging them to help save his family. Urich, an off duty fireman, responds, goes into the burning building, rescues the kid's little sister, gets blown out of a fourth story window, and breaks his back when he lands, but he saved the little girl. His heroism ICT was hitting on all cylinders, literally.

However, Urich was later discredited for his actions, because he had been drinking, even though he saved the little girl's life. He was basically stripped of his hero image. But he did achieve maximum positive development of his heroism and bravery ICTs, approaching 10.0 for both. He also improved his cowardly ICT nearing 0.0 at the same time. The strength of these ICT enhancements should carry forward to future LifeCycles.

Life-saving heroes seem to have similar motives to those of medical researchers, who commit their entire lives to finding the cure for a deadly disease. The only difference is the time required to save a life. Their sanctity of life, compassion and other related ICTs are similarly well developed, to the point of being irreversibly positive.

Severe ICT events, resulting in significant jumps in ICT development, have a tendency to create permanent ICT enhancements that a Sapien carries with it going forward. During Sapien LifeCycles, positive ICTs have a better chance of continuing to improve, while negative ICTs usually can be corrected over time with philosophical changes.

Example: As a Sapien experiences a severe ICT event, and reacts with a positive ICT response, it is referred to as character-building. In describing such events, society has given us sayings like "That builds character," and "That decision shows real character."

In reality, those age-old sayings are right on target. ICT events definitely build character, Intelligent Character Traits that is. However, they can also hurt ICT development, unfortunately.

ICT Operations

One way of thinking about an ICT is to see it as a bucket full of dormant TetraCells, waiting to be energized, positively or negatively. As an ICT develops, its TetraCells (TCs) are energized. The percent of TCs energized in an ICT NanoCell creates a unique tetronic signal emitted to the core, representing the development level of that ICT.

The Intelligent LifeCycle Theory

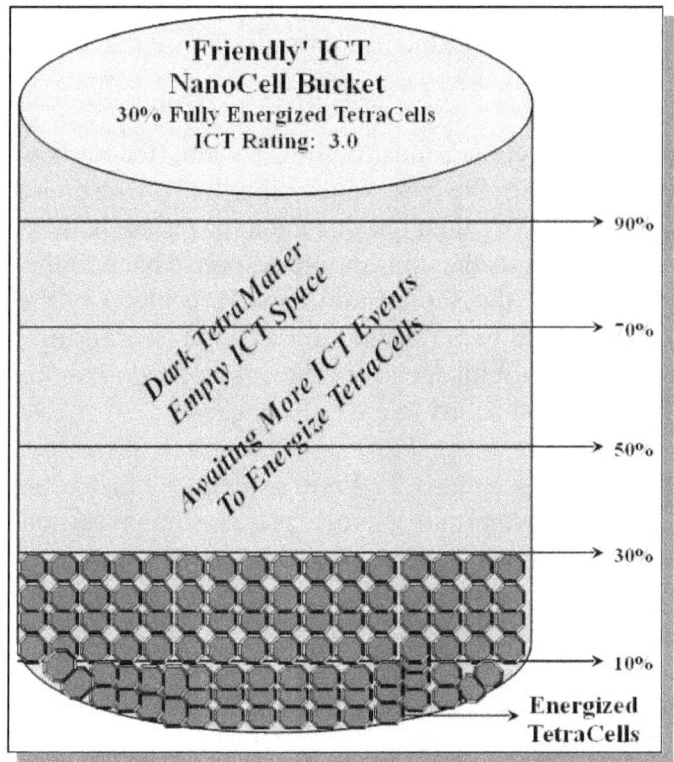

The above illustration presents a positive ICT model as a bucket, awaiting more TetraCells to be energized by LiveTime ICT events. This example indicates the Friendly ICT is about 30 percent developed, as represented by the amount of energized tetracells. As this Sapien develops further with ICT events, additional TCs will be energized representing further completion percentages.

The ICT NanoCell bucket gets filled up with energized TCs that are proportionate to its LiveTime experiences that occur in everyday life. When an ICT event occurs, the brain releases a tetroscopic enzyme, called a *Tetrazyme*, unique to each ICT affected by the event. These unique ICT Tetrazymes produce a tetronic charge that acts as a digital fingerprint for each ICT.

Within a matter of tetraseconds of an ICT event, the Sapien-Brain Bridge interfaces with the core, requesting the ICT response to the event. The Sapien core then queries the appropriate ICT, receives the response and transmits the appropriate response back to the Sapien-Brain Bridge. Once the Sapien command is received by the brain, the brain instructs the body to respond to the event, specifying verbal and physical responses. With speeds in the tetraseconds, this entire process is considered instantaneous in most instances.

Once the host body executes the brain's translated instructions from the core, the external stimuli (people, places, things) respond. If the external stimulus is not satisfied with the Sapien's response, the Sapien-Brain Bridge sends a followup query to the core for additional instructions. This is where the event impacts the ICT's development.

If the initial Sapien response was acceptable to the external stimuli, the ICT event is closed out, with no further action required. However, if the body needs further assistance from an ICT to continue with the event, the affected ICT will poll other related ICTs and maybe even the IM and conscience modules, for response options. Again, in a matter of tetraseconds, the brain is apprised of additional bodily responses.

If the event accepts the revised instruction set, then the event is closed out, otherwise a repeat of the process will continue until resolved. When the ICT event is closed out, the ICT's registry is updated with the results. If the outcome is positive, the ICT is enhanced with more Energized TCs, which is ionized dark tetramatter. If the outcome is negative, the ICT might be reduced slightly in tetracells, reflecting a new percentage of development for the affected ICTs.

The more positively developed an ICTs bucket is, the stronger the positive tetronic charge. The more negatively developed an ICT's bucket is, the stronger the negative tetronic charge. This has some similarities to the famous yin-yang theory, where the world is divided into two groups of things, people and places. This may be oversimplifying it, but yin-yang basically says that every positive thing has an opposite negative thing, both of which are reasons for the other's existence. Every positive ICT has an opposite negative ICT, but not necessarily of equal strengths.

As an ICT bucket fills up, the percentages of development are reflected in the ICT's ratings. When the positive ICT bucket is full, the ICT is developed to 100 percent. At this point in the ICTs evolutionary status, the Sapien will process all future requests for such a fully developed ICT, resulting in perfect responses.

ICTs that are less than fully developed will continue to be subject to change during events in any give LC. However, when an ICT passes the 8.0 level in development, that ICT will generally remain at that level of achievement, going forward, unless a severe ICT event occurs.

A Sapien (mind/psyche/soul/spirit) that possesses ICTs at this development level is expected to also have a number of other ICT sets with similar developmental percentages. As highly developed ICTs react with other highly developed ICTs, resultant decisions are expected to become more effective, with increasing frequency.

When this type of harmonious ICT interaction occurs, most external stimuli are more adeptly satisfied with each ICT response, on the first pass. This enviable ICT position, where many ICT sets are operating in concert, creates a curious side effect for the Sapien. Because most of its ICT decisions are correct on the first pass, with no additional feedback from external stimuli, this Sapien will not have as many opportunities to further develop many of its other ICTs. Poor Sapien.

Alright, back to the real world, in which most of live, with less than fully developed ICTs. The ICT component of the Sapien's infrastructure is, by definition, a constantly changing, highly fluid process. The complexity of ICT operations increases manifold, when considering interfaces between ICT NanoCells, the Intelligence and Conscience modules and the Sapien-Brain Bridge (SBB).

The graph below illustrates typical stages in an ICT's growth, using

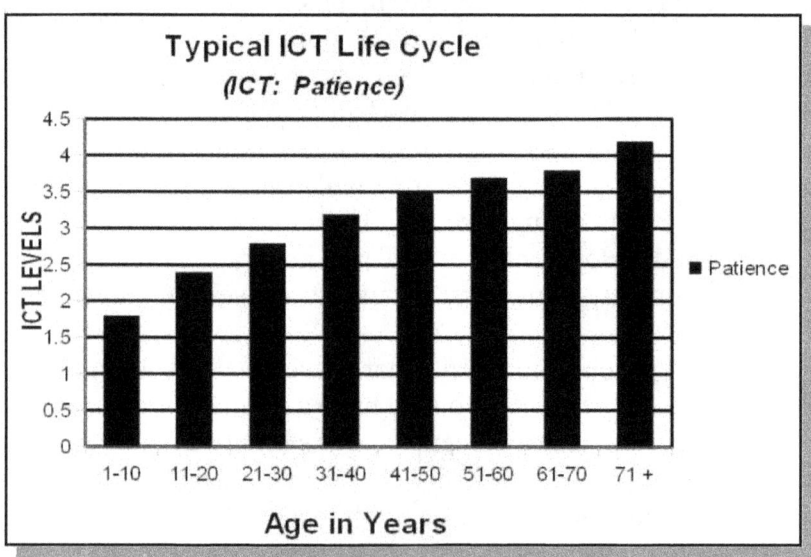

a Sapien's patience ICT, measured by its development levels during ten year increments. In most cases, as a Sapien maintains a more constant growth curve, its ICT Ratings may vary, but will generally develop upwardly on a gradual growth curve throughout any given LC.

The graph shows a Sapien coming into the world, with a patience ICT of 1.75. This Sapien showed improvements in its patience levels at every stage of its life, and ended the LC with a much improved 4.2 patience ICT. Even though this Sapien's patience ICT is still below average, it leaves plenty of room for improvement in future LCs.

Parental Overlay

During the first trimester after conception, as the fetus begins to form, a Sapien Request Order (SRO) is generated by the temporary IEF of the fetus, comprised primarily of its Parental Overlay prerequisites. As soon as the gender is determined, and all other search criteria are determined, the SRO is picked up by the nearest galaxy's UENet.

At the beginning of the second trimester, the SRO is fulfilled with a Sapien that approximates the parents' characteristics. The majority of character traits, retained by an incoming Sapien at birth, are subject to an equitable fusion between the parental overlays' ICT levels and those already developed by the incoming Sapien. ICT levels are predicated on ICT achievements from previous LCs and those of both parents.

When an ICT of the incoming Sapien is significantly lower than the parents, the new Sapien will generally begin at its lower level, since it needs additional LC time for proper development. But if the ICT is only slightly lower than the parents in that particular trait, it may be upgraded to start the LC at or near the parent's ICT level.

This minor ICT adjustment at the beginning of an LC might be a moot point in reality. In most cases, the parent, with the higher ICT level of a particular ICT, will probably train and guide the child toward the development of that ICT anyway, during growth years, so it may not be important to upgrade upon entry. Regardless, the Sapien has no choice in this process. It is the determinism theory at work.

Example: An entering Sapien has an ICT of 5.7, while the same ICT in the SRO from its parental overlay is rated at 5.9. The Sapien's ICT may be upgraded to match the parents. However, if a Sapien comes in with a 5.2 ICT that the parent's ICT is rated at 6.7, that ICT will not be upgraded to allow more needed time for proper ICT development.

When the Sapien is originally drawn into the womb, the Sapien is immediately fused with the existing energy field of the fetus, which is primarily from the parental overlay. The Sapien is then calibrated for any applicable ICT upgrades, by making automatic comparisons between the ICT Registries of the Sapien and the parental overlay.

The vast majority of Sapien requests from fetuses is for positive Sapiens, dependent and reliant upon the parent's L levels. But occasionally, the SRO might include a request for negative ICTs, usually from two parents who are highly negative, and/or evil. However, the distinction between negative and evil is an important one. Negative ICT events occur to all of us during our LCs, but most of us learn from them, so they will not be repeated.

If a Sapien continues to proffer negative responses to events without learning from them, such a Sapien might be construed as evil. But that is not necessarily the case, depending on the frequency of such infractions. An evil Sapien has had many LCs, without appreciable improvement in its ICTs, resulting in a very low overall Sapien score.

Except in special cases, LifeCycle influences on the Sapien are the dominating factors for current and future development. However, newly arriving Sapiens will be impacted to some degree by a portion of the Sapiens' parental character traits, which includes of course, the parental Sapiens' previous LCs.

A Sapien's character traits, influenced by its parent's ICT sets, will usually begin to show outwardly between twelve and eighteen months. This is the period in which the body is developing to allow the Sapien to begin controlling its responses to external stimuli. At that point, the ICTs will begin to have an impact on bodily responses.

Examples of ICT Evolution

Other than enhancements in the Sapien core, the evolution of the Sapien's ICTs is largely responsible for the Sapien's IEF Ratings and its overall development, before, during and after an LC. When a Sapien is drawn or attracted to the fetus in the womb, it brings with it the Sapien's entire ICT Set, at varying stages of development.

The starting point for an ICT is the ending point of that ICT from the last LC. This development level should closely approximate the minimum requirements needed by the fetus' parental overlays, that exist in the womb at the time of arrival of the new Sapien.

As a child grows physically, so does the child's Sapien. Experiences gained from a Sapien's LiveTime on Earth, and other IPs, affect the development of a range of specific ICTs during an LC's LiveTime.

The way an ICT responds to events during an LC, depends on its level of development at the time of the event. The outcome of such events may enhance or detract from the ICTs' previous levels. Development of ICT sets in a Sapien is a fluid process, changing throughout the LiveTime during an LC, hopefully in the positive direction.

As referenced in the following examples, ICT development is often materially impacted by physical stimuli, social constraints and environmental conditions. The way a person's Sapien responds to real-life situations directly affects the ICT Ratings, positively or negatively, depending on the outcome. LiveTime ICT events help mold the overall Individual Character Traits in a Sapien's existence.

PA-IN ICT Pair (Patience-Intolerance) *(for 2 Sapiens)*

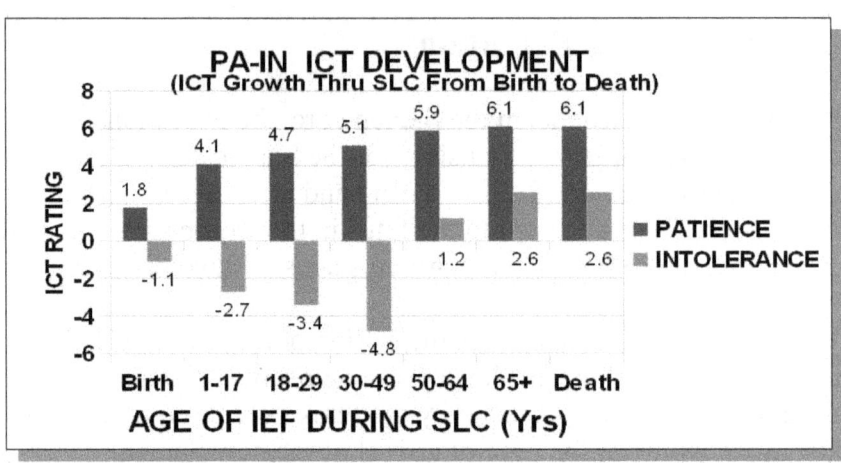

■ Example: Sandra, born with a PA-IN ICT Level of 1.8, did not have much patience at first, like most newborns. She was raised by her single mom, and worked part time to help out, since she was twelve. After high school, she began her career as a waitress, enhancing her patience ICT out of necessity. Sandra died at the age of seventy-seven with an average 6.1 PA-IN ICT Rating. Other ICTs, such as love and understanding also scored above average for this female Sapien.

■ Example: Ellen, born with a PA-IN ICT Level of -1.1, grew up in a privileged life. She always got what she wanted through her adult years and raised her two children to think they were better than most.

When she turned fifty, her life-long, live-in maid took seriously ill. Ellen devoted much of her days taking care of her friend, who died a few years later. When Ellen died at eighty-two, she had enhanced her PA-IN ICT Rating to 2.6. Other ICTs, such as conceit and vanity also rebounded to low positives, for this female Sapien.

PA-VI ICT Pair (Passivity-Violence) *(for 2 Sapiens)*

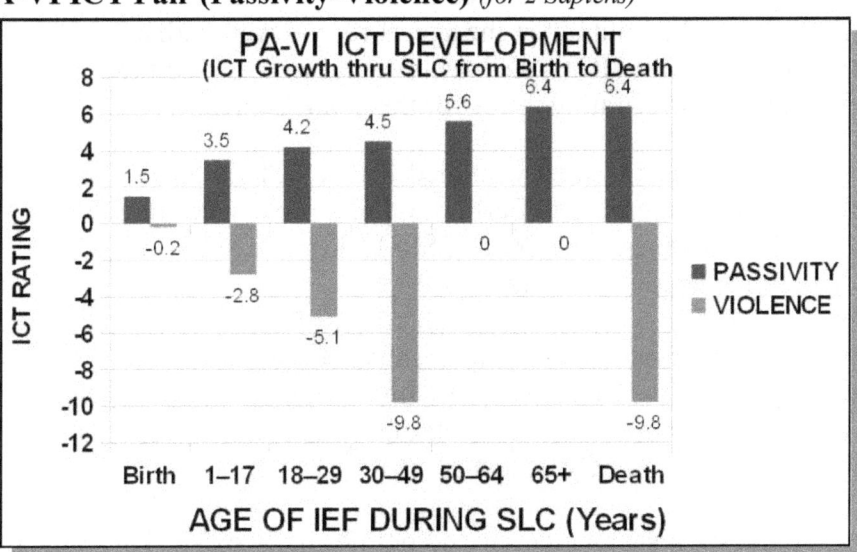

■ Example: Sam, born with an PA-VI ICT Level of 1.5, grew up in a normal family environment. Through his teenage years, Sam joined many of the school clubs, played in the band and made B's through high school. He got married after college, raised a family and avoided violence, whenever possible. Sam died at the age of seventy-three with a respectable 6.4 PA-VI ICT rating. Other ICTs, such as dignity and honor also scored high for this male Sapien.

▪ Example: Eddie, born with an PA-VI ICT level of -0.2, grew up in a violent family environment. Through his teenage years, Eddie sought peer acceptance using violence as a way to get things. At eighteen, when he became a man, he got in trouble and got a four-year degree in violence in prison.

When he was paroled, he began robbing liquor stores to get cash. He progressed with his craft and became a cheap hit man. Eddie died during a failed hit contract at the age of forty-seven with a PA-VI ICT rating of -9.8. Other ICTs, such as love and caring, also took significant negative rating drops for this male Sapien.

▪ Analysis: This murderer who died with a -9.8 violence ICT, has little chance of returning to Earth or other similarly developed IPs in another LC. The vast majority of SROs do not request, nor accept such extreme negative ICT ratings.

This Sapien may be exiled to the negative sector of the Halo, never to return again to LiveTime, except by mistake, which does happen. So in a sense, if a Sapien has too much of a negative ICT Rating, he may never get another LifeCycle again.

SROs requesting such negativity do not normally exist. This Sapien may be transferred to what current religions refer to as hell, with no more LifeCycles, and no more LiveTimes. Being exiled into oblivion is another example of the infinity rule at work.

PE-AR ICT Pair (Persuasive-Argumentative) *(1 Sapien)*

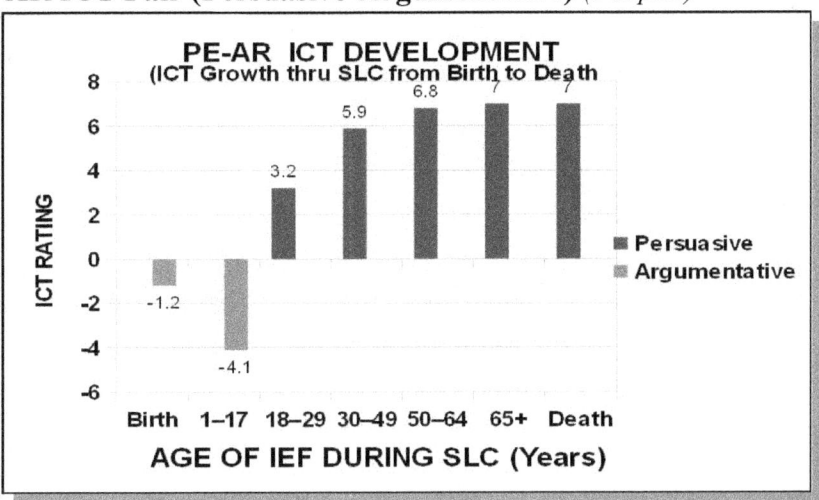

▪ Example: Little Tommy, with a 5.9 Sapien Level, was born arguing with the doctor. Through his teen years, Tommy found that he could win most arguments.

▪ The summer after graduating high school, Tom took a job selling cookware and learned more persuasive techniques. After college, Tom went on to law school and refined his persuasive abilities. He began his law career with all the right motives and intentions. However, over the years, he practiced bending the law without breaking it.

Thomas died at the age of seventy-three, with an improved PE-AR ICT of 7.0, but his Sapien suffered in other ICT areas such as honesty and deceit, finishing his LC with an unchanged L 5.9 Sapien rating. So, Tom lived his entire LifeCycle with zero Sapien improvements. As for his development as a Sapien, it is as if he never had this LC.

IN-TR ICT Pair (Independence-Trust) *(1 Sapien)*

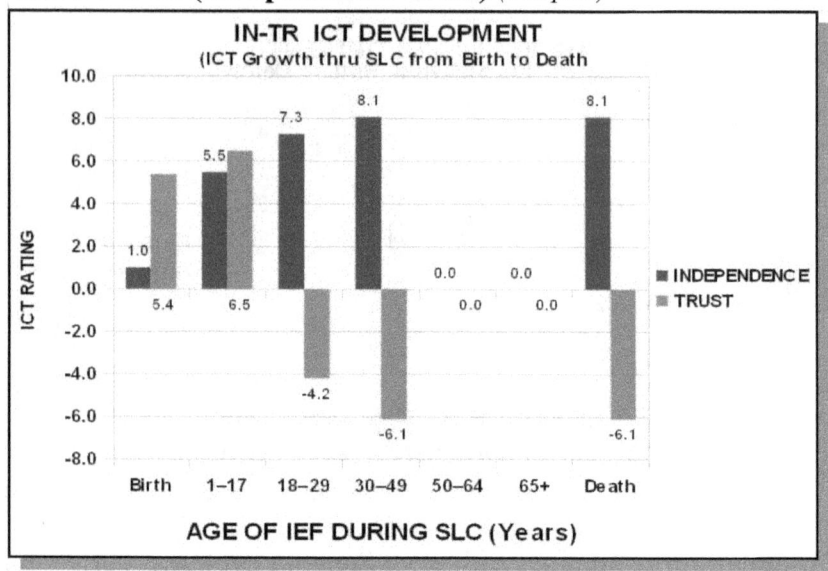

■ Example: Cowboy Joe was born in 1840 with an L3.6 Sapien, which was about average in that era. After his father and mother were murdered in their small country farmhouse, Joe was raised by his grandmother. His grandmother died when he was fifteen. Joe left home and began a career as a bronc buster, migrating from ranch to ranch, knowing he could only count on himself. When he died, at the age of forty-nine, his independence ICT had risen to an 8.1

■ However, his trust for people, or lack thereof, began to deteriorate after his grandmother died, and he went on the road. He never let anyone get close to him, and continued with his distrust until he died, with a -6.1 trust ICT and a slightly improved IEF rating of L3.8.

ICT Sets and Pairs

In addition to the ICTs used in the above examples, there are many more ICTs that were also developed, both positively and negatively, during the same LCs. All Sapiens have the same set of character traits. They are just used and developed differently, during very different LifeCycles.

Individual Character Traits (ICTs) in a humanoid-type Sapien are common to all humanoid-type Sapiens, referred to as humans on Earth. Of the many hundreds of character trait pairs inherent in every Sapien, some of the more notable ones include good/evil, love/hate, honesty/deceit, happy/sad, leader/follower, creative/mundane, quantitative/abstract, loyal/traitorous, right/wrong and corrupt/honor.

So, if all Sapiens have similar traits, there must be a set of common traits, common ICTs, that are indigenous to any intelligent species. But if all Sapiens have the same traits, how can they be unique? The differences and uniqueness in people come from the aggregate development of all ICTs operating in concert as unique character-centric Sapiens.

This is where the evolution part of the ILC theory comes in. Each Sapien has the same set of ICTs, but at different stages of evolution based on life experiences. With the trillions upon trillions of combinations possible for a Sapien's character makeup, it's easy to agree that all Sapiens are unique, since it is nearly a mathematical impossibility, otherwise. This concept is mentioned several times in the book to reinforce its importance in *The Theory*.

Sapiens evolve differently through many different LC experiences, based on their use of a common set of ICTs. The aggregate effect of all Individual Character Traits, working in concert, ensures every Sapien is indeed unique. Without this uniqueness in all Sapiens, *The Intelligent LifeCycle Theory* would make no sense.

So if we can say ICT differences exist in all Sapiens, we also must be able to measure those differences. Thus, we have created the Individual Sapien Analysis Testing (ISAT) program. For purposes of ISAT procedures, character traits are organized in like groups called ICT sets. These ICT sets are devised to provide an accurate picture of a Sapien's character traits, as a vital component to the Sapien as a whole. Such ICT sets are loosely translated by society as an individual's personality. *See ISAT chapter.*

ICT sets are comprised of representative groups of ICTs that relate to character traits involved in decision-making and situational responses. Each Set is comprised of three to five ICT pairs, grouped by emotional interpretations. Each pair includes a positive ICT with an opposite, negative ICT.

There are two types of ICT sets; Key and Supporting. However, all character traits are considered equal for purposes of evolution. During one LC journey, certain ICTs may be more dominant than others. In another life, different ICTs may be more active. During situational experiences within any given LifeCycle, different ICTs are required for different situations. Therefore, all ICTs are of equal importance to the Sapien's development and evolution.

Key ICT Sets

Even though all ICTs are equal, certain character traits are emphasized during the initial Sapien search by the subHalo to fulfill an SRO.

These Key traits are seen as basic to the successful match between the fetus' parental overlay requirements and the incoming Sapien.

After suitable matches have been accomplished, in the search for gender and overall Sapien ratings, the subHalo's SRO search continues to drill down into applicable ICT matches. Key ICTs are the first group of ICTs to match, which represent 20 percent of the Sapien SQ.

For purposes of *ISAT* ratings, there are ten Key ICT sets consisting of five ICT pairs each and considered priority search fields. This group of ICT sets carries more weight in the initial Sapien search by the subHalo. The first two ICT sets, which are definitive of ILC Rule No.1, are seen as important enough to warrant a more detailed description here.

Sanctity of Life: *"The way in which a Sapien views the importance of human life."*

The phrase *sanctity of life* refers to the idea that human life is sacred, and should not be intentionally terminated, regardless of religious convictions or low societal standards, including murder and suicide. *See Rule No.1 Disclaimer in Ten Rules of Intelligent Life.*

Prenatal terminations are considered to be more of a judgment call, individual to each Sapien. However, according to *The ILC Theory*, the Sapien does not populate the fetus, until the beginning of the second trimester of a pregnancy. So technically, an early termination or abortion during the first twelve weeks of pregnancy would not violate *Rule No.1*, since the Sapien transfer hasn't yet occurred. In theory, intelligent life begins when the Sapien is fused with the fetus, even though the Sapien's new LC doesn't actually begin until birth.

The Intelligent LifeCycle Theory

Sanctity of life, as a term, has been used in pro-life political and morality debates, concerning issues such as abortion, contraception, euthanasia, and the right to die. The sanctity phrase is a common reference in most English speaking countries, and has similar verbal equivalencies in most non-English speaking countries.

In Western cultures, sanctity of life is usually applied solely to the human species. This is in contrast to certain schools of Eastern philosophy, which believe all animal and insect life is sacred, as well.

Example: In a particular religion in India, true believers carry brushes, so they can sweep insects from their path as they walk, so as not to inadvertently step on them. I wonder what they do about mosquitos.

The ILC Theory only addresses the use of sanctity of life as it applies to intelligent life in humanoid-type beings. Animals and other non-intelligent life-forms are excluded, even though I know a guy who thinks, "dogs are people too." Unfortunately for the dog, according to *The Intelligent Life Cycle Theory*, they are not considered intelligent beings.

Dogs are cool, I love dogs, but they do not have a Sapien/soul for purposes of *The Theory*. Lesser life-forms do not have Intelligent Energy Fields, and only exist to support the needs of intelligent beings, with respect to food, beauty, companionship and entertainment, as well as maintaining the planet's ecosystem.

It is important to understand the difference between the brain with its complex capabilities and intelligence in *The Theory*. Most animals have a brain, with varying degrees of capabilities, including memory to a degree. They may seem like they have intelligence and emotions, but those characteristics are a by-product of the brain.

The Intelligent LifeCycle Theory

The ape family, human predecessors, is the most advanced species on Earth, next to man. They are not included because they do not require an Intelligent Energy Field to live. The ape brain is more developed than other animals, but not nearly as much as humans.

ILC Confirmation: Most anthropologists agree that Man is a direct descendent of the Ape. *The ILC Theory* confirms this. When the ape brain developed, over millions of years, to the point of requiring intelligence, it grew a Sapien-BrainBridge and evolved to homo sapien status. When that happened, Earth popped up on the grid and became an active node on the UENetwork, as a Sapien destination point.

The following ICT sets and pairs for Sanctity of Life are used in the *ILC ISAT* ratings. Rate yourself from 1 to 10 on each pair.

Negative (1.0) ⟶	Positive (10.0)
Set 01: Sanctity of Life I	
Antisocial	Sociable
Brutal	Humane
Violent	Passive
Cruel	Kindhearted
Disrespectful	Respectful
Set 02: Sanctity of Life II	
Evil	Goodhearted
Sinful	Virtuous
Immoral	Moral
Insensitive	Compassionate
Selfish	Selfless

The Intelligent LifeCycle Theory

Sanctity of life has been engrained into our culture, and rightfully so, ever since Moses (who may have been an L8) came down from the mountain top. With the Ten Commandments in hand, he addressed the issue in the sixth Commandment.

The compassion most people feel for other people dying and/or getting murdered is no more prominent anywhere, than in the movies. Think about it, someone dies in a movie scene on the street corner or sidewalk. The camera pulls back to an aerial view, you see many people huddling/crowding around the the dead person. That would seem to mean that sanctity of life, and probably curiosity about death, are very important to each of us, both of which are thoroughly addressed in *The Theory*.

Some of the best box-office successes have been disaster movies. You know the ones, where an event, natural or otherwise, threatens the lives of many innocent victims. While violence and death looms, the protagonist, for whom the audience is rooting, tries to save as many lives as possible.

Scenes involving doctors in hospitals, desperately trying to save a life, especially if it is the life of a good guy, are emotional experiences. The audience does not like to see death, unless of course, the death is the bad guy doing really bad things.

In the news business, especially TV news, the old saying is, "If it bleeds, it leads." Real life murders are big news. A multiple murder is an even bigger story. If the victim is a policeman or fireman, the story will lead from several angles and will get continued coverage.

The ILC Theory places significant importance on Sapien sanctity of life as the *No.1 Rule*. The exception to the sanctity of life rule is the preservation of a race and survival of the species.

If a race, or a group within a race, attempt to expand its control over other races or groups, the leaders of such a race are considered to be bad. Not only do they wage war, oftentimes in the name of religion, with violence and murder, they also violate *Rule No.2*, freedom. As they attempt to reduce or eliminate personal freedoms, these so-called leaders score very low on the sanctity of life and freedom ICT sets, as well as a myriad of other ICTs.

Conversely, if a race or group within a race is forced to engage in war for protection from aggressors, leaders of such resistant groups, are considered good, in most cases. Being a defender of Sapien freedoms is a noble goal, but sometimes a futile exercise in backward countries.

Sanctity of life is intrinsic in the Sapien evolutionary process, and is considered so precious, that early termination of a Sapien is not acceptable. Every moment of LiveTime is considered valuable in the further development and advancement of the Sapien.

When a Sapien's host body dies, there may not be another LC for that Sapien for a thousand years, or it could get recycled within a matter of only a few years. In reality, based on the current population growth of Earth, it may only be a brief period between Earthbound LCs. It does take some time for the Sapien to be assimilated back into the subHalo, inventoried and rejuvenated.

Freedom: *"The degree to which a Sapien regards his or her freedom and the extent to which the Sapien will go to protect such freedoms."*

Freedom is an innate concept in Sapien evolution, and indeed in most living things. The sense of freedom rivals that of the natural survival instinct in a species. Everyone, everything, wants to be free.

Example: Even plants that grow indoors want freedom. They lean toward the window, and we say that is because they need to get close to the light. Wrong, they want out, they want to be free.

Example: Consider a bear cub wandering into grocery store. The cub is probably just as scared as the patrons in the store. However, you can bet the little bear will do anything to keep from getting captured, running is usually preferable.

Living things need to be free. Even though freedom is just another ICT, it ranks up there as a priority character trait. Sapien differences in their interpretations of the word and its ramifications can easily be determined based on their actions to protect their freedoms. If a country's populace allows itself to be controlled by a few low-level Sapiens, who control through fear and violence, then that directly reflects on the average Sapien level of that populace.

Example: In backward societies, prevalent in some middle eastern countries, Sapiens allow themselves to lose their freedoms, because the mass populace has Sapien levels of 2.5 or lower, and are easily controllable. And their so-called leaders have higher Sapien ratings by comparison, but not much more than 4.2s.

When discussing the concept of freedom on talk shows, you may sometimes hear someone say, "That's not necessarily true, you don't know that all people want to be free." And you might summarily dismiss such commentary, but think about it.

Third world countries are generally populated with lower-level Sapiens, mostly L2s and L3s, who may not know that freedom is a right, not a gift. Such early-stage Sapiens score extremely low on the freedom scale. Citizens of these countries who fight for their freedoms are undoubtedly more developed Sapiens, L3s and L4s.

And as much as we do not like to admit it, there are, in fact, evil Sapiens in the world, Sapiens that feel they are superior to other Sapiens. Such power-hungry entities attempt to deprive others of their freedoms, in order to falsely justify their own worth. Such Sapiens may or may not evolve out of this dismal growth curve.

I suspect there have always been evil Sapiens. And I guess there may always be evil among us. Freedom is the battleground between good and evil. Wars have been fought on behalf of individual freedoms as a right of life, sacrificing millions of Sapien lives in the process.

Fortunately, as a IP's Sapien population develops and progresses to higher level averages, wars and violence will subside and personal freedoms will flourish on a global scale. Evil will be vanquished, eventually, maybe as Earth progresses to C6 IP status.

Freedom gives the Sapien the ability to maximize its capabilities and qualities during an LC. Without artificial restrictions, such as politically-repressive, socialist-based governmental controls, freedom fosters significantly positive ICT growth. Conversely, the denial of freedom is the ultimate method of control over Sapien lives.

Example: Societies around the world, regardless of governmental structure, confirm the importance of freedom as reflected in their type of punishments. The ultimate punishment is execution, which is a total denial of a Sapien's LiveTime. The next most stringent penalty is imprisonment, which is a total denial of Sapien freedoms. Both of these punishments confirm *The Theory's* position that life and freedom are paramount to existence. If they weren't, governments would not use such punishments to control the populace, by taking them away.

Freedom is an innate trait indigenous to most Sapiens. It is instinctive, but it is not hard-wired to the Sapien, like gender and survival instinct, but it is close. Freedom is one of the strongest ICT sets and one that most Sapiens cherish.

The following Freedom ICT sets/pairs are in the *ILC ISAT* program.

Negative (1.0) ⟹ **Positive (10.0)**	
Set 03: Freedom I	
Witless	Wise
Confined	Freewill
Cowardly	Courageous
Fearful	Assertive
Tired	Spirited
Set 04: Freedom II	
Fainthearted	Adventurous
Intimidated	Dauntless
Undeserving	Proud
Subordinated	Independent
Timid	Intrepid

In reality, freedom is good and worth fighting for. Unfortunately, evil exists solely to deprive those freedoms. Evil is present on Earth today, and will probably continue for some time to come. Theoretically, if we fight to preserve our freedoms in this lifetime, we will have a better shot at future societies being free, which translates into more freedom-based LifeCycles for all of us, next time.

Gender Relations: *"The ability of a Sapien to establish, nurture and maintain mature and intimate relations with Sapiens of the opposite sex."*

The longevity and success of a species is directly tied to its ability to reproduce in large enough quantities to sustain and perpetuate its own development cycle. Therefore, it is crucial that relationships between the sexes develop consistently in a positive direction.

The following ICTs for Gender Relations are used in *ISAT* Ratings.

Negative (1.0) ⟹	**Positive (10.0)**
Set 05: Gender Relations I	
Aloof	Affectionate
Indifferent	Caring
Demeaning	Deferential
Detached	Adoring
Manipulative	Loving
Set 06: Gender Relations II	
Frigidity	Sexual-normalcy
Promiscuous	Faithful
Dominating	Accepting
Jealous	Trusting
Lewdness	Prudish

Mutually beneficial gender relations are crucially important to our overall Sapien development. Intimacy involves many ICTs in a number of ICT sets outside the ones listed above.

Love, respect, trust and sexual desire are the cornerstones to relationships between male and female Sapiens. When done right, the results provide more LC opportunities for more Sapiens, as the population growth is maintained. This life-perpetuating function is imperative to the continuity of intelligent life in the entire universe.

Efficacy: *"The ability of a Sapien to produce a desired and intended result, with the willful following of fellow Sapiens."*

Efficacy traits are critical to enhancing LiveTime conditions, during LCs. In a civilized society, the direction in which Earth is hopefully going, leaders in all socioeconomic disciplines are essential. They have the ability to produce improvements in the quality of life that fosters continued Sapien growth.

The following ICT sets/pairs for Efficacy are in the *ISAT* App.

Negative (1.0) ⟹	**Positive (10.0)**
Set 07: Efficacy I	
Dependent	Risk-taker
Disorganized	Organized
Follower	Leader
Lazy	Ambitious
Reserved	Enterprising
Set 08: Efficacy II	
Ineffective	Effective
Incompetent	Competent
Indecisive	Decisive
Unimaginative	Resourceful
Insecure	Confident

The Intelligent LifeCycle Theory

Efficacy traits are most commonly associated with Sapien leaders, regardless of ethnicity, religion, wealth or location on the planet. Leaders, not to be confused with most politicians, help shape and mold the fabric of a civilized society.

Sapiens with leadership qualities, who use those qualities for the betterment of mankind, will always be needed to perpetuate and enhance positive living conditions for all Sapiens on the planet. Effective leaders in our current socioeconomic models have the opportunity to use their efficacy skills to improve the LifeCycles of Sapiens for generations to come.

Spiritual: *"The moral beliefs held by a Sapien that affect its decision-making during current LiveTime events."*

The following ICT sets/pairs for Spirituality are used in the *ILC ISAT*.

Negative (1.0) ⟹	Positive (10.0)
Set 09: Spiritual I	
Non-believer	Believer
Secular	Religious
Faithless	Devout
Godlessness	Belief in God
Irreverent	Sacredness
Set 10: Spiritual II	
Deceitful	Trustworthy
Dishonest	Honest
Immoral	Moral
Hateful	Magnanimous
Malevolent	Benevolent

As we analyze ICT sets and pairs, we find that similar words often provide very different descriptions. Ultimately, it is up to the Sapien to interpret the meaning of a word or group of words.

Example: For many people, right and wrong may have a different meaning than good and bad. Ethical and unethical may be different than moral and immoral.

Movie Quote: "Seabiscuit", 2003, Toby McGuire, Jeff Bridges, Chris Cooper. Over a campfire, Cooper asks Bridges, "Want some coffee? It's bad though". Bridges responds, "You always tell the truth?". Cooper, "Yeah, I try to."

Being truthful can sometimes be brutal. In the aforementioned scene, Cooper was brutally honest. He did not say, "It's not very good," or even , "It's pretty bad." He just said, "It's bad." The truth usually does not leave any room for interpretation, even though sometimes Sapiens try to alter the truth with misleading interpretations. Try not to alter the truth for your own benefit. The truth cannot be altered, so deal with it.

Of course, that's why we have such an expansive English language, to more accurately describe life and the truths within. More often than not, an ICT event requires many words to describe the same result, because many words can add subtle differences to an event's interpretation. Absolute truths, sadly to say, are rare occurrences in our current LifeCycles on Earth, as a C4 IP. They become more prevalent on IPs at the C6 and C7 levels.

Supporting ICT Sets

The distinction between Key ICT Sets and Supporting ICT Sets is their

The Intelligent LifeCycle Theory

priority in the initial search at the subHalo to fulfill an SRO (Sapien Request Order). Matches to key sets are the third search phase, after gender and intelligence have been satisfied. After key set searches have been satisfied, SRO criteria may require additional searches to drill down further for matches in the remaining supporting ICT sets.

Example: An acceptable range for an ICT to be considered satisfied in the search would be a +/-10 percent deviation. Even though such a deviation may be considered excessive, it is thought to be adequate. "Close enough for government work", as we used to say in the Army.

For purposes of *ISAT* scoring, there are seventy-five supporting ICT sets, consisting of three ICT pairs each, representing 40 percent of overall IEF Ratings. Each Set of ICTs is meant to foster an image of yourself, and where you rank yourself in that image. Here are a couple of examples as used in the *ISAT*.

Negative (1.0) ⟹	**Positive (10.0)**
Supporting Set 12	
Objectionable	Congenial
Obnoxious	Affable
Offensive	Likable
Supporting Set 15	
Neglectful	Focused
Oblivious	Observant
Preoccupied	Alert

Of the 512 ICTs identified, there are a few words that can be used to describe a multitude of ICT events. Fear is one of those words. It can be used to describe a number of situations with different outcomes, such as fearless, fearful, fear of failure, fear of pain, fear of heights, fear of non-acceptance, or just fear of fear.

Situations applicable to these types of words as descriptors can have a positive and/or negative impact on a number of other ICTs, affecting the Sapien in very different ways. When you are compelled to do something, or not do something, because of a fear, your actions affect many of your other ICTs. Consequently, overcoming such fears can positively affect many other ICTs, as a matter of course.

There are also words like luck, common sense and intuition, which are not actual character traits. These three traits have been designated unofficial ICTs. To deny their existence would be naïve, but they do not seem to qualify as real ICTs. A situation that benefits from a Sapien's innate ability, to use common sense, intuition or luck, can have profound effects on other ICTs, positively and negatively.

If there were a luck scale with a bell curve, the average of 5.0 would mean you are sometimes lucky, sometimes not. At the far end of the luck spectrum would be a Sapien who is unlucky at everything they do. Everything that happens to this type of Sapien is drastically skewed to the negative, fostering negative ICTs and pessimism. It is the SH Factor at work in full force, in all its infamous glory.

Conversely, when a person is thought to be a lucky person, that Sapien seems to enjoy positive results from most activities undertaken. This Sapien will exhibit more optimism, than one that is unlucky.

Consider the saying, "Maybe that will change your luck". The word 'that' intimates you can do something different to improve your luck. Well maybe, but you might also be able to gain more positive responses from your actions, by improving a couple of ICTs. And in effect, maybe you can change your luck that way.

ICT Rating Scale

Consistent with our current methodologies of measuring everything we can hear, see or touch, the ICT Rating Scale measures the Sapien's character trait development. Even though the ratings are subjective on a scale from 1 to 10, the exercise of rating ICTs provides the Sapien with a good picture of his or her current level of actual development.

Ideally, you would like to score 10.0 on all positive ICTs and score 0.0 on all negative ICTs. And of course, that is the primary goal of all intelligent life in the universe, even though the pursuit of such perfection requires countless LifeCycles to achieve.

ICT DEVELOPMENT RATING SCALE

Level	% Developed	ICT Rating	Evolution Status
L0	0%	0.00	Unused, undeveloped
L1	1% - 9%	1.0 to 1.99	Lowest, very little use
L2	10% - 29%	2.0 to 2.99	Extremely low
L3	30% - 39%	3.0 to 3.99	Low
L4	40% - 49%	4.0 to 4.99	Below average
L5	50% - 59%	5.0 to 5.99	Average
L6	60% - 69%	6.0 to 6.99	Above average
L7	70% - 79%	7.0 to 7.99	Highly developed
L8	80% - 89%	8.0 to 8.99	Extremely developed
L9	90% - 99%	9.0 to 9.99	Near Perfect
L10	100%	10.00	Perfect, no future growth

The above chart shows the various levels of Sapien development. Individual Character Traits are rated between 0 and 10. Average ICT ratings on Earth may be 4.4, whereas average ICTs on other IPs may be higher or lower. On advanced planets, average Sapiens are expected to have higher ICT ratings, 5.5, 6.2, or more. Consistent with Earth's C4 IP status, our planet is also classified as a C4 ICT planet.

ICT completion percentages reflect the number of LCs that a Sapien has experienced. Higher ICT ratings, generally indicate a greater number of LCs that the Sapien has had.

If you decide to complete your ICT Analysis with the ISAT application on our website, you may see a few interesting graphs and charts that may be helpful, like the sample below.

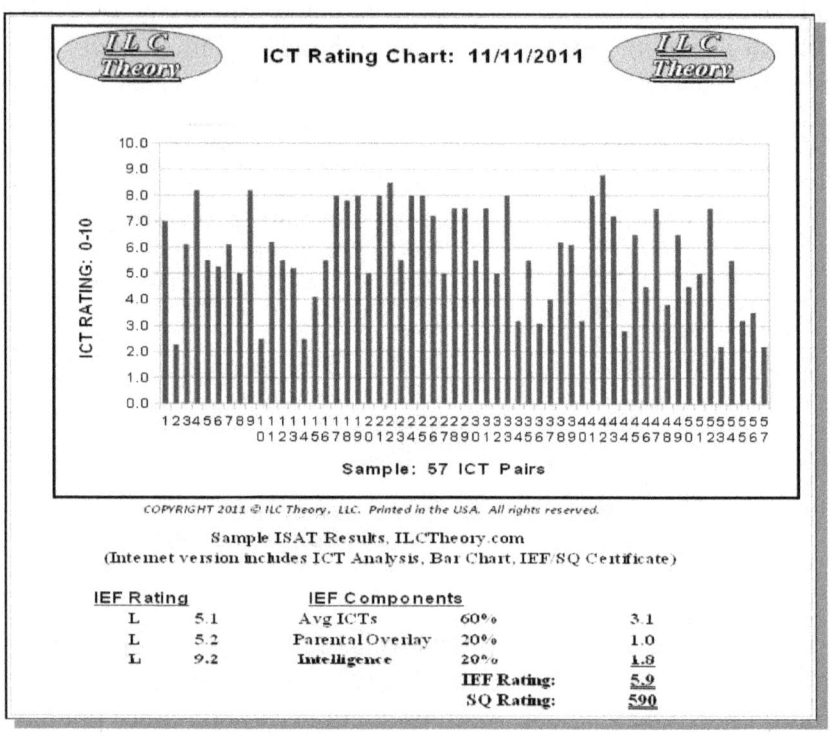

ICT Events

An ICT Event is something that occurs that affects specific ICTs in the Sapien. It can be of physical or mental origin. What creates an ICT event? Just about everything. ICT events can be significant like getting married, or average mundane things like finding a parking space. Incidentally, both of these require an above average Patience ICT, but are very different in many other ways, affecting other ICTs.

There are a number of significant ICT events that naturally occur on Earth during a typical LC. *The Theory* refers to these occurrences as milestone ICT events. These events are not necessarily life altering, but do have a substantial influence on many of a Sapien's ICT sets, as well as its future direction for further ICT development.

Milestone ICT Events, Typical SLC	
* Birth	* 1st Real Job
* 1st Day of School	* Marriage
* 1st Love	* Child Birth
* 1st Car	* Career Milestones
* 1st Time	* Divorce
* Graduate from HS	* Bankruptcy
* Graduate from College	* Retirement
* Military Service	* Death

ICT events listed above are seen as LifeCycle milestones in typical democratic countries. In lesser economically developed countries, the milestone list might be quite different, but it is still there.

The Intelligent LifeCycle Theory

Other than death, birth is the ultimate ICT event. It is determinism at its best. It is one event, over which the Sapien has little control, even though the selection process that matched the Sapien with the fetus in the first place was a result of the Sapien's ICT developments in previous LCs. So in a sense, it is determinism based on life experiences resulting from Free Will in previous LCs.

Other Milestone ICT events include the first day of school, first love, first car and first sexual encounter. These 'first' events affect ICT development, such as love, desire, confidence and happiness, and sometimes others like disappointment, rejection and jealousy.

Some of the milestones listed above may not apply to everyone, like military service and bankruptcy, but since both apply to millions of Americans, they are included. And of course, death is the ultimate ICT event in any LC. Death is either determinism or randomness, but it is definitely not free will.

During an ICT event, there can be temporary spikes in development, as shown below.

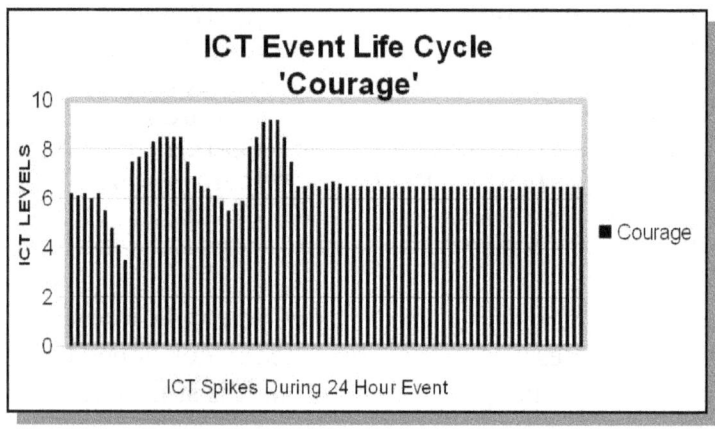

Such fluctuations in ICT ratings during an event, reflect the dynamic, fluid nature of ICT development. The net result of each event during an LC materially influences an ICT's growth cycle.

Example: In the preceding graph, this Sapien began the day with a 6.2 courage ICT. He had to give a presentation to his largest account that morning, but he was confident. When he began his pitch to a packed conference room, he immediately got negative feedback from the client concerning cost.

He stuck to his guns and emphasized the cost savings of his solution. The client continued to object. This lasted for a couple of hours. He began to acquiesce on a couple of points, basically losing some of his courage during the meeting.

But he knew in his heart, his solution was absolutely the best for the client. So instead of caving in, to placate the client, he became more adamant about the virtues of his solution. He knew, as he began taking this approach, he might lose the account.

He wavered a little after a while, but came back stronger toward the end. The meeting was adjourned. Later that night, he received a confirmation email stating he had won the business. His courage paid off.

As this man negotiated his challenging event, his courage ICT faded a little at the beginning, then spiked to 8.5 and back down to 5.5. It then spiked again to 9.2 and settled back at 6.5, a solid three-tenths of a point gain in courage, since the event began. Not bad, not bad at all.

An ICT event is one that, like the old saying goes, "builds character".

The Intelligent LifeCycle Theory

Most activities in life are character-building events to some degree. ICTs develop either positively or negatively, in response to ICT events, as the Sapien progresses through its LiveTimes.

In any given ICT event, depending on the ICT required for the event, the impact on the overall Sapien can be very dramatic or emotional. The way a Sapien deals with the event is the determining factor that either enhances or diminishes specific ICT development.

Interpretation of ICT events is certainly relative and subjective in relation to the participants. Most things are relative to interpretation and subject to that interpretation. One person sees the color blue, and another person, maybe color-blind, sees gray. It's blue to one guy, and gray to another.

Consider reality versus perception. They may all be different, but they may also all be the same, depending upon your perspective. Murder may be justifiable homicide to a person who feels like a victim, but to the court, it may be murder one. The reality of an ICT event may be somewhat different than others' perception of the same event.

Mathematicians may have different interpretations for formula results, based on the inclinations of the mathematician. Mathematical results can be interpreted differently if so inclined. Even athletics is subject to interpretation.

A top athlete at a small college may be considered the best athlete ever by the students. However, if that same athlete went to a Big Ten school, he might be considered a little above average. There are exceptions of course.

A person may be considered rich in the United States with five million dollars. Another person may be considered rich in Mexico with ten thousand pesos, four goats, two dogs, a mule and a dilapidated but functional 1967 Chevy. Reality can be perception, and perception can become reality.

However, as shown in the example below, sometimes perception and reality are indeed the same thing.

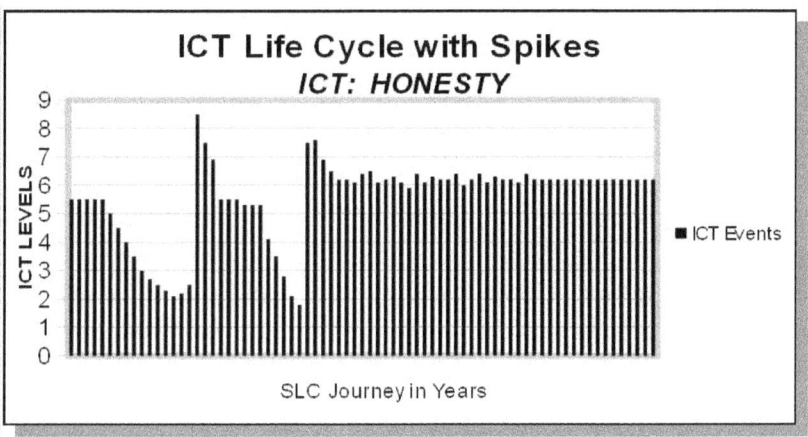

Example: The above graph illustrates the LifeCycle of a Sapien's honesty ICT. This Sapien was born with a 5.5 honesty ICT. When he reached six, he found he could lie to cover up his actions. This continued and even escalated through his teens. By this time, his honesty ICT had dropped to the mid 2s. Keep in mind, when this happens, other negative ICTs are flourishing. In this case, his deceit and manipulation ICTs dropped to -7.2 and -8.3, respectively.

When he reached seventeen, he caused an auto accident, in when his girlfriend was seriously hurt. He felt so much remorse that he had to tell the truth about drinking and driving, knowing he would get severely reprimanded, if not incarcerated. His honesty ICT jumped above 8 and hovered above 6 for a while.

Later, he took a job with a large corporation and began a serious relationship with a woman. He began stringing her along, while he played the field. He promised her love, marriage and children. One night, his girlfriend caught him in bed with another woman. She admonished him for his deceit. When he awoke alone the next morning, he went outside to get the paper. He stared in horror at his car. It was destroyed with red paint all over, spelling out some pretty nasty emotions, windows broken, and garbage strewn everywhere. Guess who the perpetrator was?

He felt remorse for treating his girlfriend badly. And to make matters worse, he had let his insurance lapse. He swore, from then on, he would never lie again. He kept his promise and finished his LC with a 6.2 in Honesty, which was up nearly $7/10^{th}$ of a point since birth. Sometimes it takes a significant negative ICT event to correct a weakness in a Sapien's ICTs.

Throughout history and the evolution of mankind, there have been many significant ICT events that have affected many millions of Sapiens around the globe. Global events in recent history include the invention of the automobile, WWI, the 1929 stock market crash, WWII, the invention of the computer, the Korean War, man walking on moon and the Vietnam War.

Now of course, we have 9/11 and the ensuing wars in Iraq and Afghanistan as current global events that continue to shape Sapiens and their ICTs. Not to minimize the impact all the other global ICT events had on our Intelligent LifeCycles, but the one that seems to deserve additional analysis is 9/11, because it is current.

9/11 ICT Event Analysis

The tragedy of the Islamic terrorist attacks against the United States, on September 11, 2001, was a monumental ICT event, similar in global impact to the Japanese bombing of Pearl Harbor on December 7, 1941. It was such a significantly infamous ICT event that it deserves an infamous analysis here.

It is obvious what the Islamic Muslim extremists' message was by the date chosen for their mass murder agenda. September 11 signifies a major wake-up call for civilized Western cultures. September 11 was chosen to represent a 9 1 1 emergency call to all Jihads that the war with the Infidels had begun.

These mass-murdering Islamist Muslim terrorists have left no doubt about their intentions, and have publicly declared as much, on more than a few occasions. Their evil plan (and make no mistake about it, it is pure evil) is world domination, pure and simple, and in the name of Allah no less. Hiding behind a ridiculously vengeful god may have worked for them five hundred years ago, but not today.

This one event directly violated six of the *Ten Rules of Intelligent Life*, and indirectly violated the other four. These international criminals, who forcibly commandeered those four commercial airliners on that fateful day, were extreme radical Islamist Muslim terrorists. They were low-level Sapiens with SQs in the low 200s at best.

Because of their extremely low Sapien ratings, these terrorists were easily misinformed, misguided and manipulated into blindly obeying their radical Islamic Muslim terrorist leaders, who incidentally are no more than 3.4 Sapiens themselves. These radical Muslim leaders, responsible for 9/11, control their followers through fear and absolutely stupid religious beliefs. They think that if they can control the ICT sets of the 1.3 billion underdeveloped Sapiens in their faith, they can then control the world. Wrong!

They espouse that the only way any of them can reach paradise is to kill (eradicate) as many of the infidels (Americans) as possible, and sacrifice themselves in the process. And when they accomplish that feat for Allah, they will be admitted to paradise as martyrs, and be given 72 virgins each. I mean really, how stupid can you get?

Those Sapiens need to be recycled back to the C1 and C2 Planets, from which they undoubtedly came. Let them grow up there, and come back to Earth in a few hundred years. Earth, as a Class 4 IP (C4), generally pulls from C3 to C5 IPs for our net Sapien increase (births minus deaths).

C1 and C2 planets, which develop L1 and L2 Sapiens, have been fueling the massive population explosion in the middle east for the last half a century. With inferior Sapiens, leaders in that part of the world, with only slightly higher IEF ratings, feel they can control the world in the name of Allah. Get over it, that is not going to happen.

Please understand, these observations are made here with great disappointment and sorrow, not from a vengeful nor malicious perspective. If any of these lower-level Sapiens from the middle east read this book, maybe these words will help them understand their wrongful ways and help them elevate their own ICTs toward peace and harmony, instead of violence and murder during this LifeCycle.

In the mean time, the net Sapien growth rate in Muslim countries will continue to foster parents whose SROs favor L2 selections, because that's the average of their parental overlays, for now. With an average of 8.8 children per family in these regions, their net birth rate far outstrips their death rate for reusable Sapiens. So these new Sapiens must come from L1 and L2 IPs, and/or from the L0 Sapien reserve in the MilkyWay subHalo.

As their cultures and societies evolve, the average Sapiens of the parents in these backward nations will begin to increase, thus increasing the level of Sapiens in their SROs. When the parents in these regions reach L4 Sapien levels, their SROs will begin to request L4 Sapiens, which should reverse this negative Sapien requirement for newborns.

Sapiens, who are as deficient in their ICT development as the 9/11 terrorists were, may be doomed to a cave man's existence, at least for the next few LCs. With less frequent LCs on remote planets, going backward to such primitive living conditions might be paramount to hell for such Sapiens.

The caveat to all this is the fact that, as these extreme Muslim radicals get more exposed to Western culture, the radical natures of their offspring will begin to be neutralized. Unknowingly, the next generation of Muslims will begin to spend time developing their positive ICTs, because of this exposure to the West, instead of just the negative ones mandated by their leaders, in the name of Allah.

That is the good news. The bad news is, this neutralization process of radical Muslim extremist views may take a number of LifeCycles to take effect. I am sure that Earth is not the first intelligent planet in the universe to confront this type of evil. And I believe as it pertains to this issue, good will prevail over evil on Earth.

The impact that 9/11 had on the flight crews, passengers, hostages and terrorists probably covers most ICT sets of those directly involved. This one, senseless and idiotic act negatively affected hundreds of millions of people, worldwide. ICT evolution that day was extensive, both positive and negative, ranging from heroic to cowardly, from courageous to murderous.

The infamous 9/11 ICT event includes all four theories of mankind's evolution. Major ICT events that occurred on those planes, before and during the crashes, dramatically impacted many Sapiens' ICTs.

Determinism was the first of the four to surface. It was predetermined by the ruthless leaders, what was to happen. The terrorist hijackers had no control over their actions. As lower-level Sapiens, they were just outgunned, metaphorically, by their leaders, who had long before predetermined their deaths.

Randomness became a component, when the crew and passengers boarded the planes. Even though the flights were preselected by the terrorist leaders, it was coincidental to their plan that those crew members and those passengers were on those planes.

Free Will was exercised, when the passengers decided to take back one of the planes or die trying. They made a choice to crash the jet into the ground, instead of hitting the White House. They used their free will to fight against the terrorist murderers, who were unbelievably infringing on their freedoms and right to life. And in doing so, they gave up their own lives to fight against evil, and saved thousands of lives in Washington. As compared to the terrorists, who gave away their free will, and blindly followed such violent, murderous and plainly idiotic commands of their supposed leaders.

And from *The Intelligent LifeCycle's* perspective, this tragic ICT event was responsible for a number of significant ICT developments to occur, some good and some evil. Passengers on the doomed planes exhibited major ICTs of heroism, bravery, sanctity of life, compassion, and goodness among many others. The murdering terrorists exhibited a few ICTs, all negative, including violence and deceit with pure evil intentions.

Passengers prayed to one god to not be killed. Terrorist hijackers prayed to another god to help them kill the infidels. What is wrong with this picture? This could best be described as a true struggle of good against evil.

Evil injects itself into Earth's culture through population explosions in low-level Sapien countries, such as those in the middle east with highly repressed populations and even more repressive governmental regimes. Those countries cannot sustain their highly explosive population growth just from previous L1 and L2 Sapien deaths in the middle east. They must get them from other, less developed planets, with high violence and low sanctity of life cultures.

The struggle of good against evil, as personified in the hideous 9/11 tragedy, is far from over. We must always continue to fight against those who transgress on our freedoms. And if we do, we will make Earth a better place for all of our future LCs.

Other ICT Event Observations

The following are observations of ICT events and their effects on a variety of Sapien ICTs. These are just observations, not to be misconstrued as indicative of all Sapiens. Maybe they will help, as you complete your *ISAT*, maybe not.

ICT Event Observation 1: A man and a woman fall in love. It seems to be a match between 'key ICTs' that they both have in common. Men and women are initially attracted to those of the opposite sex who exhibit similar ICT strengths. Sometimes the same ICTs that attracted them to one another, in the first place, become liabilities in their relationship, indirectly competing with the other.

Conversely, when men and women meet, and they complement each others' ICT sets, their ICT match seems to be more complete. And inversely, when men and women mistake physical attractions for ICT attractions, their love may begin to fade as the physical attraction fades with age. If lovers' ICTs do not at least match, or even better yet complement the other's, then the ICT Match may be wrong for both.

Movie Quote: "*The Bounty Hunter*", 2010, Jennifer Aniston, Gerard Butler. Aniston gets analyzed by her mother, "Look sweetie, you married a man because he drove you crazy, and then you divorced him for the same reason."

ICT Event Observation 2: During an ICT event, temperance and restraint are sometimes the best ICTs to deal with a situation. Sometimes, a temper can preclude other ICTs from benefiting as a result of an event. Ideally, you would like to improve your positive ICTs and reduce your negative ones, as a result of an event. As the old saying goes, "You can't get rid of your temper by losing it."

ICT Event Observation 3: When considering your ICT set, it might be a common fallacy to think your negative or underdeveloped ICTs are merely the result of a mismatch at birth. For the most part, other than mismatched gender selections, that would be wrong, since the subHalo search programs are sufficiently detailed enough to allow fairly accurate matches between Sapiens and their parental overlays.

It is easy to say, "It's not my fault", whether you say it aloud or just to yourself. Placing blame for your actions on a mismatch in the Sapien order fulfillment process does no good for you or the people around you. If you learn from your ICT events, take responsibility for your actions and enhance your ICTs when possible, your Sapien will naturally improve, and make it better for you in your next LifeCycle.

Movie Quote: In *"Malone"*, 1987, Burt Reynolds, Lauren Hutton, as they are being chased by the bad guys, Hutton says "We picked up a tail." Reynolds, riding shotgun, closes his eyes and responds, "That's not my problem, you're driving."

ICT Event Observation 4: When, not if, but when you make mistakes in this life, this LC, your reactions and the way you handle them are the defining moments following an event. Albeit, some mistakes are more major than others. If you genuinely regret your mistakes, have real remorse for your actions, and learn from them, your affected ICTs may still suffer, but they also may bounce back much faster.

If your feelings of remorse are genuine, your next LC should be better. Remember, faking remorse about your wrongful actions may actually make the ICT development even more negative. The reason is simple. With fake remorse, you are just as likely to do it again. But with real remorse, you learn from the event and have a much better shot at not repeating it again in future LCs.

ICT Event Observation 5: The birth process, as a monumental ICT event in the LC, sometimes does experience errors. The subHalo and UENet are not infallible. Gender mismatches do occur, which are beyond the control of the Sapien. A male fetus may be sent a female Sapien, and vice versa when a female fetus receives a male Sapien. In such cases, gays and lesbians can legitimately say, "It's not my fault."

ICT Event Observation 6: As a result of the 9/11 disaster, the radical Muslim terrorists, leaders and followers, may be doomed to less frequent LCs, quite possibly on lesser developed C1 and C2 planets, from which they came. When such terrorist groups, obviously comprised of lower-level Sapiens, claim responsibility for their murderous actions, as if it were a right, their admissions are much more hurtful to their ICT development than feigning remorse.

Their ICTs are damaged even further beyond the event itself. Their sanctity of life ICTs have dropped entirely off the chart. It may take hundreds of future LCs for these types of Sapiens to reach any semblance of normalcy. Their future plight of less frequent LiveTimes on C1 and C2 IPs might be considered a form of hell, purgatory, limbo or some combination thereof.

ICT Event Observation 7: They say confession is good for the soul. That is actually fairly accurate, since a Sapien's honesty with himself or herself may improve or enhance ICTs that need correcting. Regardless of whether it is a religious confession or one to yourself, the self realization affects other ICTs as well, as long as the admission or confession is genuine. In doing so, the ICT event itself may have a positive impact on a Sapien's honesty ICT, supporting the concept that such behavior builds character.

Caution: Artificial improvement of ICTs, just for the sake of thinking you are enhancing your ICTs, is not enough. It can't be faked. It has to be genuine ICT development, not contrived. If the reaction, like remorse, is genuine, then certain Tetrazymes are released that energize

TetraCells in the proper ICT NanoCell. If the reaction of remorse is not genuine, the brain releases negative ICT Tetrazymes, which negatively affect the ICT even further.

ICT Event Observation 8: As we go through our LCs, the more technologically advanced a civilization becomes, the more ICT events we will have, from which to benefit. Emotional exposure, to a wider range of events, should increase opportunities for the Sapien to further develop its ICT sets.

Technological advancements may seem like they would enable the Sapien to improve his or her ICTs faster, because of the increased number of ICT events. In reality, it may not have any effect on a Sapien's rate of improvement. Real character choices and real character changes cannot be enhanced at artificial rates because of technology.

ICT Event Observation 9: A parent in today's culture is exposed to a number of ICT events that a non-parent does not experience. They gain valuable ICT development, good and bad, through marriage, family, children and broader financial obligations.

Conversely, single adults may be exposed to a different set of ICT events during their LC, affecting ICTs like independence, freedom and self awareness. So during any given LC, all Sapiens have similar opportunities to positively develop ICTs, different or otherwise.

ICT Event Observation 10: Because Sapien development is based on LiveTime experiences, a Sapien's ICT development may be enhanced slightly more from an affluent home, than from parents who are poor. As a Sapien matures in a financially secure environment, it will be exposed to many more people, places and things, than the one raised under meager conditions.

However, a Sapien child with a highly developed efficacy ICT set, raised in a lower economically challenged family, can rise above its comfort level of ICT development and become more successful, because of it. Examples of both conditions are numerous in the advanced sociopolitical system we have today.

ICT Event Observation 11: An ICT event that results in a person using abusive, hurtful language toward another, especially between races within a species, fosters a myriad of ICTs, with mostly negative ramifications. ICTs, such as pride, compassion, confidence, respect, and sensitivity are significantly negatively affected by this type of behavior toward others.

When a white guy calls a black guy a nigger, or a black guy calls a white guy a honky, or they both call a Mexican a spic, or they call an Italian a wop, or if a guy calls his wife a whore, it is very hurtful to the receiving Sapien. And as important, it is also very hurtful to the sending Sapien's ICTs. Best advice, don't do that.

Movie Quote: "Forces of Nature", 1999, Sandra Bullock, Ben Affleck, a character, they picked up along the way, is talking about how he found his wife singing in the shower, with his brother. He summarized his wife's morality ICTs, when he concluded, "Yeah, that lying, whoring, adulterating pig."

There are always possible exceptions to the use of hurtful language. Some events or series of events may require more direct verbal reactions. If you are having to face such significantly negative ICTs in your spouse as above, you may feel justified in such a critique. And many may agree with you, especially if she really seems to be all those things. But please, try to refrain, the operative word here is *try*.

ICT Event Observation 12: Sexual relations is such a strong ICT set, it has several seemingly oxymoron-type ICTs revolving around it. If you are promiscuous, you are oversexed. If you are frigid, you are undersexed. What is sexual-normalcy?

What is normal sexual desire? Once a day, once a month, twice a year, or maybe twice an hour is normal. Extremely high sexual appetite is seen as a negative trait. Low sexual desire and celibacy are considered abnormal sexual patterns. It is all relative to the individual. A low sexual desire may not be bad. It may mean you have already covered that in previous lives. If you have a high sexual appetite, it may indicate you haven't conquered sex yet, to know what moderation is.

ICT Event Observation 13: If you are a gender-misplaced Sapien in this LC, sexual-related ICTs are such strong traits, that you try to correct your gender, your sexual orientation, through a homosexual lifestyle. And understandably so, if your Sapien is really the opposite sex. In the case of a gender mismatch, the odds are dramatically in your favor of getting the right sex next time.

ICT Event Observation 14: A little levity here. It is fun to watch movies with major ICT events that provide for significant character development, under extraordinary circumstances. When you are about to experience an ICT event, wouldn't it be great, if you actually had background music in the scenes you're playing out, like they do in the movies? Sad songs when you are depressed. Upbeat tempos when you are feeling strong. Talk about motivation and drama, ICTs on steroids!

ICT Event Observation 15: Emotions are external responses to ICT events, and are part of the ICT itself. When someone gets emotional, their affected ICTs are basically proclaiming that they are pretty serious about the event. When this happens, do not ignore it. Step back a bit and analyze the event, if possible. Emotions are symptoms of a situation. ICTs are the delivery system to resolve the emotions.

ICT Event Observation 16: Understanding the differences between character traits and habits is important. Drinking is a physical habit to survive. The act of drinking is habitual, a character trait. Hunger is a physical attribute. The way you handle hunger is a character trait. ICT events, involving these traits, often affect many other ICTs, such as patience, anger, discipline, selfishness, pleasure and pain.

ICT Event Observation 17: Just as there are physical differences between men and women, there are also ICT differences between men and women. The way a female Sapien reacts to a situation may be 180 degrees from the way a male would. This is neither good nor bad, it all depends on the situation. Sometimes a male response is best, and sometimes a female response is best.

Both sexes are guilty of occasionally misjudging the way the other sex handles an event. Unfortunately, it is a natural instinct for a Sapien to be critical of other Sapiens that are different. This is not necessarily good, but natural. ICT differences between the sexes do exist in all Sapiens, to some degree.

Movie Quote: "V.I. Warshawski", 1991, Kathleen Turner, Angela Goethals. Turner gives a young girl some advice, "Never underestimate a man's ability to underestimate a woman."

ICT Event Observation 18: ICTs involving Attention Deficit Disorder (ADD) relate to a Sapien being inattentive, selfish, easily distracted and disorganized, resulting in procrastination and forgetfulness. These ICTs seem to describe a personality more than a disorder. ADP, Attention Deficit Personality, may be more appropriate.

ADP may even be an advantage in a Sapien's life pursuit, such as an entrepreneur striving to achieve the American dream. The thought processes of the idealistic entrepreneur focuses on the big picture, as opposed to the details. ADPs have a tendency to be more optimistic, as they see the opportunities first, instead of the negatives. In contrast to a detail-oriented person, who sees problems and negatives first, which is also vital to success. ADPs sometimes also possess other traits that may not be beneficial to such an occupation, such as the inability to commit, and a lack of a sense of completion.

ICT Event Observation 19: The more educated a Sapien becomes, the more developed its ICTs generally become, but not necessarily proportionately. Keep in mind, there are always exceptions, depending on the situation. Education breeds civility and denounces violence, theft and deceit. This could explain why there is a disproportionate crime rate among disenfranchised, minority races. However, to use the down trodden as a scape goat for committing bad acts is a cop-out, to say the least.

ICT Event Observation 20: As with any ICT event, the benefits to be derived depends on the Sapien's responses to the event. The most difficult decisions sometimes test a person's belief systems. If you are more concerned with your character, than with your reputation, then you understand that your character is what you are, while your reputation is only the way others perceive you to be. Be true to yourself, be true to your Sapien, and you can't go wrong.

ICT Recap

All Sapiens are similar, but unique. All have different physical and mental capabilities, during any given LC. However, all Sapiens have the same sets of Individual Character Traits. Some Sapiens have alot to work with, regarding the physical body, which includes the brain, and some don't. Just as each Sapien is unique, each ICT, although the same for every Sapien, is also unique, relative to its percentage development.

With so many ICTs and so many different combinations of ICT development, it is no wonder that everyone is different. This uniqueness of all Sapiens makes it equally amazing that there is so much conformity within the species. If you look around, you may notice that sometimes people do some pretty strange things, just to be accepted or liked by other Sapiens.

Even though Sapiens are all made up of the same ICTs, the variable of ICT development combinations for each Sapien makes the difference, good and bad. This is not to minimize a Sapien's negative actions and thoughts. Bad is bad, even though most negative ICTs can be corrected, given enough LifeCycles.

During our current lifetime, a Sapien, within certain constraints in today's socioeconomic climate, has the ability to improve itself through experiences gained, which fosters growth. Depending on the sociopolitical atmosphere of a country, some Sapiens have more freedoms to pursue ICT development than others.

As you work on your ICT development, it is okay to make mistakes. That's how your Sapien improves, as long as you try to learn from them. A mistake can improve any number of ICTs, such as compassion and humility. You are doing fine, as long as you keep the ICT development going in the right direction.

There is an inherent problem in working on your ICTs. It requires a conscious thought process to focus on things non-material. Such a mindset usually does not take shape until a person reaches fifty or sixty. When you are young, you do not think about it, because you are too busy living life, raising a family, making money, doing things, having fun.

This is certainly understandable and justified to some degree. Often, however, a person, during their adult growth years, eighteen to fifty, may feel inordinately in control of life. They think they have no faults, no deficient ICTs, and will live forever, a commendable feeling, however foolish it may be. Many of us were in the same mindset at that age. By attaching such a stigma to your Sapien growth, you may have many ICTs that are ignored and do not benefit from positive development.

Having said that however, it is virtually impossible for a Sapien to actively work on more than a few ICTs at once. All you can do in this lifetime is to work on the ICTs that you can, and focus on the others during your next LC trip. The more developed a Sapien's ICTs become during this life, the more likely that Sapien is to experience favorable conditions in future LCs.

At whatever age it occurs, when a person begins to assess their ICT development structure, he or she will usually find one or more ICTs that need some serious attention. Such ICTs may have been pivotal in the current LC, either positively or negatively. Some ICTs, needing help, may have previously been totally ignored. Regardless, if you have the opportunity to improve an ICT, try to do so. It will help you during this lifetime, as well as in your future LCs.

Everyone has their own development path for their Sapien evolution. Try not to begrudge others, if they have more financial success, or more achievements, during this LC. A person that does not fit traditional societal views of success (money, fame, possessions) has probably developed ICTs that quite possibly elude a more successful person. All ICT development is important and will carry a Sapien in good stead into the future.

During a LifeCycle, normal ICT growth, if there is such a thing, involves ICT enhancements, however small. ICTs develop gradually through a Sapien's early years. During adult years, ICT development grows at a little faster pace, peaking in the fifty to sixty year range. After retirement, further ICT development generally dwindles, which relates to a reduction in personal motivations to experience new things. It is a physical thing, as the brain ages, even though the Intelligence Module (IM) of the Sapien remains intact.

Since we are a society of numbers, intent on measuring anything and everything, *The ILC Theory* includes a method to measure the development of a Sapien and its ICTs. The *ISAT* (Individual Sapien Analysis Testing) program was devised to do just that.

A number of ICT sets and ICT pairs were grouped together to elicit certain perspectives on life, enabling a Sapien's self-analysis. By scoring yourself on a scale from one to ten on each of the ICT sets and pairs, you should be able to see your strengths, and more importantly your weaknesses, the areas where you could improve.

Ideally, when you attain full development, your positive ICTs are 10s and your negative ICTs are 0s. Of course, that is not necessarily a practical goal, so on your way to perfection, just try to improve those character traits you can, when you can. *(See ICT Lists in Appendix)*

As you develop your ICTs, it is best not to embellish enhancement levels. You may have an inclination to artificially improve your *ISAT* score for a better position in your next LC, or just achieve a higher *ISAT* score for bragging rights. If you try to fool your LC Registry with a higher *ISAT* to improve the selection process of your next LC, it might actually be detrimental to certain ICTs, such as honesty and deceit.

The Sapien's core has a built-in moral barometer, a truth-o-meter, called the conscience. It will resist attempts to falsely improve ICTs, without the Sapien going through the true LiveTime rigors of experiences, that foster valid ICT enhancements. The *ISAT* exercise is strictly for your own benefit, if you approach it with honesty and candor. Like the old saying goes, "You can't fool Mother Nature."

Sometimes, when things do not seem to be going right, you may get frustrated and want to quit. You feel like you have had enough. When this happens, try focusing on some of your positive ICTs and the good things in your life, it will pass.

Movie Quote: "Regarding Henry", 1991, Harrison Ford, Annette Bening. After a slow recovery from being shot in the head, Ford's secretary tried to help, as she pours cream in his coffee. He watches her pour. She says, as a parent would, "When you have enough, you say when." After some lengthy rehab work, he finally regains his composure and says, "When".

The Intelligent LifeCycle Theory

The Intelligent LifeCycle Theory

 HALO & subHalos

When *The Theory* first began taking shape, one of its most vital components, for lack of a better description, was called the Universal Energy Field (UEF). Sapiens, which are considered pure intelligent energy, are drawn to and transported from their LCs, via the UENet, to the mass energy field in the universe, the UEF.

Although the UEF component answered the question about where you go when you die, the name seemed to portray too much of a harsh, clinical image. To match the name with the functionality, Halo was chosen, representing something more desirable and soothing, yet all encompassing.

As described in Wikipedia, the free encyclopedia, "a dark matter halo is a hypothetical component of a galaxy, which extends beyond the edge of the visible galaxy and dominates the total mass. Since they consist of dark matter, halos cannot be observed directly, but their existence is inferred through their effects on the motions of stars and gas in galaxies. Dark matter halos play a key role in current models of galaxy formation and evolution."

According to Webster's, Halo is "a region of space surrounding a galaxy... is believed to contain a great deal of dark matter". Also Webster's says a halo is, "the aura of glory, veneration, or sentiment surrounding an idealized person or thing."

Consistent with our acronym-intensive methodology, HALO was born, and defined as the Holistically Ascending Lifecycle Oasis. When considering the definitions and descriptions currently accepted in today's scientific community, Halo integrates into *The ILC Theory* very nicely in a number of ways.

Two key words in the HALO acronym add to its functionality and scope. Webster's defines *holistic* as "relating to or concerned with wholes or with complete systems rather than with the analysis of, treatment of, or dissection into parts." Webster's also states that *oasis* is considered "a time or experience that is pleasant and restful, something that provides refuge, relief." Add *ascending lifecycle* to the mix and the HALO acronym accurately describes its role as the home to all intelligence in the universe.

The functionality of the Halo within the scope of *The Theory* is similar to that of heaven in most religions today. The Halo, like heaven, is where the Sapien/soul goes when you die. However, that's where the similarity ends. The Halo is also the place where Sapiens originate before LiveTime births.

The Halo system is also the place where the Sapien goes to rest between lives/LCs and to get rejuvenated. But more importantly, the Halo protects the intelligence of the universe by surrounding it with "a great deal of dark matter", more specifically "super-dense dark matter". Similar to Earth's electromagnetic field, this protects the Halo from external interference by galactic forces damaging the universal energy field, such as intense heat, radiation and meteoric collisions.

The Halo protects the UEF and subHalos protect the subUEFs. If not for the Halo and the subHalos, the entire ILC system would be in great jeopardy, and intelligent life, as we know it, may cease to exist.

Think of it as an impenetrable aura of super-dense dark matter surrounding the Halo at the center of each galaxy. To pass through such an impenetrable shield, the UENet system has a resident dark matter neutralizer (DMN) application. This app runs 24/7 and engulfs its StarSpeed communications network, allowing it to carry its tetronic transmissions through the protective Halo and out into the real world.

Halo Basics

The ILC Halo is home to the host UEF and the L10 Control Board. It is at the center of the center-most galaxy in the universe. However, if our universe is in fact infinitely large, there can be no center point. Similar in context to mathematical theory that says, if a number series is one to infinity, there can be no center number, no average.

By positioning the host Halo at the center of our universe, *The ILC Theory* stipulates there are other universes beyond ours, each with their own Halo, subHalo infrastructure, UENet and universe center. Following the same 10^{11} rule Earth scientists have used to estimate the size and scope of our universe and its galaxies, there would be 10^{11} universes that comprise a Superverse, and 10^{11} superverses beyond that, and so on. This further establishes that the scope of *The Intelligent LifeCycle Theory* is 'true Infinity'.

Here is another test of your belief in the concept of infinity. If infinity is real, which *The Theory* stipulates is the First Natural Law of the Universe, there can be no end to space and no end to the celestial bodies that occupy it. Regardless of the artificial parameters we may place on a galaxy or universe, there is always something beyond that.

So, if our universe is among many other universes in the cosmos, then our universe is in fact, finite and measurable. Thus the Halo for our universe is centrally located at the center of ILC Galaxy Number 003548599337, which is theoretically equidistant in any direction to the edge of the visible universe.

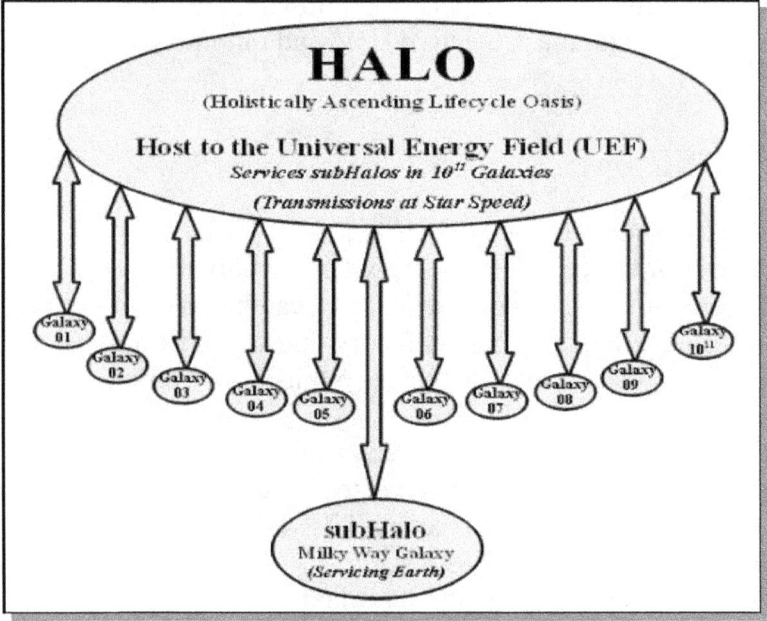

The above flowchart shows the dedicated Halo connections to all 10^{11} galaxies in the universe. The host Halo system provides service and support to the Milky Way subHalo that services Earth.

The Halo is ultimately responsible for the availability, delivery and recycling of Sapiens in the universe. The Halo is equivalent to what most religions refer to as heaven. The L10 Board of 'perfect Sapiens' would be the equivalent to what most religions refer to as God, Allah or the Supreme Being, even though there are multiple L10s.

The host Halo oversees all of the 10^{11} (100 billion) subHalos that service individual galaxies. The ILC Halo is also home to Retired L8s and L9s, not participating in the Rotating or Roving L8/L9 programs.

Halo Organization

Other than a small contingent of retired L10s, Halo Sapien population is comprised exclusively of L8 and L9 Sapiens, known in religious circles as wise men or wise women and angels, respectively. The majority of L8s and L9s are permanent residents of the Halo, as they enjoy eternal retirement. This inherent benefit rewards those Sapiens who have progressed from L1s to L8s or L9s, over many, many LCs.

Since there are no L8 or L9 parents breeding on any IP, requests for L8 or L9 Sapiens are non-existent. These advanced Sapiens have several options to pursue during their retirement millenniums. They can accept retirement and reside in the host Halo forever in total peace and bliss. Or they can participate in various Halo administrative and operational programs available to L8s and L9s.

Historically, there seems to have never been a shortage of advanced Sapiens applying to run ILC operations. By accepting additional assignments as an L8 or L9, instead of permanent retirement which is

The Intelligent LifeCycle Theory

well deserved, a Sapien has the opportunity to continue its ICT and IM development to further its overall Sapien level.

In the sophisticated environment of the Halo and subHalos, advanced Sapiens perform many tasks that are crucial to *The Intelligent Life Cycle*, as we know it today. Even though the majority of systems, subsystems, networks and subnets are completely automated, running on cruise control, the systems are not infallible.

The Organizational Chart below identifies several operational and administrative layers required for infinite perpetuation of the host Halo system. Continued successful operation of the Halo system is crucial to the successful operation of the subHalos it services.

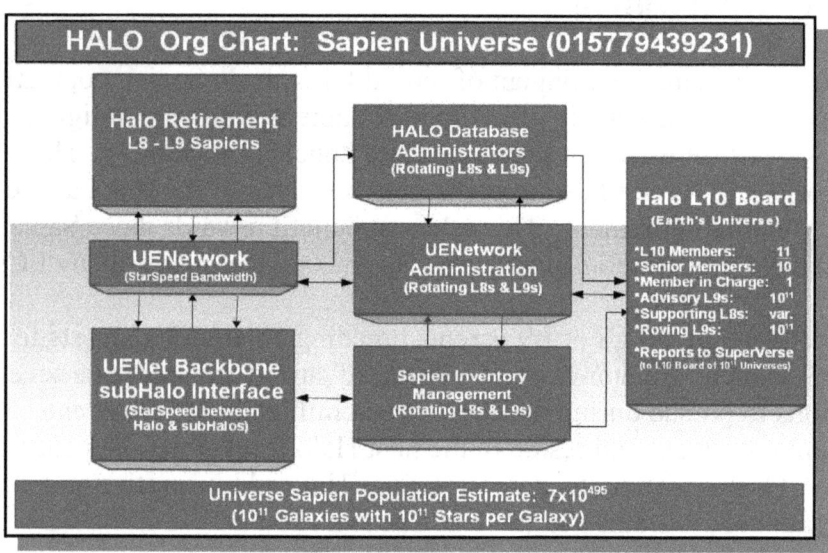

The Halo Org Chart is shown as a horizontal reporting structure instead of vertical, which emphasizes the fact that all Sapiens are considered equal. This philosophy instills the overriding feeling among all advanced Sapiens that it is a team effort, even though each level of Halo personnel does report to the next level to ensure the successful continuity of Halo operations.

The Halo L10 board is comprised of eleven L10 Sapiens, consisting of ten Senior Members and one Member In Charge (MIC). Each senior L10 represents his or her quadrant of the universe. The ten seniors, representing the ten quadrants of the universe, are supported by a small contingent of other L10s from the same quadrant that selected him or her for the job.

The MIC (or L10IC) is selected by the L10 senior members. When an MIC wishes to permanently retire, the remaining ten Seniors unanimously promote one of their own to the top job. This leaves a vacancy, which is filled by another L10 from the same quadrant vacated by the new MIC.

Until an L10 formally retires, he or she has a small contingent of L9s available for support, research and advice. L9 support contingencies generally are drawn from the L10's quadrant. Occasionally there may be cross-over L9s with multiple-quadrant LCs in their history.

The L9 Advisory Board consists of an L9 representative from each subHalo. L9 Advisers are available, when needed, to offer their recommendations and develop solutions to issues that arise from their respective subHalo galaxies. In addition, there is generally a large contingent of Supporting L8s, resident in the Halo, to assist L9s and L10s in most operational functions.

If these advanced Sapiens were L4s and L5s, like many of today's politicians, the L10 board would be ripe with political maneuvering.

However, since L8s through L10s are all highly advanced Sapiens, such lowly, egocentric attitudes do not exist in the Halo. But because they are, after all, mere Sapiens, there might be the occasional situation where an L9 might attempt to jockey for position, in furtherance of a cause.

Other than that, there is no bickering and no politicking in the Halo. Generally, all L8s, L9s and L10s work together to ensure the integrity of the universal Sapien evolutionary system. Keep in mind, L8s, L9s and L10s are perfect or near perfect intelligent beings.

To reach that level of Sapien development, their individual LC count is in the thousands, if not millions. In addition, time spent in Halo management for such advanced Sapiens can easily add another few millenniums to their resumes.

With the volume of Sapien traffic and Halo communications traversing the UENet, 24/7, judgment calls are required regularly by controlling L8 and L9 Sapiens. It is just because of this extremely high volume of traffic, that there are currently about 5 percent mismatched Sapiens to LC requests. *See Sapien/Intelligent Energy Field chapter.*

Halo operational & administrative support is provided by selected L8s and L9s, responsible for database and network administration, Sapien inventory management and Halo retirement. Sapiens in these positions are regularly rotated in and out to allow Sapien RestTime in between Halo assignments.

subHalo Organization

SubHalos have galactic responsibility and are located at the center of each galaxy. SubHalos service individual IPs in their respective galaxies, at the center of each galaxy. They also protect the subHalo infrastructure and all resident Sapiens from external spatial forces.

For practical purposes, subHalos regulate all Sapiens through a natural hierarchical database scheme. While resident in the subHalo, in between LCs, Sapiens are grouped according to physical location in the universe and their Sapien ratings.

As shown, a subHalo is responsible for servicing intelligent planets in a galaxy. Earth's subHalo services the entire MilkyWay Galaxy.

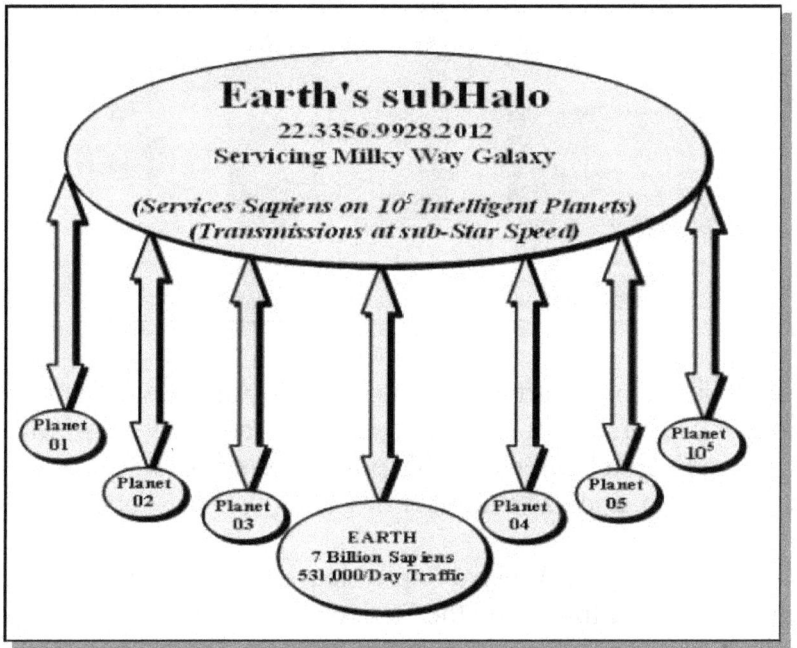

Sapiens are grouped according to Sapien development, L1s with L1s, L5s with L5s and so on. It is another natural law of the universe.

Intelligent beings tend to congregate with like beings. Sapiens in subHalos are grouped according to the natural hierarchical needs of the Sapien database system. Grouping Sapiens by their unique tetronic charges facilitates the fulfillment process for Sapien requests.

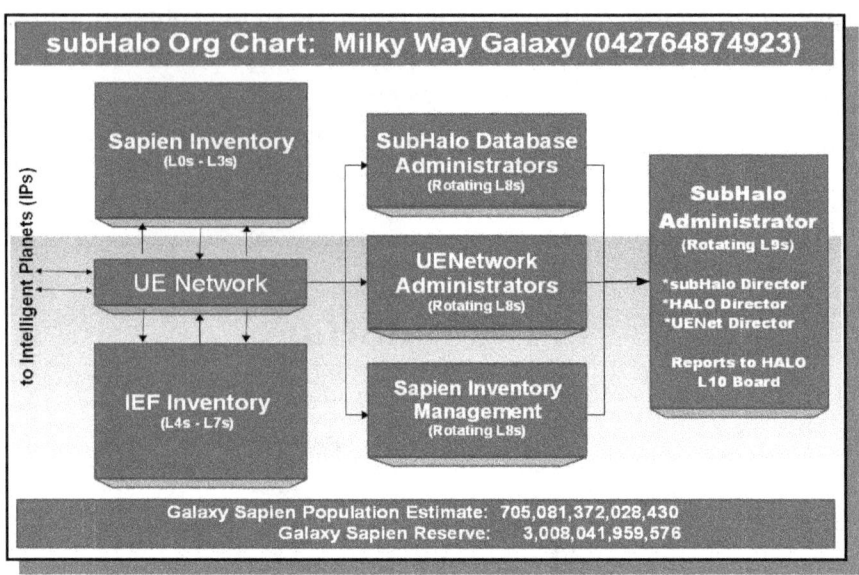

As shown in the org chart above, the subHalo Administrator, a Rotating L9, oversees all subHalo operations, and serves as Halo Director and UENet Director. This position reports to the L10 Board of the host Halo, and has a number of L8 Sapiens as support staff.

It is all about physics. When a Sapien leaves the physical body, it instantly travels (attracted by the Sapien's unique address and ending tetronic charge) to the nearest galactic subHalo. It is then inventoried, classified and assigned to the appropriate Sapien L Level for rejuvenation prior to the next LC assignment.

When a Sapien returns to the subHalo after an LC, he or she retains the mental persona of the physical person from the LC, until the next assignment. If you were Joe or Jolene in your previous LC, you would be Joe or Jolene during your subHalo stay.

To accommodate the inflow and outflow of Sapiens, management of the subHalo is organized by functionality, similar to the Halo. Rotating L8s are responsible for database administration, Sapien inventory management and UENet administration. L8 administrators are also supported by other L8s to assist in operations.

Sapiens are stored in 'L Sections' of the subHalo, according to their level of development. The Sapien inventory is separated into two primary groups, L0s to L3s and L4s to L7s. Sapiens, within the primary groups, are assigned to areas specific to their development levels and housed aggregately, L4s with L4s, L5s with L5s, and so on.

All subHalos sit on the UENet backbone to provide maximum network integrity, performance and throughput. As shown in the previous org chart, Sapien inventory is maintained nearest to the UENet backbone to ensure rapid turnaround times for Sapien arrivals and departures.

Rotating L8s & L9s

As shown in both Org Charts, management duties in both the host Halo and the subHalo are assumed by Rotating L8s and Rotating L9s. Sapien Halo assignments average a few years or more, in Earth time. When an L8 or L9 rotates out, the Sapien is replaced by the next Rotating L on the list. After finishing a stint in Halo admin, the Sapien gets much deserved, quality time to relax before rotating back in.

The Intelligent LifeCycle Theory

The amount of Halo RestTime for these advanced Sapiens varies with each Sapien. One Sapien might want to re-engage as soon as the next available slot opens up. Another Sapien may wish to take a few hundred years off. Others may elect to permanently retire, after their first stint in Halo duty. Retirement socials are held periodically in each subHalo to recognize all recent advanced Sapiens entering permanent retirement. Participation in these events is generally limited to the other L8s and L9s in similar Halo programs.

The advanced Sapien Halo programs allow participants substantial flexibility by design. This is because within all Halo retirement programs, assignments for extra credit are strictly voluntary. When a Sapien decides he or she does not need nor want any further development and elects to retire, he or she is held in the highest esteem by all other advanced Sapiens for their individual contributions to the evolution of intelligent life in the universe.

If a retired Sapien decides later he or she is bored and wants to rejoin the 'Rotating L' program, the welcome mat is always out, of course. However, the Sapien would be placed at the bottom of the Halo assignment waiting list, which is always full, in all fairness to other awaiting advanced Sapiens.

Rotating Ls infrequently, but occasionally, take assignments in different galaxies. Since Sapiens are race and species neutral, this is certainly possible. Sapiens with multiple galaxies in their LC registries, which are rare, are more likely to get subHalo assignments requiring galactic relocation between galaxies. Such moves by Rotating Ls do require some additional database tweaking. However, the first few sets of numbers in the Sapien's permanent tetronic address always includes the Sapien's originating subHalo and planet.

Roving L8s & L9s

Although Roving Ls do not show up on the subHalo Org Chart, they are assigned to and work from specific subHalos, covering specific galaxies. Roving L9s get their Halo Intervention Transfer (HIT) assignments, as a result of communications between themselves, the applicable subHalo L9 and the L10 board. L9s report directly to the L10 Board, as shown in the Halo organizational chart. Cross-over HITs are infrequent, but do occur, when a Roving L9 accepts an assignment in another galaxy from its home galaxy.

When a Roving L9 gets notified of a planet going the wrong direction in its Sapien development cycle, it triggers a request for assistance to the Halo. This generally occurs a few times in an intelligent planet's history, and usually during the planets early development stages.

When an IP reaches an aggregate Sapien level of 3.0 or higher, the average Sapien level of its Sapien Request Orders (SROs) will usually increase, as a matter of course. This occurs because of the majority of positive Sapiens in all subHalos versus negative ones.

The vast majority of Sapiens will gradually progress positively in their individual Sapien ratings over many LCs. When an IP reaches the C3 level with a Sapien Index of 300, its population growth curve is not expected to require any further L9 interventions.

Roving L8s are sponsored by their Roving L9s, the subHalo managing L9 and the L10 board. When an IP begins showing Sapien level decreases in its Sapien Request Orders (SROs), a Roving L8 HIT may be requested to get things back on track, before warranting an L9 HIT.

Such HITs occur automatically, when an IP has three consecutive LC generations of SROs that decrease in Sapien levels. In the early stages of an IPs Sapien development, which is when HITs are generally needed, LifeCycles are generally in the thirty to forty year range. So theoretically, if a planet shows decreasing Sapien level requests for a hundred years or so, it triggers a HIT.

Example: Earth currently has an average Sapien population of L4.4, with a Sapien Index of 440. This has been achieved with one L9 HIT (Jesus) and one L8 HIT (Moses) over thirty-five hundred years.

Other than Moses, there may have been a couple of other Roving L8s in Earth's history. Names like Mohammed, Gandhi, and even Noah have been discussed. Incidentally, Noah was only an L3, but that was considered good in those days.

Negative L1s & L2s

SubHalo Sapiens in RestTime are normally grouped and classified by their ratings and their galactic locations. However, there is a type of Sapien that requires another level of scrutiny, when determining its location within the subHalo rest area, and its future LC assignments.

A Sapien that has maintained a critically low overall L1 or L2 rating, after many LCs with little improvement, may be categorized as a negative or evil Sapien. Sapiens that have little, if any, positive development in their ICTs, but have a relatively developed Intelligence Module (IM), after ten LCs, are considered incorrigible and beyond redemption, to use a religious term.

Sapiens with many LCs and extremely negative ratings in ICTs, such as violence, murder and deceit, are drawn to a separate section in the subHalo. This section, which only attracts such Sapiens, is referred to as the Sapien Abrogation Pit (SAP). This is the place in the subHalo where consistently negative and deficient Sapiens are drawn. This subHalo RestTime section is analogous to the concept of hell.

Depending upon their deficiencies, Sapiens in this group will generally receive fewer LC assignments. And the majority of those will be to C1 and C2 planets, since the vast majority of Sapien requests from more advanced planets would not accept such negative traits.

However, on C4 planets such as Earth, there are countries where such negative Sapiens, referred to as SAPs, are not only accepted, but requested by the parental overlays of the region. Some third world countries, specifically in the Middle East, are populated with lesser developed Sapiens, who become parents that request similarly developed Sapiens for their offspring.

L2 parents, unknowingly of course, will always request L2 Sapiens for their children, based on their own SQs, because that is the parental overlay SRO they generate at conception. And in regions that are populated with lesser developed Sapiens, like the Middle East, it is a self-perpetuating cycle, until the children break out and begin developing their own Sapiens positively. Once a Sapien surpasses L3 development regardless of its LC count, it is considered a positive Sapien, and is not expected to digress much during future LCs.

Sapien moves between L Groups in the subHalo are not based on moral standards or beliefs. Sapiens are drawn to applicable subHalo sections, based purely on their unique tetronic charge. Over time, SAPs may possibly improve their negative ICTs and progress back into normal Sapien classifications again, after many more LCs, or not.

subHalo Inventory Management 101

The primary purpose of the subHalo is to effectively manage the incoming and outgoing traffic of Sapiens between IPs and the subHalo. This is basic inventory management.

Other than the complexity of the network and the sheer volume of Sapiens, the ILC system fits a classic database model, perfect for servicing client worlds . It is all based on the specific tetronic charge that is emitted from each Sapien, which provides addressing schemes and the current Sapien development level.

When death occurs, the brain releases the Sapien of its Tetrical bond (a trillion times the speed/capacity of an electrical connection), severing the Sapien Brain-Bridge. This triggers an automatic update in the Sapien's LC Registry, logging in the specifics of the LC that just ended. This is all done in a matter of tetraseconds.

At that point, the Sapien emits its own unique signal of availability, or LC Termination. The nearest sub-Halo, which is constantly polling its IPs, detects the LC termination signal from the expired Sapien via its UENet Sapien retrieval program.

Once detected, the Sapien is instantly drawn up to the nearest sub-Halo for reconditioning and rejuvenation, prior to selection for another LC. In some cases, the Sapien may be rechanneled to another sub-Halo in another galaxy, based on its Sapien Rating and certain ICT Ratings. However, Sapien transfers between subHalos are infrequent.

As soon as the Sapien is acquired, via the UENet (Universal Energy

Network) at StarSpeed (trillion times the speed of light), the sub-Halo records the Sapien's vitals for inventory. Sapiens are then categorized and grouped according to their addressing schemes and Sapien ratings.

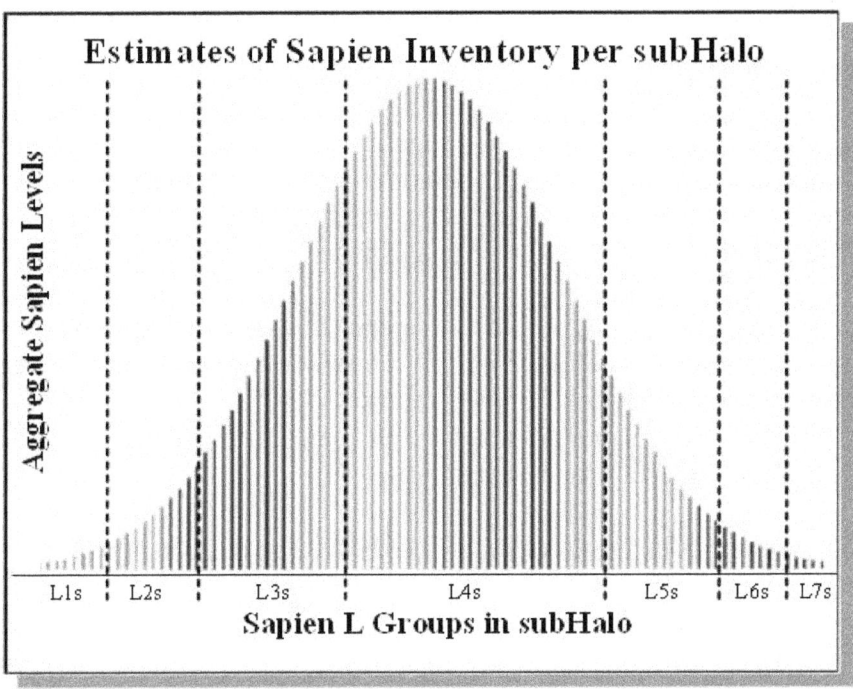

The above illustration is that of a traditional bell curve view of the Sapien levels, as they exist during RestTime in a typical subHalo. It provides estimates of Sapien development levels in a typical subHalo, which should be indicative of the universe's Sapien population.

L sectors of the Sapien database provide for natural groupings, according to Sapien Ratings and addressing data. L5 Sapiens from Earth are transferred to the subHalo RestTime sector that is home to

Earth L5s. L4s from XYZ IP are sent to the XYZ L4 sector, and so on. Database substructures are maintained according to Sapien tetronic charges. In each subHalo, there are 7×10^5 sectors, representing each IP in the galaxy with seven active Sapien levels, L1 to L7 for each IP.

The previous bell curve is skewed to the left of center. This shows the average Sapien population in the subHalo to be about a 4.2 rating. The Sapien inventory, in a subHalo, ranges from L1 to L7, since L8s and L9s are no longer in general circulation. With an estimated average Sapien level of L4.2 in the subHalos, this indicates the subHalos, and by default the universe, are a little less than fifty percent developed.

Earth Sapiens, with an estimated average of L4.4, seem to be a little more developed than the average IP. However, we are below average in the number of L5 to L7 Sapiens currently on the planet. With 95 percent of Earth's Sapien population estimated to be between L2 and L4, this indicates Earth is top heavy in L4s.

The good news is, it seems Earth may be poised to make the leap from a C4 IP to a C5 IP with a Sapien average above L5.0, sometime in the next couple of hundred years or so. By definition, this will increase the development level requested by Earth Sapiens. As average Sapien levels continue to increase on Earth, improved LC living conditions for future LiveTime journeys are expected to benefit Sapien populations globally. And as living conditions are enhanced, through technology advancements, Sapiens are afforded more diverse ICT events to further develop their Individual Character Traits (ICTs).

SubHalo distribution of Sapien inventory is primarily directed back to the originating planet. When needed, subHalo directors may reallocate Sapien inventory from one IP sector of the subHalo to another planet, with similar Sapien level requirements. This occurs, when the species on an IP begins to experience a rapid population growth rate, that cannot be sustained purely from that IPs existing Sapien inventory.

When an IP progresses from a C3 to a C4 planet, births begin to exceed deaths. This happens because C4 IPs start to experience higher population growth rates with longer average LifeCycles, as their populace migrates from rural environments to cities and medical research extends life. To satisfy such high-growth Sapien requirements, subHalo selection criteria for this stage of planet would expand to other similar worlds with a lesser developed Sapien base.

For those Sapiens who cross over between IPs, the subHalo inventory management system tracks the moves. It has a constantly changing registry that logs all Sapien activity, including LC entries and exits, LC counts and Sapien L groups. Sapien transfers, in and out of subHalos, are part of the continual 24/7 inventory management program. That is in Earth time. On some planet's, it may be a 28/8 operation.

subHalo Locations *(serving the universe and a Galaxy near you)*

Scientific data indicates that super-massive black holes are present at the center of every galaxy. Black holes are the perfect location for sub-Halos, since the very nature of a black hole provides protection for the subHalo and UENet from outside interference.

These super-massive black holes, centrally located in the nucleus of each galaxy, host the subHalo Sapien traffic for each galaxy. The black hole's super-dense superstructure, filled with dark tetramatter, provides protection for the massive storage requirements of that subHalo's Sapien database.

Larger galaxies may have two black holes that support two subHalos, even though *The ILC Theory* assumes one subHalo per galaxy. Such super galaxies may also have multiple subNets to accommodate the sheer size of Sapien traffic for that galaxy.

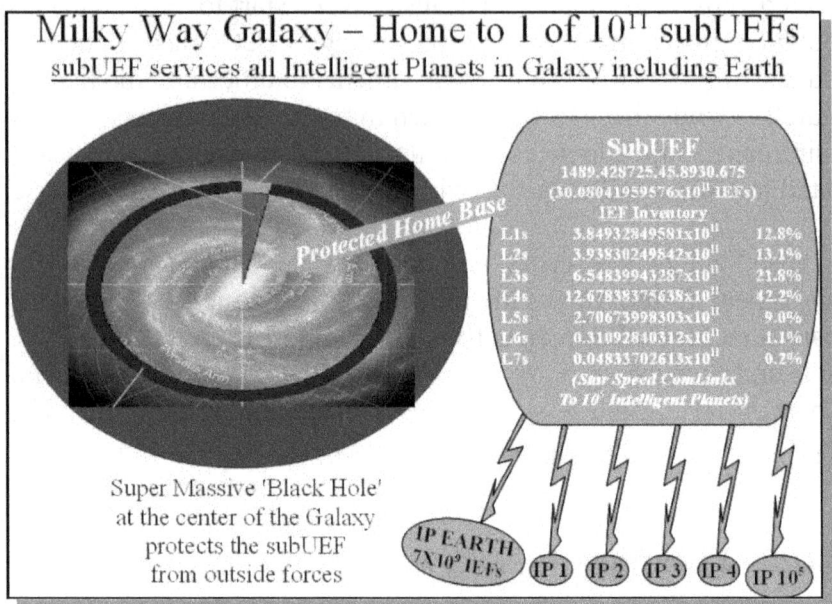

ILC Collectible: The above illustration represents an earlier version of what we now call the subHalo in the MilkyWay Galaxy. It shows estimated populations of Sapien L groups, which were initially called IEFs (Intelligent Energy Fields). Halo was originally called the UEF (Universal Energy Field), subHalos were called subUEFs.

Assuming there are 10^{11} galaxies in the universe, current scientific knowledge would indicate there are also at least 10^{11} super-dense black holes in the universe. Other than theoretical statistics, we know very little about black holes, there operations nor their purpose. *The Theory* provides just such a purpose for the existence of black holes.

ILC Discovery: The primary purpose of a black hole at the center of each galaxy, other than potentially stabilizing gravitational forces in the universe, is to provide a home for and protection of our subHalos

On July 21, 2007, the above photo, courtesy of Wikipedia, was taken by ESO astronomer Yuri Beletsky. A wide band of stars and dust clouds is seen, spanning more than 100 degrees in the sky. This is the Milky Way, our Galaxy. A beam of light in the photo identifies the location of the subHalo for the Milky Way Galaxy at the center of the galaxy's black hole.

The Intelligent LifeCycle Theory

Halo and subHalo Populations

When considering the Sapien population of the universe, we must look at several components. Halo and subHalo reserves, Sapien retirees and LiveTime Sapiens on all IPs in the universe. Even though nearly all Sapien transfers and storage is conducted at the subHalo level, the Halo has ultimate responsibility for the development of all Sapiens in the universe.

The Sapien count for the MilkyWay subHalo is estimated to be 705,081,372,028,430, assuming Earth is average size. That is over seven hundred trillion Sapiens living their LCs on IPs in the MilkyWay subHalo, with over three trillion Sapiens in reserve during RestTimes.

We can extrapolate that number to other galaxies in the universe, to get the Sapien count for the universe. These numbers are estimates of course, but are based on current knowledge of intelligent planets and their respective populations in the universe. The Sapien population of our universe, No. 015779439231 in the Superverse, can be estimated mathematically. To calculate the total Sapien population in the universe, we must consider several Sapien groups.

We can estimate the LiveTime Sapiens that are currently in LCs on intelligent planets in the universe by the following: 10^{11} galaxies x 10^5 IPs/galaxy x (7×10^9) Sapiens/IP = 7×10^{25} Sapiens in the universe. That is a seven with twenty-five zeros, commonly known as seventy septillion. *See Large Number Naming Conventions in Appendix.*

Of course, to get an accurate Sapien count, we must also include Sapiens in subHalos during RestTime between LCs, as well as the retired, rotating and roving L8s and L9s in the Halo and subHalos. And let's not forget the L0s, who are waiting in each subHalo for their first LC. The Sapien count for RestTime Sapiens is expected to at least equal that of LiveTime Sapiens. It is estimated there are nearly 7×10^{27} Sapiens, or seven octillion Sapiens in our known universe.

And that is just in our universe. If there are multiple universes, an estimate of the number of universes would need to be consistent with the 10^{11} rule used in calculating the size of our universe. Therefore, the Superverse consists of 10^{11} universes.

If our universe is average in size and Sapien population, an estimate of the Superverse would equate to $7 \times 10^{27} \times 10^{11}$ universes, or 7×10^{38} Sapiens in all the universes. Therefore, we estimate the Sapien population of all universes in the superverse to be approximately seven hundred undecillion. Of course, this assumes we can place a limit on something so infinite.

During discussions about Sapien populations, a question arose, "What happens when a world suddenly ceases to support life?" This is a question that is not that far removed from reality.

During the evolutionary cycle of a planet, there are boom times and there are bust times. At any point in time, a planet either supports intelligent life, or is does not. All planets go through these cycles.

Every few million years or so, planets are purged of life by solar flares, meteoric collisions, changes in axis rotation, and/or global atmospheric and gravitational changes. Earth has already gone through this cycle and will undoubtedly go through the same cycle again. Hopefully it will not happen any time soon, but when that happens, Earth will be *de-listed* as an Active IP, until the next cycle.

Recent media coverage of end-of-the-world stories loom on the

The Intelligent LifeCycle Theory

horizon for the remainder of 2012. Such stories are certainly sensational and entertaining. However, *The ILC Theory* does not subscribe to the Apocalypse 2012 notion that the Earth will end this year. Don't worry about it. (However, if it does, then never mind.)

Upon the sudden death of a world's population, all resident Sapiens from that world are drawn up to the appropriate subHalo to be recycled to other worlds, as they are needed. Such an immediate influx of a few billion Sapiens would undoubtedly tax the system.

The volume of Sapien traffic already going through a subHalo is in the tens of billions per day. Such a global extinction event of a planet's entire population can easily be handled at the subHalo level.

There are a couple of side benefits to be derived from such a catastrophic event, if that is possible. Remember, the extinction of intelligent life on a planet, although infrequent, is not that uncommon of an event in the universe. Of course when you expand the scope to include the Superverse, it occurs more frequently in sheer numbers.

When an IP suddenly goes dark, the subHalo receives an immediate windfall of a few billion more Sapiens available for LC assignments. And the subHalo will no longer need to service that IP for a few million years or so, freeing up those Sapiens to respond to other IPs' Sapien requests. Both of these subHalo enhancements certainly help alleviate pressures on the Sapien pipeline that services the galaxy.

Sapien Request Order (SRO)

The *Intelligent Life Cycle* of a Sapien begins with the Sapien Request Order (SRO), which may sound like an oxymoron, but it works. A

Sapien is being requested, so that the subHalo can fulfill the order, one document for both, saves the trees.

After conception, the fetus begins to develop, according to the hereditary physical components of the parental overlay, which is created from both parents. As soon as the gender of the fetus is identifiable by the formation of the X/Y chromosomes, the SRO is created by merging the parental overlay specifications with the fetus' gender and addressing information. The SRO is then transmitted to the nearest subHalo with the fetus' expected time of arrival.

The SRO address identifies the location destination of the Sapien requested. The address, such as 1.042764874923.032985.003.03., represents the subHalo, star, planet and country of the originating fetus. Supporting detail for the SRO includes fetus gender, as well as IM and ICT averages of both parents. The request to the subHalo is to match as closely as possible the traits and intelligence of the parental overlay with those of the Sapien to be selected.

As the new fetus approaches the end of its first trimester of pregnancy, which is the time when it needs its own energy field, a followup signal is sent from the womb to the subHalo. The new transmission indicates the timing needed for the Sapien transfer from the subHalo to the womb, usually before the second trimester begins. The little fetus will continue with its own development, while awaiting the Sapien arrival.

Sapien Selection Process

The Sapien selection process at the subHalo begins as soon as the SRO is received, requesting a Sapien transfer. The initial Sapien selection process begins with the location specs, identifying the destination of the intended Sapien. The next key search is for gender.

Once these two primary search parameters are met, the subHalo program then searches available RestTime Sapiens, for IM (Intelligence Module) and ICT development percentage matches. When the subHalo selection program is complete, the Sapien is then sent to Earth to fuse with the intended fetus.

At this point, the Sapiens LC Registry is updated with the new LC entry, as is the subHalo's records. The last two fields are added to the Sapien address, indicating Sapien LC count and Sapien Quotient (SQ).

In this case, the Sapien selected has ten previous LCs, and an L5.3 Sapien rating. This results in the Sapien's new addressing scheme, 1.042764874923.032985.003.03.10.530, which is attached to the Sapien and registered in the subHalo's Sapien transfer log for inventory purposes.

This process of Sapien selection is responsible for the offspring exhibiting similar intelligence and character traits to those of the parents. The Sapien IM and ICT similarities are the result of the subHalo Sapien selection program choosing a Sapien that closely resembles the mental characteristics of the parents. Physical similarities between the parents and the child are of course the product of physical DNA pass through.

If you are somewhat reticent about the prospects for your next LifeCycle, do not fret. Instead of thinking about what you have not done with your LC this time, just think about what you have done.

Envision the positive traits your Sapien has developed during this life. Most Sapiens have at least a few positive ICT strengths they can identify, which may help in their Sapien selection for the next LC, or maybe not. Don't worry about it, that's life.

Movie Quote: "The Long Kiss Goodbye", 1996, starring Geena Davis and Samuel L. Jackson. During a moment of truth, Jackson, as an ex-cop, ex-con and private investigator, laments about his life. He has an epiphany of sorts, when he suddenly realizes, "Ya know, I've never done one thing right in my life...., and that takes skill."

Give that some thought. Your current LC has probably enhanced your Sapien ratings more than you think. There will always be other Sapiens not as developed as you. And there will always be Sapiens more developed than you. Both scenarios are directly proportional to a Sapien's number of LCs to date. The more LCs a Sapien has equates to more fully developed ICTs and IM.

During the selection process, errors are occasionally made with respect to traits of selected Sapien. Normally L0s are sent to C1 developing worlds. L7s are usually sent to the most advanced C7 planets.

The subHalo Sapien selection program, however, is not infallible, which results in occasional mismatches between the parental overlay and the incoming Sapien. Sometimes the SH Factor (Sh*t Happens) intrudes into the process, and the match between parents and child are not even close. The vast majority of Sapien selections result in extremely good matches between parents and their baby Sapiens.

Sapien Exit Request (SER)

At death, when the physical body can no longer sustain life, the Sapien-BrainBridge's tetronic bond is broken. The Sapien immediately transmits a signal to the subHalo for an LC termination pickup. The signal is immediately received, since the UENet program is constantly searching for Sapien Exit Requests (SERs), on a 24/7 basis, throughout the galaxy.

The Sapien is then pulled up into the nearest subHalo over the UENet at StarSpeed. Resembling the instantaneous travel as portrayed in *"Jonathon Livingston Seagull"*, the Sapien is transferred to the subHalo in less than a second of Earth time. Once received at the subHalo, the Sapien is then processed, inventoried and listed as available for future LCs.

As a result of improvements and enhancements to its ICTs and IM during its previous LC, the Sapien leaves the subHalo with a new unique Sapien address. This new address reflects changes from its previous birth, both in character trait development and innate intelligence.

The Sapien's tetronic charge will exhibit new data for the last two fields, representing the new number of LCs, and the ending Sapien rating from the previous LC. The new Sapien ID would then appear as, 1.042764874923.032985.003.03.11.570, replacing the previous 1.042764874923.032985.003.03.10.530 address.

Think of the Sapien's tetronic charge as an Internet address. Each one is unique, at least temporarily until you disconnect. When you reconnect, you are assigned a new Internet address, with the first couple of fields representing your Internet provider remaining intact.

If you have a dedicated Internet connection, you have a permanent address, such as 10.230.45.1003. This scenario would occur when a Sapien evolves to L8 and L9 status, with an 'always on' tetronic connection to the Halo or subHalo.

During each LC, the Sapien has a unique address, which reflects the actual Sapien L rating, in combination with the Sapien's addressing scheme. Each Sapien is absolutely unique, because of its LiveTime ICT events and the impact its LCs had on individual ICTs.

Example: An L5 Sapien may actually possess a tetronic charge of 5.634974089329303000233, which we would classify as an L5, or more specifically an L5.6. When you combine this Sapien's tetronic charge with its addressing scheme, the resultant Sapien address is indeed unique.

subHalo RestTime

The largest section of the subHalo is used for Sapien RestTimes. This is the subHalo section that Sapiens enjoy as they await their next LCs.

After a Sapien is drawn up to the subHalo and processed, it is assigned a position in the L group that is consistent with its own development. This assignment to the subHalo's RestTime function allows the Sapien time to relax, after a long and sometimes grueling seventy plus years of LiveTime on Earth.

Think of RestTime in the subHalo as a permanent dream state. All elements of the Sapien are fully functional without a body. Sapiens can relive moments in their previous LC by viewing their memory files, but only those memories that were saved, and only those memories from the previous LC. During RestTime, the Sapien maintains the same persona, as that of the person it was in the last LifeCycle, which is useful during communications between Sapiens in the subHalo. They can also access their LC Registry for cursory details of their other previous LCs to date.

After a good long rest, or possibly a very short one, a Sapien is selected for another LC. The Sapien is then transferred to the outgoing preparation group, with other Sapiens awaiting their next LCs. Each Sapien must undergo a set routine of reconditioning before getting subHalo approval to reenter LiveTime in the next LC. It is pleasurable, painless and slightly time consuming, but it is mandatory. And after all, it is a system that has worked for trillions of years.

Prior to recycling, the Sapien's ICT sets and IM get re-calibrated, reflecting ICT and IM improvements from the last LC. At that point, the Sapien's record is updated in the subHalo database, with the new address and Sapien data for inventory accounting.

The first phase of reconditioning is Sapien memory upload. Memories of key ICT events from the previous LC that were stored in the Sapien's short term memory are uploaded to the subHalo's LC Library. The Sapien's LC Registry is then updated with data and a few relevant video images from the LC.

The second phase of reconditioning is Sapien Rejuvenation. Following the years spent in the previous LC and subHalo RestTime since, the Sapien needs to be re-energized for the next LC assignment. The time required for a Sapien to get 'rejuvied' is dependent upon the complexity of the Sapien's evolution.

A Sapien with a higher LC count and more advanced ICTs and IM will generally take longer to get re-energized, than a lower developed Sapien with fewer LCs. During the rejuvenation process, a Sapien's memory from the previous LC is sometimes partially or wholly erased, as a result of intense tetrical restoration.

After the Sapien has been successfully rejuvied, it goes to the third phase of LC prep, Memory Deletions. Even though all or part of a Sapien's memories from the previous LC were deleted during rejuvenation, it undergoes another round of memory deletion programs. This is done to ensure all memories of the previous life are permanently erased from the Sapien before being downloaded to its next LifeCycle. During this final phase, prior to recycling, the Sapien's parental overlay module is also cleared to accommodate new data from parents in the new LC.

When the Sapien is totally rejuvenated, it is tagged as available for the next outgoing LC slot in its category. The new revised Sapien configuration will remain with the Sapien, while it is a resident at the subHalo during the remainder of its RestTime.

This recycling process includes all four evolution theories. The Sapien selection criteria provided by the parental overlay indicates the presence of *Determinism*. The improvements in a Sapien's traits from previous LCs, that qualify it for a specific LC, results from the Sapien's *Free Will* in those previous Cycles. The final selection process of getting cued up for the next available slot may represent *Randomness*. And of course, the entire process of Sapien recycling represents *Intergyism* (Intelligent energy-ism), which was first introduced in *The Intelligent LifeCycle Theory*.

A Sapien's ending ICT and IM levels are the next LC's starting point. They will continue to develop through the next LC, until LC termination, at which time the process starts all over again.

Sapien Communications During RestTime

During RestTime, a Sapien gets to experience the mental-only part of the *Intelligent Life Cycle (ILC)*. And it is fascinating, to say the least. Sapiens at rest can communicate with other Sapiens at rest, through a phenomena, we on Earth call, Extra Sensory Perception (ESP), or mental telepathy.

It takes a little time for Sapiens to perfect the ESP techniques that allow them to mentally project their physical image to others. Until they master the ability to project, they communicate only by audio to other Sapiens, who are already fully functional, metaphysically.

Example: As a new arrival to an L5 subHalo group, you communicate with others in your group, through verbal ESP type messaging only. When you perfect the visual projection technique, it is like a coming-out party. The other Sapiens in your group now get to see what you looked like in your last LC. And they have the benefit of seeing your expressions and body language, as you talk about life, as if you were physically present. It is infinitely cool.

A Sapien can relive some of his or hers ICT events from memory, and share them with others, through a very advanced form of mental telepathy. It is like you are telling your story, but instead of the spoken word, you are able to use full audio/video replications of your story.

Every time a Sapien returns to the subHalo for its RestTime, the Sapien retains the persona and experiential memories of the previous LC. When a Sapien interacts with other Sapiens in the subHalo, he or she exhibits all ICT and IM characteristics existent in their person at the time of their last LC termination.

Sapiens resting in subHalos do have the ability to interact with other mental-only Sapiens, but normally only with those Sapiens within the same L Group. Such interactions do not have any affect on ICT and IM development. The ratings a Sapien has, when he or she enters the subHalo, are the ending points from the previous LC, and will become the starting point for that Sapien in the next LC. Only LiveTime ICT events have an impact on a Sapien's development.

When a newly arriving Sapien begins to communicate with other Sapiens, he or she cannot stop talking and asking questions about the sudden transfer from Earth to the subHalo, from the physical form to the metaphysical realm. This usually lasts for a day or two, until reality sinks in, and the Sapien becomes comfortable with the life-after-death situation.

Sapiens interact and communicate with other Sapiens in rest mode, covering a variety of topics. They share stories about their preceding LCs, the memories of which remain intact, until they are erased and reset to zero, prior to the next LC assignment. Sometimes Sapiens discuss their subHalo accommodations, their dream states, length of subHalo stays and next LC prospects.

Metaphysical communications is quite a trip, the first time especially. You do not have a physical body. But you do have memories of your previous life and body, as well as the newly-acquired knowledge of the real *Intelligent Life Cycle*.

Halo Recap

In the far reaches of space, at speeds unknown to common man, via the Universal Energy Network (UENet), there exists a place where all

Sapiens wish to reach. The host Halo is the final destination, to which all Sapiens strive to become a part.

The Halo is the final repository for perfect and near perfect Sapiens. For most Sapiens, their transition to the Halo will eventually occur, over countless LC journeys to and from their respective subHalos. For some, the 'negative Ls', the journey to the top may never materialize.

The Halo is ultimately responsible for all intelligent life in the universe. Its 24/7 or 28/8 operation is supported by subHalos in every galaxy, the primary objective of which is to service the intelligent life requirements in each galaxy.

SubHalos provide a way station of sorts to all Sapiens as they continue to evolve in their development. SubHalos manage the natural evolution of a Sapien, as it progresses from an L1 to an L7. When a Sapien makes the jump to L8 status, the Sapien then assumes residence in the host Halo. From the Halo, L8 and L9 advanced Sapiens have the opportunity to materially affect the evolution and continuity of intelligent life in the universe.

Think of the Halo as the home page of the Universal Energy Field's website. This is the place from which an advanced Sapien can effectively navigate across multiple platforms to assist in Halo and subHalo operations, and/or enjoy retirement from active life.

As the trillions of Sapiens in the universe rotate in and out of their respective subHalos and LCs, they continue to develop their character traits as intelligent beings. Change is the name of the game in Sapien evolution, hopefully in the positive direction. It is definitely a fluid and highly dynamic environment.

Example: The subHalo systems manage all Sapien traffic to and from IPs in the universe. The subHalo, responsible for the Milky Way Galaxy, services hundreds of thousands of Sapiens per day, just on Earth. Multiply those traffic levels by the billions of intelligent planets in the universe, and you can visualize the vast scope of the Halo system, and its supporting subHalos.

Aggregately, subHalos recycle Sapiens from a number of different intelligent life species in the universe, in various humanoid-type host bodies, on planets that support intelligent life. Even though there is a remote possibility of insect intelligence on some far off planet, as seen in sci-fi movies, the Halo and UENet address only humanoid-type intelligent beings as Sapiens.

The Halo is at the core of the origin of the universe, if there ever was an origin. Halo operations is infinity on steroids with a twist. It is infinite in scope with finite components, and ultimately it had no beginning and has no end.

The Intelligent LifeCycle Theory

Universal Energy Network

The Universal Energy Network (UENet) is the transportation system used for Sapien travel, and the communications backbone of the universe. UENet operations are controlled from the UENet sector of the host Halo and its Universal Energy Field (UEF).

The master network consists of 10^{11} subNets servicing each galaxy's subHalo. Each galaxy subNet is comprised of planetary subNets to service the Intelligent Planets (IPs) in each galaxy, such as Earth, with multiple nodes servicing each IP.

The UENet is responsible for transporting Sapiens from the subHalos to their respective planets to begin their LifeCycles. Such Sapien transfers usually occur within the same galaxy, and usually to the same planet, as their previous LCs, except in the case of C1 and C2 IPs, which are used to service C3 and C4 planets.

Conversely, the UENet is also used to pickup expired Sapiens. As Sapien LCs terminate, they are picked up by the nearest UENet node and returned to the appropriate sector in their home subHalos for rejuvenation and RestTime, prior to the next LiveTime LifeCycle.

The UENet is a 24/7 network operation, servicing intelligent planets in the universe at StarSpeed. Since some UENet traffic traverses the spatial void (1 atom/cubic meter) between galaxies, UENet transfer rates increase significantly between sub-Halos and the host Halo.

The UENet has been in operation since infinity began, which is a profound oxymoron, if you can imagine that. It had no beginning and it has no end. When and where the UENet began is immaterial. What is important is that it continues to function as the carrier of intelligent life throughout the universe.

UENet Operations

Although the UENet is the communications backbone of the universe, its primary function is to transport Sapiens to and from planets and subHalos. The communications that precedes Sapien selection for a LifeCycle is the Sapien Request Order (SRO), which the subUENet receives and transmits to the subHalo for fulfillment. The UENet is constantly polling all galaxies for SROs and SERs, 24/7 or 28/8.

The SRO is generated by the parental overlay's temporary life force in the fetus. It is then sent via its unique tetronic charge to the nearest subUENet node that services the applicable planet.

Once received by the UENet, the SRO is then sent to the applicable subHalo for fulfillment. As soon as a successful match is completed by selecting the proper Sapien for the SRO, the selected Sapien is then transmitted to the originating planet and fused with the intended fetus.

When the Sapien's LC is terminated (death), the Sapien's core immediately generates a Sapien Exit Request (SER) to the nearest subNet available for Sapien pickup. The UENet then transmits the expired Sapien to the appropriate subHalo for processing.

Another use for the UENet is to transmit statistical and performance data between planets, subHalos and the Halo. Such data, tracking all SROs and SERs through the system, is constantly analyzed, evaluated and accrued for summary reports between the subHalos and the Halo.

At any moment in time, the UENet allows subHalo management the ability to have an accurate Sapien count for the galaxy. UENet data management includes Sapien levels, locations and Sapien status.

All Sapiens are inventoried, whether they are in LiveTimes on an IP, being processed in the subHalo as incoming Sapiens, in subHalo Rest Time, or being processed in the subHalo as outgoing Sapiens. This gives L9ICs in each galaxy a comprehensive Sapien inventory database from which to effectively manage daily subHalo operations.

A planet's performance is measured to ensure the Sapien development of a planet is evolving positively. Generally, when an IP reaches C3 status with average Sapien ratings in the L3 range, the planet is not subject to as much frequent scrutiny by the L10 board in the Halo.

However, when a planet seems to be going the wrong direction in Sapien development, the SRO/SER summary reports generated by the UENet begin to show deficient Sapien level transfers. As Sapien in/out traffic goes negative, an alert is sent via the UENet from the subHalo to the Halo identifying the deficient average Sapien ratings.

When the aggregate Sapien average of SROs and SERs decrease sufficiently, it indicates a dangerous reversal trend in Sapien development on the planet. When this occurs, intervention may be

The Intelligent LifeCycle Theory

needed to correct the evolutionary direction of a planet's Sapien population. Intervention is usually needed during the early stages of an IP's development, as a C2 IP.

As needed, generally once or twice during the early growth of an IP, the Halo may decide to select a Roving L8 or Roving L9 to assist and to intervene. In such cases, the advanced Sapien selected is sent to the planet in the same manner as other Sapiens, via the UENet to the fetus to begin the Halo Intervention Transfer, or HIT assignment.

Other than the infrequent Roving Ls, 100 percent of Sapien selections and 100 percent of Sapien transfers over the UENet are 100 percent automated, for lack of a better word. The UENet programs, developed trillions of years ago, are digitally-based applications that transport Sapiens to and from LiveTimes and applicable subHalos.

Currently, the UENet's planetary subNet that services Earth processes over two hundred million total Sapien transfers per year. Earth's volume of UENet traffic, including births requiring Sapien deliveries and deaths requiring Sapien pickups, is estimated to be over five hundred and fifty thousand per day.

As shown below, birth rates far exceed death rates on Earth.

2005-2010 Stats	Sapien Traffic: Earth		
	Per Year	Per Day	Per Hour
CBR (Crude Birth Rate)	142,100,000	389,315	16,221
CDR (Crude Death Rate)	59,500,000	163,013	6,792
Net Sapien Growth	82,600,000	226,301	9,429
Total Sapien Traffic	201,600,000	552,328	23,013

This means Earth, as a C4 IP, is presently a net importer of Sapiens from other IPs in the MilkyWay galaxy. Such interplanetary Sapien transfers to address Earth's net growth rate are needed to service the explosive populations in certain countries, as previously discussed.

The UENet subnet that services the MilkyWay subHalo, as shown below, handles over 20 trillion Sapien transfers per year. This includes all birth deliveries and death pickups. Using Earth as the average IP in the galaxy, the UENet completes an estimated fifty-five billion Sapien transfers in the MilkyWay galaxy per day.

Sapien Traffic: MilkyWay Galaxy	
(10^5 IPs/Galaxy)	
2005-2010 Est.	Per Year
CBR (Crude Birth Rate)	14,313,151,852,177
CDR (Crude Death Rate)	5,993,191,662,241
Net Sapien Growth	8,319,960,189,936
Total Sapien Traffic	20,306,343,514,418

Because of the sheer size of the universe, it seems meaningless to extrapolate the MilkyWay numbers into total Sapien numbers for the universe as a whole. However, for the record, our known universe, as currently defined, is home to over 70.51 septillion Sapiens, or more specifically 70,508,137,202,843,000,000,000,000 Sapiens. Scientific notation would show this number as 7.0508137202843e+25, or simply 7.051×10^{25} Sapiens in our known universe.

When you think about these kinds of numbers, infinity comes to mind again. Even though most Earth scientists believe in the possibility and in fact the probability of infinity, they have nonetheless tried to define the scope of its existence.

The position scientists take on infinity may seem like an oxymoron, as do many explanations surrounding the word. They say infinity exists, but also claim the universe is finite and measurable. This is best exhibited by scientists' wide acceptance of the theory that there are only 10^{11} galaxies in the universe. Of course that is just a round number used for calculations, but by doing so, they have attempted to define the universe in finite terms.

However, if there is a limit (10^{11} galaxies) to the universe, and infinity does exist, what's past this universe? The only logical answer, to this infinite question, is more universes with more UENets. This concept, by definition, must be the default solution in order to effectively perpetuate the growth of intelligent life throughout the universe and indeed throughout time itself.

There is one way to describe the scope of infinity. Just as you would make the case, and rightfully so, that infinity has no end, you must also make the same case that infinity had no beginning. I know infinity is a tough concept to comprehend, but think about it.

UENet Organization

The Universal Energy Network is administered, monitored and operated by semi-retired L8 and L9 advanced Sapiens. The majority of advanced Ls accept these assignments within their home galaxy's subHalo and subUENet operations. Although not that frequent, occasionally an advanced L may be transferred between galaxies, to accommodate work load differences as they arise.

Instead of accepting retirement in the Halo for all eternity, some advanced Sapiens opt to continue in administrative functions. Because these functions are so vital to the successful continuity of intelligent life, such advanced Sapiens are able to gain experiences that allow them to continue with their own ICT development.

As shown in the organizational chart below, the UENet management hierarchy is comprised of an L9 Controller and a number of L8s in specific roles of responsibility. The functions of these positions replicate similar duties to those required in most technology database management systems.

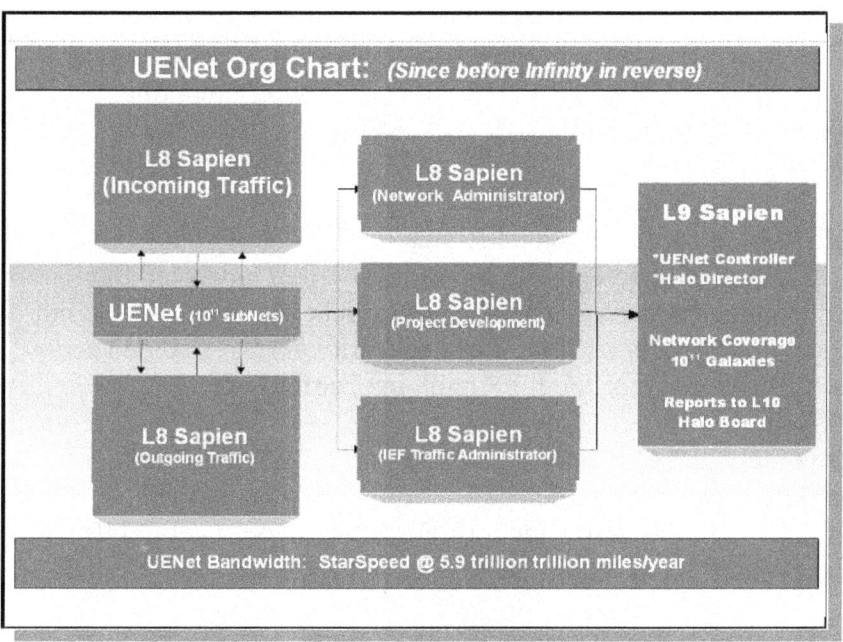

The Sapien with the most direct responsibility for UENet operations is the L9 Controller, who reports directly to the Halo L10 Board. This position requires an L9.0 or higher Sapien, angel status. Advanced L9 Sapiens, with L9.5 or higher ratings, are considered to be more applicable to this all important role,

The UENet Controller's position is filled with advanced Rotating L9s, who rotate in and out of the office every few years or so. The UENet controller function is thought of as a high-stress job, by most Sapiens familiar with its operations. There seems to be unilateral agreement among higher-level Sapiens that only a Sapien with angel status can withstand the pressure.

Occasionally an L9 might remain in this position for more than a few years. However, some have been known to take full retirement after only a few months of active duty as the UENet L9 Controller. A few months may not seem very long for a tour of duty like this, but think about it. Can you imagine the pressure, if you had sole responsibility for the safe transportation of all intelligent life in the universe?

High-stress is probably an understatement. But of course, that's how we lesser developed Sapiens perceive it. More advanced Sapiens, such as L9s, may not perceive it to be stressful at all. Well maybe, but whatever the stress level is, it is a necessity. It can also be very gratifying as well for the L9 Sapien in charge.

Fortunately, the L9IC (L9 In Charge) has a formal hierarchical structure with which to delegate administrative and operational duties of the UENet. Support functions are filled by semi-retired, Rotating L8s, generally with assignment tours longer than that of the L9IC.

Administrative and operational L8s in the UENet handle daily Sapien captures and deliveries, to and from the one hundred billion galactic subNets and their respective intelligent planets. Although just as vital, L8 administration may not be as stressful a position as the L9IC.

Rotating L8s function as network administrators in each of the 10^{11} subNets servicing each galaxy in the universe. SubNet L8s are resident in their respective subHalos, regardless of galaxy of origin.

Rotating Ls provide support to their respective subHalo L9ICs in each galaxy. They report directly to the L8 traffic administrator in the Halo, who in turn reports directly to the UENet L9 Controller.

A cadre of qualified L8s have always been available to manage UENet operations in the hundred billion subNets servicing galaxies around the universe. While most L8s and L9s firmly retire to the Halo, these Rotating Ls pursue continued development in hopes of evolving to higher Sapien status eventually. Sapiens that take this approach have definitely developed a good understanding and acceptance of infinity.

UENet Speeds and Feeds

The speed and capacity of the UENet, by design, must be able to handle extremely large amounts of perpetual traffic, 24/7 or 28/8 as the case may be. Transmission speeds of the UENet are undetectable by our current technology standards.

Such extremely high bandwidths are needed to carry the volume of Sapien traffic at any given time throughout the universe, within short durations of time. Even though such distances and speeds seem unimaginable with our current technology, we still have the need to further define the phenomena of LightSpeed, and now StarSpeed.

If it could be measured, UENet transport speeds between worlds, subHalos and the Halo are somewhere in the neighborhood of a trillion times the speed of light. Even though this is way beyond our current scientific knowledge base as humans, think of the UENet as something akin to a black hole type conduit between subHalos and their IPs. Visualize how Hollywood has portrayed these mystical black holes in movies, traveling at instantaneous speeds. It is something like that, minus all the glitz and glitter.

Since UENet speeds are measured in multiples of light speed, it is important to understand the comparison between the two. Someday, probably not in the next few hundred LifeCycles, but sometime in the distant future, Earth humans may be able to comprehend and replicate StarSpeed. But before that time comes, we must first understand and be able to replicate LightSpeed.

Example: Light from the Sun takes about 8 minutes to reach the Earth, after leaving the Sun's surface. That's a 92 million mile trip in only a few minutes, at the speed of light. LightSpeed is so unbelievable, consider this. Light, being generated at the Sun's core, is deflected so many times during its journey to the surface, it takes about 5,000 years to reach the Sun's surface, and then only 8 minutes to get to Earth.

In theory, if the Sun suddenly stopped generating light at its core, we might not even know about it, when it happens. Assuming the abrupt change was undetected, and it did not affect Earth's gravitational nor atmospheric forces, it would be 5,000 years and 8 minutes before we Earth Sapiens would find out, just about the time the Earth went dark.

If we could replicate LightSpeed, space travel to distances within our own solar system would easily be attainable. However, when you consider the vast reaches of space, it would require speeds much greater than light to effectively navigate to IPs just within the MilkyWay galaxy, not to mention the rest of the universe.

You may think communications, and indeed travel, at this level is impossible. According to Earth's current scientific knowledge, you would be right. The popular premise is that nothing can go faster than the speed of light. If it did, it would become light itself.

The illustration below shows the straight-line distance from Earth to the Sun, approximately 150 million kilometers or 92 million miles. At this distance, it takes light about 8.32 minutes to reach Earth from the Sun, but only 120 nanoseconds on the UENet at StarSpeed.

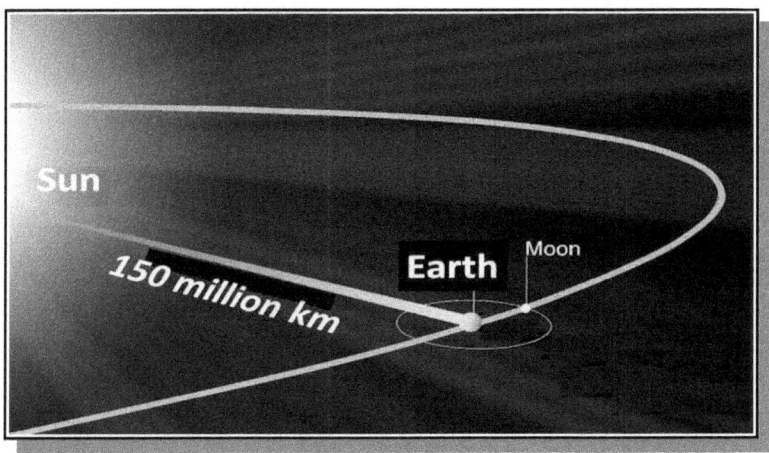

There is a theory that says, you may even go back in time, if you exceed LightSpeed, creating a monumental paradox. I never understood that one. It seems that if you traveled faster than light, wouldn't you go forward in time and not backward?

Another theory purports to the concept of bending time as a possible solution to space travel. It is thought that such time warps, if possible, would obviate the need for faster than light speeds, by circumventing time and by default circumventing space itself.

Given these types of facts and theories, it allows Earth humans the ability to discuss such concepts logically and scientifically. Within the realm of the accepted language of physics, these discussions should add some credence to the possibility that such speeds and technologies do indeed exist, and are someday attainable.

Time & Distance Equivalents

Abbrev.	Time Span	Distance Traveled
ls	1 light-second	187,000 miles
lm	1 light-minute	11.2 million miles
lh	1 light-hour	673.1 million miles
ld	1 light-day	16.2 billion miles
ms	1 light-month	484.6 billion miles
ly	1 light-year	5.9 trillion miles
parsec	3.26 light years	19 trillion miles
Kly	1,000 light-years	5.9 thousand trillion miles
Mly	1 million(10^6) light-years	5.9 million trillion miles
Gly	1 billion (10^9) light-years	5.9 billion trillion miles
Tly	1 trillion (10^{12}) light-years	5.9 trillion trillion miles
SSY	StarSpeed (UENet speed - 1 Tly)	5.9 trillion trillion miles

Nanosecond = 1 billionth of a second   Tetrasecond = 1 trillionth of a second

The above chart equates LightSpeed durations to distances traveled. The most familiar one is the light-year (ly), which is the distance light travels in one year. The highlight of the chart is the StarSpeed Year (SSY), the effective bandwidth of the UENet throughout the universe. SSY, with a capital Y, is equivalent to a trillion light-years, or 1 Tly.

Other ways to define StarSpeed include, 5.9×10^{24} miles per year, and/or 5.9 trillion trillion miles per year. The UENet, transmitting at StarSpeed, is considered to be a network that is robust enough to effectively handle seventy septillion Sapien transfers, if needed.

To equate StarSpeed to our current measurement of miles per hour, for the record, StarSpeed travels at 673,515,981,735,160,000,000 miles per hour. More succinctly, StarSpeed is described as 6.74×10^{20} miles/hour or 674 million trillion miles/hr.

StarSpeed allows virtually instantaneous travel. If you find it difficult to comprehend such velocities, think about our current level of communications. Right now, we can instantly talk to people across the country and around the world.

With today's digital communications technology, we can also see the other party with live video feeds. This level of transmission is accomplished via voice/data links that are at high transfer rates, but well below the speed of light, and way below StarSpeed.

Using the analogy of our current technology may make it a little easier to comprehend such speeds. As we see the need for increased travel speeds and can imagine such speeds, it becomes obvious that instantaneous travel by Sapiens over the UENet is not only practical, but absolutely a prerequisite to space travel.

Sapien transfers can only be handled with StarSpeed connectivity, or greater. Some may consider UENet's StarSpeed analogous to another theory of star travel from the 1970s, astral projection.

Astral projection is purported to allow a person the ability to experience instantaneous travel through out-of-body experiences, or 'thought-travel'. Astral projection may be similar in concept to StarSpeed, except that in the case of Sapien transfers, the Sapien has no control over the transport nor its destination. Whereas astral projection allows the traveler total control of the trip.

The Intelligent LifeCycle Theory

StarSpeed is relatively instantaneous, requiring only 0.82 seconds from Earth to the center of the MilkyWay, which is the home of our galaxy's subHalo. However, due to the extremely lengthy distances in space, it still takes seventeen days at StarSpeed to travel the 46.5 billion light-years to the edge of the universe, as we know it.

As currently defined, light travels 5.9 trillion miles in a year, referred to as one light-year. Currently, UENet's StarSpeed travels about a trillion times the speed of light, which is absolutely necessary for the transfer of matter, energy and information through space.

LIGHT SPEEDS & UENet SPEEDS

From Earth to:	Distance (miles)	Light Speed	UENet Speed
The Moon	250,000	1.31 seconds	1.3 tetraseconds
The Sun	92 million	8.32 minutes	120 nanoseconds
Milky Way Center	153×10^{15}	26 Kly	0.82 seconds
Edge of Universe	274×10^{21}	46.5 Gly	17 days

Distances measured in fractions of a light-year usually involve objects within a star system. Distances in light-years are generally used between stars and galaxies.

The above data comparisons are important to understand the real significance of such a network as the UENet. In comparison to current Earth technology standards, our most distant space probe, the Voyager1, logged sixteen light-hours away from Earth as of 2011. At its current speed of about 38,000 mph, it will take 17,500 years to reach the distance that light travels in one year.

The only way for LiveTime Sapiens to reach other stars and other planets with Sapien civilizations is with the advent of StarSpeed. And StarSpeed, or some equivalency thereof as a prerequisite for travel to the stars, is the only way Sapien travel can exist between intelligent planets and subHalos. Without StarSpeed, there would be no *Intelligent LifeCycle Theory*.

The chart below converts miles to light years, and extrapolates that into actual travel time, comparing LightSpeed to StarSpeed.

SPEEDS & DISTANCES OF THE UNIVERSE

Light-Speed (miles/yr)		**StarSpeed via UENet (miles/yr)**
5,900,000,000,000		5,900,000,000,000,000,000,000,000
5.9 trillion		5.9 trillion trillion
(59×10^{11})		(59×10^{23})
	Earth to:	
Travel Time	**Center of Milky Way (miles)**	**Travel Time**
26 thousand light-years	153,400,000,000,000,000	0.8205 seconds
(26 Kly)	(1.534×10^{17})	
	Earth to:	
Travel Time	**Edge of Universe (miles)**	**Travel Time**
46.5 billion light-years	274,350,000,000,000,000,000,000	16.98 days
(46.5 Gly)	(2.7435×10^{23})	

UENet Reliability

Basically, the Universal Energy Network has unlimited bandwidth, transferring energy at a trillion times the speed of light with high-end performance measured in tetraseconds. UENet uptime and accuracy levels are estimated to provide 99.999997 percent resource availability. The UENet is not perfect, nor infallible, but it is close.

The Intelligent LifeCycle Theory

The UENet normally does not carry much Sapien traffic between galaxies, and little if any between universes. The vast majority of UENet traffic exists primarily between the subHalos and IPs. With network downtimes estimated in the 0.000003 percent range, the UENet shows significant reliability. Even so, it does experience some network outages, infrequent as they are. But hey, that's life.

The flowchart below shows the UENet servicing 10^{11} galaxies, including twenty trillion Sapiens per year in the Milky Way Galaxy.

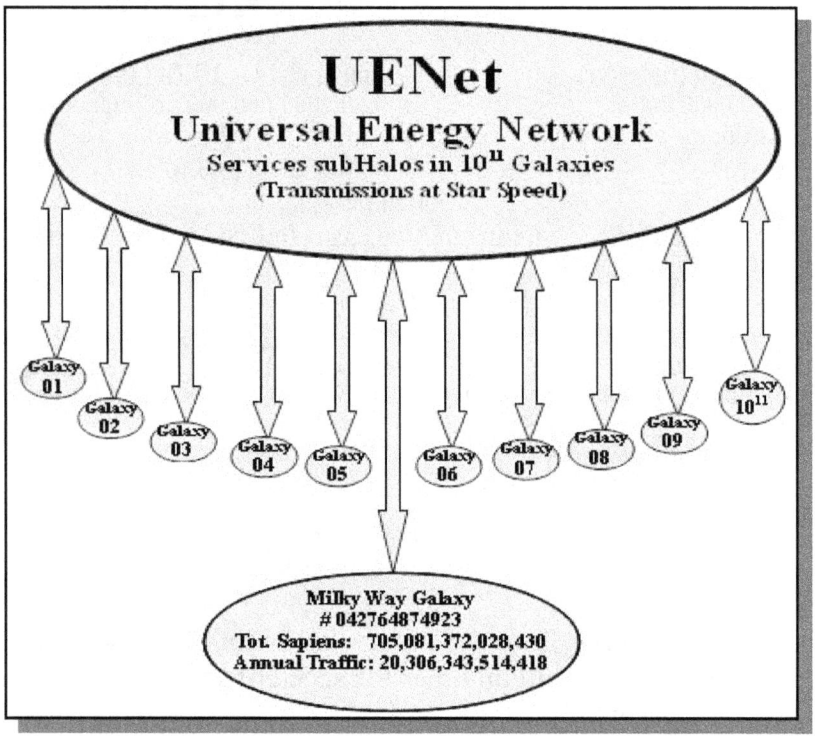

Scientists believe that the spatial void between galaxies is in fact empty space. This emptiness is filled with a tenuous gas of an average density that is less than one atom per cubic meter. Because of this emptiness in outer space, UENet StarSpeed is possible. Its reliability attests to its significant uptime.

In addition, UENet speeds are possible because of dark matter, which accounts for about 90 percent of the mass of most galaxies. Dark matter, the opposite of 'anti-matter', is very dense and compressed, providing least resistance to UENet transfers at high speeds.

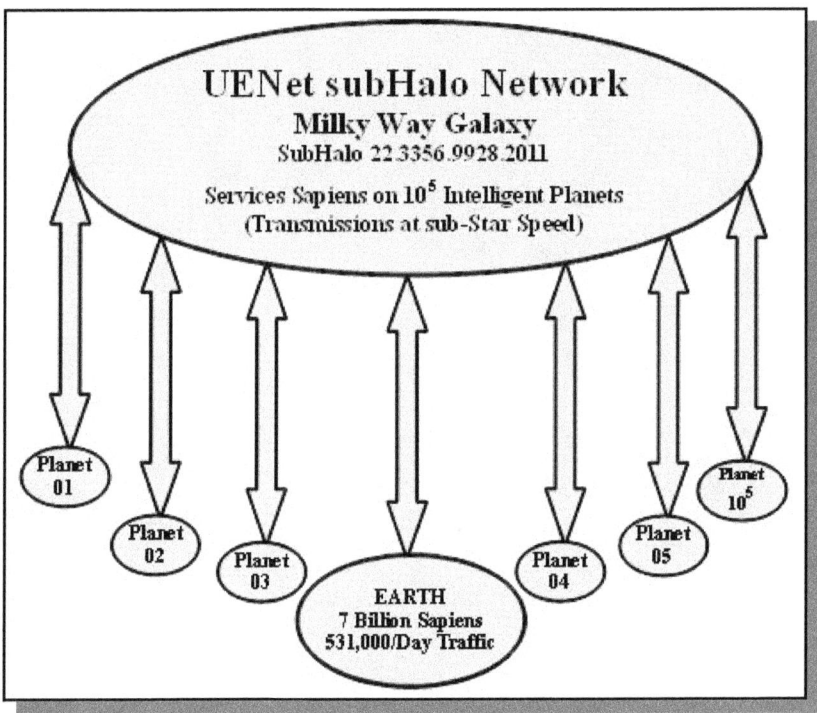

The flowchart above illustrates the UENet subHalo Network servicing one hundred thousand intelligent planets (10^5 IPs) in the MilkyWay galaxy, with average Earth traffic of 531,000 Sapiens per day.

The UENet, as an extremely sophisticated delivery system, is solely responsible for the safe transportation of all Sapiens in the universe, between their LiveTimes on intelligent planets and their home subHalos. The UENet is the Intelligence Network Backbone of the Universe.

8. Sapien LifeCycle

A Sapien's LifeCycle (LC) is the LiveTime event of a Sapien following that Sapien's previous life. This part of *The Theory* is similar to other reincarnation theories, in that the Sapien (soul/spirit) is recycled. But that of course, is where the similarities end. A LifeCycle is the vehicle available to the Sapien to perpetuate its own existence and continue its ICT and IM development.

The reasoning behind the reincarnation component of *The ILC Theory* is based purely on the laws of physics and the natural laws of the universe, not on religious precepts. The purpose of an LC is to continually grow and develop intelligence in the universe. And in doing so, an LC becomes its own self-fulfilling prophecy. *The ILC Theory* is a pragmatic way of analyzing life after death.

Darwin's Theory of Evolution is assumed by *The ILC Theory* to be an accurate portrayal of the evolution of mankind, as we know it on Earth. However, Darwin, as all others have done before and since, postulates only on the development of mankind as a physical entity.

The Intelligent LifeCycle Theory

According to Darwin, lifeforms evolved over millions of years in many different directions, creating many different species of living organisms. A branching pattern of evolution resulted as species developed. One branch of the physical evolution evolved into Primates, which ultimately evolved into *homo sapiens.*

Considering our progress as an intelligent species, there are some that think human evolution has come full circle. And that physically, we are reverting to our predecessors physical demeanor, albeit with a much higher intelligence level. The following illustration came from a viral email some years ago depicting the evolution of mankind.

As we evaluate the physical evolution of man (and woman), the illustration above is an interesting way of looking at it. From a certain perspective, this depiction may seem valid. Did we come full circle, as physical beings? Kind of, but not really. As a species, we still walk upright, breathe oxygen, drink water and provide a brain for our Sapiens to navigate life. It is simply the way our natural physical evolution has occurred, as a species.

Specifically, it is the way mankind has evolved on Earth, the third planet from the Sun, in the MilkyWay galaxy, over the last million years or so. On other intelligent planets (IPs), physical evolution of the host body may develop differently. Of the millions of IPs in the universe, it is expected that indeed there are many versions of physical evolution of species that support and require intelligent life.

LifeCycle Basics

That is the physical side of the story. *The ILC Theory* picks up, where the others have left off. To provide intelligent functionality to a physical species, the Sapien (soul) is considered to be metaphysical, for lack of a better term.

As described in this book, the intelligence component of the LifeCycle evolves separately and apart from the host body it occupies, during any given LC. When a species on a planet develops to the point of requiring an intelligent energy source for continued development, the species adapts. A new fetus, during initial development following conception, grows a tetroscopic Sapien-BrainBridge that emits signals picked up by the subHalo, indicating the need for intelligent life.

The Intelligent LifeCycle Theory provides logic and rationale to the entire LifeCycle and reincarnation processes. It also dismisses reincarnation folklore, illustrating how it is not possible for you to come back as a dog, or goat, or anything less than a humanoid. The Sapien is an intelligent entity and cannot exist in an animal or other lifeform that does not require nor support intelligence.

During a lifetime, during an LC, a Sapien develops and hopefully improves its character traits as an intelligent being. When the host body (which includes the brain) expires for that lifetime, the Sapien may be recycled later in another host body, to once again experience that most exalted possession of all, LiveTime.

When a virgin Sapien (L0.0) is first introduced to a lifeform, for its first lifetime on record, it usually occurs on early-development stage planets. This is the initial period of development of a planet, as it begins to support intelligent life, during the first million years or so.

Example: A prehistoric caveman or woman, a million years ago, would be considered a Sapien's first LiveTime. The Sapien's first LC is considered the originating IP home base of the Sapien. Earth and the MilkyWay galaxy become the first of many permanent entries in this Sapien's LC Registry.

When the subHalo receives an SRO (Sapien Request Order) for an L1 Sapien, a new Intelligent Energy Field (IEF) is selected at random, from the subHalo's vast reserve of L0s. To complete the Sapien upgrade from an L0 to an L1, the intelligence and all character traits of the Sapien are calibrated to the default setting of 10 percent development across the board. Thus, a Sapien is sent to its first life with basic, but primitive, levels of its IM and ICT set development.

After the first LifeCycle, referred to as the Sapien's LC1, LiveTimes of all future lives are referred to as subsequent LifeCycles, LCs or just Cycles. The history, of a Sapien's LC journeys, is permanently recorded in the LC Registry in the Sapien core.

The recycling of Sapiens, to and from host bodies on intelligent planets, creates intelligent energy traffic analogous to streams of light going through the universe. By today's technology standards, such traffic is not visible to humans, nor measurable by any scientific technology we employ today. Sapien journeys, to and from their LCs on IPs, utilize the UENet for transport at StarSpeed, a trillion times the speed of light, which is almost instantaneous, hence non-detectable.

As the population explosion begins on developing planets, Sapien LCs become more frequent (less time between LCs). The subHalo inventory requirements to service high-growth planets increase when a net birth rate exceeds the death rate.

Since 1950, the CBR (crude birth rate) has been two to three times the CDR (crude death rate) on Earth. Between 2005 and 2010, the CBR was 20.3 births per thousand people per year, with a CDR of 8.5, resulting in 11.8 net population growth per thousand per year. This means that during that period, Earth required 20.3 incoming Sapiens per thousand people and only gave up 8.5 outgoing Sapiens per thousand, resulting in a net deficit of 11.8 Sapiens per thousand, to be filled by C2 to C3 IPs.

When the birth rate far exceeds the death rate on a planet, such as on Earth over the last century, the planet begins to experience a rapid, net population growth. Because of this, new LC assignments for Sapiens become more frequent returns to Earth. Keep in mind, the Sapien has limited memory storage capacity, so there are no conflicts from previous lives to interfere with future LCs.

Because of the deficiency of deaths required to service births on Earth, we must pull Sapiens from other planets to fill the void. And as much as possible, Sapiens from Earth will generally continue to be recycled to and from Earth. Under current socioeconomic and sociopolitical conditions, Earth Sapiens are expected to continue with LCs on Earth, until they get diverted to more advanced planets, as they progress to L6 and L7 status.

The majority of Sapiens, whose LCs expire on high-growth planets such as Earth, will generally get returned to the same planet for future LC assignments. On an IP with a high, net population growth curve, repeat LC trips to the same planet are more common than not. However, when the population of a planet exceeds that planet's available Sapien inventory, like Earth, the subHalo must recycle Sapiens to that planet from other less developed planets.

Example: Earth, as a C4 Intelligent Planet, will normally attract L3 to L5 Sapiens from other less-developed C2 and C3 planets, to augment its high population growth needs. SubHalos service many, many more C2 and C3 IPs than C4s, to be able to accommodate C4 IP growth.

On a C4 IP, repeat Sapien LCs to the same planet generally continue, until the Sapien reaches L6 or L7 status. At that point, the Sapien might require relocation for future LCs to more advanced planetary systems for continued development.

More advanced civilizations on C6 and C7 IPs have more advanced medical technologies than Earth. And with advanced medical procedures such as organ transplants (including the brain) and artificial limbs, the lifespan of a planet's population is extended, which ultimately results in a longer lifespan and reduced birth rate.

Average lifespans of one or two hundred years is probable in more advanced societies, on more advanced planetary systems. The real breakthrough in extending the physical life of a species will be in the area of brain transplants, since the brain evidently has a shelf life consistent with Earth's average LC duration of seventy plus years. *See "ReIndexing The Brain" in Appendix.*

As medical research increases the average lifespan available to Sapiens during their LC travels on more advanced planets, the question becomes one of non-stop endurance. How long can a Sapien sustain its LiveTime without a break?

Without periodic rejuvenation in the subHalo between LCs, can the Sapien effectively manage an LC's LiveTime of five hundred years or more? Or is a Sapien's LC more effective, more productive, with a duration of a hundred or so years? If Earth is considered a little above average developed planet, then the average lifespan of all LCs in the universe would also be around seventy years or so, at this point in the evolution of the universe.

Sapien Selection Process for LCs

Upon a successful conception, the tetracells from the parental overlay form a temporary IEF in the fetus. This temporary energy field in the little fetus contains applicable IM and ICT development percentages of both parents. Once the XX and XY chromosomes are detected in the fetus, confirming the gender, the temporary IEF then transmits its requirements needed to match a Sapien with traits similar to those of the parents. In most cases, the Sapien-BrainBridge (SBB) develops much faster than the brain, since it must communicate with the UENet before other organs are fully formed.

The SBB signal, from the barely formed fetus, is then picked up instantaneously by the nearest UENet node, responsible for the subHalo traffic in the appropriate galaxy. The subHalo attempts to match, as closely as possible, the intelligence levels and character traits of the parents in selecting the right Sapien for the impending LC.

A Sapien's unique tetronic charge, consisting of its unique combination of ICT development and IM levels, never matches exactly those of the parental overlay in the fetus. However, the selection process does result in Sapien LC placements that are near matches. It is estimated that LC assignments with near matches occur over 90 percent of the time.

The remaining 10 percent of Sapien placements are considered mismatched LCs. Approximately 5 percent are gender-mismatched assignments, where the sex of the incoming Sapien is not the same as the fetus. The other 5 percent consists of ICT and IM mismatches, either significantly higher or significantly lower than the parents.

This selection process is conducive to Sapien growth, since its new LC provides the Sapien with parents of similar development levels. Such a scenario gives the Sapien an identifiable connection in its new world, through its parents. This theoretically gives the Sapien needed and acceptable guidance during its early growth years. Regardless of whether the Sapien grows up with two parents, or one or even none, the Sapien maintains some semblance of an innate connection to its parental overlay during the LC.

During the Sapien selection process, preceding the actual transfer to a fetus, the gender of the Sapien is the first characteristic to match. The Intelligence Module (IM) and Key ICTs that are important/compatible to the parental hosts are then included in the final selection process.

After a Sapien is selected for a specific LC assignment, it is then cued up for transport. If the selected Sapien is a new arrival in the subHalo, with very little RestTime, it may not have completed its rejuvenation program yet. This is not a factor, since it normally requires only a short period for the average Sapien to rejuvenate.

Once the Sapien has been rejuvied, it is transported from the subHalo to the nearest node on the UENet that services the target planet. After its Sapien ID is updated with the new destination address as the next LC in its LC Registry, it is then transported via StarSpeed and fused with the Sapien-BrainBridge in the awaiting fetus.

The whole Sapien selection process operates on tetronic attractions between Sapiens with similar tetrical charge profiles. Until a Sapien reaches L8 development, wisdom status, the selection and fulfillment process for LCs is 100 percent mathematical, with no input from the Sapien.

However, once a Sapien is born and enters LiveTime in another LC, the Sapien will begin to have some control over its life, through the exercise of free will, increasingly so with age. Historically speaking, during an LC on Earth, Sapiens tend to evolve into and gravitate toward LC groups, based on the timing of their births.

In current day vernacular, such LC groups are referred to as generations, or eras. LifeCycle groups are thought to have some ICTs in common, based on their age group. In reality though, ICT sets, that may be credited to a certain age group, are generally more of a result of socioeconomic and sociopolitical influence on Sapiens through exposure to the same mini-cultures within the generation.

Having said that however, if certain ICT sets are emphasized and seen as representative of a generation of Sapiens, it could indicate a shift in societal views of a generation, hopefully for the positive. When an entire group of Sapiens move in unison to whatever degree, as long as it is positive, that in itself represents an evolution in acceptable Sapien behavior. As generations of Sapiens develop and participate as members of particular LC groups, the average ISAT and SQ levels of Sapiens will reflect such evolving habits and thoughts, again hopefully in the positive direction.

Example: Following WWII, people born in the late 1940s and early 1950s were originally called 'war babies'. As they grew into the 1960s, they became synonymous with the 'love generation', with slogans like "make love, not war." Later they became the 'baby boomers'. Now of course, it is the 'aging baby boomers'.

Each generation of Sapiens, and eras within generations, are thought to share some semblance of commonality in their character traits. This primarily occurs as a result of societal influences on individuals during their generational growth, and not necessarily because all Sapiens within an age group are the same.

There is evidence to support claims that say generational and era-related age groups exist purely for business and marketing purposes. It gives businesses the ability to cater to consumer groups based on preconceived notions of the groups' buying behavior. Of course, living in a free-market economy, that is no surprise.

Members of such generational LC groups do seem to exhibit similar outward characteristics. But it would not be accurate to identify a group of Sapiens with certain ICT sets, because of prevalence in generational behavior. Each Sapien remains unique, in its overall IM and ICT development, as a result of different ICT events during the Sapien's LCs.

As Sapiens grow during their LCs, the natural evolution of mankind, as we know it, has always been to constantly improve living conditions over previous generations. With a higher standard of living, Sapiens tend to enjoy further enhancements to their ICTs, and indirectly improve their IM ratings.

As a culture and society develops into a more civilized structure, the increased SQ levels tend to steer Sapiens away from violence as a solution to Sapien interactions. Because of this, the chances that a Sapien, with violent tendencies and other negative ICTs, will get recycled to peace-oriented societies decreases with each generation.

Earth Sapiens with tragically low violence-oriented ICTs may get sequestered after their current LC to lower level planets that need violent-oriented Sapiens. Such Sapiens with significantly unimproved negative ICTs may never get recycled to Earth again.

The reasoning for this, again, is pure physics and mathematics. As a society progresses past the violence stage, the parental overlay component in SROs ultimately cease accepting negative ICT levels.

For Sapiens who have experienced modern day Earth LCs, it might be construed as a sort of hell, to be exiled to the lower-level Sapien section in the subHalo for eternity. This section of the subHalo is referred to as the 'F' section, referring to 'terminally failed' Sapiens, instead of being classified with normal low L level designations.

However, there are two LifeCycle avenues available to terminally failed Sapiens. Such critically negative Sapiens may get future LC assignments to early-stage developing planets, in what we would call prehistoric times.

Or they could be recycled to more violent cultures on Earth, such as a few middle eastern countries. Either of these options might be construed as a form of hell or punishment for the negativity a Sapien had on *The Intelligent LifeCycle*, during current and previous LCs.

Example: Charles Manson probably started his current LC, as a low-level Sapien, with most ICTs significantly negatively developed or non-existent, but with a relatively high IM. His negative ICTs were so divergent from his parents, that his LifeCycle has become a classic case of a mismatched Sapien, due to negative and incompatible ICT ratings.

He used his above average intelligence to exploit his negative ICTs and foster allegiances from other 'like' Sapiens. Textbooks have been written about his negative manipulation skills. In Manson's case, the subHalo Sapien selection process failed. His parental overlay's character trait requirements were significantly compromised for whatever reason, when his Sapien arrived in the womb.

When Manson's current LC is terminated, his Sapien may eventually get rechanneled to an early growth stage planet, fighting to survive in prehistoric times. Or he could be permanently assigned to the 'F' section of the subHalo, as terminally failed. Of course, there is always the possibility that he could get recycled to the Middle East rather immediately, where Sapien requirements match such character traits of diminished capacity.

But in reality, Sapiens in those countries are not necessarily of diminished capacity, that is just where they are in their own LifeCycle evolution. It is the SH Factor at work, full bore. Unfortunately, Earth has progressed to the point that it provides LifeCycle platforms for lower developed Sapiens to participate in above average cultures. This is the new culture clash, and it is happening now in many countries around the world.

The good news is that unless a Sapien has severe serial violent tendencies, its ICTs can be improved. So for negative Sapiens reading this, it is never too late to change. And it would be better to change sooner than later, before actually becoming non-recyclable.

The really good news is that most of us are relatively cool in our LifeCycles to date. We have lived and are living relatively good lives, as we improve our ICTs. The vast majority of Sapiens reading this book, should feel fairly comfortable that their next LC will be as good or better than this one.

Remember, financial rewards, possessions and notoriety are not measurements of a Sapien's LC success. ICT and IM development are the only factors used in determining the worth of a LifeCycle on a Sapien's rating.

As you may have surmised by now, the Sapien selection process is a critical component to the perpetuation of intelligent life. The vehicle within this process is known as the Sapien Request Order (SRO), which includes the parental overlay's requirements for IM and ICT development in the child.

A fine-tuned Sapien selection process, in all subHalos, ensures the continuance of Sapien LiveTimes on all intelligent planets. And with constant improvement and growth of its Sapien population, Earth, as an intelligent planet, is destined to become a C7 IP someday, if Earth's physical LifeCycle allows us the time to develop.

It may not seem mysterious or romantic enough, but we really do not have any control over the selection of our LifeCycles. When we travel from one life to the next, it is purely an attraction between energy fields, utilizing and adhering to the natural laws of physics that apply to all things in the universe.

You may have heard people say that they were put here on Earth for a reason. Well in reality, everyone is here for a specific reason. Every LC is a result of successful gender, ICT and IM matches between the incoming Sapien and the fetus' parental overlay. That is the reason for your individual LifeCycle this time. Next time, there will be different matches, but there is always a reason that is unique to each LC.

LifeCycle History *(Earth: 1 million BC - today)*

In analyzing an IP's LifeCycle history, given that there are millions upon millions of planets that support intelligent life equal to or greater than Earth, the questions are basic. What is the origin of intelligent life? When and where did the first LifeCycle occur?"

These are valid questions. However, specific answers to these questions are in a sense, meaningless for our purposes. All we can do is to evaluate the history of intelligent life on Earth, and extrapolate that evolutionary process in theory to IPs in the rest of the universe.

How and when it all began is immaterial to *The Theory*. Suffice to say, it was trillions and trillions of years ago, on some planet, in some galaxy, in some universe, somewhere, as a result of some sort of tetronic mutation that occurred naturally over trillions of years. The origin of intelligent life in the universe, given an infinite number of possibilities, may be similar to *Darwinism* in concept, but with infinite scope, and no clear understanding of its beginning.

So as we analyze Sapien history on Earth, and by supposition LC history in the universe, a few observations seem to clarify the validity of various components of *The Theory*. Intelligent LifeCycles, as we have defined them, are dynamic and constantly evolving, as the

The Intelligent LifeCycle Theory

physical things in the LCs evolve.

During the evolution of life in general, there seems to be the need for 'like things' to congregate with other like things. This attraction between like things seems to be another natural law of the universe. It certainly dispels, to some degree, the notion that opposites attract, except for tetro-magnetic fields of course.

This natural attraction between like things applies to people, objects, ideas and in fact geography. You do not see too many mountains in the desert, just as you don't see too much sand in the farmlands. Trees within a forest tend to grow near other trees.

Most tall buildings congregate with other tall buildings in central business districts, thus architectural ideas and concepts tend to congregate with like structures. Of course, this concept is based on efficiencies and economies of scale. Architects and builders have created other examples of this concept with residential subdivisions.

The fact is, Sapiens, during our current LCs, have designed and constructed like buildings in like geographic areas. There seems to be a trend here, just as nature has done with our global geography.

This suggests that it may be a natural order of things in life, for like things to congregate in like groups. This phenomena indeed extends to animal, fish, fowl and human species. Monkeys hang with other monkeys. Giraffes hang out with other giraffes. Sparrows fly with other sparrows. Shrimp swim with other shrimp. It is the natural order of living things to congregate with likes. It is certainly more than just strength in numbers, or safety in groups.

Sapiens certainly congregate in groups within the species, during their

LiveTimes. And because Sapiens represent the intelligent species on the planet, they also must congregate with other like Sapiens, both philosophically, mentally and physically. There are many types of Sapiens, composed of different races, nationalities and cultures.

Sometimes it may be difficult to remember that all Sapiens are equal, even though their development levels during this LC are different. All Sapiens have the same right to live, even though they are different. This of course precludes evil Sapiens, who are on their own negative LifeCycle, hopefully spiraling downward toward extinction.

Movie Quote: "Rhinestone", 1984, Sylvester Stallone, Dolly Parton. Parton's sleazy boss keeps trying to hit on her. Her response left no doubt about her feelings. As she unleashes her anger on the lecherous club owner, Dolly concludes, "There are two kinds of people in this world, and you ain't one of 'em."

The following is a brief ILC version of Earth's history during our current IP's LifeCycle.

Circa: 1 to 2 million BC   Avg Sapien Level: 1.1
During the early days of Sapien LCs on Earth, prehistoric man congregated by families and groups of families within very small geographic regions. As the Sapien Intelligence Module (IM) developed, slowly and methodically, these L1 Sapiens focused primarily on physical things to survive, without any regard to making life better, and little or no room for ICT development.

Basically, ICTs took a backseat to survival instinct and intelligence. This was the natural order of things in those days, and understandably so. Since there was little interaction between people, there was little need for character traits.

The primary motivational factor for Sapien communications was food, food and more food. Hunting, fishing, gathering and preparing the food was a full time job for men and women. Children helped when they could.

<u>Circa: 500,000 BC</u>　　　　　　　　　<u>Avg Sapien Level: 1.5</u>
As men and women began living together in larger groups, they combined their still-primitive intellect to create a better world for the group. They moved out of their caves, built huts and forged narrow trails, congregating primarily for food gathering, water retrieval and survival from the elements. They began procreating geometrically into larger groups.

At that point in the natural evolution of homo sapiens on Earth, it became apparent that certain character traits might be important. ICTs such as love and trust, began to emerge, to offset traits like hate and deceit, which unfortunately also began to surface. As these basic ICTs developed, they were impacted, positively and negatively out of necessity, by the Sapien's survival instinct, which is resident in all Sapiens.

<u>Circa: 100,000 BC</u>　　　　　　　　　<u>Avg Sapien Level: 1.8</u>
Over time, after thousands of LC generations had passed, Sapiens began to congregate based on such basic character traits. In reality, it became the good guys against the bad guys. Fortunately, there were and are significantly more good guys than bad guys.

Within a window of only a few thousands years, Sapiens were developing around the globe, on different continents, at varying rates in varying degrees of civilization. Physical races of humans developed according to their group's geographic location on the globe.

Circa: 10,000 BC   Avg Sapien Level: 2.1
As Sapiens continued to evolve on Earth, their growth was reflected in the quality of life improvements they contributed, from LC to LC. They built rock roads, invented buggies to pull behind horses and began congregating in greater numbers to what would later be called townships.

People no longer had a need to congregate for safety purposes, or for food and water resources. They began congregating according to likes, which included not only nationality, but also racial, occupational and philosophical commonalities.

Circa: 1,500 BC   Avg Sapien Level: 2.5
About fifteen hundred years before Christ, a Sapien began a new LC in the body of baby Moses. He grew to adulthood, and began seeing the evolution of mankind going the wrong way. In an attempt to correct humankind's evolutionary direction, Moses, as a Roving L8 which was of course unknown to him, came down from the mountain top with *"The Ten Commandments"*.

This helped establish religion as the basis for society to further develop positively, rather than negatively. However, it did not seem to be enough, as Earth continued its spiraling moral decline. Those times were very detrimental to the positive development of Sapien ICTs.

Circa: 1BC to 1AD   Avg Sapien Level: 2.8
Some fifteen hundred years after Moses, Jesus Christ was born. As he grew into adulthood, Jesus, a Roving L9, developed a large following. He preached good over evil, and gave his life (his current LC) to show humanity that it had to stand up against evil, at all costs.

In an attempt to get humankind back on track as a positive Sapien development planet, Jesus taught the word of God. Commands such as do not lie, cheat or steal, and especially do not kill were some of the cornerstones of his message to his Sapien followers, who were on average approaching L3 Sapien development levels.

This time, the intervention worked, and mankind began to regain its development toward more positive goals, based on religious values, as a matter of course. Evil was still rampant, however, but good was definitely fighting back.

Over the millennium and beyond, Jesus became the leading figure in religious history. Can you imagine what Earth would be like today, had evil prevailed over good in Earth's early days of development?

<u>Circa: 1500</u> <u>Avg Sapien Level: 3.2</u>
Over the next few hundred years, as civilizations evolved on Earth, Sapiens began to get exposure to a wider, more diverse set of ICT events during their LC trips. Religions grew and expanded with more formal leadership, and became accepted within certain societal constraints.

Civilizations began formulating with an increased rule of law, whether it was administered by a king, his court or various levels of tyrants. During these times, Sapiens could exercise free will, on a limited basis, depending on the whims of ruling leaders and/or tyrants.

The Ten Commandments seemed to be a good basis from which to formulate the laws of society. So it was written. However, the actual interpretation of laws in those days was very subjective, at best. Sapien LCs were oftentimes prematurely terminated on personal whims of the ruling elite and/or on quasi-political grounds.

Specific geographic boundaries had developed, identifying what later became the nations of the world. Civilizations that were then separated by lines on a map began developing their own versions of law and order, with varying degrees of effectiveness and fairness.

LCs of the ruling class, although allowing a pampered lifestyle, did not provide much in the way of ICT-building experiences. For the subordinate masses, their LCs fostered many more ICT events for ICT development, much more so than their master elite Sapiens. This 'under class' began to develop into what we call today the middle class.

However, it is important to remember in today's terminology, middle class is purely an economical inference. And its relativity as a class distinction is somewhat different between countries. According to *ILC Theory* doctrine, such a distinction does not exist within Sapien ranks.

All Sapiens are considered equal, even though some LCs make some Sapiens appear more important than others. In such cases, perception is not necessarily reality. All Sapiens are equal, but are at varying degrees of development. If there is a middle class of Sapiens, it would be based on LC experiential data, not on earthly possessions. From a pure statistical perspective, the middle class on Earth during this era would have fallen into the L3 Sapien ranks.

<u>Circa: 1800</u> <u>Avg Sapien Level: 3.5</u>
When Earth passed the C3 level, it began attracting a small percentage of Sapiens from the L4 and L5 ranks. This continued over the next couple of hundred years and began to position Earth as a positive IP for mid-level Sapien development.

During this period, Sapien development continued with a steady

The Intelligent LifeCycle Theory

growth curve in the positive direction. Sapien enhancements became commonplace as more ICT events presented more ICT development opportunities during the average lifespan, which was increasing as our medical and technology advancements evolved.

Sapien development of Earth's LC history is estimated as follows:

Century	Year	Avg Sapien IEF
16th	1500	Level: 3.2
17th	1600	Level: 3.3
18th	1700	Level: 3.4
19th	1800	Level: 3.5
20th	1900	Level: 3.9
21st	2000	Level: 4.4

<u>Circa: 2000</u>   <u>Avg Sapien Level: 4.4</u>
As Earth Sapiens began to expand their use of science for solutions to improve the quality of life, in the late twentieth and early twenty-first centuries, more SROs were beginning to request Sapiens from higher L5 subHalo sectors. As technology developed exponentially, LCs provided Sapiens with increasing numbers of significantly diverse ICT events, from which to further develop their ICT sets.

During this era, Sapien growth increased in most areas of ICT and IM development. When Earth passed the L4.0 Sapien level in the latter half of the twentieth century, advancing to C4 IP status, Sapien development was unsurpassed in quality and number of LC transfers. As Earth celebrated Y2K, at the turn of the twenty-first century, the 1990's technology explosion was in full swing.

With the advent of the Internet and all its supporting technologies, Sapiens began to be dramatically impacted during their LCs. ICT

The Intelligent LifeCycle Theory

events appeared to be everywhere, both positively and negatively. Sapiens have more opportunities today to improve their ICTs, IM and overall Sapien ratings than ever before in Earth's LC history.

If the nations on Earth continue on the current path, more countries are expected to develop toward democracies with greater freedoms for their citizens. This will spawn a new level of Sapien development not previously known to millions of Sapiens in those countries.

When our advanced civilizations successfully reign in violence and hatred on a global basis, Earth will then progress to the next level of intelligent energy. The average Sapien's IEF rating is expected to pass the L5 level by the end of this century. Earth is expected to advance to C5 IP status with an average Sapien IEF rating of 5.3 by 2100.

Century	Year	Avg Sapien IEF
22nd	2100	Level: 5.3
23rd	2200	Level: 6.2
24th	2300	Level: 7.1

By the time Earth evolves into C6 IP status, with a preponderance of L6 Sapiens, LiveTime ICT events involving such negative traits will be greatly reduced. When Earth reaches C7 IP status, such negative Sapien traits will no longer exist, during LCs to this now highly advanced intelligent planet.

The evolution of Sapien intelligence in the universe is slow and methodical, but omnipresent throughout history. ICT and IM growth requires many LCs to develop and mature. Sapien improvements, during any given LC may seem insignificant. However, it is important to understand that as long as your Sapien improves from LC to LC, you are ahead of the game.

Good versus Evil

It is expected that the struggle between good and evil is omnipresent on IPs throughout the universe, especially on C1-C4 planets. We are indeed fortunate to have evolved with more positive Sapiens than negative ones on Earth. So, in order to maintain the integrity of ILC methodology, consider the following analysis as proof that there are substantially more good Sapiens in the universe, than bad ones.

Proof of Concept: Sapiens begin their first LC as an L1.0, with IMs and ICTs set at minimal default settings of 10 percent, on a C1 early-developed planet. As the Sapien engages external stimuli (ICT events) during the first few LCs, its ICTs develop positively or negatively, based on an infinite number of combinations of interactions between the Sapiens' ICTs and events.

As the Sapien's IM develops, it begins to learn that good results outweigh bad, and that pleasure is better than pain. And thus, more ICTs develop positively than negatively. And with any respectable statistical model, there will always be deviants from the norm.

There is and probably always will be a small percentage of bad Sapiens, so as to adhere to statistical standards. These bad eggs are actually misnamed, since all Sapiens begin equal as L1s, good eggs. It is the Sapien's reactions and responses to ICT events, during its early development LCs, that foster the direction in growth of Sapien traits, positively and/or negatively. Most Sapiens innately learn that good is better than bad, some do not.

Fortunately, initial Sapien design, trillions and trillions of years ago, preferred pleasure to pain, positive results to negative ones, happiness to sadness. These were the traits thought to be required to best develop intelligence in the universe.

As the Sapien population grows on a planet, there should be, according to mathematical probabilities, a preponderance of positive Sapien transfers. Since there are more positive Sapiens procreating on the planet, they will, unknowingly of course, be submitting positive SROs. There are also more positively developed Sapiens in the subHalos to service rapid population growth.

As the number of positive Sapiens on a planet increases, their positive SROs increase exponentially over negative ones. Another added kicker to this mini-theory is the fact that negative Sapiens may get recycled to lesser developed planets, so there will be even less negative Sapiens in the subHalos, from which to select.

So, it becomes a self-fulfilling axiom, from which there is little deviation. If someone wanted to spend the time, they could probably calculate the exact percentage and numbers of good guys and bad guys. **End, Proof of Concept**

Once a civilization has a majority of positively developed Sapiens, the physical struggle of good against evil becomes less prevalent in average Sapien LiveTimes. However, the mental struggle continues within the Sapien population, sometimes not knowing what is right and what is not.

For our purposes here on Earth, at this time in our planet's history, the eternal struggle of good over evil, whether it be physical or mental, is unfortunately expected to be with us for some time. This adversity between good and evil is expected to be under control by the time a planet gets upgraded in classification to C5, when the planet's average Sapien rating surpasses L5.0.

Earth, currently a mid-level C4 IP, is expected to have relative but not total control of the good/evil paradigm. But Earth is not out of the woods yet. We, countries with free societies, continue to face terrorist threats, and possible revived nuclear threats from a few unstable, psychotic and tyrant-controlled governments.

However, Earth does seem to be developing fairly well, considering the many facets of so many different socioeconomic models in so many different countries in the world. Earth is past the point of no return in positive Sapien development. Unless some rogue mass-murdering leader somewhere successfully nukes the world, Earth will continue to improve as a higher level IP for the foreseeable future. According to *The Theory*, the good guys will win.

Well, that is the ILC good versus evil pitch, a struggle which will unfortunately continue to exist on Earth, at least for the next few LC generations. When Earth progresses to the average Sapien level of L5 and evolves as a C5 IP, ICTs such as violence, hatred, deceit and other negative traits are expected to have been diminished significantly across all races and national boundaries.

Available Sapien Hosts

Of the millions of planets hosting intelligent life, LC travel is not restricted just to Earth. Sapiens are constantly moving in and out of different planetary worlds, as a matter of course. Theoretically, Sapiens can be sent to any IP in the universe, assuming IM and ICT matches occur, regardless of world, race and even species.

The ILC Theory encompasses all intelligent life forms on similar intelligent life-supporting IPs. Specifically, *The Theory* focuses on oxygen, water and food dependency of humanoid-type beings, who function with brains, requiring thought processes and self mobility. Other physical characteristics of a host species include two legs, two arms, strength, dexterity and male/female procreation.

Intelligent asexual species, if at all possible, have been discussed but are not included in *The Theory*. The physical process of asexual reproduction does not seem to lend itself to an intelligent species. There are too many variables and too many ways to fail as a species.

Such qualified host bodies on other planets may not physically resemble humans on Earth. However, they are expected to function in a similar fashion with the above characteristics required for physical and mental intelligent life growth. The physical form of a Sapien's host is not important, since a Sapien does not retain any memory of its previous LC experiences. Memories that could have been in very diametrically opposing physical worlds may not be functional in future LCs, if physical forms were important.

Memories of previous LCs would not be productive and would only get in the way of further Sapien development. LCs provide constant ICT development for a Sapien. Regardless of the differences in physical characteristics of the hosting species and the host planet, Sapiens are qualified to travel to any IP in the universe for an LC.

In reality however, Sapiens are generally recycled back and forth from the same planets, when possible. This seems to provide a better environment for Sapien development. Even though the Sapien will have no memory of its previous lives on any planet, its ICT and IM development may more easily adapt to familiar ecosystems.

Other than physical travel during LCs, Sapien travel is twofold. Upon an LC termination, Sapiens travel the UENet from the LC's planet to the appropriate subHalo. After a Sapien is sufficiently rejuvenated in the subHalo, it then becomes available for another LC assignment. Once selected, the Sapien again traverses back through the UENet to start its next LC, generally on the same planet as the previous life.

RestTime Between LCs

The time spent between LifeCycles is certainly an unknown variable, depending on the planet of origin. A Sapien could remain in RestTime mode in the subHalo for thousands of years between LCs. Or, it might get a new LC assignment within a matter of months, after a successful rejuvenation period in the subHalo.

Example: LifeCycle assignments, from early-stage IPs (C1-C2), are less frequent than those from high population growth IPs (C3-C4), such as Earth.

Chances are, if you're reading this book, you are an Earth Sapien during this LC with at least an L4 Sapien rating. Because of the current population growth rate on our planet, your next LC is expected to be a return to Earth within a couple of years, if not before.

Sometimes RestTime may be extended in the subHalo, if the Sapien recently returned from an exhaustive LC. However, the amount of RestTime between LCs is definitely an unknown quantity, possibly ranging from months to years to eternity. Because of this uncertainty in subsequent LifeCycles, mankind should continue to treat each life,

The Intelligent LifeCycle Theory

each LC, as a sacred endowment.

The reason mankind should treat life so special is because sanctity of life is so precious, and life is so uncertain as to its longevity. When a Sapien's LC expires or is terminated, and the Sapien goes to the subHalo to be rejuvied, the timing of the next LC is questionable at best.

Whether the Sapien returns to Earth or is sent to another planet, the RestTime in the subHalo is always a variable. Generally, the timing of the recycled Sapien is not immediate. After rejuvenation, which may require a few months, depending upon the complexity of the expired LC, the Sapien returns to the availability roster in the subHalo to await the next LC.

A rejuvied Sapien functions as a brand new little energy field, when recycled. The growth and learning curves of all human infants are similar during the early years of a Sapien's LC. However, the Sapien's Individual Character Traits (ICTs) and Intelligent Module (IM) retain developmental levels from the Sapien's previous LCs.

Example: If a Sapien had an aggregate SQ of 483, when its LC expired, the Sapien will remain an L4.83 while in the subHalo. The Sapien will begin the next LC as an L4.83 with an SQ of 483.

During RestTimes after being rejuvenated, Sapiens can and do on a selective basis communicate with other Sapiens in rest mode. This generally occurs between Sapiens in the same subHalo sector, L4s and L4s, L5s and L5s and so on.

Since Sapiens in the subHalo do not have physical bodies, their communication resembles our concepts of mental telepathy and extra sensory perception. The strength and power of such communications in the subHalo between Sapiens more closely resembles something like ESP x 10^{11} magnitude.

Communication between Sapiens in the subHalo is a very mentally visual style that's way beyond our current comprehension. And for lack of actual LiveTime ICT events, Sapiens in rest mode do not experience any ICT or IM improvements during their subHalo stays.

The illustration below shows a normal Sapien progression between LiveTime LCs and subHalo RestTimes. Both are variables depending upon the Sapien and the IP.

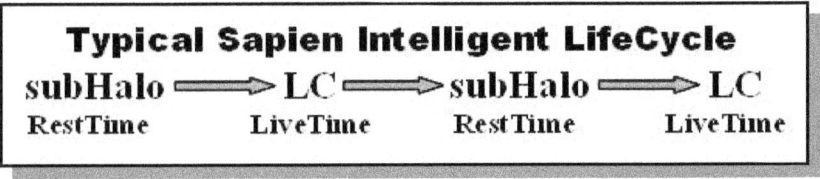

A typical Sapien LifeCycle may have equal amounts of RestTime and LiveTime after it has progressed to the L4 status, because of the increasing need for Sapiens on high-growth L4 IPs. However, lower level L1 to L2 Sapiens generally have more RestTime between LCs.

As we continue to develop on Earth, with such a high population growth rate, our current LC generation is expected to receive future LC assignments back to Earth, more frequently. In fact, as our planet develops upward through its C4 IP status, LiveTime durations of Sapien LCs are expected to substantially exceed the decreasing availability of RestTime between LCs.

Decreased RestTime between LCs happens out of necessity to fulfill increasing numbers of SROs on Earth, from available Earth Sapiens as much as possible. This phenomenon is known as the *C4 Stretch*.

The C4 Stretch is the lengthy period in a C4 IPs LifeCycle, in which the planet experiences a high net Sapien growth rate for an extended period of time, as births far exceed deaths. This Stretch in a C4 IP's history could last for a number of LC generations. Because of the high net growth, the SRO fulfillment process must be augmented by large numbers of Sapiens from other less developed planetary systems.

As of this writing, Earth is currently in the middle of it's C4 Stretch, which began sometime in the mid to late 1800's. During this period, the RestTime for Earth Sapiens is generally equal to the required rejuvenation period with little actual RestTime, before returning to Earth for another LC assignment. This IP phase is expected to continue until Earth nears C5 IP status, at which time, the net Sapien growth rate is expected to begin a gradual decline.

Scope of LifeCycles

Earth primarily provides quality LC opportunities to Sapiens across the three most populated Sapien levels, L3 through L5, since Earth is a C4 IP. Over the last half century, SRO requests have increased dramatically for L2 Sapiens from many backward, middle-eastern type countries.

These lower-level Sapien requests with IMs of 3.0 or less originate from parental overlays with lower-level Sapien ratings. Many L2s in this situation may still have their conscience switch in the 'off' position, with very few LCs to their credit so far.

However, given a proper match between Sapien and parents, a Sapien is more likely to achieve meaningful ICT improvements and resultant IM enhancements. With similar Sapien tetronic charges, the Sapien child may benefit from parental ICT growth that had occurred, since their original SRO was submitted before birth.

Example: An L4 Sapien sent to L4 parents may experience greater ICT improvements than a mismatched L6 Sapien sent to L3 parents. The same generally holds true for mismatched L2 Sapiens sent to L5 parents. Even though mismatches sometimes occur, it remains the responsibility of the individual Sapien to improve his or her ICTs or remain stagnant, during any given LifeCycle.

During an LC, when a Sapien reaches a new level of development, it affects its future selection possibilities. When a Sapien progresses from L3 to L4 status, that Sapien will then be available for L3 to L5 SROs. This compares to the Sapien's previous selection range of parents with L2 to L4 status, as an L3 Sapien at rest.

Sapien selection is generally confined to Sapiens within one level, either way, of the SRO. If an L4 SRO is not able to be filled within the proper time frame with an L4 Sapien, the subHalo may logically fill the request with an L3 or an L5 Sapien.

SRO fulfillments outside the one-level Sapien rule are infrequent. The reason is pure tetronic attraction. A C4 Sapien's tetronic charge is either too strong for matches from L1 to L2 parents, or too weak for matches from L6 to L7 parents.

Sapiens retain their IEF Level Ratings anywhere in the universe. However, most LC assignment for most Sapiens will be requested by parental units with similar ratings from the same or similar worlds.

Sapien development should continue for Sapiens on Earth through additional LiveTime experiences from future LCs. When a Sapien reaches L7 status, future LCs might be steered toward C6 and C7 IPs.

Once a Sapien reaches IEF Level 8 status, it has obtained Wisdom. It then transfers from its home subHalo to the Halo, since it has no more need for LCs. *See Halo chapter.*

Most worlds do not have the ability to request L8 Sapiens, since there are generally no L8 parents to submit such highly advanced SROs. It is not very likely that there are any L8s currently among us on Earth in the twenty-first century. There has only been a couple of L8s in Earth's history to date. *See Religion chapter.*

Mid-level IPs, such as Earth, are not likely to have Sapiens that can produce a strong enough tetronic attraction within a fetus that would attract a more advanced Sapien. For this reason, Earth does not get many L7s, for now. As Earth progresses to higher C levels as an intelligent planet, the scope of Sapien availability may include more L7 Sapiens, as a natural benefit of Earth's IP evolution.

LC Registry

The LC Registry is the component of the Sapien core that records and tracks each LiveTime LC that is experienced by the Sapien. Depending upon the number of LC entries, the LC Registry may be comprised of multiple nanocells. Each entry becomes a permanent part of the log of LC activity unique to each Sapien in the universe.

The chart below illustrates type of data accumulated in a Sapiens' LC

Registry for four of its 15 LCs. This example is of a 1563 Sapien, which means this is its 15th LC, with a current Sapien IEF of 6.3.

4 of Sapien 1563's LifeCycles			
Sapien Address: 1.342764874923.132985.003.22.15-6.3			
LC 01	LC 09	LC 14	LC 15
Born an L1.0, as all new IEF's, 1st time out, pure survival instincts, FOOD! Died 22, as L1.9 IEF	Born L3.6, 14th century gypsy, lived by his wits. Died 37 with an L4.2 IEF	Born L5.1, became a lounge singer, married, divorced twice, 1 child, good ICT development. Died 54, L5.7 IEF	Born L5.7, 2 yrs since last LifeCycle, Entrepreneur, some success. Current LC Open
1 mil B.C.	1345	1891	1947

This Sapien began as an L1.0 Caveman during his 1st LifeCycle. He developed to an L5.7 thru 14 LCs with further development in his current LifeCycle to L6.3 IEF.

Except for new entries, the LC Registry is a static historical record and cannot be altered. Once an LC is completed, the LCs new entry data is recorded and becomes a part of the permanent LC Registry.

In the chart above, this 1563 Sapien began its first LC as an L1.0 with LiveTime as a prehistoric caveman in one million BC. After several more LCs, 1563 began his ninth LC as an L3.6, becoming a fourteenth century gypsy. By the fourteenth LC, 1563 had developed his IEF to an L5.1 level. He became an unsuccessful lounge singer in the 1930's and 1940's, married twice with one child, and died in 1945.

The Intelligent LifeCycle Theory

His fifteenth LC began as an L5.7 in 1947. During the current LC, his ICT development is expected to pass the L6 level, as his LC remains 'Open'. Since 1563's current LC began only two years after his fourteenth LC expired, it is expected that his sixteenth LC will be available soon after the current LC expires.

SLC Registry

	-----Beginning-------				--------Ending--------		
SLC#	Date	IEF	Galaxy/Star/Planet/Loc.	Occupation	Date	SLC	IEF
01	1mil BC	1.1	MW/Sun/Earth/mountains	Caveman	999,981BC	19Yrs	1.9
02	1721 BC	1.9	MW/Sun/Earth/plains	Herdsman	1692 BC	29Yrs	2.2
03	0121	2.2	MW/Sun/Earth/Greece	Beggar	0146	25Yrs	2.3
04	0322	2.3	MW/Sun/Earth/Greece	Fisherman	0353	31Yrs	2.5
05	0588	2.5	MW/Sun/Earth/Italy	Swordsman	0607	19Yrs	2.5
06	0746	2.5	MW/Sun/Earth/England	Servant	0788	42Yrs	3.1
07	0953	3.1	MW/Sun/Earth/England	Sheepherder	1004	51Yrs	3.5
08	1127	3.5	MW/Sun/Earth/France	Joker	1175	48Yrs	3.9
09	1345	3.6	MW/Sun/Earth/Spain	Gypsy	1382	37Yrs	4.2
10	1477	4.2	MW/Sun/Earth/England	Sailor	1513	36Yrs	4.4
11	1599	4.4	MW/Sun/Earth/England	Explorer	1646	47Yrs	4.6
12	1703	4.6	MW/Sun/Earth/USA	Shoemaker	1758	55Yrs	4.8
13	1801	4.8	MW/Sun/Earth/USA	Cowboy	1850	49Yrs	5.1
14	1891	5.1	MW/Sun/Earth/USA	Singer	1945	54yrs	5.7
15	1947	5.7	MW/Sun/Earth/USA	Entrepreneur	open	open	6.3

The chart above represents Sapien 1563's Summary Report of its fifteen LCs. Dates are expressed in Earth terms for comparison purposes.

All LifeCycle data retained by the Sapien is summarized in the LC Registry, as shown in the preceding report. Data stored for all LCs include pertinent facts about the lives that are relevant to the Sapien's development. The registry is updated twice per LC, at birth and at death. Once recorded, the LC data is locked and cannot be altered.

Because memories require massive amounts of storage, only relevant summary information about previous lives is saved in the LC Registry. A Sapien's memory tetracells are limited in quantity and capacity. Only salient LC details are included for each LiveTime journey, as shown in these charts.

One video file, as we refer to it in concept, is attached to each LC entry, optimized for brevity so as to describe the clarity of purpose of the LifeCycle. These mentally visual images briefly recall only those key experiences during LiveTime that characterize the salient highlights or lowlights of the life.

The LC Registry is not easily accessible by its Sapien owner, at least consciously. Subconsciously though, previous details about specific lives can be recalled, while in a semi-hypnotic state induced by a therapist, known as a regression. *See LC Regressions in Appendix.*

As a side note, Sapiens who are intimate with *The ILC Theory* have begun to refer to LCs as just, Cycles. In the above example, 1563 has had 14 Cycles previously and is currently enjoying his fifteenth Cycle. However, the word LifeCycle does seem to convey a more appropriate meaning to the lifetime event.

Sapien ID

Just as people on Earth have different IDs, such as drivers licenses and passports, Sapiens have their own identification for subHalo inventory purposes. A Sapien's unique digital address is comprised of designations representing its evolution.

The Intelligent LifeCycle Theory

SAPIEN ADDRESSING SCHEME

HALO[1]	1.
subHalo - Milky Way[2]	042764874923.
Star System - Sun[3]	032985.
Planet - Earth[4]	03.
Country - USA[5]	003.
LifeCycles[6]	10.
Current SQ Rating[7]	530

Sample Sapien Address: 1.042764874923.032985.03.003.10.530

The chart above illustrates the alpha-numeric equivalency of 1563's Sapien ID, which delineates locations in the universe and LC data.

The first two alpha characters in the Sapien's address represent the gender of the Sapien, XX for female and XY for male. The second field represents our known and existing universe, with a 1. For Sapiens in other universes, their IEF addresses would begin with 2.,3., 4., and so on.

The third field represents the home galaxy of the applicable subHalo. In this example, the MilkyWay galaxy, which is one of one hundred billion galaxies in our universe, is represented with a twelve digit number to accommodate 10^{11} galaxies.

The fourth descriptor is a six-digit number to accommodate our Sun, which is one of an estimated one hundred thousand intelligent star systems in our galaxy. The fifth field shows Earth, as the third planet from the Sun.

The sixth field represents the country of origin for the Sapien, indicating nationality in most cases, except for nationals from one country migrating to another. The birth place is the key descriptor in this field. You may notice, there is no reference to race. Sapien descriptors are race and ethnicity neutral.

The seventh field lists the number of the current LC, while the eighth field represents the current IEF Sapien rating. For the vast majority of Earth Sapiens, the only addressing components that change from LC to LC are the last three fields in the address. If a Sapien is transferred to another galaxy, its address would reflect the new location's data in all fields except for the first two, which remain unchanged.

Since we assume all Sapiens are unique, then they must also have unique descriptors in their individual address. *The Theory* provides this. The eighth descriptor field in a Sapien's address is the Sapien's complete tetronic charge as it relates to the Sapien's development rating. In this case, the last descriptor in 1563 Sapien's address, instead of 6.3, might be 6.322987348710092, as an exact level of attainment, which renders the entire address totally unique.

LC Memories

Memories of previous lives include brief details as shown in the previous charts. To conserve storage resources in the core, the Sapien only saves relevant details about previous lives in the LC Registry. Because the registry is embedded deep inside your Sapien's core, it is not easily accessible.

Like most components of *The ILC Theory*, selections as to which memories are stored are based on science and logic. Memories are chosen for permanent storage according to their importance to the Sapien during the LifeCycle. These are not necessarily the same memories the brain stores as important events to the person.

During an ICT event, the Sapien core measures the amount and intensity of tetrazymes being generated to create quantities of tetracells for ICT and IM improvements. Events are saved in descending order according to the magnitude of the event, as measured by the amount of tetracells generated by or taken from the ICTs.

ICT events foster specific Sapien tetronic charges to/from ICTs and IM, the strength of which is the delineating factor that rates the importance of the event to be stored. It is an automatic function of the system. Only major ICT events that are representative of the LC are saved.

The majority of current LC experiences will not be retained in your Sapien's memory, because of limited storage capacities. If you think about it, memories, events from previous LCs, people and places, would create significant hardships and conflicts during future LCs.

More in-depth LC memories would also create severe conflicts for the Sapien in decision making. If previous life experiences were remembered, they would undoubtedly cloud the issue during the decision-making process. This could also thwart Sapien ICT development, by creating massive doubt with conflicting memories and resulting in indecisiveness and non-decision making. So in the case of previous LC memories, less is better.

When you think about your Sapien not retaining memory of your current life after you die, please do not feel like you are losing what you gained during this life, namely knowledge, abilities and friends. To the contrary, you do retain the advancements you made, during this lifetime, in your ICT and IM modules, just not specific memories, other than data stored in the LC Registry.

Enhancements to your overall Sapien development, gained during this LC trip, will hold you in good stead for future LiveTimes. Such gains might even improve the results of your next LC selection process. So when you go to the next life, you are carrying the net results of your experiences from this life and all of your other LCs.

LC Regressions of Past Lives

Regressions are used as investigative tools to learn more about your Sapien's experiences during previous lives. The regression process puts the brain into a semi-hypnotic state. This is done to put your brain and its mental capacities temporarily at rest.

While you are regressed, there is an absence of outside influences on your Sapien's resources. When this happens, all of your non-critical systems are shut down. This allows an increased mental focus on your LC Registry, so you can discover your personal LC history.

If you get regressed, and we highly recommend that you do, please do not expect that in any of your LCs, you were a famous person. That is always a possibility of course, but it is certainly not the norm.

Think about it. There are only a few thousand or so really famous people in history, and there are billions of Sapiens currently alive on Earth. The mathematical probability of you being reincarnated from one of the famous people is quite small. And that is not a negative inference at all.

To the contrary, famous people sometimes have less opportunities, to improve their ICTs and IMs, than average citizens. Oftentimes, being famous means that others surrounding the famous Sapien may be consciously trying to protect him or her from outside influences, during the LiveTime.

This, by definition, reduces the number of ICT events available to the famous Sapien for self improvement. And as a result, the Sapien's ability to enhance its ICTs may be detrimentally affected, just because he or she is famous, during their protected LiveTime.

On the other hand, lifestyles of the rich and/or famous do seem to provide character-building opportunities in other ways. During their hectic lives, they will be exposed to different types of events with different results, positive and negative, than those of us not so famous.

Regardless, famous people in the past did exist. Hitler, Napoleon, Einstein, Reagan, Monroe, Madam Curie, to name a few, all lived a life that made them famous, or infamous, during one LifeCycle. Chances are, their Sapiens may be among us today, navigating their own current LCs, as they continue with their own LC schedules.

However, infamous personages such as Hitler and Napoleon may be back on the C1 or C2 IPs, from whence they came. On the other hand, they may be alive and well in the middle east.

Remember, famous Sapiens also existed before, in previous LCs themselves, just like you and I, the non-famous ones. In reality, famous Sapiens basically hit it lucky with their famous LC.

Statistically speaking, the chance of achieving such notoriety in an LC are approximately one hundred thousandth of one percent or less, based on Sapien populations on Earth.

This is not meant to minimize famous Sapien accomplishments, not at all. Successes in LCs, for the most part, are highly commendable and cherished. It is these successes that have made it better for the rest of us during our own LCs. Successful Sapiens were able to use their ICT and IM levels, some less developed than others, to their advantage during an LC, in a time that was conducive to their particular combination of ICTs and IM.

It is obvious that being a famous person would not be the Sapien's first time at the dance. During a famous LC, the Sapien fortunately ended up at the right place, at the right time, during a time that could benefit from the Sapien's specific ICT and IM levels.

The vast majority of us in our previous LCs were average people, just enjoying our LiveTimes, and hopefully improving our Sapiens, just as most of us do today. Although we did not know it at the time, we were slowly and methodically enhancing our ICTs for the next life. Without any applause, we just did it. And as a result of that growth, we are theoretically better off during this LC than the last.

Reincarnation is usually portrayed in motion pictures through weird, crazy, cult-type individuals, who are not to be taken seriously. A character in a movie might be depicted as believing she was Cleopatra in a previous life. Along with other disillusioned memories of undue importance, this character is normally portrayed as a crazy person, or certainly less than normal.

Maybe this book will help change that view to a more realistic approach to life after death. Hopefully, it will move opinions about reincarnation away from the crazy mentality and toward thought-provoking intelligent dialogue. This might generate a more realistic iconic image for this most important phenomenon.

During a regression, a person might describe people, places and things from a different era in great detail. When this happens, believers point to it as a means of rationalizing why the LC was real. They say that if it were not a real memory, then how could this person remember such detail about something with which they've had no experience?

On the surface, this would seem to make sense. However, the Sapien can only recall selected events and images that are stored in its LC Registry, as shown previously. So if that is the case, then how does a person recall such detail of an era?

As a Sapien is being regressed, in a semi-hypnotic state, it begins to describe its previous lives. In reality, it can only recall incidents that are recorded in the brief entries in its LC Registry. To augment the Sapien's memory of previous LC lives, data in the brain's physical memory, during the regression, is accessed to extrapolate current Sapien memories onto previous events.

When this occurs, fabrications may be inadvertently created to fill in the details of the LC picture. These embellished supporting facts and observations, as verbally described by the regressed Sapien, are generally done in the subconscious.

Detailed accounts of previous lives, more often than not, will result from the brain's memory of actual events that may be similar, or from books read and/or movies seen. Such fabricated memories are not necessarily a bad thing, if they help complete the picture of the LC.

And for the record, most of these detailed stories are not thought to have been fabricated intentionally. Such detailed memories are fabricated subconsciously by the unfettered strength of the human brain. During a regression, the process basically assumes control of all internal brain functions, temporarily, to allow the Sapien to 'drill down' to its LC Registry for recall.

Recurring Relationships in LCs

It has been a romantic notion for a long time that you could possibly reunite with another person from this life, in the next one. Although highly unlikely, given the enormous odds against it happening, it is theoretically possible. It might not be the exact next LC. But there is always the possibility that you may meet again in the far distant future, in another LC. There's that infinity deal again.

These ideas about an afterlife, probably considered folklore by some, have become a part of our everyday language. At least in the movies, when one guy says to his friend, right before they have a gun battle, with low odds of survival, "See ya on the other side.", or "See ya in the next life."

So is that life imitating art, or art imitating life? Of course, *The Theory* agrees with the latter.

Another perspective to this romantic mental exercise has developed from the scenario of a person meeting someone in this life, that they knew in a previous life. Again, the odds are against that happening, but it has given rise to some debate. It is possible, but highly unlikely.

The Intelligent LifeCycle Theory

Strangers meet for the first time. One or both instantly feel some semblance of familiarity with the other, when one says, "Don't I know you?", or "Haven't we met before?"

Other than being used as pickup lines, these questions might actually have some significant meaning in your LC history. Although the odds are dramatically against this scenario happening, it is possible, as remote as it might be. You guessed it, infinity.

However, the more technologically advanced our communications and transportation systems become on Earth, the better the possibility that such remote events could occur in future LCs. Even with more complex societal avenues available to interrelate with other Sapiens during this LC, the odds are still dramatically against it.

In our current sociological agenda, a person might be attracted to others, who have similar Sapien Ratings and ICT makeup, through professional circles. Best friends, lovers, loves, suitors and mentors have all evolved from such business surroundings, involving similar characteristics and interests.

So theoretically, if one person is attracted to a certain cultural environment, then it stands to reason that the person who is thought to have been known before, might also have similar interests. And, if they have similar interests and the recycling factor is timely, they could be in the same social and/or business circles.

As romantic as this notion is, the reality of this scenario is quite different. The odds of actually meeting another Sapien again in another LC are extremely low. And if you did, you wouldn't remember it anyway, sorry.

The Theory unfortunately dispels this popular romantic version of reincarnation, where you meet again in another life. Not only is the timing super critical, the destination planet must be the same and the location on the planet would need to be the same or near enough for the chance to meet again.

If timing and location are similar for both Sapiens, when they fuse with the fetuses in the next concurrent LC, then the ICTs might take over. As they grow, the two Sapiens may drift toward each other in the same professional and/or social circles. Sapiens do congregate with other 'like' Sapiens during their LiveTimes. Theoretically, it is possible to meet someone in another life that you knew before, but not likely.

Example: A married Sapien dies. His wife passes many years later. By the time her LC expires and she goes to the subHalo, her deceased husband, of many years before, has already been recycled, rejuvied and assigned to his next LC. He's probably a teenager by then.

There is another component to folklore and myths surrounding Intelligent LifeCycles that also needs to be dispelled. People may think they are here on Earth to do something, specific or non-specific. Or, they may feel they are here for a reason. They are all right, but not for the reasons thought.

In reality, everyone is here for a reason, a very specific one. Every LC is determined by the subHalo selection process. Because Sapien and ICT Ratings are unique to each LC assignment, the Sapien selected for the LC is chosen for a very specific reason, the LC Sapien match. The successful match between the Sapien and the fetus's SRO is the reason for the Sapien's birth, period.

For a long time, maybe since the beginning of whenever, people have often wondered, why they are here. They ponder about the reason for their existence. What does it all mean?

Well...., it means exactly what you make it to mean. Once your LC begins, it is all up to you to find out why you are here this time. The natural inclination is for the Sapien to gravitate toward those things that utilize existing developed ICTs. Taking advantage of the character traits you already have is good. You might also consider developing some of your other ICTs that may need help. Just a thought.

Possibility of Ghosts

For centuries, ghost stories have been told, sometimes around bond fires, and usually to frighten the listeners. For centuries, artists have painted graveyards with ghosts rising from the graves. Occasionally, ghost sightings are reported, generally in a specific place or house. Thus, the term *haunted house* became part of our vernacular.

According to *The ILC Theory*, there are a couple of reasons why ghosts may be a reality. And in accordance with our scientifically-based methodology, there are specific factors that could cause such a phenomenon.

Just as there is a small error rate in the subHalo's Sapien selection process, resulting in gender, ICT and IM mismatches, there are occasionally errors in incoming traffic to the UENet. Although extremely rare, there is the possibility of an error occurring in the collection program, which is responsible for expired Sapien retrieval. Errors in UENet collection routines do occur, but very infrequently.

An expired Sapien pickup error could occur, when the Sapien's core has been damaged, maybe during the death event itself. When this occurs, the Sapien must remain on Earth after death without a body, as a Sapien waiting for pickup, or as a ghost, as we so affectionately call them. The damage prevents the Sapien from successfully transmitting its Sapien Exit Request (SER) to the UENet with a strong enough signal to be received by the UENet for pick up.

When this happens, the Sapien has basically missed the train, and has no choice but to wait. As the misconnection with the UENet occurs, the Sapien may have to wait around for its signal strength to rejuvenate itself before the next pickup. This may only take a few seconds, a couple of hours, days, maybe even months. If it is irreparable, infinity seems unlikely, but an option.

This could be loosely interpreted as a form of limbo, in reference to the religious concept of 'in-between' worlds. As a Sapien waits for the UENet and does not immediately get picked up, it is literally between the Earth world and the subHalo world. This would be analogous to your modem going down and not being able to get on the Internet. The Net is up, only you are down.

If an expired Sapien misses the UENet pickup for transport to the subHalo, it attempts to repair its positive/negative ionic imbalance in its core. This is a basic rejuvenation program, resident in all Sapiens. It restarts the core communications module for SER retransmission. Once the core is rejuvied and a stronger signal is sent, the Sapien is pulled into the UENet for transport to the subHalo.

During this wait time, a Sapien could be considered a form of ghost. As for living Sapiens being able to visually see expired Sapiens waiting for their pickup, there is much speculation and just as much

The Intelligent LifeCycle Theory

physical proof that this might be possible.

Another reason for a missed Sapien pickup is UENet downtime. There is always the remote possibility that a node on the UENet backbone goes down. Such blips in the network's performance might only last for a few tetraseconds.

Depending on the severity of the network break, such infrequent downtime might last longer. This would be analogous to your Internet Service Provider (ISP) going down and nobody on your network having Internet access. The Net is down, so you and others on the same circuit are down.

Longer lapses in UENet downtime could explain other ghost sightings, such as groups of ghosts in mass sightings. If a number of Sapiens die together, and they all miss their UENet connections at the same time, the only logical conclusion is network downtime.

Network downtime, as infrequent as it is, explains group ghost sightings and hauntings. This could be applicable to a mass disaster, such as a cruise ship full of passengers sinking at the same time, as the UENet nodes goes down. Hundreds of passengers die, all with healthy Sapien cores. Because of the network being down, expired Sapiens must wait for the network to repair itself and return for their pickup.

Many movies have been produced and many books have been written about this phenomenon, ghosts at sea. Reclamation workers have reported ghost sightings on sunken ships, and as suddenly as they appeared, they abruptly began disappearing. This could be explained by timing issues, as the UENet came back online, its retrieval program once again began collecting the expired Sapiens, who had been waiting for pickup.

ILC Discovery: There are two known possibilities, as remote as they may be, for ghosts to exist: (1) A Sapien's core is weakened and fails to transmit a strong enough signal to the UENet, which delays pickup; (2) A retrieval node on the UENet goes down, resulting in mass expired Sapien pickup delays.

In movies, ghosts are portrayed as not wanting to go into the light, not wanting to let go. But actually it is just the opposite, they are trying to get to the light, but cannot get there. They want to go. They do not have a body anymore, so they are in a perpetual dream state, and they are alone.

When the UENet fails to pickup an expired Sapien in time, the Sapien hangs out in a constant dream state without a body, waiting for the subUENet pickup. In the case of *"Poltergeist"*, 1982, starring Jo Beth Williams and Craig T. Nelson, the ghosts were trying to get to the light (UENet), to go home (subHalo). But they could not make the jump, because of a defective signal or maybe a negative signal that was not accepted by the UENet, so they needed little Carol Ann to take them to the light.

Fortunately, the vast majority of Sapien cores are infinitely healthy, and the performance and accuracy of the UENet is estimated to be 99.999997 percent accurate. This means that the possibility of you becoming a ghost when you die, is extremely slim.

LifeCycle Recap

Critical to *The Theory*, the Sapien LifeCycle (LC) is the logical vehicle used to perpetuate the evolution of intelligence throughout the universe. It provides LiveTime experiential events for Sapien growth on an historically perpetual basis.

A Sapien's growth begins with its first assignment as an L1.0 intelligent being on an intelligent planet. This inaugural journey is sometimes referred to as the Sapien's Original LifeCycle (OLC), but is most commonly called the Sapien's L1. This becomes the home base for the Sapien's galaxy, star and planetary systems.

Generally, a Sapien's first LC assignment from the subHalo is its birth on a C1 intelligent planet. As a C1 IP develops at a sufficiently rapid pace, future LCs of a Sapien will generally continue on the same planet, as its original birth. However, if a Sapien develops its ICTs and IM faster than its home planet can accommodate, it may begin to receive assignments to higher C-level IPs, C3s and C4s.

The Intelligent LifeCycle Theory provides the basis for the natural evolution of intelligence in the universe. Through a sequential series of LCs, a Sapien can improve its development levels, as its ICTs respond to LiveTime events.

As a Sapien ends an LC, returns to its subHalo, gets rejuvied and awaits its next cycle, the Sapien carries with it, its ending Sapien ratings from its previous LC. These are the development levels from which the Sapien will be selected for the next LC, and the starting point for the Sapien in its new LiveTime.

Generally, Sapien ratings do not decrease between LCs. They do not go backward with reverse development. That is not to say however, that a Sapien might not digress negatively in certain ICTs. Generally, a Sapien that ends a Cycle with an L4.3 rating will begin its next LC with an L4.3 rating. The exception to the rule might be a Sapien experiencing such a significantly negative event that it reverses gains from previous LCs in applicable ICTs.

In the overall scheme of things, you might think time is irrelevant, since we are talking about infinity. However, as it relates to Sapien growth, it is just the opposite. Time is everything, LiveTime that is.

The length of an LC's LiveTime is uncertain at best, and in the grand scheme of things, relatively short. Sapiens do not know how long their current life will be, when it will end, or when the next one will begin. It is up to the Sapien to make the most of the LiveTime it gets during this LC.

When you consider the rarity of your LC LiveTime, a couple of common phrases take on a whole new meaning. Phrases such as "don't waste precious time on that" or simply "don't waste your time" are subconsciously stating a very pragmatic fact of life.

During an LC, time is a very limited and valued commodity. Every moment on Earth is considered precious time that you don't want to lose or waste. After all, you might not get recycled again for some time. Then again, you might get another LC assignment within a few months after rejuvenation, you just don't know. This is the primary reason for rule No. Six in the *Ten Rules of Intelligent Life*.

Even so, the good news is that Earth's population growth rate is currently out-stripping Sapien inventory availability from normal expired Sapien recycling. Because of this, there is a good chance your next LC on Earth may be sooner than later. And it should be better than this one, at least for purposes of Sapien growth and development, not necessarily for social status nor financial wealth.

Example: As in the earlier example of Sapien 1563, his first LC was approximately one million BC as a caveman on Earth. His next LC was not until around 1700 BC. Another eighteen hundred years went by before his third LC in 121 AD. Then his LCs began occurring more frequently, every hundred years or so, as Earth's population grew. In 1945 as Earth's population growth curve intensified with the "baby boom generation", 1563 died after his fourteenth LC and was reborn in 1947 for his fifteenth LC, only two years later.

A Sapien who has had fifteen LCs might encapsulate a saying that has been around for some time in religious and other circles. An old man might be described as, "an old soul, who's been around". That might be appropriate in 1563's case, then again it might be presumptuous to think that could be the case after only fifteen LCs. After all, fifteen LCs in terms of infinity is a drop in the bucket.

Other sayings such as "not in this lifetime" add to the mystique of an afterlife. The most common translation of this phrase is "no". However, the fact that it referred to the possibility of "not now, but maybe in another lifetime" indicates that thoughts of subsequent LifeCycles have become accepted into our vocabulary.

Another saying, somewhat of an oxymoron, is "nobody should die alone." Someone might use this to describe a person who does not have a partner or soulmate, or family or friends. Maybe you yourself have grimaced at the thought of dying alone.

Well, have no fear. This old adage, although a sentimental thought, is an unlikely premise. In reality, everybody does in fact die alone, and the operative noun here is *body*.

Funerals are for the living, not the dead, who are long gone by then.

End of life ceremonies allow other Sapiens the chance to express their sadness and sometimes anger or confusion at the loss of a friend or loved one. Of course, attendance at a funeral is thought to show respect for the dead. Once again, they are dead, so it is actually a way of showing respect for the living left behind. However, it is a necessary part of the grieving process that Sapiens must go through in life.

Example: The following dialogue proves the point that you definitely die alone. First guy says, "Poor man, he's going to die alone." Second guy responds, "Everyone dies alone." First guy, "That's not true." Second guy, "Unless of course, you wanna die with him". First guy, "No of course not." Second guy, "Well there ya go, everyone dies alone."

A funeral is definitely an ICT event, even if it is not yours. Given the situation, some Individual Character Traits (ICTs) may benefit from such negative events.

At the other end of the LC spectrum, are the newborn, the babies that perpetuate our lineage as intelligent beings. *The Theory* provides a rather unique perspective on babies. Infants are just little bitty baby people, about to begin another LC of their own. So if you have the opportunity, give the little baby Sapiens encouragement and wish them good luck on their long trip ahead.

As we grow and further develop our traits, there is another popular saying worthy of note, "look on the bright side". For the most part, this is meant to comfort a person during a not-so-positive event. When you get older, you may feel there is no bright side. Situations that previously could have benefited from such a statement, may no longer be of interest. You may feel like you just want to be left alone, to

The Intelligent LifeCycle Theory

finish out your LC in peace. And that is fine, you have certainly earned the right to some peace and quiet.

However, if you have the energy and the spirit, your retirement years do not have to be void of character development. You may still have time to achieve a little more ICT development, and maybe even have some fun doing it during this LC.

After all, your purpose in life is not only to enhance your ICTs and have fun doing it, but also to provide whatever contributions you can that will help improve the living conditions of Sapiens on the planet. Regardless of your occupation during this LC, you have the ability to contribute just by doing your job, whatever that job is.

A janitor, a mailman and a store owner all contribute to our quality of life, just as a heart surgeon, a psychologist and a high school principal do. All Sapiens are created equal. It is character development that makes the difference. "Skill sets are learned, ICT sets are earned."

In pursuing your ICT development, during any given LC, there are ICTs you can improve and those you cannot. You can take some solace in the fact that during any given LC, all Sapiens have ICTs they might not be able to address. There will always be ICTs that will have to wait for improvement. Do not worry, you will have plenty of time in future LCs to work on them.

The universe has taken a few trillion years to get where we are today. Depending on your perspective, it may seem high or it may seem low, to think the universe is only about forty percent developed, both physically and metaphysically.

If that is the case, then we should have another few trillion years left before the universe is fully developed. Even though time is very precious to Sapiens during LCs as a measurement of intelligence in the universe, time is irrelevant at best, considering infinity of course.

So in lieu of infinity, the most we can do is focus on each LC as we get them, this one specifically. You can never go wrong, if you just get out there and try to make a difference during your LC, hopefully a positive difference.

Conversely, sometimes you may feel that your LC just is not working out, no matter how hard you try. But that is okay. I know it is easy to say that, so I will say it again, "That is okay." Regardless of your achievements in life, or lack thereof, societal standards are not the ultimate authority on Sapien development.

If you have had it hard during this LC, your Sapien ratings may benefit significantly from your trials and tribulations. The harder you try at life, the more enhanced your ICTs may become, as you deal with sometimes negative ICT events during your LiveTime.

And as your ICTs improve, so does your Intelligence Module (IM) as a matter of course. The added bonus of improving your Sapien ratings during this life is that, by doing so, you will be enhancing your selection prospects for your next LC.

The Intelligent LifeCycle Theory

Intelligent Planets & The Universe

As we look at Intelligent Planets and their spatial relationships within the universe, it is easy to get overwhelmed with the vastness of space. It may be helpful to first look at our own IP's history of theories and philosophies that have evolved since our known civilization began.

Over the last few thousand years, there have been a number of theories about Earth. As Sapien levels increased with each century, so did the sophistication levels of theories about Earth, some of which would later become the foundation for modern day astrophysics.

One of the first theories, if not the first, was that the Earth was flat, with little if any reference to the stars in the sky. The stars were merely decorations in the sky that provided some light during nighttime hours.

As scientists continued to look skyward, they ultimately agreed the Earth was spherical. With this new concept, astronomers began developing the geocentric model, which stated that the sphere we call Earth is indeed the very center of the universe. This theory concluded that all other objects orbit around the Earth in the same orbital patterns every day. An adjunct to this theory was the idea that the Earth was stable, completely at rest and motionless in space.

The geocentric model was the accepted theory for the universe for over fifteen hundred years in civilizations such as ancient Greece. As a result, ancient philosophers, including Aristotle and Ptolemy, thought the sun, moon, stars and visible planets all circled the Earth.

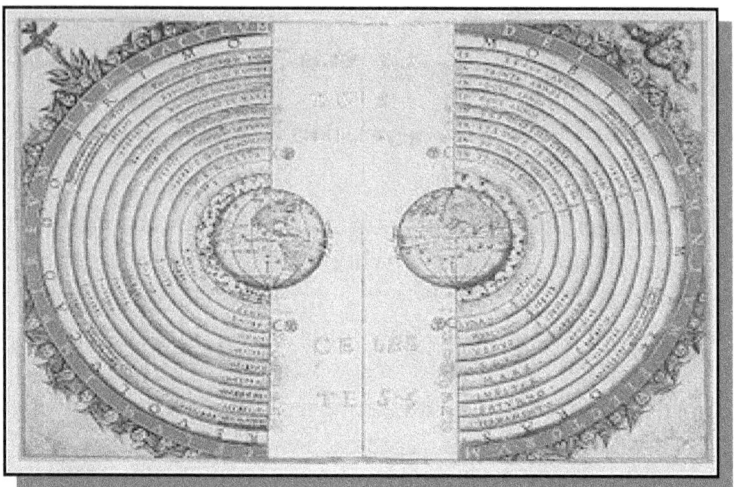

"Figure of the heavenly bodies", an illustration of the Ptolemaic geocentric system by Portuguese cosmographer and cartographer Bartolomeu Velho, 1568. The artist's rendition of all objects revolving around Earth as the center of the universe.

The ancient Greeks believed that the motions of the planets were circular and not elliptical. Ptolemy's geocentric model was used to develop astrological charts for nearly two millenniums.

This viewpoint remained unchallenged in Western culture until the late sixteenth and early seventeenth centuries. Astronomers of the day, such as Copernicus, Galileo and Kepler, all began to replace the geocentric model with a heliocentric model, which became the basis of current astrological assumptions.

However, migration to the concept of the Earth not being the center of the universe met with some resistance at first. Theologians were reticent to accept any theory that was seen as a possible contradiction to certain sections of the Bible. And there remained, of course, a small contingent of staunch geocentric believers that still thought everything in the universe revolved around the Earth.

Thoughts about life on other planets in the universe have evolved into popular themes of successful sci-fi motion pictures over the last century. As shown below, the first known science fiction genre movie was released in 1905 entitled, *"A Trip to the Moon"*.

This early sci-fi film was a black and white, silent French film (only fourteen minutes long), depicting space travel to the moon. Using 1904 state-of-the-art animation techniques, the film showed this now well-known image of the bullet-shaped capsule landing sharply in the eye of the Man on the Moon.

Since then, science fiction movies have become the top box office hits, by far, of all motion picture genres. The fascination with this genre indicates our Sapiens' keen interest in outer space and the possibility of life elsewhere in the universe.

Now, let's fast-forward to current day reality. As agreed upon by most scientists today, our universe has at least one hundred billion galaxies (10^{11}). Each galaxy has over one hundred billion stars, with individual planets revolving around them, some of which support intelligent life, like Earth. So how does Earth fit into the grand scheme of things?

According to the IAU (International Astronomical Union) in their 2006 white paper, our Solar System has eight Planets: Mercury, Venus, Earth, Mars, Jupiter, Saturn, Uranus and Neptune. Pluto, which was considered a planet since its discovery in 1930, was de-listed by the IAU as a planet after seventy-six years of being taught in schools that it was the ninth planet in our solar system. Our sun now has five dwarf planets, including Pluto.

Earth, with a circumference of only twenty-five thousand miles at the equator, is considered a relatively small planet. Even so, Earth is used as the average IP size with a population of seven billion in our ILC models. Our calculations use these conservatively estimated averages to project levels of intelligent life throughout the universe, even though there are many planets in the universe much larger than Earth.

The ILC Theory does not attempt to analyze, evaluate, predict or answer questions about the physical evolution of the universe, the origin of life, or the beginning of time. *The Theory* does, however, answer questions about the advancement and evolution of intelligent life that populates planets in the universe, as the planets themselves evolve.

Conditions on planetary systems, and availability of intelligent planets for Sapien LifeCycles (LCs), are both critical to *The Theory*. Because of our basic assumptions requiring planetary hosts, we must consider the physical realm in which our Sapiens' LiveTimes are spent. As Sapiens go through their own LifeCycles, so do the billions of planets throughout the universe.

Planetary Life Cycle

There seems to be a natural evolution in the growth cycle of life-supporting planets. They are born, they live and they die. Over time, all planets are expected to complete this cycle. Earth, like all other intelligent planets, will someday come to an end, but hopefully not for another billion years or so.

With only a few degrees change in Earth's orbit around the Sun, Earth might drift too close to the Sun and burn up, or move too far away from the Sun and freeze. Or a huge meteor collision, known as a galactic collision, could occur and totally destroy Earth.

As drastic as those possibilities seem, they are in fact possibilities that do occur during a typical planetary evolutionary cycle. Planets live and planets die. Their orbits change back, and they live again. And then they die again. It is the Planetary Life Cycle (PLC). Just as Sapiens have recurring LCs, planets have recurring PLCs.

The difference is that Sapiens improve from LC to LC, retain and carry forward their developed character and intelligence traits. Planets do not. They start from scratch every time and build their ecological habitat that someday will support intelligent life, once again.

Another difference between a Sapien's LC and a Planet's PLC, is the duration of the cycles. Sapiens have relatively short LifeCycle durations, traditionally lasting for less than a hundred years. Planets, on the other hand, have very lengthy Life Cycles, measured in the millions of years.

There are many categories and subgroups of planets in the universe. For ILC purposes however, there are basically three classes of planets currently orbiting stars in the universe. A planet's ability to support life is directly proportional to a planet's distance from its sun. It is this distance from its light and heat source provided by a sun that dictates whether a planet can proffer an ecological habitat that will support life.

The chart below identifies the three classes of planets, as defined in *The Theory*.

IP Classification	Planet description
Class A Planet	Barren, does not support life
Class B Planet	Supports life, Organism development, vegetation and wildlife
Class C Planet	Supports Intelligent Life, which feeds on Class B-type inhabitants

As shown above, a planet either supports life, or it does not. Class A planets are relatively barren, with no capability of supporting life, because they are either too close to their sun, or they are too far away.

The Intelligent LifeCycle Theory

Class B planets do support life, but not intelligent life.

Class C planets support intelligent life and other lifeforms that provide food and nourishment for intelligent life growth. Sapiens can only exist on Class C planets, thus the term intelligent planet.

Since Class C planets are the ones that support intelligent life, *The Theory* focuses solely on them. Class A and B planets may evolve someday into life-supporting Class C planets, as Earth has done more than once. But for our purposes, only current Class C planets are considered relevant to *The ILC Theory*.

As shown in the chart below, the typical planetary life cycle progesses through the three classifications as previously stated. A planet begins as a barren planet, since it is either too close or too far from its sun. As its orbital patterns change, it may evolve into a planet that supports life, and then to one that supports intelligent life, and back to one that does not support any life.

Typical Planetary LifeCycle			
Class A ⟹	Class B ⟹	Class C ⟹	Class A
Barren	Life	Intelligent Life	Barren
	subHalo Status		
IP Inactive	IP Inactive	IP ACTIVE	IP Inactive

There sure seems to be a pattern developing here. Whether it is a Sapien's LifeCycle or a Planetary Life Cycle, or maybe even a Solar Life Cycle, the entities have similar growth patterns. They are born, they live and they die. And then they do it all over again. The only difference is the duration of the Cycles.

The Intelligent LifeCycle Theory

This is of course a rudimentary analysis of the LifeCycle of living things in the universe, but an important one. Some say this adds significant credibility to *The Theory's* position that we, as intelligent life entities, will also continue to get recycled, the same as the stars and planets that support us.

Intelligent Planets (IPs)

According to ILC projections, there are hundreds of thousands of Intelligent Planets in each galaxy. And that extrapolates into billions of IPs in the universe, all at different levels of development.

The growth periods during an IP's evolution are, coincidentally, very similar to the planet's Sapien evolution. IP LifeCycles fit a similar bell curve type evolution to their Sapien counterparts. The majority of planetary growth occurs in the middle classifications, as indicated by the hierarchy levels of Class C IP levels below.

Intelligent Planet (IP) Classifications

IP Rating	Sapien Range	Avg Sapien	IP Index
Class C1	L1s - L2s	L1.5	150
Class C2	L1s - L3s	L2.1	210
Class C3	L2s - L5s	L3.2	320
Class C4	L3s - L7s	L4.4	440
Class C5	L4s - L7s	L5.5	550
Class C6	L5s - L7s	L6.4	640
Class C7	L6s - L7s	L7.1	710

Class C IPs are divided into seven classifications that identify the level of Sapiens that occupy the host planet. The age of the planet and the living environment are the two things responsible for IP Class C ratings, which are divided into Sapien L Groups.

Using the stages of a Sapien's LiveTime as a reference, a planet's developmental stage progresses from its embryo phase as a Class C1 IP to its child stage as a C2. As it advances to C3 status, the IP begins to exhibit attributes inherently consistent with the beginning of a Sapien's teenage years.

When an IP progresses to a Class C4 like Earth, it reflects Sapien traits consistent with the ending of adolescence and the beginning of adulthood. At this point, the IP has evolved into a planet where anything is thought to be possible, as evidenced by the IP's technology explosion, indicative of all IPs during C4 evolution.

Like teenagers approaching adulthood, C4 IPs may have the optimistic ideals of older teens, but also lack the experience that only comes with a lengthy adulthood. This phase of an IP's Life Cycle usually fosters many mistakes and ill-conceived notions as to the IP's proper direction of development. Phases in Earth's evolution thus far have already been experienced, and will likely continue, as we grow toward C5 IP status.

So you might say, Earth is a young adult in the grand scheme of intelligent planets in the universe. Some IPs are far more advanced and civilized than Earth (C5 to C7 IPs), while there are many more planets less developed than Earth (C1 to C3 IPs).

Generally, the older the IP, the more developed its Sapien population will be. And the more advanced the Sapien base becomes, the better the living conditions for its inhabitants will be.

Class C1 and C2 IPs request L1, L2 and L3 Sapiens, since those are the common Sapien levels of the parental overlays' development on those planets. A C1 IP is usually the entry point for L0 Sapiens to enter the evolutionary development cycle of intelligent life.

When an L1 Sapien is requested, the Sapien Request Order (SRO) is generally fulfilled with a brand new, uncirculated Sapien, an L0.0, which is immediately upgraded to L1 status at birth. An unlimited or infinite supply of L0s is thought to be resident in each subHalo. These virgin Sapiens are available 24/7 to begin their own LCs, while priming the pump for Sapien evolution on newly emerging IPs.

As planetary systems evolve to higher levels of Sapien occupancy, they provide platforms for more advanced Sapiens to be born. When an IP progresses to a C3, its rate of Sapien growth begins to accelerate, commensurate with its ability to support increased Sapien population.

High growth periods for a planet naturally occur as a planet develops from Class C3 to C4 (Earth) and then to C5. If a planet lives long enough, it might develop into a C6 or C7 IP, but the odds are not in favor of the planet. That is the reason there are substantially fewer advanced worlds. Only a few million intelligent planets have lived long enough for that level of Sapien evolution.

Even if an IP lives for a billion years or more, it will ultimately expire with its own Life Extinction Level Event (LELE). In ILC parlance, a LELE is the event resulting in the death of a planet, where all life on an IP is extinguished.

This ultimate ICT event, for billions of Sapiens, renders the planet incapable of supporting life, oftentimes as a result of a shift in its axis or a significant change in its orbital pattern around its sun. Earth is thought to have already gone through this phenomenon, at least once in our recorded history, when the dinosaurs suddenly became extinct.

When an IP abruptly ceases supporting life, after a catastrophic LELE, the nearest subHalo must absorb the billions of Sapiens from the planet, all with premature simultaneous LC terminations, en masse. Such an event is called a Sapien Grab. It requires the Sapien population of the expired IP to be assimilated into the subHalo database sectors en masse, after being reclassified and rejuvied with some RestTime, before the next available LC to other compatible IPs.

Before extinction occurs, an IP by default will continue to develop as a life-supporting world, as it naturally evolves to higher C levels. When an IP successfully transcends from a Class 3 to a Class 4 IP, it does so as a direct result from improvements in two Sapien traits. Those are the violence and sanctity of life ICTs. Improvements in these two ICTs are the most visible evidence of an IPs escalation in Class.

As a planet like Earth progresses from its original status as a C1 IP, millions of years before, to a more advanced C4/C5 IP status, its acceptance of violence as a solution to social problems decreases. And conversely, its value in the sanctity of life improves.

Improvements in Sapien averages of these two characteristics also affect the Sapien levels that are attracted to the planet. And by doing so, it directly enhances the IP's average Sapien levels, which allow it to continue to move up in Class C standings. The indirect result is enhanced living conditions for its Sapien inhabitants.

In intelligent worlds like Earth, a Sapien with evil tendencies and a majority of negative ICTs may find it easier to exist, survive and mature, more so than in societies that are more advanced. So an environment like Earth is primed for evil Sapiens because it is an advanced society, but not so advanced morally and technologically, as we might think we are. However, the existence of evil Sapiens is a very small percentage of most IP's Sapien population, and reduces further as the IP progresses in Class.

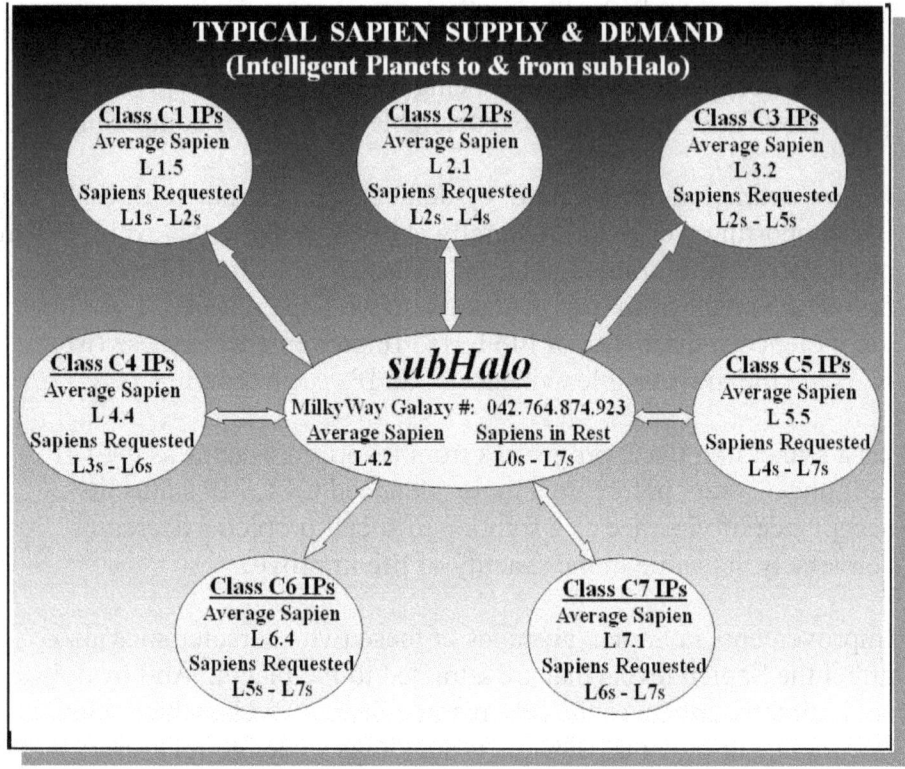

As shown above, each Class C IP, in its evolutionary cycle, requires varying levels of Sapiens for continued growth. At the same time, each IP Class provides specific levels of Sapiens from which to draw for the more advanced IPs. Worlds with lower C ratings, until they reach C3 status or above, will always be developing Sapien levels that feed other planetary systems with more advanced requirements.

A planet's Sapien population growth rate begins to explode by the time the IP makes it to the C4 level. Such population explosions generally continue through the early stages of its history as a Class C5 IP before it starts to subside.

During this normal IP Life Cycle, a planet's Sapien birth rate far exceeds its death rate. When this occurs, Sapien transfers are required for many of its births from less developed planets.

At this point, the question occasionally arises as to the methodology used that would statistically allow high-growth IPs the ability to sustain such growth. If there are more people alive today on Earth than have ever died in totality throughout Earth's history, then how can we sustain our Sapien growth rate?

C4 IPs, like Earth, can only sustain such growth rates by attracting Sapiens from other C2-C3 IPs. Sapien transfers between IPs within a galaxy are not uncommon at the C4 IP level to meet the demand. The subHalo will continue to draw Sapiens from other IPs to augment its recycling of Sapiens on Earth, until Earth reaches a C5 IP Rating.

As Earth progresses in its development, its net population growth will begin dropping with less need to import from other worlds. This is expected to occur sometime during the early to middle stages of Earth's C5 tenure, as our average life expectancy increases to well over one hundred years per LifeCycle.

Once an IP surpasses the zero gain in birth rate (less births than deaths), it then becomes a supplier of Sapiens to other C4 to C6 IPs with higher growth rate requirements. At that point in our planet's evolution, Earth as a C5 will become a new source for Sapiens to other more advanced IPs, as it was in its early days as a C1/C2 IP. Once again, we can see a noticeable trend of intelligent life in the universe, that is unending in its scope.

When an IP reaches the C5 level, the evil Sapien factor still exists, but with less of an impact on overall living conditions on the planet. As a planet progresses to C6 status, the violence factor continues dropping to very low levels and all but totally disappears by the time a planet reaches the C7 IP level.

When this happens, the Sapiens' sanctity of life ICTs are at their highest point of development. So much so, that when violence occurs on such advanced IPs, it is a major news story, continuously covered by all popular media venues of the era, since it is so rare.

Not to sound like a broken record, but it does help to think in terms of infinity. There are billions of intelligent planets in our universe, ranging from C1 to C7 IPs.

And they are all feeding the evolutionary cycle of intelligent life in the universe, from C1 planets with an average life expectancy of twenty-two years, to the C7 IP with Sapiens living hundreds of years during one LC. And subHalos will always have an infinite supply of L0s to fill in the gaps.

IP Index

The IP Index is the overall rating for the average Sapien level of a planet multiplied by one hundred. Similar to a Sapien's SQ rating, the IP Index translates a planet's Sapien development level into a single number that is more easily categorized and monitored statistically. The IP Index almost sounds like a commodities exchange indicator, in which you could also buy and sell futures. Maybe it is on a C7 IP.

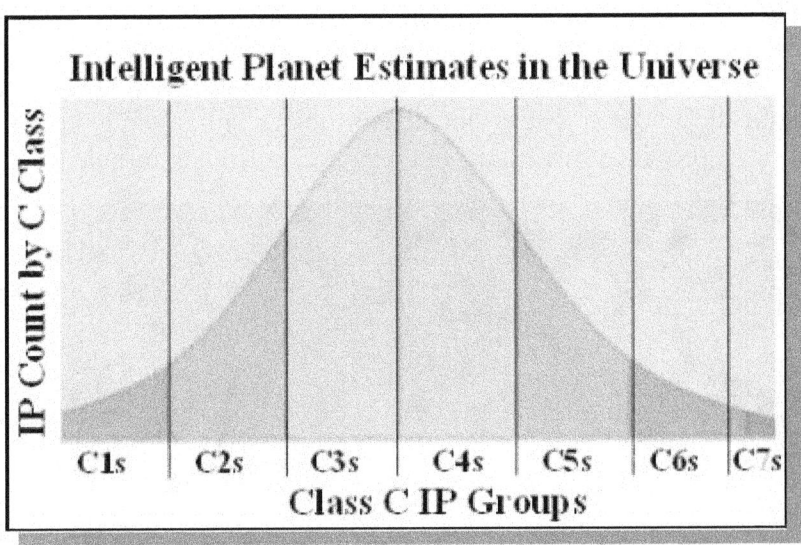

As shown in the above graph, the distribution of intelligent planets in the universe follows some semblance of a normal bell curve. As would be expected, since the universe is thought to be less than fifty percent developed in intelligence, the graph shows a predominance of IPs in the C3 to C4 range.

Example: Earth, as a C4 IP, with an average Sapien of L4.4, translates into an IP Index of 440. Millions of years ago, when Earth was a C1 planet, its IP Index was in the 100 to 199 range. The majority of Sapien transfers occur on C3-C4 planets with an IP Index ranging from 300 to 499, primarily hosting L2 to L5 Sapiens.

Galaxies in the universe

The following photos and artist renderings of The MilkyWay galaxy, 042.764.874.923, pinpoint the location of Earth's subHalo, which traditional religions refer to functionally as heaven. Each image shows what science has dubbed the black hole at the center of the galaxy. The subHalo for each galaxy, located at the center of each galaxy's black hole, provides safeguards and protection from external stimuli.

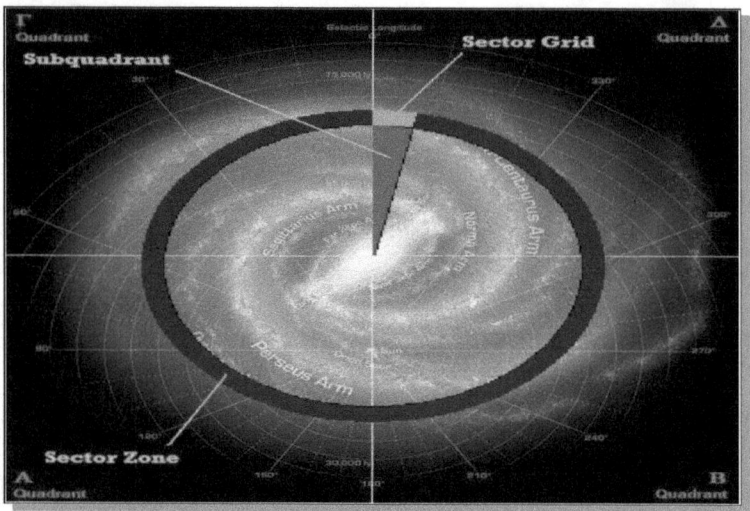

Artist's conception of the Milky Way's spiral structure with two major stellar arms and a central bar, using infrared images from NASA's Spitzer Space Telescope.

Galaxies across the universe come in many sizes. The MilkyWay galaxy is roughly one hundred thousand light-years in diameter. Our nearest sister galaxy, the Andromeda Galaxy, is located roughly 2.5 million light-years away.

There are more than one hundred billion (10^{11}) galaxies in the observable universe. Typical galaxies range from dwarfs with as few as ten million (10^7) stars to giant galaxies with one trillion (10^{12}) stars, all orbiting a galaxy's center of mass. Some scientific projections attest to estimates that include more than one hundred and seventy billion (1.7×10^{11}) galaxies in the observable universe.

A recent study by astronomers estimated that the observable universe now contains three hundred sextillion (3×10^{23}) stars, even though many still believe in the 10^{11} progression theory. To be conservative, ILC projections use the 10^{11} rule, which equates to ten sextillion (1×10^{22}) stars in our universe, just to be on the safe side.

NGC 4414, a typical spiral galaxy in the constellation Coma Berenices, is about fifty-five thousand light-years in diameter and approximately sixty million light-years away from Earth. Credit: NASA/ESA Hubble Space Telescope.

Although it is not fully understood yet, dark matter appears to account for about 90 percent of the mass of most galaxies. And super-dense dark matter seems to be prevalent surrounding the black hole in each galaxy, providing additional protection for the subHalos.

Size of the universe

The universe is certainly immense and theoretically infinite in volume. The region visible from Earth (the observable universe) is a sphere with a radius of about forty-six billion light-years. By comparison, the diameter of a typical galaxy is only thirty thousand light-years, and the typical distance between two neighboring galaxies is about 3 million light-years. The universe is a big place.

So how can we measure something so large, and possibly infinite in scope? There are certain assumptions that should be made in order to measure the finite attributes of something that in fact may be infinite.

Assuming there are only 10^{11} galaxies in the universe, and there are only 10^{11} stars per galaxy, there would be 10^{22} stars, or ten billion trillion stars in the universe, as we know it. This assumes of course that there is only universe.

Using the conservative assumption of 10^{22} stars in the universe, we can conservatively calculate the number of intelligent planets available for Sapien LifeCycles. We can then logically estimate the number of intelligent planets equal to or greater than Earth, to dispel such ancient theories that Earth is alone.

To continue our conservative approach, we can drill down further by assuming that only one-one hundredth of 1 percent of all stars have planets around them that support life. And only one-one hundredth of 1 percent of those planets support intelligent life. There would be ten billion planets with intelligent life equal to or greater Earth.

Of that number, if we assumed only one-one hundredth of 1 percent of

The Intelligent LifeCycle Theory

those planets have intelligent life greater than Earth, there would be one million planets with more advanced intelligent life than Earth.

Not only are we not alone, there are many more intelligent planets like Earth in the observable universe. Billions more.

SIZE OF THE UNIVERSE	
Conservative ILC Assumptions	
No. of Stars in Universe: 10 Sextillion (10^{22})	10,000,000,000,000,000,000,000
99.99% of Star Systems Cannot Support Life	0.01%
Stars with min.1 Planet Supporting Life	1,000,000,000,000,000,000
	1 quintillion (10^{18}) Planets
99.99% of those Cannot Support Intelligent Life	0.01%
Planets Supporting Intelligent Life	100,000,000,000,000
	100 trillion (10^{12}) Planets
99.99% of those with Less Intelligence than Earth	0.01%
Intelligent Planets => than Earth	10,000,000,000
	10 billion (10^9) Planets
00.01% of those with more Intelligence than Earth	0.01%
Intelligent Planets more advanced than Earth	1,000,000
If Earth is more advanced than 99.999999% of all IPs in the Universe, there are 1 million planets more advanced than earth. If Earth is more advanced than only 99% of all Intelligent Planets, there would be more than 1 trillion planets more intelligent than Earth.	
"WE ARE DEFINITELY NOT ALONE!"	

The above chart conservatively shows the probabilities and expected number of intelligent planets that exist in our universe. Most scientists seem to agree that these calculations are indeed conservative.

Example: If Earth only ranks in the top one thousandth of 1 percent of developed worlds, it would be more advanced than 99.999 percent of all intelligent planets in the universe. This conservative assumption identifies ten trillion IPs equal to Earth's level of development, and one billion planets that are more advanced than Earth.

If we agree that these conservative estimates are possibilities, it does present a very wide range in the number of IPs that are like Earth, within our current IP Class, almost unimaginable. Considering such highly conservative estimates, *The ILC Theory* predicts that one million to one billion intelligent planets are currently more advanced than Earth.

For purposes of our calculations however, we must assume a finite size of the universe, which most think is not the case. Many scientists feel the universe is indeed infinite in scope, even though they continue to attempt to define its infinite boundaries with finite calculations. *(Think about that one.)*

Regardless of such assumptions, our universe should be considered in the category of big-time infinity. It is unbelievably huge, constantly moving and constantly expanding. At some point, it becomes meaningless to make any further projections, since the ones we are already dealing with are way beyond our existing comprehension.

Age and Shape of the Universe

The best current estimate of the age of the universe is 13.75 ± 0.13 billion years. However, if the universe is infinite, then that estimate is only the starting point. It is not known if something existed before the moment of the Big Bang.

The Intelligent LifeCycle Theory

For all intents and purposes, our universe is finite in size. And even more so with the addition of the Superverse concept, of which our universe is one of the 10^{11} universe members.

The ILC Theory describes the universe as an Nfinitoid, which is defined as, "the holistic entity, encompassing all intelligent life in a universe, with no beginning and no end, but with a definitive and expansive scope". So as a result, *The Theory* projects there are at least 10^{11} Nfinitoids in the superverse, each of which support trillions upon trillions of Sapiens. *See ILC Terminology in Appendix.*

As shown below, there are three possible geometries to describe the shape of the universe: Closed, Open and Flat, from top to bottom.

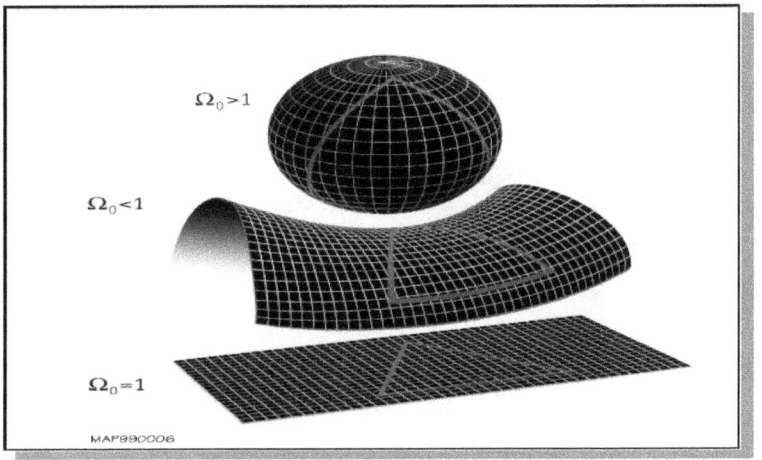

Permission of NASA Official: Gary Hinshaw

The closed universe is of finite size and, due to its curvature, traveling far enough in one direction will lead back to one's starting point. The open and flat universes are infinite, and traveling in a constant direction will never lead back to the same point, theoretically.

All three theories seem to be saying the same thing. The universe is infinite but finite, which may be more logical than such an oxymoronic phrase would otherwise indicate. Such theories seem to fill an innate need we Sapiens have to measure and quantify everything, including our ever-expanding universe.

The following pie chart indicates the composition of different types of entities that exist in the universe. With approximately 95 percent of the universe in the form of dark matter and dark energy, all of the stars in all of the galaxies occupy less than 1 percent of Space.

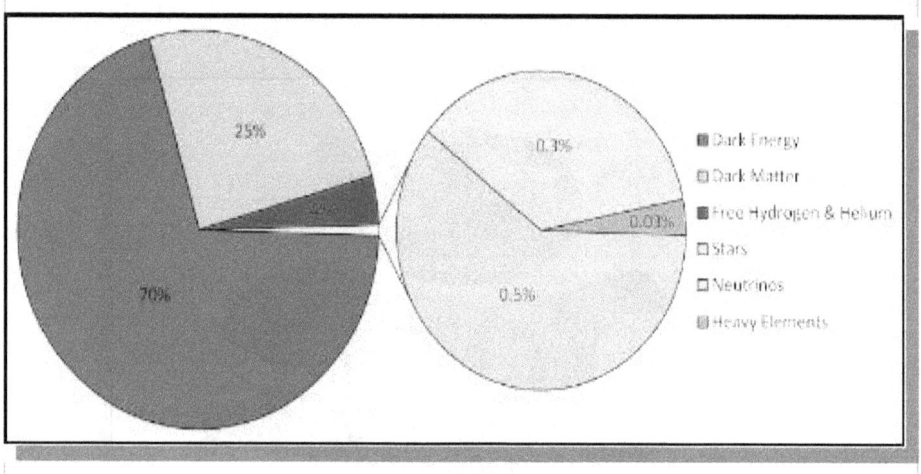

Scientists speculate that dark energy accounts for about 70 percent of the space in the universe. Such extensive amounts of little-known dark energy remains one of the great mysteries in astrophysics.

Big Bang Theory

The Big Bang Theory refers to the physical evolution of the universe. Its basic premise states that everything originated from a single cell. There are some that even say it all began from nothing. You think infinity is hard to imagine, try getting your hands around that one.

Since its creation in the early twentieth century, the Big Bang Theory has become one of the more prominent spatial paradigms surrounding the origination of the universe. Even though it espouses infinity, it negates it by saying the universe actually had a beginning.

Regardless of whether it all started from one cell or from nothing, if the universe had a beginning, it could indicate the universe is indeed a finite entity. However, as proponents of Infinity, *The Theory* further stipulates that, although the universe may have had a finite beginning, its future is indeed infinite.

According to the Big Bang model, the universe expanded from an extremely dense and hot gaseous state and continues to expand today. It speculates further that space itself is expanding, carrying galaxies with it, like spots on a balloon as it inflates.

More recent analysis indicates this original state existed approximately 13.7 billion years ago. This is considered to be the age of the known universe, and the time that the Big Bang occurred.

Religious leaders have always been at odds with the principles of the Big Bang, simply because they do not separate the physical origins of the universe from the intelligent life component. *The ILC Theory* does not address the origin of the physical universe, nor the origin of intelligent life in the universe, for that matter.

Having said that however, *The Theory* vehemently disagrees with the Big Bang Theory and its estimated age of the universe as only a few billions years old. If the future of our existence is in fact infinite in scope, then the same must also apply to our past. Infinity is ageless.

Suffice it to say, however and whenever it all started, it was long ago, trillions and trillions of years ago, if in fact, there ever was an original starting point. According to infinity, there never was a beginning, just as there will never be an end.

Superverse *(A Super Nfinitoid)*

The Superverse is the universe of universes. It has evolved in *The Theory*, as a result of identifying certain finite attributes of our existing universe, which directly implies there is more than one universe.

Example: The black hole is at the center of a galaxy, surrounded by the galaxy's cluster of stars. Since the universe is a large cluster of galaxies, it is expected that the superverse is an extremely large cluster of universes. And of course, this analogy could be carried out to infinity, with multiple superverses, and so on.

Another feature that points to our universe as being finite, is the black hole that has to exist at the center of any Nfinitoid. And according to *The ILC Theory,* the black hole, at the center of our universe, is home to the Halo that services our subHalos.

So if our universe has a center, it would, by definition, illustrate that our universe is finite, with measurable dimensions. And if our universe is finite with boundaries, the question always remains, "What is beyond the edge of our universe?"

Posing this question implies there may be other universes, beyond our universe. And these universes, like ours, exist with their own large clusters of galaxies, each of which is comprised of billions of star clusters. When you look at something in space, there is always something else beyond that. So what is beyond the edge of our universe? Simple answer, more universes.

The illustration below shows how multiple universes could be stacked on top of the others, assuming they all occupy different spatial voids, with no time dimension overlapping.

A depiction of a multiverse with seven universes, which are separate spacetime continua, each with different physical laws, and maybe different dimensions. Entitled "Vectorization of Multiverse", by Wikipedia contributor, Lokal Profil.

The Theory refers to this cluster of universes as the Superverse. Depending upon the size of and the distance to these other universes, it could require more extraordinary travel speeds that are afforded us by the UENet. To reach other universes, we may need a much faster network, possibly SuperStarSpeed (SSS), or Googol StarSpeed (GSS), which would be StarSpeed^{100}. Using Einstein's formula $E = MC^2$, GSS would equate to $E = MC^{114}$, where C equals the speed of light.

If there are multiple universes that coexist with ours, separated by trillions upon trillions of light-years, travel between universes may not be practical. However, there would still need to be multiple L10 boards residing in Halos for each universe, and possibly a separate L10 board for the superverse itself.

There could be the possibility of multiple universes occupying the same spatial void, but in different time dimensions. The same spatial void within the same time dimension being occupied by two different universes, could cause a time warp, or more specifically a Time Dimension Warp (TDW). The possible existence of a time warp scenario seems to create an infinite number of possibilities in defining the universe. This is important, if the time warp negatively affects or disrupts the theoretical concept of the space-time continuum.

If we used this multiverse illustration, making it consistent with *The Theory's* methodology, there would be 10^{11} universe platters, representing one hundred billion universes in the superverse. Prior to the above multiverse and *The Theory's* introduction of the superverse, the universe was considered to represent true infinity.

With the expansion of the 10^{11} Theory to include the superverse (10^{11} universes), our universe then becomes finite and the superverse becomes infinite. Or does it? What is outside of the superverse? For the record, more superverses of course. Infinity has no limits.

The Intelligent LifeCycle Theory

To conform to the *The Theory's* numbering scheme, individual universe numbers and addresses within the Superverse would need to be able to accommodate 10^{11} universes. If that is the case, our universe may actually be referred to as universe 054.345.832.143. The other universes would have similarly unique addresses that reflect their position in the superverse of one hundred billion universes.

ILC Discovery: Take the 10^{11} theory past the number of galaxies in our universe to the next step. If there are 10^{11} universes (one hundred billion) in the Superverse, this equates to 10^{22} galaxies and 10^{33} stars in the superverse, a decillion of stars.

Using these assumptions, there would ultimately be 7×10^{44} Sapiens on IPs throughout the superverse, or seven billion decillion Sapiens. Such quantities are super large but finite, so they are measurable. These *ILC projections* are so large and seemingly infinite in scope, they might best be described as *Quantifiable Infinity*.

The Intelligent LifeCycle Theory

10. Body & Sapien

During its evolution, *The ILC Theory* has defined, measured, dissected and analyzed the Sapien and all of its vital components. This chapter discusses body and Sapien interfaces and their evolution as they respond to the other.

For the Sapien to experience LiveTime during an LC, it must occupy a host body. Species that qualify as hosts are those that require an Intelligent Energy Field (IEF) to live and function as an advanced species.

According to *The Theory*, applicable host species have certain physical attributes required for Sapien growth. The host species breathes oxygen, requires water and food to survive, and has similar tolerances to heat and cold as we do. Hosts are warm temperatured beings with physical agility and mobility. They have a brain, walk upright on two of four appendages, and reproduce sexually between the male and female of the species.

The Intelligent LifeCycle Theory

There are some lower species on the evolutionary scale that possess some of the qualities of a host, including a brain, but do not require intelligence to live. Such species, specifically in the ape family, use their brain with limited memory solely to function without requiring a Sapien. They only have a physical energy field, and cannot accommodate an IEF, since they lack a Sapien-BrainBridge.

When a species evolves to the point of requiring an intelligent energy source, it grows a Sapien-BrainBridge. This occurred on Earth, when the human species evolved from the ape family. At that moment in time, the planet and the species became active in the MilkyWay subHalo, somewhere in the one to two million year BC range, according to archeological facts and known calendar assumptions.

With this occurrence, Earth became an active IP in the MilkyWay subHalo network once again. Earth and the human species were activated as a Sapien source and a Sapien user. If it were the planet's first experience as an IP, a new IP account had to be setup identifying the planet as both pickup and destination points on the UENet. If it were an IP like Earth, which is expected to have had multiple IP Life Cycles, the subHalo account for the planet was merely re-activated.

Once a species is defined as an intelligent being, the LifeCycles of its Sapiens are controlled by two primary factors. The parental gene pool is responsible for the physical attributes of the host body. The parental overlay, as defined in the SRO, is responsible for initial mental attributes of the fetus. Once the SRO is fulfilled, the selected Sapien, with its own ICT set and IM, is then fused with the host body for the Sapien's new LifeCycle.

The incoming Sapien begins to adapt to its new body and its new surroundings, when it first arrives in the fetus. This usually begins to occur during the second trimester, even though the Sapien's new LC does not actually begin until birth.

As the host body develops during its childhood growth years, the Sapien's Individual Character Traits (ICTs) and Intelligence Module (IM) begin to surface in their words and actions. The Sapien must adapt to each LC, just as the host body does. It is all new stuff to the Sapien and the host. As the body's brain learns and matures, the Sapien's ICT and IM responses begin to surface, forming the basis of his or her personality.

During the Sapien's teen years, its ICT and IM responses to ICT events begin to materialize much faster, to the point that sometimes it is a little confusing to the teen. As a teen becomes increasingly exposed to a wider range of ICT events, at a faster clip, the brain may sometimes lag behind the Sapien's core of ICT and IM instructions, which is based on the Sapien's previous LCs. Thus, we sometimes have confused and/or confusing teenagers.

As the brain catches up with the Sapien's ICT set and IM during adulthood, the character and personality of the Sapien becomes undeniable with observable and finite qualities. At this point, these are the traits of the Sapien from its previous LC, plus any minor changes since his or her birth.

Early adulthood allows the Sapien's true ICTs to be recognizable and seen by others, as the young adult begins to exhibit more personable words and actions. Other people's reactions to the way the Sapien responds to life are generally good indicators that may reflect some good traits, some that need work and some that are almost non-existent.

Such is the state of the art in young adult Sapien development. This is the point in the LifeCycle, when the Sapien usually tries to capitalize on his or her good ICTs and delays any work on the ones that need help to pursue precious LiveTime ICT events.

A Sapien's ICT development and IM enhancements continue through the adult years as the host body ages. During the early adult years, a Sapien may concentrate on physical conditioning, education and having fun. As the body begins aging through the later adult years, the Sapien begins to shift its thought processes to life accomplishments, and character traits developed.

When the Sapien reaches its retirement years, ICT development may continue, but at a lesser pace. ICT events that positively or negatively affect Sapien evolution tend to be less frequent during retirement. However, ICT events, during the host body's aging years, may still have a significant impact on overall Sapien development.

As an intelligent being, a Sapien will always have character traits, as well as bodily attributes, that are less than fully developed. This level of imperfection will always be with us, until of course, we reach L8 or L9 status and reside in the Halo, after millenniums of LCs.

During the host body's final aging process of the Sapien LifeCycle, conflicts sometimes arise between the physical attributes of the body and the mental traits of the Sapien. As mentioned before, the Sapien remains alive and well during all stages of LiveTime. However in later years as frustrating as it may be, the Sapien is restricted to some degree by the physical elements of the body in dealing with daily life, such as coordination and memory.

At this point, a Sapien's understanding and acceptance of his or her physical deterioration may make the final stages of the LC journey more amenable. We Sapiens are certainly constrained by the physical life cycle of the human body. This is the natural order of things, and acceptance is the key.

When death occurs, the bodily functions cease, which includes the brain. This automatically releases the Sapien from the body by breaking the Sapien-BrainBridge connection and terminating its current LifeCycle. Within a few tetraseconds after death, the Sapien then transmits its Sapien Exit Request (SER), which is picked up by the UENet, and is then sent to its home base, in Earth's case, the MilkyWay subHalo.

Sapien-BrainBridge

The Sapien-BrainBridge (SBB or the Bridge) is a tetrical connection between Sapien and brain. It relays ICT and IM responses to ICT events from the Sapien core directly to the neurological centers of the brain. The Bridge also receives the brain's feedback on the event as it unfolds. It forwards those messages back to the Sapien core for redistribution to applicable ICTs and IM for processing and further responses.

During an ICT event, the brain transmits positive or negative tetrazymes to the Bridge, which are then sent to the Sapien for responses. These unique tetroscopic enzymes go to the Sapien core, and are then converted to a specific tetrical charge that is unique to each specific ICT. When tetrazymes reach the core and are relayed to a specific ICT, the TetraCells (TCs) in the ICT are energized to new levels, higher or lower, depending on the gravity of the situation. This increases the percentage of TCs in each ICT bucket, reflecting the percentage of overall ICT development in real time.

The Sapien-BrainBridge is also fused to the brain's sensory nerve portal. This allows the Sapien to receive stimulus input from the body's five senses. Once received, these sensory messages are processed by the core, its IM and the appropriate ICTs. Applicable responses are then returned to the Bridge for the brain's bodily reactions to events.

They say "the eyes are the windows to the Sapien". Although an interesting metaphor, this phrase is more of a hyperbole used to create an emotional image. If the eyes are considered the windows to the soul, when you look into the eyes, do you see the soul in there? No of course not, because it is not visible to the human eye or any other detection technology we have today.

However, you may sometimes have the feeling you can see someone else's thoughts, when you look into their eyes. Although not practical nor feasible, it is theoretically possible. If you could make the connection between the eyes and the Bridge, you might be able to get directly into the Sapien core, and see its thoughts. Good luck.

Currently, a Sapien has total use of its host body for seventy plus years on the average. When the brain and other body parts begin having trouble functioning, ICT sets and other Sapien components find it more difficult to communicate with the host. However, the Sapien is still alive and well and absorbing information, even if it cannot seem to communicate much to the brain anymore, because of deterioration to the Brain and subsequently the Bridge connection.

The reason lower animals (human food sources) do not possess a Sapien is because they do not have a Sapien-BrainBridge, which provides the interface between the host brain and the Sapien core. Until they grow a Sapien-BrainBridge, a species functions exclusively from its brain and its survival instincts.

Lesser species with smaller brains do have some memory that accounts for the domestication of wild animals as well as Sapien pets, like dogs and cats. They have just enough brain power to remember basic patterns of life that allow them to live more comfortably and interact favorably with Sapiens. Lower-level species have a physical energy field for their daily activities of food gathering and survival but not an Intelligent Energy Field (IEF) required to engage in abstract thought.

The brain, a physical component of the body, has a default setting that is without intelligence, which works for lesser species. Lesser species of beings found on a planet do not have or need energy fields to grow and function. Their raw survival instincts from the brain rule their existence. Many lesser species are used as food sources for Sapiens, governed by survival in the form of hunger and starvation.

Example: Caveman Sapiens saw lesser species purely as food. Their basic motto in life was, "Kill 'em 'n Eat 'em." A secondary motto equally as important was, "If you can't eat 'em, don't kill 'em, unless they're trying to kill you."

Brain & Memory

The brain is the amazing, computer-like organ that controls the physical functions of the body, stores current lifetime memories and makes millions of calculations every minute that allow humans to live. The host brain is infinitely more sophisticated than current computer technology.

The Intelligent LifeCycle Theory

The host brain is similar to the Sapien's ICT set, in that every Sapien has one. We all have the same brain lobes, just as we all have the same ICTs with which to evolve. Differences in Sapiens occur because of the various levels of brain, IM and ICT development that exists within each Sapien during any given LC.

The differences in brain capacities between humans are measured (or attempted to be measured) through a multitude of mental testing mechanisms, such as IQ tests, SATs, LSATs and others. As an intelligent species, Sapiens seem to have the need to quantify and categorize anything and everything associated with our bodies and our lives.

To understand the inner workings of the brain, some of the best medical and scientific Sapiens in the world have used science to further our understanding of the different areas (lobes) of the brain. They have created a technology referred to as functional Magnetic Resonance Imaging (fMRI), which scans the different brain lobes with radio waves and magnetic fields, measuring blood flow to various regions of the brain. The consensus of opinion is that increased blood flow to a particular lobe of the brain during an ICT event indicates increased brain activity, which should identify the functionality of the various areas of the brain.

However, such tests and their resultant data have not been conclusive to date. fMRI research, although extremely valuable, has not been able to provide the location in the brain where memories are stored or how the transfer of memory data is actually accomplished. As scientists continue probing the boundaries of NanoScience and ultimately TetroScience, they may eventually find answers that can prolong Sapien life expectancy by hundreds of years.

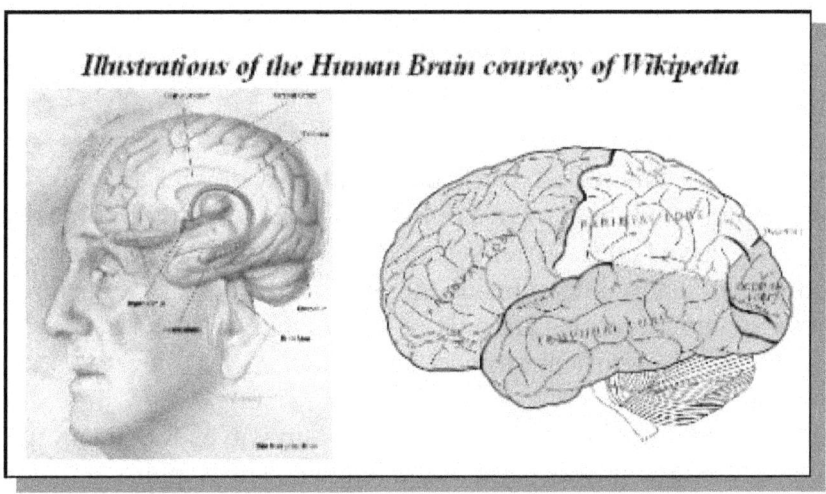

Basically, scientists do not really know how or where the brain stores its memory information. They do know, however, which parts of the brain register increased activity through radio waves and magnetic fields, which could possibly indicate memory storage functions. The fMRI (functional Magnetic Resonance Imaging) may have the ability to measure the brain's energized TetraCells. Maybe *The ILC Theory* will add a new dimension for scientists to consider, as they continue their research on the brain and its memory function, or maybe not.

Regardless of how memory cells in the brain work, they are solely responsible for recording everything about the current LC. Brain tetracells capture details of sights and sounds, images and facts, and store them for recall to be used in future ICT events.

Detailed memory, although crucial to physical existence, is not part of the Sapien. Memories of past LCs would not be useful during current and future LCs, which may have possibly occurred on other worlds with totally different cultures. Also, if the Sapien stored past LC memories, it would create undue overhead on the Sapien, with trillions of memory images that may be immaterial and even detrimental to future LCs.

Theoretically, this added overhead would slow down Sapien ICT development and the Sapien's portability to and from the subHalo and future LC LiveTimes. Brief selected memories of past LCs are recorded and stored deep inside the Sapien's LifeCycle Registry. These Sapien memories are only of events that occurred in previous LCs that had a significant impact on the LC.

During an LC, the brain, as it produces brain waves for functionality, is considered the power plant of the Sapien. The Sapien's power plant continually provides actionable requests and instructions to the core via the Bridge during all waking hours.

The brain stores all images of everything you've ever experienced during your current LC. Although all the details are there (images, scenes, experiences), it may be difficult to find details of an event among the trillions of terabytes of brain storage.

Example: If you cannot remember some detail of an event in your current LC, think of it as a photograph. If you have a big photograph with lots of action and people, you have the whole picture. You may not notice some small detail in the photo, until you go back and look for that detail again, but it is there. Memories are forever, at least during your current LC. The only thing that changes is your accessibility to those memories during your LC.

The memory portion of the brain is where *"ReIndexing The Brain"* could benefit, resulting in a Sapien lifespan on Earth being prolonged by possibly hundreds of years. Depending on the re-indexing method used, it may not be that effective on the brain's database after the first or second time, but useful nonetheless. *See 'ReIndexing The Brain' in the Appendix.*

Photographic memory is a physical attribute of the brain and not yet fully understood by science. People who have photographic memories will tell you they do not know how they do it, they just see images. It is a physical brain thing, not a character trait. Wouldn't it be great, if you could develop a photographic memory like other ICTs? Of course, it would only be applicable to your current LC. This would fall into the same category as mental telepathy and ESP, about which we know very little, so far.

Unlike the Sapien, the brain is programmable. It can be taught about the timings of its body movements and its reactions to LiveTime events. Based on such programming, the brain can easily replicate repetitive tasks during its current LC without further Sapien input.

Our current scientific knowledge of the brain comes from measuring brain activity during ICT events. This is done by attaching electrodes to certain lobes of the brain to measure increased brain waves during the event. Electrodes monitor energy eruptions in the brain, which scientists think are increased measurable brain waves, resulting from the presence of an ICT event.

When brain wave eruptions occur and are measured, it may record the existence of an ICT event and the event's effect on the brain, but not necessarily the exact location in the brain, where it is stored. Brain wave analysis is similar in interpretation to seismic anomalies in oilfield exploration. The seismic data may indicate the presence of oil, but it does not identify the exact location of the reserves. Memories are like oil reserves. We know they are there, but the exact location remains a question. And as in the search for oil, once we find the memory, we know we can drill down and retrieve it, but only for this current LifeCycle.

Human Conditions

There are many human conditions we all must negotiate during our LCs, good and bad. Some may be deficient and are remedied through science and medicine. Other conditions may be beyond repair, with little if any scientific or medical remedy available.

The human condition we are all most interested in improving is, of course, the body's aging process. Through science and medicine, we have found ways to extend the aging curve. But the fact remains, the body is destructible and has a finite shelf life. We have found ways to prolong the Sapien lifespan on Earth, and will continue to do so, but will probably never find a cure that eliminates aging. But hey, that's life, literally, deal with it.

Today, many conditions that affect human Sapiens do not have a cure, or even a logical explanation for their occurrences. Even though *The ILC Theory* does not provide any remedies for a Sapien's bodily conditions, it does provide logic and reasoning that identifies the cause of a few of them. Such deficient human conditions may be categorized as birth defects and/or mental illnesses.

Other than traditional illnesses and diseases ranging from coughs to cancer, there are two impairments that affect a Sapien's control over his or her body. The infrastructure of the Sapien may be damaged, during LiveTime or during death. Or the Sapien-BrainBridge may be fully or partially broken by accident during the LC or at birth.

Fortunately, because of the super-dense halo of dark matter that surrounds the Sapien and protects it from external stimuli, damage to the Sapien itself is extremely rare. Even in instances of nuclear explosions, the reliability and integrity of the Sapien infrastructure is thought to have a 99.99 percent rating.

Add to that the tetrasecond response rate of the UENet, and you get 99.9 percent with twelve 9s behind it. This would equate to an unimaginable Sapien infrastructure failure rate of 00.0000000000001 percent, or one in a hundred trillion. The Sapien and its core are relatively indestructible, and remain unscathed between LC's.

Since we always need to consider the concept of infinity, however, we need to add that anything is possible. If and when such a Sapien disaster occurs, it is expected that the disruption in Sapien integrity would be reparable, during the initial processing stage upon reentry to the subHalo. This would then result in a 0.00 percent Sapien infrastructure failure rate, as close to a sure thing as you will ever get. Basically, host bodies die, but Sapiens are forever.

So assuming the Sapien itself is damage-proof, the only other way a Sapien might be compromised is through its connection to the host body. The Sapien-BrainBridge, which is the interface between Sapien and body, may be damaged or broken at birth. If damaged or broken, the Bridge would no longer be available for Sapien communications to the host body.

A damaged or broken Bridge would inhibit and/or prohibit Sapien core instructions from being interpreted by the brain. This could result in a person who has a healthy Sapien but has little or no access to it. So the body operates almost entirely from its untrained brain, depending upon the severity of the break.

The Theory addresses the inherent cause-and-effect impact a disruptive Sapien-BrainBridge might have on the Sapien and the host body. Physical problems with the Bridge could explain some of our less understood human conditions, such as autism, Savantism, Alzheimer's, dementia, comas, morning sickness, Attention Deficit Disorder (ADD) and Obsessive Compulsive Disorder (OCD).

The Bridge has short-term memory that is capable of handling multiple, simultaneous ICT events through to their conclusions. Similar to RAM storage in today's computers, Bridge memory is dynamic and resets to zero during sleep (when turned off), ready for the next waking ICT event.

If there is a defective memory module in the Bridge, its restricted storage could result in attempting to handle the same amount of events simultaneously with less time for each event. With significantly less time in memory to reach an event conclusion, Bridge memory may prematurely clear to bring in the next ICT applicable to the event. This may result in the Bridge continually swapping information and thoughts in and out of storage more rapidly than required for an event to be concluded.

Consequently, it may outwardly appear the person has attention span issues. So we label it ADD. But more often than not, ADD is a result of low percentage development in certain ICT groups that include attention span, concentration and focus, all of which can be improved upon.

Because of restricted memory capacity, the Bridge might only allow a few ICTs to get through to conclusion, so the body exhibits only partial responses. An event might not receive full analysis by all applicable ICTs.

One or two ICTs may tend to dominate certain types of events, with no other counter-balancing ICTs getting through because of less available Bridge bandwidth. Human conditions, such as OCD, could be caused by defective Bridge issues. But like ADD, obsessive compulsive tendencies are more attributed to deficiencies in certain ICTs, than to a defective Bridge.

We, as a civilization, have decided that things not in compliance with our aggregate definition of normalcy are by definition abnormal. We especially like to use that approach when it comes to naming such social conditions in humans. If it is not easily defined, categorized and quantified, we call it a disorder.

What is a disorder anyway? For a disorder to exist, that means there must be an order somewhere. Where is the order in social acceptance? If there is an order in our civilization, it is obviously constructed by mankind, according to preconceived normalities. Doesn't that make it an artificial order? And if that is true, doesn't that also make an abnormality, an artificial disorder?

Conditions like ADD and OCD are predominantly due to a Sapien's deficient ICT development in a few traits. If that is the case, it would seem more appropriate to refer to such conditions as Attention Deficit Personality (ADP) and Obsessive Compulsive Personality (OCP). Labeling these type of conditions as disorders seems a little drastic. They should more appropriately be referred to as personality types.

ADP attributes are common among entrepreneurs and writers, who usually focus on the big picture. They spend whatever time is necessary to complete an event and move on to the next, no more and no less. Such attributes are seen as advantages in some business situations. It does not seem productive to try to establish such arbitrary norms that preclude legitimate ICT issues and call it normal.

Actual brain-related diseases may also be explained by a defective Bridge, such as certain types of dementia like Alzheimer's. This disease primarily affects elderly people. A certain type of age-related break in the Bridge can dramatically impact Sapien communications with the short term-memory area of the brain.

When the Bridge connection to short-term memory is severed, the individual may have very little memory of current events. With nothing but long-term memories available, the Sapien's memory recall capability of long ago events may flourish in great detail as memories are recounted, as if they were yesterday.

If the interface between Sapien and brain is damaged, the person will seem to be handicapped on the outside, even though he or she has a perfectly good Sapien still intact on the inside. Keep in mind, this is the first time a Sapien has had to negotiate aging, as far as the Sapien knows.

Other human conditions that can be explained by a defective Sapien-BrainBridge include autism and savantism. Both of these afflictions can be directly attributed to a partial or full break in the Sapien-BrainBridge.

Autism is thought to be a neurological disease. Some experts say, "nothing gets through to the person". Others say, "everything gets through". They are both right. *The Theory* believes that everything gets through to the brain of an autistic person. But very little gets through the Bridge to the Sapien Core for ICT and IM feedback.

All external stimuli (sight, smell, sound, taste, touch) gets through to the brain. But since the Bridge is down, nothing or very little gets through to the Sapien core. And without ICT and IM instructions from the core back through the Bridge to the brain, it cannot process any of the input it receives externally. The person is alive and well physically but has no noticeable character traits that allow it to function in society.

Even though the Sapien remains intact, it cannot communicate ICT or IM instructions to the brain because of the break in the Bridge. The Sapien tries to communicate but cannot. If the break is partial, sights and sounds may get through to the core for processing, but the defective Sapien-BrainBridge may stop some ICT or IM responses from being received by the brain.

When this happens, it is understandable that the Sapien with the defective Bridge may get a little frustrated and not even be able to show it. Occasionally, you may see an autistic person go into a rage. That is the Sapien inside that is exhibiting its extreme frustration because it has no control over its LC and does not know why. The Sapien continually receives images and information from the brain, but then can only sit back and watch as its ICT events unfold having no way to affect any outcome.

Savantism is a rare human condition that results from a near total break in the Sapien-BrainBridge at or near birth. The Bridge was intact long enough prior to birth, so the Sapien-Brain fusion occurred, meaning the Sapien was stuck for the duration of the LC.

ILC Discovery: Autism and savantism, usually associated with autism, is a direct result of a damaged Sapien-BrainBridge, which restricts normal communications between the Sapien and the brain. The Sapien is normal, but its tetrical connection to the brain is not.

With significantly reduced bandwidth, the Bridge only allows the IM and a couple of ICTs to get through to the brain. If the Sapien's IM is more advanced, the person may exhibit extraordinary mathematical or musical skills. This unfortunate Sapien may not exhibit many social skills since none of its ICTs can get through to the brain. A Sapien in this condition may also exhibit extreme mood swings, as a result of its frustration from having no control over its cherished LifeCycle.

Children with autism and savantism may still be able to understand, if it is only a partial break. So, if you believe in *The ILC Theory,* and if you think it would help, tell them, it is not their fault. It is a bad connection in their Bridge, which is extremely rare. And they will have a better life in their next LC, sorry.

Such understanding may sometimes have a calming effect on the Sapien. It might help them deal with the duration of their current LC. The odds are definitely in their favor of having a better LifeCycle next time, and with a body that has a good, strong Sapien-BrainBridge.

As painful as it may be to continue such a life, the Sapien should always remember Rule No1. Premature termination of a LifeCycle is bad, so the child is stuck with this LC, this time. The Sapien may still be able to show some improvement in ICTs and IM during the LC. Even during such a secluded LC, the Sapien may experience some ICT events in their lives that do get through to their Sapien core and thereby affect Sapien development.

Who knows? Maybe the cure for neurological diseases, such as autism and Alzheimer's will be found, if not now, maybe in future LCs.

ILC Discovery: The cure for autism and other neurological diseases in the future may be a tetroscopic surgery procedure to repair the Sapien-BrainBridge. Tetroscopic brain surgery to fix the Sapien interface does sounds logical.

When a partial Bridge break occurs, and only one or two ICTs and partial IM can get through, the totality of brain resources becomes focused entirely on one or two ICTs, and/or IM. That explains why a certain ICT or two may become more acute visibly, since existing brain power does not need to be reserved for all the other ICTs.

ILC Discovery: Occasionally, a Bridge may be fully functional but experiencing intermittent power surges, distorting ICT and IM translations from the Bridge to the brain. A Sapien with such irregular Bridge disruptions, resulting in sporadic losses of data, is affectionately referred to as a scatter-brain.

A break in the Bridge may also be the cause for a person going into a coma. An irreparable break in the Bridge would result in a permanent coma. When that happens, the Sapien is irrevocably released from the connection, and the Sapien sends out its SER for pickup. The question then becomes, "When is the SBB irreparably damaged?"

A partial Bridge break, however, might be reparable, either through tetroscopic surgery or as in some cases, the Bridge healing itself with its own tetracell regeneration application. If the break is minor, the Sapien-BrainBridge may be down temporarily while the Bridge regenerates itself.

ILC Discovery: When a Sapien-BrainBridge breaks causing a coma, the person may be considered alive, but brain dead, if it is a severe or total break. If it is a minor break, the person may suddenly come back to life as soon as damage repair to the Bridge is complete. And the Sapien has no memory of the coma event, since the Bridge was down and nothing got through to the core until it was repaired.

Another very prevalent human condition in *The Intelligent Life Cycle* is a mother's morning sickness. This is a mother's bodily defense mechanism to prevent germs and toxins from reaching the fetus during the early weeks of pregnancy. It is thought to be a physical trait that protects the fetus against toxins that are ingested by the mother. True enough.

During the first three months of pregnancy, the fetus has not yet built up its own immune systems. So the mother expels these toxins through nausea, or morning sickness, before they reach the fetus.

By the end of the first twelve weeks, the fetus' susceptibility to toxins is greatly reduced as it builds up its own defenses. The mother's morning sickness had protected it, while it built up its own immune systems.

Yes, all true. That is the explanation for the host body's physical reaction to pregnancy. Now for *The Theory's* take on morning sickness.

During the first trimester of pregnancy, since the requested Sapien has not yet arrived, the mother must share her own energy field with the fetus as it grows. At a certain point, generally by the beginning of the second trimester, the mother cannot survive, if she continues to share her own energy field, as the fetus' energy needs increase with growth.

Of course, the reason for the twelve week lag time between conception and Sapien infusion is to ensure fetal viability to prevent needless Sapien transfers at the subHalo level. And as it turns out, the Sapien arrival is the primary reason a mother stops having morning sickness.

When a fetus makes it to the twelfth week, fetal viability is seen as complete. With this determination, the Sapien, as specified in the SRO, is sent from the subHalo to the womb via the UENet.

Once the Sapien is fused with the semi-immune fetus around the twelfth week of pregnancy, it is able to more effectively ward off toxins, since the little fetus now has its own energy field. The mother's body ceases its nausea regimen as she reclaims her full energy field. With her energy field restored, the mother begins to become voracious, as if she were eating for two people, which of course she is.

ILC Discovery: When a pregnant woman stops having morning sickness, her unborn baby's Sapien has arrived. Given that fact, we should be able to estimate the time of arrival of the requested Sapien to coincide with the cessation of the mother's morning sickness. To carry this thought one step further, the actual age of a Sapien's LC would be the chronological birth age plus twenty-four weeks.

Evolution of Humankind

Most theories on the evolution of humankind treat the Homo sapien as one entity, without regard to the two distinct and separate components, the host body and the Sapien. This is understandable of course, since that has always been the perception, except for certain strict religious interpretations. *The ILC Theory* provides definitive standards based upon scientific precepts and methodologies as to the development, perpetuation and evolution of intelligent life in the universe, separate and apart from the physical body, regardless of intelligent species.

According to *Wikipedia*, "Humans are known taxonomically as *Homo sapiens* (Latin for 'wise man' or 'knowing man'). They have a highly developed brain and are capable of abstract reasoning, language, individual communications, introspective thought and problem solving. This mental capability, combined with an erect body type that frees the hands to manipulate objects, has allowed humans to make far greater use of tools than any other living species on Earth."

This is an important description, because the human body on Earth is the vehicle that supports Sapien LCs on Earth. It is the vessel that allows Sapiens to develop their ICTs and IM during LiveTime assignments. The degree to which traits can be developed during an LC depends to an extent on the physical capabilities of the host body, which includes the brain. Without the physical body, there would be no Sapien evolution, on any planet, in any galaxy or in any universe.

We call the intelligent species on Earth, human beings. Other IPs undoubtedly have different names for their intelligent beings that represent similar meanings and qualities. Humans, the intelligent species on Earth, evolved from the primate families.

Although the evolution of primates can be traced back sixty-five million years, studies indicate a much later transition to the intelligent species of humans. According to paleontologists and archeologists, the final evolutionary break between humans and the remaining members of the great ape family occurred 4 to 8 million years ago.

ILC Discovery: The reason humans broke away from the great ape family in their evolutionary cycle several million years ago is because the new species of humans developed their Sapien-BrainBridge at that time. In doing so, Earth was re-activated in the MilkyWay subHalo as an Active IP approximately two to four million years ago, once again.

During our Earth's current IP LifeCycle, intelligent life has flourished for the last few million contiguous years. The Sapien population of humankind has continued to develop, slowly at first and accelerating to current birth rates.

As Sapiens on Earth developed from L1s to L4s, Earth progressed from a C1 IP a few million years ago, to the C4 IP status it now holds. With an average 440 SQ today, Sapiens have developed Earth's standard of living significantly over the last few thousand years, and more substantially over the last two hundred years.

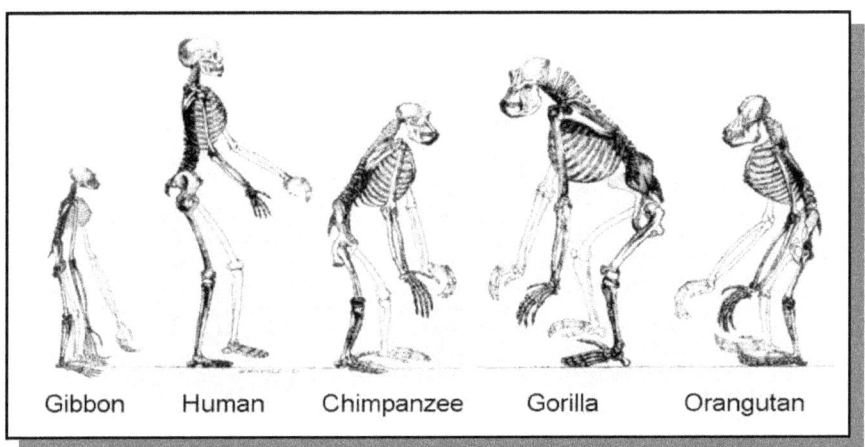

Gibbon   Human   Chimpanzee   Gorilla   Orangutan

The above illustration reflects the similarities and differences of certain primate families that have a brain and walk upright on two legs. The primary difference between these primates is the Sapien-BrainBridge, which requires an Intelligent Energy Field. The human, who has evolved from the rest with the cultivation of the Bridge, is the only species that requires a Sapien.

Coincidentally, it was just about two hundred years ago that little Charlie Darwin was born. Noted Sapien, Charles Robert Darwin (February 12, 1809 – April 19, 1882), became an English theorist. His unifying theory of life sciences, specifically the evolution of mankind commonly known as *Darwin's Theory of Evolution* was certainly counter to existing theory on the subject in those days.

Charles Darwin, as depicted in an editorial cartoon in 1871.

Darwin's theory stated that all species of life descend over time from common ancestors. He proposed the scientific theory that this branching pattern of evolution resulted from a process that he called 'natural selection'.

Darwin published his theory of evolution in his 1859 book, *"On the Origin of Species"*. By the mid twentieth century, Darwin's theories on evolution were generally accepted by most scientists and the public at large.

Darwin's scientific theories explained life's physical evolution, as well as the diversity of life, but not necessarily intelligent life. He, like all others, made no distinction between the physical evolution and the Sapien evolution. To date, science treats both as one and the same.

That's where *The Intelligent LifeCycle Theory* becomes a player. The physical evolution of mankind conveniently coincides very nicely with the metaphysical evolution of the Sapien. Actually, it is the development of Sapien ICTs and IMs that have elevated man's existence on this planet.

The body could not have achieved mankind's accomplishments on Earth without the Sapien. And the Sapien could not have developed without the body. It is literally one of those symbiotic relationship deals, at full-tilt boogie, 24/7, forever.

This is of course until Earth moves into its next IP Cycle, that being one of no life on the planet, which would trigger the de-listing of Earth as an Active IP once again. Then after another few million years or so, Earth will come back to life, start all over again with its physical evolution, and ultimately develop into a re-activated IP again.

As Earth progressed to its current level of Sapien development, across many different sociopolitical and geographical boundaries, ICT events that influence Sapien LCs vary just as widely. In different parts of the world, certain mannerisms, customs and ideologies tend to be race and country specific.

This results in physical and/or environmental influences on a Sapien during an LC. Such seemingly inherent character traits of a race are merely learned behavior, not true ICTs. Remember, Sapiens are gender specific, but race, color and ethnicity neutral.

An important factor in the development of a Sapien's ICTs during an LC is to understand and accept the physical limits of the body, which includes the brain. One of the primary purposes for a Sapien during its LC is to try to improve its ICTs whenever possible. And in doing so, it is most beneficial to try to minimize the impact environmentally influenced ICT events have on a Sapien's overall development.

The best scenario is when a Sapien attempts to work on those ICTs that need help and live a decent life without blaming others for his or her lot in life. When this occurs in a LifeCycle, enhancements in a Sapien's ICTs happen as a matter of course. However, when a Sapien tries to blame others for life's inequities without taking responsibility, it negatively affects a myriad of its ICTs. This could be an accurate assessment of a few of our current political leaders.

Dependent upon societal and technological advancements that tend to improve civilizations, the average Sapien lifespan has increased from around thirty-five years, only a few hundred years ago, to over seventy years today. It is probably a very good bet, that some day the average Sapien lifespan will exceed one hundred years.

As science and technology continue to develop, Earth Sapiens may live longer. Further in the future, if Earth is given the time, average lifespans may reach several hundred years. But since time in relation to spatial infinities has no relevance, the average Sapien LC on an IP is directly proportional to the host body's ability to endure life.

And what about the deficiencies inherent in intelligent life, the physical and mental inequities of life? Life, by definition, is not meant to be simple, nor fair. Sapiens must deal with the hardships of life, to survive and grow, while adhering to the *"Ten Rules of Intelligent Life"*, as much as possible.

Sapien-BrainBridge malfunctions, which today are considered mental impairments, directly impact the quality of life. The physical side of a Sapien's LC is equally important to achieving meaningful ICT growth.

If you were born with an irreconcilable physical deficiency that impairs your ability to experience ICT events like other Sapiens during your LiveTime, that is truly unfortunate. However, if you accept your physical condition as inevitable for this LC, you may have mental opportunities and ICT events not normally available to others for your Sapien growth during this LifeCycle.

It is certainly easier to say than do, but it really is all up to you. Whether it be a physical deficiency or a socioeconomic one, Sapiens always have the free will to improve during an LC.

We have shown how *"The ILC Theory"* functions by incorporating the other three life cycle theories at various stages of life, *Determinism, Free Will and Randomness*. A physically defective host body, at birth or by accident during LiveTime, is another example of a Sapien experiencing the negative impact of randomness, referred to in *The Theory* as the *SH Factor*. None of us can escape the SH Factor in our LCs, even though some experience it more than others.

Since physical impairments are relatively rare, the only reason for such a condition is pure 'luck of the draw'. You may take some solace in knowing, there is a 99.99 percent probability that your next LifeCycle will be to a healthy host body. Remember, whether they are physical, mental or socioeconomic, life's hardships really do build character.

Comedian Quote: Robin Williams, in one of his standup monologs, comments on God's design of the human body. "It seems like he could've done a little better job at designing the body. I mean, gimme a break, he put a major waste disposal plant near a recreation area, what's up with that?"

As much as we talk about the body and Sapien being separate entities, we must never lose sight of the fact that both are 100 percent dependent upon the other. The symbiotic relationship between the Body and the Sapien is paramount to Sapien development.

The Theory & Religion

Traditional, organized religions play a very important role in mankind's evolutionary process. Different religions have different belief systems, but most have two positive attributes. Religions answer the question about the afterlife, so people can focus on the day-to-day issues of life. And most religions generally preach good, moral principles that if followed, will result in living a better life.

However, if all religions are valid, and all have a god, then why would one religion hate another religion? Why would one god hate another god? Why would members of one religion kill members of another religion just because of their religious beliefs? Why have nations propagated wars with global consequences purely because of religious differences, instead of fostering global peace?

Some religions, it seems, are based on false premises and false beliefs with no consideration for the sanctity of life and represent a pretty significant misdirection in the evolution of mankind. Maybe there are multiple gods, a good god and a bad god. Not likely, but there is definitely something wrong with this picture. If you believe in a god, then doesn't it make sense that such a higher being would be benevolent, caring and loving, not violent, vengeful and hateful?

Example: A religion that seems to agree with only one or maybe two of the *Ten Rules of Intelligent Life* that apply to all Sapien life is Islam, which is espoused by over a billion worshipers to be the only belief. All others are damned.

That is quite a religion. Think about it. If you are a Muslim man under Islam, and you go out and kill the infidels (non-Muslims), then when you die, you go to paradise and get seventy-two virgins. Give me a break. How crazy is that? And what about the women? What do they get?

Granted, that is an extremist position within the Islam religion. But it openly exists in a religion that is accepted by over a billion people. The biggest concern *The Theory* has with Islam, other than the threat of Western civilization's extinction, is its inherent repression of ICT and IM development of its followers.

Loss of personal freedoms dramatically reduces any potential ICT and IM improvements gained during an LC. It is almost as if those Sapiens under Islamic control never really had real LifeCycles.

Unfortunately they will have little if any chance for real improvements in their ICTs and IMs this time. And quite possibly because of such repressive regimes, lesser-developed Sapiens in those cultures may stray toward negative or evil tendencies with their ICT development.

What does that mean? Well, it might mean people that hold those

The Intelligent LifeCycle Theory

views are probably L2 and L3 Sapiens, for starters. At least *The Theory* is based on physics and the natural laws of the universe, not on some prehistoric fear philosophy and violent control tactics.

There are many religions and belief structures on Earth, most of which do pray to a single god and believe in a heaven/hell scenario and/or some form of an afterlife. The following is a list of the major religions on Earth and estimates of the number of believers per religion, as reported by *Religion Facts* in their 2011 *"Big Religion Chart"*.

Religion	**Origin**	**Members**	**God/Prophet**	**Afterlife**
Christianity	30 AD, Israel	2.0 billion	One God	Heaven/Hell
Islam	622 AD, Saudi Arabia	1.3 billion	Allah	Paradise/Hell
Atheism	Ancient Greece	1.1 billion	none	none
Hinduism	Indigenous to India	900 million	Brahman	Reincarnation
Chinese	Indigenous to China	394 million	yin and yang	Reincarnation
Buddhism	520 BC	360 million	Buddha	Reincarnation
Judaism	1300 BC, Hebrews	14 million	Yahweh	Heaven-Lite
Mormonism	1830 AD, New York	12 million	The Father	Heaven/Hell

Religion Facts, currently tracks forty-three separate belief systems, including fourteen recognized religions that espouse some form of reincarnation-lite. Someday, maybe they will track *The ILC Theory*, not as a religion, but as a fact of life.

The Theory wholeheartedly embraces the First Amendment, freedom of religion, because of all the positive attributes that it entails. All religions should have the right to exist, even the misguided, violence-oriented Muslim groups, at their own peril.

As a side note, *The Theory* also supports wholeheartedly the Second Amendment. After all, Earth is still only classified as a C4-IP, with an

The Intelligent LifeCycle Theory

L4.4 average Sapien population. We have not yet progressed far enough as a civilization to have the luxury of not needing personal physical protection against the evil that still exists on our planet. But we will get there.

Imagine in some future LifeCycle, we live in a world that is totally void of all violence, fear and deceit, and prevalent in personal freedoms, love and trust. Civilization on Earth is definitely headed in the right direction, but we have a long way to go. And our progress is measurable, via average SROs and SERs.

When Earth makes the jump to a C5 IP, such negative ICTs will hopefully continue to subside and should continue to decrease through its C6 IP development. However, Earth's culture may not be completely rid of such evil traits, until our Sapien population elevates the planet to C7 IP status.

At this point, *The Theory* needs to further explain several key occurrences in our planet's history. The subHalo that services a developing planet such as Earth has all available data from the hundreds of millions of Sapiens going in and out of their LiveTimes on Earth every year. And from that data, the development progress of the planet is measured.

When a planet like Earth, which is seen as a good Sapien evolution platform, begins to develop negatively instead of positively, the subHalo L9 In Charge (L9IC) may request an intervention. As a planet continues to evolve in the wrong direction, a HIT (Halo Intervention Transfer) assignment may be necessary to get the planet back on track as a good, positive Sapien provider.

When an intelligent planet's Sapien averages begin to drop, it is recognizable at the subHalo level by the averages of its SROs and SERs. By monitoring the in/out Sapien traffic of an IP, an overall drop in average Sapien requirements is easily identified. If Sapien development on an IP remains stagnant for too long, it might be the precursor to negative leanings in the future.

In communications with the Halo's L10 control board, the subHalo L9IC might request assistance from a *Roving L*. Roving L8s/L9s go between worlds that need help in developing in the right direction as an intelligent planets. A Roving L8 might first be chosen to perform the HIT, if the IP is considered to be a relative risk but not sufficient to warrant an L9 HIT.

Around 1500 BC, *Moses*, a Roving L8 from the MilkyWay subHalo, was sent to Earth to help the planet's positive growth. His goal, unbeknownst to him, was to foster a more favorable evolutionary environment for Sapiens.

When he came down from the mountain top with the Ten Commandments, he did so to help ensure the Sapien development cycle on Earth would be based on good, moral and ethical principles. The goal of the subHalo is to develop its Sapien population and the Sapien population of its tens of thousands of intelligent planets toward a positive maturation, not a negative, evil one.

Evidently, the Ten Commandments were not sufficient to get Earth back on track. In today's terms, we needed 'a heavy-hitter'. Some fifteen hundred years later, a second HIT was seen as necessary. *Jesus Christ*, a Roving L9 was selected and sent to Earth.

Jesus occupied the body of a mortal man. He was born, he lived and he died. We have been taught that he made the ultimate sacrifice for mankind, dying on the cross for all of our sins. But what he really did was to show from example that we cannot give in to the evil that unfortunately exists in the universe.

Jesus did a tremendous job at getting Earth back on track as a good Sapien development hub. We still have evil among us of course, but that percentage should continue to reduce itself proportionate to the good Sapien population trying to live their daily lives the right way, with proper moral and ethical standards.

Christians believe there will be a second coming of Christ on Earth. *The Theory* believes this will not be necessary. However, considering the propagation of evil doctrines through the spread of certain Muslim sectors, Earth may require another HIT assignment. Conversely, such a major ICT event may not be needed, since freedom-loving Sapiens are so firmly entrenched in current cultures around the world so as to repel such backward encroachments on Sapien freedoms.

Earth is considered an intelligent planet with a solid evolutionary platform for effective and positive Sapien growth that may not need a third HIT. Other possible HITs in our history have been considered, with names like Noah and Gandhi. However, it is the opinion of *The ILC Theory* that Moses and Christ were the only two Roving Ls to HIT Earth during the Earth's current IP LifeCycle. Incidentally, Noah with his ark was probably an L3, which was good in those days.

So what are the alternatives to *The Intelligent LifeCycle Theory*? Do you believe that your soul (Sapien) just appears in the womb and just as quickly disappears when you die? Or is the soul sent from god to the embryo and upon death returns to god for all eternity? Or do you believe the Sapien (soul) is dynamic, constantly growing and developing through multiple LiveTimes?

The Intelligent LifeCycle Theory

If the scientific approach to intelligent life redistribution makes sense, then *The ILC Theory*, which contains many of the components of most mainstream religions, makes sense. Please keep in mind, *The ILC Theory* is just that, a theory, not a religion.

If you believe your Sapien was put on this planet one time for one life, and at the end of that life, you either go to heaven or hell, that is fine, that is your belief. It gives you something to believe in, something to take away the fear of death. As painful as it may seem, death should not be feared. It is just the portal to the next LC.

It sure seems hard to believe that we are put on this Earth for one short period, and we either make it work or we do not. And we either go to heaven or hell when this one life is over. That just can't be right. We spend seventy plus years developing our person (Sapien), and then it's over. Doesn't that seem like a significant waste of time and energy?

We spend our whole lives developing as human beings, and then we expect to go to heaven and as an incomplete entity at best. Or if we are bad, then we go to hell with no shot at redemption. That seems too black and white for such an important, highly dynamic, highly fluid phenomena such as intelligent life in the universe.

Traditional religions are to be applauded of course. As early as only a few thousand years ago, with the advent of the Ten Commandments, religion has led the way in forging our legal system of rights and wrongs and punishing those who commit crimes against humanity.

The Ten Commandments are intrinsic doctrines in our laws. They help us to be a better, more civilized, more advanced society and species. They have allowed Earth to become a more positive breeding ground for positive Sapien development in the universe.

Traditional religions, along with *The ILC Theory*, address the fact that people have the need to believe in something bigger than themselves, or a higher power. *The Theory* offers a logical explanation for that higher power based on physics and the natural laws of the universe.

For those people who do not believe in a god, *The Theory* offers a new belief structure that answers questions about the afterlife, based on science instead of pure faith. And as important, it answers the question of why we are truly here.

The Intelligent LifeCycle Theory is about the perpetuation and evolution of intelligent life in the universe. It can provide an alternative belief system for those who want to know what happens after death, without it being based on blind faith.

The Theory is based on some semblance of statistical analysis, scientific data, reasoning and logic. It makes sense. *The ILC Theory* does seem to transcend other religious beliefs, but at the same time, it also supports many traditional religious standards and five of the original Ten Commandments.

Other religious leaders, such as Mahatma Gandhi, the thirteen Dalai Lamas, Mohammed and others throughout history may have been highly developed L7s. And as highly developed L7s in an L3/L4 world environment, they had significant impact on millions of lives.

Religious leaders are Sapiens that proclaim good shall prevail over evil and morality is better than depravity. In the case of Mohammed, the issue becomes a questionable precept at best.

If a god instructs its flock to eradicate all non-Muslim believers, all infidels, then that god would be ruling its congregation through fear and violence. I think not. Instead of a god advocating violence and death, shouldn't a god be benevolent and caring and advocate peace?

Consistent with *The Theory*, some have said that the Father, Son and the Holy Ghost are represented by the controlling L10 board, a Roving L9 and the subHalo, where the Sapien goes after death. In theory, this type of comparison, although interesting, should only be considered from the functionality perspective. In that sense, the functions of the three components may be similar, minus the religious overtones.

According to the bible, at thirty-eight, Jesus, a Roving L9, had the "day of reckoning" confrontation with the devil when he was tested for forty days and forty nights. This proved that he could endure anything and would continue to stand up against the devil, against evil. In religious history, this forty day ordeal firmly positioned Jesus as the Son of God in religious sectors in many parts of the world.

When Roving Ls take LifeCycle assignments around the universe, they must go through the same rigors of other Sapiens. They must be born, they must live and grow, and then they must die. It is the normal *Intelligent LifeCycle* in the universe.

Such advanced L8 and L9 Sapiens must mature within the cultures afforded them in the worlds that they are sent to help. So as these advanced Sapiens grow into adulthood, they begin to empathize with the lower level Sapien population of a world, as they themselves struggle with the cruel realities of life. They introduce moral concepts that need to be followed to get a planet's evolution of life back on track toward a positive development curve.

The Intelligent LifeCycle Theory

The following is Rembrandt's 1659 rendition of Moses coming down from the mountain top with the Ten Commandments.

From the Yorck Project: *10.000 Meisterwerke der Malerei*, 2002. ISBN 3936122202. Distributed by Direct Media Publishing.

If you believe in a god, shouldn't you believe he or she is benevolent, not violent? And shouldn't he or she want our Spirits to continue to evolve, longer than a mere seventy plus years in one lifetime?

To put it all in perspective, according to *The Intelligent LifeCycle Theory*, the Halo L10 board members, god status Sapiens, who now control the universe, were L1s at one time, trillions and trillions of years ago. We can only speculate how, where and when it all began.

The Intelligent LifeCycle Theory

Individual Sapien Analysis Testing

All Individual Character Traits (ICTs) are common to all Sapiens. However, the combination of all ICTs interacting together, each with varying degrees of development, is what makes each Sapien unique. And that is why we can quantify and measure Sapien development with the *Individual Sapien Analysis Testing (ISAT)* system.

A Sapien's ICTs develop over many LifeCycles, hopefully in the positive direction. Groups of ICTs (ICT sets), most commonly referred to as personality or emotions, can be scored to arrive at an overall Sapien development level. Sapien scores and ratings generally indicate the percentage of the Sapien's character traits, parental influence and intelligence that it has developed to date.

Example: A Sapien with an overall IEF rating of L5.4 has developed about 54 percent of its capacity as an intelligent entity. The same Sapien may have a 6.7 rating for its patience ICT, which means the Sapien's patience is about two-thirds developed.

The Intelligent LifeCycle Theory

There are two ways to complete your ISAT.

1. Manually:
   a) Read the groups of Negative ICTs and Positive ICTs associated with each ICT set.
   b) Rate yourself on a point scale from 1 to 10 for each ICT set, with at least one decimal, 5.5 for example. If you wish, you can drill down further with your self-analysis by rating each individual ICT pair under each ICT set. You might want to just rate yourself for each ICT set as a group, your first time. You can fine tune it later and use it to track your own progress during this LC.
   c) Complete the ten KEY ICT sets. Calculate the average and multiply by 20 percent.
   d) Complete the seventy-five Supporting ICT sets. Calculate the average and multiply by 40 percent.
   e) Make estimates of your parents ISAT ratings, unless your parents already have their SQs. Average both parents Sapien L ratings for your parental overlay and multiply by 20 percent.
   f) Rate your intelligence by converting your IQ to IM and multiply your IM by 20 percent. *(See IQ & Intelligence Module in Appendix)*
   g) Total your weighted scores from c through f above. This is your IEF Rating, representing your level of development as a Sapien.
   h) Multiply your IEF by 100. This is your current SQ Score.

Example: Your average Key ICT score is 5.45 with an average Supporting ICT score of 5.65. Your estimate of your father's overall IEF was 4.60 and your mother's IEF was 4.40, for an average 4.50 parental overlay rating at the time of your birth. Your Intelligence Module is 7.10. Your IEF Level would then be an L5.67. You would be considered a 5.7 Sapien with an SQ of 567, and probably have eight to ten LCs under your belt.

2. Online:
   a) Go to our website: www.ILCTheory.com
   b) Sign up as an ILC Member.
   c) Complete your own interactive ISAT ratings.
   d) The ISAT App will do all the calculations for you and create graphs, charts and your SQ Certificate.
   e) Save and print your personalized SQ Certificate and personal development graphs and charts, with your SQ score in PDF format suitable for framing.

As you analyze and rate your Sapien's development levels, please keep in mind, L7s are considered highly evolved Sapiens. A Sapien with an L8 IEF is considered to have reached pure wisdom. An L9 Sapien is considered angel status. With the exception of Roving L8s and L9s, these two Sapien levels are no longer in circulation and may only recycle through an intelligent world's evolution a few times in a planet's history.

And an L10 is perfection personified. As one of the controllers of the universe, who hasn't been in circulation for some time, it is not likely an L10 Sapien would appear on a planet like Earth.

When you are evaluating your ICTs, you may legitimately score a 9.0 or higher on a specific ICT, as unlikely as it might be, if you truly believe you are near perfect with regard to that ICT. Even so, scoring that high on an entire ICT set is not that probable, in reality.

Keep in mind, there are no bad scores or good scores. Your ISAT ratings represent where you are in your own Sapien development journey over many LifeCycles to date. There seems to be a direct relationship between ISAT Scores and the number of LCs. *See Sapien Chapter, Sapien Development Levels for LC estimates.*

Normal Distribution Bell Curve for SQ

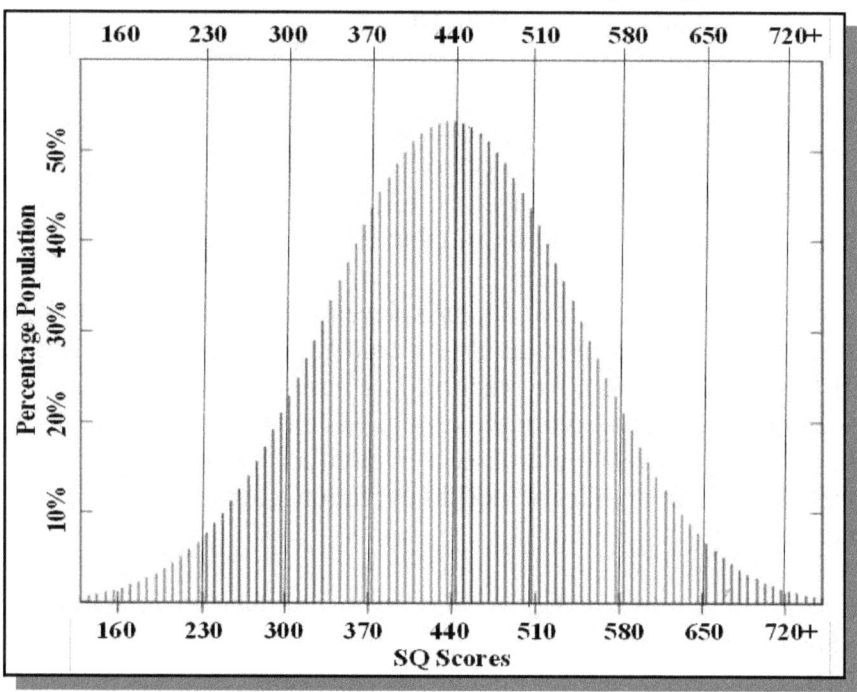

According to the bell curve above, Earth's Sapien population is expected to consist of approximately 95 percent with SQ Scores between 230 and 650. Although the SQ rating system is subjective, scoring results are estimates at best. However, the range of its parameters is sufficient for ILC purposes.

SQ scores, like IQ scores, fit very neatly into a standard bell curve graphical representation. However, SQs are unlike IQs in that they measure Individual Character Trait development as well as Intelligence.

The reason for doing the ISAT is not just to get your Sapien score and an estimate of your LCs. This process gives you the opportunity to properly evaluate your character traits so that you can identify which ones need help in developing. You will benefit more from this exercise, if you are brutally honest with your personal assessments, than you would by just posting an artificially high score.

Movie Quote: "Burlesque", 2010, Cher, Christina Aguilera. Cher speaks to her ex-husband about his ICTs, "Look. You've got some fine qualities, and then you have some iffy qualities. But you've never been a phony."

There are eighty-five ICT sets, representing over five hundred Individual Character Traits. The ISAT App is very straight forward. It is an exercise that is well worth your time, and it's fun too. Read the groups of positive and negative ICTs related to each ICT set. Rate how you perceive yourself in relation to these groups of words from 1 to 10.

The Individual Character Traits of a Sapien represent nearly 80 percent of the Sapien Rating Score. ICTs are divided into two groups: Key ICTs (20 percent), and Supporting ICTs (40 percent). In addition, the parental overlay's ICT sets, which represent the majority of their ratings, account for another 20 percent. This is included in the ISAT, since the parental overlay was used as minimum SRO targets for the initial Sapien match as well as directly affecting the Sapien's development from birth to early adulthood.

The Sapien's intelligence component (20 percent) does not have any ICTs in its structure. However, it does directly impact the development of most ICTs throughout its LC evolution.

There are ten Key ICT sets that are considered to be more important to the proper development of the Sapien, even though all ICTs are created equal. In addition, there are seventy-five ICT sets that support ICT development. Each ICT set is comprised of multiple ICT pairs, with which to evaluate the Sapien's character trait development levels.

Evaluating your own ICT sets will provide you with a good picture of your overall Sapien development to date. This in turn will give you an idea of how many LifeCycles you have had so far.

Just take your time and have some fun. Rate yourself on a scale of 1 to 10 as to how you perceive yourself, as earnestly as possible. Remember this self-analysis will only be beneficial, if you are as honest with yourself as possible. There are no good or bad scores, as long as you are honest with yourself without fabricating artificially high ICT levels. Anyone can do that. The soul-searching aspect of the evaluation process is what is important.

Movie Quote: "People vs. Larry Flynt", 1996, Woody Harrelson, Courtney Love. Harrelson talks to his brother about a new dancer in his topless club that looks too young. The brother says, "She's got an ID". Harrelson replies, "Hell, my dog can get an ID..... for my goat."

KEY ICT SETS

SANCTITY OF LIFE
"The way in which a Sapien views the importance of human life."

       <u>**Negative (1.0)**</u> ⟶ <u>**Positive (10.0)**</u>

Set 01: Sanctity of Life I
Antisocial	Sociable
Brutal	Humane
Violent	Passive
Cruel	Kindhearted
Disrespectful	Respectful

                                             Set 01 Rating: _____

Set 02: Sanctity of Life II
Evil	Goodhearted
Sinful	Virtuous
Immoral	Moral
Insensitive	Compassionate
Selfish	Selfless

                                             Set 02 Rating: _____

FREEDOM
"The degree to which a Sapien regards his or her freedoms."

Set 03: Freedom I
Witless	Wise
Confined	Freewill
Cowardly	Courageous
Fearful	Assertive
Tired	Spirited

                                             Set 03 Rating: _____

Negative (1.0) ━━━▶ **Positive (10.0)**

Set 04: Freedom II
    Fainthearted   Adventurous
    Intimidated   Dauntless
    Undeserving   Proud
    Subordinated   Independent
    Timid   Intrepid
                                    Set 04 Rating: _____

GENDER RELATIONS
"The ability of a Sapien to establish, nurture and maintain mature and intimate relations with another Sapien."

Set 05: Gender Relations I
    Aloof   Affectionate
    Indifferent   Caring
    Demeaning   Deferential
    Detached   Adoring
    Manipulative   Loving
                                    Set 05 Rating: _____

Set 06: Gender Relations II
    Frigidity   Sexual-normalcy
    Promiscuous   Faithful
    Dominating   Accepting
    Jealous   Trusting
    Lewdness   Prudish
                                    Set 06 Rating: _____

EFFICACY

"The ability of a Sapien to produce a desired and intended result, with the willful following of fellow Sapiens, critical to enhancing LiveTime conditions during LCs."

<u>Negative (1.0)</u> ━━━▶ **<u>Positive (10.0)</u>**

Set 07: Efficacy I

Dependent	Risk-taker
Disorganized	Organized
Follower	Leader
Lazy	Ambitious
Reserved	Enterprising

Set 07 Rating: _____

Set 08: Efficacy II

Ineffective	Effective
Incompetent	Competent
Indecisive	Decisive
Unimaginative	Resourceful
Insecure	Confident

Set 08 Rating: _____

SPIRITUAL

"The moral beliefs held by a Sapien that affect its decision-making during current LiveTime events."

Set 09: Spiritual I

Non-believer	Believer
Secular	Religious
Faithless	Devout
Godlessness	Belief in God
Irreverent	Sacredness

Set 09 Rating: _____

The Intelligent LifeCycle Theory

Negative (1.0) ━━━▶ **Positive (10.0)**

Set 10: Spiritual II
    Deceitful   Trustworthy
    Dishonest   Honest
    Immoral   Moral
    Hateful   Magnanimous
    Malevolent   Benevolent
                                     Set 10 Rating: _____

That concludes the five Key ICT sets that are used as primary ICT matches between the parental overlay and your SRO prior to birth. Key ICT sets represents 20 percent of your overall ISAT Score.

The following seventy-five supporting ICT sets are as important in providing your overall ISAT scoring and ultimately a well-balanced, growth-oriented future. Supporting ICT sets account for 40 percent of your overall ISAT Score.

SUPPORTING ICT SETS

Negative (1.0) ⟶ **Positive (10.0)**

Set 11	Caustic Inhospitable Introverted	Amiable Hospitable Extroverted **Set 11 Rating:** _____
Set 12	Objectionable Obnoxious Offensive	Congenial Affable Likable **Set 12 Rating:** _____
Set 13	Reclusive Sad Unfriendly	Gregarious Happy Friendly **Set 13 Rating:** _____
Set 14	Absentminded Daydreaming Distracted	Engaged Immersed Attentive **Set 14 Rating:** _____
Set 15	Neglectful Oblivious Preoccupied	Focused Observant Alert **Set 15 Rating:** _____
Set 16	Complacent Hapless Obstinate	Aggressive Tenacious Felicitous **Set 16 Rating:** _____

	Negative (1.0) ⟶	**Positive (10.0)**
Set 17	Hesitant Conflicted Reticent	Eager Hopeful Willing **Set 17 Rating:** _____
Set 18	Barbaric Combative Confrontational	Kindhearted Passive Patient **Set 18 Rating:** _____
Set 19	Destructive Hostile Fatalistic	Tolerant Peaceful Idealistic **Set 19 Rating:** _____
Set 20	Pugnacious Contentious Argumentative	Conciliatory Pacific Peaceable **Set 20 Rating:** _____
Set 21	Boring Dull Fearful	Daring Visionary** Fearless **Set 21 Rating:** _____
Set 22	Spineless Timid Uninspired	Valiant Bold Innovative **Set 22 Rating:** _____

The Intelligent LifeCycle Theory

	Negative (1.0) ⟶	**Positive (10.0)**
Set 23	Disagreeable Distrustful Envious	Agreeable Trusting Altruistic **Set 23 Rating:** _____
Set 24	Careless Impetuous Impulsive	Careful Diligent Meticulous **Set 24 Rating:** _____
Set 25	Negligent Reckless Oblivious	Watchful Cautious Observant **Set 25 Rating:** _____
Set 26	Inconsiderate Insensitive Rude	Considerate Sensitive Polite **Set 26 Rating:** _____
Set 27	Tacky Tactless Thoughtless	Dignified Tactful Thoughtful **Set 27 Rating:** _____
Set 28	Unkind Vulgar Quarrelsome	Sweet Genteel Cordial **Set 28 Rating:** _____

The Intelligent LifeCycle Theory

	Negative (1.0) ⟶	**Positive (10.0)**
Set 29	Crude Foolish Imprudent	Sophisticated Shrewd Prudent **Set 29 Rating:** _____
Set 30	Indiscreet Indiscriminant Undiplomatic	Discreet Discriminant Diplomatic **Set 30 Rating:** _____
Set 31	Dumb Unperceptive Brainless	Sapient Clever Brainy **Set 31 Rating:** _____
Set 32	Bland Dull Unproductive	Creative Keen Imaginative **Set 32 Rating:** _____
Set 33	Fraudulent Imitative Misleading	Genuine Promethean Truthful **Set 33 Rating:** _____
Set 34	Petty Liberal Narrow-minded	Charitable Conservative Broad-minded **Set 34 Rating:** _____

The Intelligent LifeCycle Theory

	Negative (1.0) ⟶	**Positive (10.0)**
Set 35	Abstract Vacillating Doubtful	Precise Purposeful Exacting **Set 35 Rating:** _____
Set 36	Apprehensive Lackadaisical Vague	Deliberate Incisive Thorough **Set 36 Rating:** _____
Set 37	Impatient Insatiable Irritable	Accepting Satisfied Genial **Set 37 Rating:** _____
Set 38	Corrupt Criminal Decadent	Incorruptible Unimpeachable Principled **Set 38 Rating:** _____
Set 39	Deceitful Disgraceful Hypocritical	Truthful Commendable Earnest **Set 39 Rating:** _____
Set 40	Dishonorable Immoral Sinful	Honorable Moral Virtuous **Set 40 Rating:** _____

Negative (1.0) ⟶ **Positive (10.0)**

Set 41 Sly Straightforward
  Sneaky Candid
  Shameful Shameless
    Set 41 Rating: _____

Set 42 Unconscionable Conscionable
  Unethical Ethical
  Unscrupulous Scrupulous
    Set 42 Rating: _____

Set 43 Belligerent Serene
  Complaining Tolerant
  Confrontational Amicable
    Set 43 Rating: _____

Set 44 Cowardly Brave
  Unheroic Heroic
  Weak Strong
    Set 44 Rating: _____

Set 45 Fainthearted Stalwart
  Gutless Determined
  Inconspicuous Audacious
    Set 45 Rating: _____

Set 46 Untrustworthy Trustworthy
  Traitorous Loyal
  Unreliable Reliable
    Set 46 Rating: _____

The Intelligent LifeCycle Theory

	Negative (1.0) ⟹	**Positive (10.0)**
Set 47	Dry Frownful Pathos	Witty Comical Humorous **Set 47 Rating:** _____
Set 48	Anguish Tormented Cursed	Cheerful Jovial Joyous **Set 48 Rating:** _____
Set 49	Sarcastic Sober Sorrowful	Funny Playful Fun **Set 49 Rating:** _____
Set 50	Arrogant Brash Conceited	Humble Quiet Humility **Set 50 Rating:** _____
Set 51	Egotistic Pompous Pretentious	Demure Temperate Modesty **Set 51 Rating:** _____
Set 52	Submissive Subservient Undisciplined	Impotent Initiative Disciplined **Set 52 Rating:** _____

Negative (1.0) ⟶ **Positive (10.0)**

Set 53	Anger Infuriating Enraged	Tranquil Comforting Tempered **Set 53 Rating:** _____
Set 54	Mischievous Rowdy Uncivil	Composed Inconspicuous Civil **Set 54 Rating:** _____
Set 55	Abomination Coldhearted Cruel	Love Warmhearted Gentle **Set 55 Rating:** _____
Set 56	Cynical Pessimistic Defeatist	Sentimental Optimistic Transcendent **Set 56 Rating:** _____
Set 57	Flirtatious Secretive Promiscuous	Innocent Overt Homogeneous **Set 57 Rating:** _____
Set 58	Spiteful Exasperating Malicious	Sympathetic Calm Gracious **Set 58 Rating:** _____

	Negative (1.0) ⟶	**Positive (10.0)**
Set 59	Frigid Abstinence Nuisance	Sultry Intimate Passionate **Set 59 Rating:** _____
Set 60	Unromantic Indifferent Weary	Romantic Devoted Spirited **Set 60 Rating:** _____
Set 61	Obscene Abusive Loathing	Mannerly Innocuous Pleasing **Set 61 Rating:** _____
Set 62	Lascivious Lewd Nymphomania	Wholesome Decent Celibate **Set 62 Rating:** _____
Set 63	Promiscuous Undersexed Undesirable	Chaste Horny Desirable **Set 63 Rating:** _____
Set 64	Self-centered Shallow Shy	Self-assured Analytical Assured **Set 64 Rating:** _____

The Intelligent LifeCycle Theory

	Negative (1.0) ⟶ **Positive (10.0)**	
Set 65	Spendthrift Extravagant Lavish	Economical Prudent Wise **Set 65 Rating:** _____
Set 66	Miserly Cheapskate Stingy	Thrifty Sensible Frugal **Set 66 Rating:** _____
Set 67	Addictive Compulsive Obsessive	Controllable Resistible Willful **Set 67 Rating:** _____
Set 68	Subdued Unresponsive Obedient	Liberated Responsive Self-reliant **Set 68 Rating:** _____
Set 69	Inexperienced Ineffective Inefficient	Experienced Proficient Efficient **Set 69 Rating:** _____
Set 70	Inept Shallow Slow-witted	Capable Well-rounded Sharp **Set 70 Rating:** _____

	Negative (1.0) ⟶	**Positive (10.0)**
Set 71	Cynic Diffident Fearful	Visionary Unabashed Risk-taker **Set 71 Rating:** _____
Set 72	Carefree Disorganized Haphazard	Methodical Organized Structured **Set 72 Rating:** _____
Set 73	Apathetic Coldblooded Detrimental	Concerned Warmblooded Benign **Set 73 Rating:** _____
Set 74	Disinterested Dispassionate Halfhearted	Zealous Passionate Gung Ho **Set 74 Rating:** _____
Set 75	Angry Antagonistic Apathetic	Content Empathetic Understanding **Set 75 Rating:** _____
Set 76	Unmotivated Undiscriminating Undemanding	Driven Meticulous Fastidious **Set 76 Rating:** _____

	Negative (1.0) ⟶	**Positive (10.0)**
Set 77	Impersonal Unemotional Lax	Demonstrative Emotional Discerning **Set 77 Rating:** _____
Set 78	Petty Narrow-minded Biased	Objective Open-minded Unbiased **Set 78 Rating:** _____
Set 79	Impractical Dreamer Unrealistic	Practical Pragmatist Realistic **Set 79 Rating:** _____
Set 80	Unmanageable Unruly Immature	Manageable Reserved Mature **Set 80 Rating:** _____
Set 81	Indignant Moody Neurotic	Amenable Serene Sensible **Set 81 Rating:** _____
Set 82	Temper Unpleasant Depressed	Restrained Pleasant Euphoric **Set 82 Rating:** _____

The Intelligent LifeCycle Theory

	Negative (1.0) ⟶ **Positive (10.0)**	
Set 83	Boisterous	Restrained
	Cocky	Prideful
	Defiant	Cooperative
		Set 83 Rating: _____
Set 84	Disrespectful	Respectful
	Offensive	Courteous
	Ungrateful	Gracious
		Set 84 Rating: _____
Set 85	Jealous	Trusting
	Suspicious	Understanding
	Possessive	Permissive
		Set 85 Rating: _____

The Intelligent LifeCycle Theory

ISAT Summary

Key ICT Rating: *(10 ICT Sets)* _____
To calculate your average key ICT rating, total all of your key ICT set ratings, divide by 10 and multiply by 20 percent.

Supporting ICT Rating: *(75 ICT Sets)* _____
To calculate your average supporting ICT rating, total all of your supporting ICT set ratings, divide by 75 and multiply by 40 percent.

Parental Overlay Rating: _____
To calculate your parents' average overall Sapien ratings at the time of your birth, add estimates of both parents' IEF ratings, divide by 2 and multiply by 20 percent.

Note: If your parents have already completed their own ISATs, you can use their accredited IEF ratings. However, if you wish to drill down even further, you can reduce your parental overlay average IEF ratings to compensate for enhancements they may have made in their own ICTs during this life, since your birth. This will give you a more accurate assessment of your Sapien level, since your parental overlay component at the time of your birth was included in your original SRO, at an early stage during their own ICT development in this LC.

Intelligence Module Rating: _____
Rate your intelligence by converting your IQ to IM, then multiply by 20 percent. *Refer to IQ and Intelligence Module in Appendix.*

IEF-ISAT Rating: _____
Add the four weighted ratings above. This is your overall IEF Level and ISAT Rating.

SQ Score: _____
Multiply your IEF by 100. This is your Sapien Quotient.

ILC Theory Summation

There are many facets to *The Intelligent Life Cycle Theory*, so much that it required this 450 page book to explain it all. *The Theory*, in its totality, combines many elements of psychology, religion, science and technology to effectively tell the story of intelligent life in the universe.

The ILC Theory goes way beyond today's reincarnation beliefs. It adds logic, reasoning, functionality and scientific infrastructure to the concept of living multiple times. It is a comprehensive theory about the development, evolution and perpetuation of intelligent life in the universe and beyond.

Traditionally, there have been three schools of thought pertaining to the evolution of mankind: *Determinism, Randomness* and *Free Will*. If *The ILC Theory* was considered the fourth theory of the evolution of mankind, it might be called *Intergyism* (intelligent energy-ism).

As it applies to intelligent life throughout the universe, *The Theory's* methodology, reasoning and scientific relevance applies only to the mental aspects of the intelligent living species, and not the physical. This is assuming, of course, the body and soul are separate entities, which is the cornerstone of most religions.

Maybe *The ILC Theory* is the way in which intelligent life concepts are introduced into a world's culture as a planet evolves past traditional religious beliefs. *The Theory* does seem to fit right in with a number of evolutionary trends we have identified that makes it the next logical step in understanding the meaning of life.

The ILC Theory Summation is more of a philosophical one than the traditional summary format. But to satisfy the need for an actual summary of points included in this book, consider the following brief synopsis of *The Theory*.

Of all the factors that collectively work together to make *The ILC Theory* understandable, believable and acceptable, there are **eleven components** that are critical to operations. All of which are equally as important. None of which can be sacrificed without dramatically damaging the evolution and continuity of intelligent life in the universe.

The ***Sapien*** is the mental and intellectual part of a living being, one that requires intelligence to function. It is the Intelligent Energy Field (IEF) that occupies a physical host body. The Sapien is most commonly referred to on Earth as the soul, mind or spirit.

The basic assumption of *The ILC Theory* is that the Sapien is separate from the physical body. And since the Sapien is pure energy, intelligent energy, it cannot be created nor destroyed, only transferred between hosts.

The *Halo*, functionally similar to heaven, is the place where all advanced Sapiens go to retire after many, many *LifeCycles (LCs)*. The Halo is supported by *subHalos* in every galaxy in the universe. The 10^{11} subHalos are responsible for Sapien LifeCycle selections within their respective galaxies and database management of Sapiens during their RestTimes between LCs.

The LifeCycle of a Sapien begins, when a female Sapien is impregnated. The fetus in the womb begins to develop, based on a temporary energy field provided by both parents, called the parental overlay. As soon as the X and Y chromosomes are identifiable, indicating male or female, the parental overlay in the fetus transmits a *Sapien Request Order (SRO)* to the nearest subHalo, via the *Universal Energy Network (UENet)*.

The SRO specifies the Sapien qualities requested for the little fetus in the womb, specifically *Individual Character Trait (ICT)* and *Intelligence Module (IM)* development levels. The subHalo program searches all Sapiens in RestTime that meet SRO requirements with previous LC experience on the applicable *Intelligent Planet (IP)*.

Once a Sapien has been selected, the subHalo fulfills the SRO and sends the chosen Sapien to the IP to fill the energy void in the womb and fuse with the fetus via the UENet. This usually occurs by the end of the first trimester, when the mother can no longer sustain her own energy needs and the growing needs of the fetus.

Given a successful Sapien match and a successful birth, the child grows up exhibiting similar character traits and intelligence to those of its parents. As the physical body matures, the **Sapien Core** takes over and manages the maturation of its ICTs and Intelligence, according to the IP's socioeconomic environment.

As the person matures into adulthood, its ICTs and IM evolve as well. The character traits inherent in the Sapien's configuration adapt and respond to LiveTime ICT events, that shape its development as an intelligent being.

When the person dies, the Sapien's LC is terminated. Within a few tetraseconds, the Sapien-Brain Bridge disconnects, generating the **Sapien Exit Request (SER)**, which is sent to the UENet for pickup. Within another few tetraseconds, the Sapien is drawn back to the subHalo, for rest and rejuvenation. After which, the Sapien's LifeCycle process starts all over again.

Well, that's the mechanics of *The Theory*. Now, let's consider a few philosophical interpretations relating to how *The Intelligent LifeCycle Theory* impacts your life, your current LC and how you can use it to make your life better.

Other than birth and death, there are two things that occur during every LifeCycle, two things that are incontrovertible. The first absolute: every LC provides the Sapien with a unique combination of ICT events, from which to negotiate and hopefully benefit. And thus by definition, each new LC creates new opportunities in life, every time. So we have something to look forward to in our next cycle.

The second constant in every LifeCycle: you will make mistakes. You will unavoidably do things you regret in every LC, guaranteed. Because as we know, no one is perfect, not even close. If they were, they would already reside in the Halo or subHalo, as an L8 or L9.

The bottom line is this. Every Sapien, during every LC, will make mistakes (plural). And every Sapien, during every LC, will have regrets. That's life, but that's also what builds character.

So when you make your mistakes, and you are truly remorseful and genuinely take responsibility for your actions, your ICTs will improve as a result. With enhanced ICTs, your next LC should be better, not necessarily socially or financially, but better.

The vast majority of Sapiens in the universe develop their ICTs and IMs positively. Unfortunately, there are some Sapiens who develop negatively from LC to LC. It is like the yin-yang philosophy, in which everything has an opposite counterpart where positive and negative forces coexist.

The Theory's position on the good/evil issue is simple. According to ILC history, there has always been and will always be evil Sapiens among us. As an IP develops social and scientific advancements, the percentage of evil Sapiens decreases on the planet over time, as Earth has done over the last few hundred years.

Evil and violence become less of a factor in a planet's Sapien growth once technological advancements begin to shape society. However, because of the technology explosion, evil thoughts and actions become more powerful and more acute, much faster.

The good news is, we can use technology to combat evil without having to commit tens of thousands of troops to the timeless struggle of good versus evil. By increasing the exposure of Western culture to third world countries, over time, the Sapien populations of those backward regions will begin to adopt the ideals of freedom. And by doing so, average Sapien ratings will improve. If we can raise the average Sapien levels in certain third world countries, Earth should be able to make the jump from our current Class 4 (C4) rating to a C5 IP.

To accomplish this, the Sapien citizenry of repressed countries around the world will need to dramatically increase their awareness of human rights and demand more personal freedoms. This movement, which has already begun in a number of developing countries, will continue to create more turmoil in the streets.

Sapiens, who were previously restricted in their freedoms, will attempt to take more control over their LCs in increasing numbers. This global movement toward Sapien freedoms, however slow as it may seem, celebrates several of the *Ten Rules of Intelligent Life*. This is good.

By today's standards however, evil still has a sizable position in Earth's current evolution. Even though it will continue to decrease, evil will be with us for at least another few LC generations. Evil will not be completely eradicated from our societies, until Earth progresses to the Class 7 IP level. But hey, that's life, deal with it.

Fortunately, the vast majority of Sapiens progress through their LCs, positively developing their character traits and intelligence. Most of us choose right over wrong, good over evil, honesty over deceit and improvement over debasement. And that is what builds character, Individual Character Traits that is. But hey, that's life too, enjoy it.

Intelligent life as we know it has been around for trillions of years on trillions of planets. In all probability, there are different species of physical lifeforms that host Sapien LCs on some planets. However, the human lifeform on Earth seems to be a good species capable of building worlds that provide Sapiens with quality LiveTimes during their LCs.

Because of its physical capabilities, which includes the brain, homo sapiens, or variations thereof, are expected to be one of the more dominant physical lifeforms that support intelligent life. Over the last few thousand millenniums, Earth-type homo sapiens are thought to have been replicated as the dominant species on many other intelligent worlds around the universe. Such worlds have proven to be excellent evolution platforms for Sapien development and are expected to continue as the planets progress in their individual C levels.

Following such discussions, the same questions invariably arise. How and when did it all start? How was the Halo originally formed? And what is the origin of Sapien intelligence? Well, if you believe there is an endless universe or possibly multiple universes, the answers to such questions become more complex. The truth is, nobody knows, at least no Sapien below L8 status.

When you consider infinity, with reference to time and space, the question of origination becomes a moot point and immaterial. Infinity applies to *The Theory* in one simple statement. "Intelligent life in the universe had no beginning, and has no end."

"The Intelligent Life Cycle Theory" describes, analyzes and rationalizes the current system from which we have evolved over trillions of years. This is the same system with which we will continue to evolve for the next few trillion years. *The ILC Theory* is "infinity on steroids" but quantifiable, if you can imagine that.

This infinite but quantifiable theory can be used as an analytical tool to enhance current and future LCs. Here's the part where we get personal. And after all, if *The ILC Theory* is valid, it can be used to evaluate your current life and help improve some of your ICTs that need attention. And by doing so, it should help enhance your future LCs as a matter of course.

As you begin to understand the ramifications of *The Theory* and how it affects you in your current life, you have the opportunity to see your life from a fresh perspective. And by doing so, you have the opportunity to make adjustments to your current LC for possible improvements that could also enhance your future LifeCycles.

When you monitor your ICTs, you cannot help but improve them. No matter what your situation in life, it can always get better. And it will, if you work on your ICTs. You will not only improve your current LiveTime during this LC, but you will enhance your possibilities for a better LC next time.

As you come to the realization that you have certain good character traits and some deficient ones too, you are half the way there. The next step is to focus on those ICTs that you can improve during this LC and possibly delay work on others maybe not as critical. Keep in mind, you will have many more future LCs to work on the rest of them.

The key to ICT improvement is the ability to take responsibility for your words and actions. Consider the slogan, "the buck stops here". When you adopt this philosophy, ICT improvements will begin to automatically evolve. You may have a natural inclination to place blame for your actions on others. You may want to blame your lot in life as the reason for your lack of success. You may want to use *The ILC Theory* as a crutch to justify why it is not your fault. Do not do this. It only impedes your ICT development. And it may also be detrimental to your overall Sapien growth, which could negatively affect your future LCs.

Once you have identified certain traits that need improvement, you should consciously work on them. Individual Character Traits do not improve themselves. With the proper attitude, enhancing your ICTs is not work, it is very gratifying. Improving ICTs is good.

Every Sapien in the universe not yet elevated to L8 status or higher has varying degrees of negative ICTs. Having a negative ICT does not mean you are evil. If you have a number of negative ICTs, you are not necessarily evil, if you work to improve on them. By working on them and attempting to improve them in itself means you are not evil.

However, if you really think you are evil, you just might be. But that condition is not necessarily irreversible. You can turn evil into good, by working on those evil character traits. If not, your future may be fewer LCs that are further apart, on C1 or C2 IPs. It is your decision.

For most Sapiens though, improving ICTs is very attainable. At the end of an LC, we hope we have made positive enhancements to our Sapiens' development, when possible. Success or failure of a Sapien's LC is not related to economic success.

A poor Sapien may experience different challenges during LiveTime, than if he or she were rich. Even though ICT events for rich and poor may differ somewhat in magnitude, opportunities to develop Sapien character traits in any given LC are equal, regardless of economic status in society.

If you are at the top of your game during this LC, congratulations. You became successful, made lots of money and lots of friends, theoretical and otherwise. That is good. Hopefully, your success contributed to better living conditions for other Sapiens during their own LCs.

Financial success has a tendency to make an LC more enjoyable. However, sometimes money may create more hardships and difficulties for a Sapien, just because he or she is rich. Adversity breeds character trait advancement, whether you are rich or poor.

If you are rich this time, enjoy it while it lasts. If you are poor, enjoy those things you do have. Your next LC will most assuredly be different. And if you improved your Sapien this trip, your next one should be better, not necessarily financially, but better. It is all up to you.

As you evaluate your successes and failures during your current LC, you should be able to gain a better understanding of your strengths and weaknesses and how they affect your everyday life. When you get the opportunity, try to capitalize on your strong ICTs and work on improving your weak ones.

Your success as a Sapien is not contingent upon financial rewards, societal acclaim nor individual recognition. It is dependent upon your ability to positively enhance your Sapien traits. This is especially important if traditional religions are right, and you only have one shot at life, which *The Theory* disputes, of course.

So given the fact that you will have more LCs to come, do not spend too much time worrying about your hardships. Try to benefit from them, Sapien-wise. It is just part of the trip, part of the ride, part of the package. Your next LC should be better, if you improve your Sapien traits during this life. Of course, it could be much worse, if you are in fact an evil Sapien. But one thing is for sure, it will not be boring.

One of the things that makes life not so boring is the SH Factor. It is omnipresent in all of our LCs. When, not if, but when Sh*t Happens, it usually connotes having a bad day. But now that you are aware of the SH Factor's existence, you may be able to accept it more easily, when it happens, even though it is by definition unexpected.

Theoretically, the SH Factor can hit you at random or appear as a result of bad luck in some aspect of your personal life. Regardless, ICT events that encompass the SH Factor may have some socially redeeming quality, however minute it may be. All you can do is try to make the best of it, smile and move on.

On the bright side, random events do occasionally end with positive results. Either way, ICT events build ICTs. Or to put it another way, Sh*t builds character, learn from it.

At some point in your life, you will attempt to judge what kind of contributions you have made during your current LC. If you are somebody like Steve Jobs, who contributed greatly to technology advancements, which translated into improved living conditions for millions of Sapiens, good for you.

If you are a janitor at a local high school, a realtor, a dentist or a teacher, your contributions may be more local in nature but just as important. If you improve your own Sapien traits while positively affecting LCs of others, your LiveTime, this time, will be considered a success, regardless of your monetary rewards or lack thereof.

It is important to understand that your Sapien rating is not intelligence-centric. Your IM accounts for only 20 percent of your overall rating.

The other 80 percent is comprised of ICT development levels, resulting from your parental overlay and your own ICT events during this LC and all your previous LCs.

High intelligence does not necessarily equate to a high Sapien Quotient (SQ), just as lower intelligence ratings do not necessarily equate to a lower SQ. This is life, and it is certainly complex. But it can also very enjoyable and gratifying, if done right.

Sapien ratings and their respective SQs represent pure statistical analysis, which identify averages and deviations from the average, or norm. If you think you are the norm, then you may in fact be the average. And that is good. It makes you a standard-bearer of the norm. Your contributions to life can be as significant as any other Sapien in any LiveTime on any IP in the universe.

An average, normal Sapien can have just as much of a positive impact on others around him or her as anyone else. And when you positively affect another Sapien's LC, that is very good, for them and for you. That is certainly a realistic goal for any Sapien to achieve during any LifeCycle.

The reality of life, however, is somewhat subjective. Much of life is relative to a Sapien's individual LiveTime experiences. What may be good for one Sapien may not be so good for another, depending on the Sapiens' individual and unique perspectives. How a Sapien perceives an ICT event dictates his or her responses to such external stimuli.

A Sapien with a 6.2 rating for a specific ICT may react to an event differently than a Sapien with a lower developed rating in that same ICT. That is what determines the degree of subjectivity, sometimes referred to as relative subjectivity.

Example: One Sapien may think a three-story building is tall, whereas another may see it as average. One person may think a million dollars is alot of money, while another may consider it chump-change.

A Sapien's individual life experiences will determine his or her comfort level during events from which to make decisions. Generally, the more unusual an event is to a Sapien, the more uncomfortable the Sapien is with decision-making during that event. It is this comfort zone that fosters an innate need and desire for Sapiens to associate with like Sapiens to live and function in familiar surroundings.

When someone says, "Look at that guy, he must be from another planet." Well in reality, maybe he is. His crude, rude or violent behavior may indicate he is from a C2 planet, where barely-formed ICTs are the norm. Or maybe this LiveTime was just his next LC since his days on Earth in the fifteenth century. Many things in life are open to interpretation, to some degree, depending upon different Sapien perspectives.

Interpreting Sapien characteristics is an interesting mental exercise, especially in motion pictures, where character development is more acute, usually within two hours or less. One of the key reasons a movie is successful is because of its deep, Sapien-searching character development. The more an audience emotionally relates to a movie's characters, the more enjoyable it is for the audience, and the more successful the movie will become, theoretically.

Major movies, as they are called, are those that have effectively included a full range of ICT developmental situations as integral components of the storyline. The more an audience can relate to a character's ICT events, the more enjoyable the movie.

Example: The movie "Titanic" is an excellent example of major ICT development ranges between the characters. The highs and lows of ICT evolution within the movie's characters make you want to watch the movie again and again, if for no other reason than to appreciate the full impact of its characters' growth. ICTs evolve from the highest of highs to the lowest of lows, occasionally within the same character and especially during the sinking sequences. Watching such a movie might, it its own right, become an ICT event for the viewer.

The Theory gives new meaning to the phrase character development as it applies to motion picture genre. And plot development in movies is more enjoyable to watch from the unique perspective of tracking ICT development of the lead characters.

As you become more cognizant of ICT development, you may begin to more methodically look inward to evaluate your own progress. After you complete your ISAT and get a realistic Sapien rating with identifiable character deficiencies, you may want to consider events in your life that have gotten you to this place in your LC.

During every LifeCycle, there are tradeoffs. Choices you have made in the direction of your life have precluded other options available to you. During your LC, decisions you make directly impact your sphere of people, places and things. As you consider this thought process, try not to think in terms of "If I had only done that," or "If I'd gone that direction, everything would be different." There are only three answers to such reflections: yes, no and maybe.

Yes, your LifeCycle decisions, if you could change them, would result in different outcomes, by definition. That does not necessarily mean, however, that the outcomes, although different, would be better, or worse. They would just be different.

If you lament over past decisions that are no longer relevant, you miss the big picture. Decisions you make are the culmination of all of your ICTs working together with your IM at that moment in time to try to reach the best possible outcome for you in any given situation.

As you come to the realization that your accomplishments and non-accomplishments are all integral parts of your LC's history, you may get a renewed feeling of personal freedom. The freedom that comes with realizing your past is just that, an unchangeable past, and the future is yet to come. Where you go from there is all up to you.

As you look back on your life to date, you may notice some of the tradeoffs you have made and begin to accept them. You are the Sapien you have evolved into so far. And the physical attributes of the body you occupy are also you, this time. Both of these things are incontrovertible.

With this realization, you may begin to feel a certain calmness about life as you accept the realities of your current LC. This should not infer, by any means, that you should lose your motivation or future momentum. To the contrary, at any age and at any point in your LC, you have relative control over your own destiny to make decisions that will enhance your Sapien development. This is your life. This is your LC. Make the most of it, going forward.

With the acceptance of your current LC scenario, you may gain some semblance of inner peace with the knowledge that you can continue to move forward at whatever pace with which you are comfortable, and that is okay. Tranquility and serenity are valuable commodities to be cherished. However, they should not to be used as cop-outs to avoid further Sapien improvements. Continued Sapien evolution is good at whatever age.

As you understand the ramifications of *The ILC Theory* on your existing life, you may gain a new perspective on your current LC. There is some solace in knowing what is going to happen at the end of your current LC journey. According to *The Theory*, unless you are truly an evil Sapien, you will have more LifeCycles, and they will be equal to or better than your current one and probably on Earth. So with that out of the way, you can concentrate on more ICT experiences during your current LiveTime.

Movie Quote: "*Something's Gotta Give*", 2003, Jack Nicholson, Diane Keaton. As the two contemplate their lives, Keaton says, "It sure goes by fast, doesn't it?" Nicholson retorts, "It goes by in the blink of an eye". In ILC parlance, with the proper attitude, life could go by, "with the wink of an eye", until the next time.

Reincarnation, of course, is an integral part of *The ILC Theory*, but only a part. It is the process on which the ILC system is based. The recycling of such a valuable intelligent entity as the Sapien makes sense, both philosophically and scientifically.

If reincarnation were not possible, it sure would be a tremendous waste of time, energy and intelligence assets. In current terminology, if reincarnation did not exist, it would invariably be referred to as 'a major waste of time and money'.

However, money is useless in the ethereal world. A Sapien's SQ is the only currency needed in the Halo and subHalo systems. SQ ratings are used in subHalo database management criteria, Sapien locations during subHalo RestTimes and future LC selections.

When you consider life-after-death options, *The ILC Theory* provides promise that there is indeed a life after death, and another one, and another one, and so on. Other than the traditional religious concept of heaven, and *The Theory's* concept of Halo and subHalo systems, the only other possibility on this topic would be the One-Shot-Deal theory, (OSD).

The OSD theory says that intelligent life is given to a person on a one shot deal basis. You are born, you live, and you die. And that is it. You only get one shot at life. It is a one shot deal. Your existence is purely genetic. Since you do not have a Sapien or soul, your brain is wholly responsible for your mental growth and your actions during that growth. For seventy plus years, you flourish, then you perish.

Movie Quote: "The Natural", 1984, Robert Redford, Robert Duvall, Glenn Close. Redford tries to explain why he quit baseball, and why he dropped out of sight for years. Redford summarizes his LifeCycle to Close, "We all have two lives, the life we learn with and the life we live with after that."

Redford's words, although very true during any given LifeCycle, fail to capture the fact that intelligent life, as we think we know it, is too sophisticated to be left up to mere genetics. And if it was, it sure seems like a phenomenal waste of intelligence to throw it all away after such a short period of growth during one lifetime on Earth, good or bad.

Movie Quote: "Seabiscuit", 2003, Toby McGuire, Jeff Bridges, Chris Cooper. When Bridges asks Cooper why he is mending his horse's broken leg, since the horse cannot race anymore, Cooper replies, "You don't throw a whole life away, just cause it's banged up a little."

Regardless of your situation in life, it can improve. If you capitalize on your strong ICTs and improve those that need help, it will get better with each LC. All Sapiens get a little banged up during their normal LifeCycle evolution. The trick is to not let it get you down and try to improve those character traits you can. You will have plenty of opportunities to improve the other ICTs during LCs to come.

Coincidentally, Cooper and Bridges repeat the same line in two different scenes, indicating its importance to the storyline. The second time was in reference to McGuire's condition as Seabiscuit's jockey, with a broken leg. So it is worth repeating. "You don't throw a whole life away, just cause it gets banged up a little."

Movie Quote: *"Seabiscuit"*, 2003, Toby McGuire, Jeff Bridges, Chris Cooper. Bridges remarks to reporters about his little horse's racing prospects, when he explains, "Everybody loses a couple, and you either pack up and ya go home, or ya keep fighting."

This type of positive mental attitude goes well with *The Theory*. When you get banged up in life, you jump up, dust yourself off, and keep going. Anything less would be an injustice to your LiveTime. In reality, when you get banged up, it means you are trying. You are not merely going through life as a spectator, you are trying to make a difference. Run your own race. Do it your own way.

ILC Quote: A noted American philosopher offers his personal perspective on life. He has requested this to be written on his tombstone. "Life is not a journey to the grave, with the intention of arriving safely in a pretty and well preserved body, but rather to skid in broadside, thoroughly used up, totally worn out, and proclaiming wow, what a ride!"

The Intelligent LifeCycle Theory

The goal of *The Intelligent LifeCycle Theory* is to instill some modicum of logic and rationale to the saga of intelligent life in the universe. *The Theory* proudly states that you can be good, without religion. You can have moral values and principles outside of religion, just as you have inside it. You can improve your traits with belief in the natural laws of physics and the universal laws of intelligent life. If everyone understood *The ILC Theory*, there might be less violence and hatred in the world.

Be forewarned however that, just because you believe in *The ILC Theory*, and are reading this book, it will not by itself improve your Sapien ratings. Although this level of philosophical and strategic thought process should give your Intelligence Module a boost. If you evaluate your own current life situation and use the concepts presented in this book, you should be able to improve some of your own ICTs this LifeCycle and enhance your Sapien ratings for your next LC.

Movie Quote: "*Seabiscuit*", 2003, starring Jeff Bridges, Toby McGuire, Chris Cooper. Bridges as the owner of the legendary thoroughbred sums up life very easily. "This is not the end, this is just the beginning. It's all about the future."

If this is the beginning, and it is all about the future, then we certainly have alot to look forward to. And we hope, during this life as well as our future LCs, we can individually make meaningful contributions to the advancement of Sapien life. But for now, just relax, enjoy life and work on those ICTs.

Movie Quote: "*Moneyball*", 2011, starring Brad Pitt, Jonah Hill. Always hoping to win the World Series as Oakland A's GM, Pitt listens to a tape of his teen daughter singing a song, she wrote just for him.

Her ending lyrics are profound for her young age, when she sings, "Ya gotta let it gohhhh....., and just enjoy the showwww. Just enjoy the show."

It does not matter whether you are an L4 or an L6, if you feel you have a relatively good life, just keep living your life, doing what you're doing. Have fun, and do more to improve in areas you can. Try to be good, try not to hurt anyone, and just enjoy the show.

Have fun and good luck, see you around the universe.

THE END
(or is it Just The Beginning, you decide)
NEXT

About The Author

When we were discussing the approach to this chapter, there were a couple of options to consider. Should it be written in the third person, or first person? Should it be written by someone else, with seemingly inauthentic bravado to increase sales? Or should it be written by me, with boring descriptions of my life's accomplishments and failures?

I decided to write it in a non-traditional approach, keeping with the tradition of *The ILC Theory*, but in the first person. I want to give you my personal interpretation, from a user's perspective, of my current and previous LifeCycles without laborious and unimportant detail.

To set the stage, I feel compelled to first offer an encapsulated version of my current LC with some personal comments and observations about life. Then I'll explain how *The Intelligent LifeCycle Theory* first began and offer some personal analysis of my previous LifeCycles.

Current LifeCycle

I was a typical small town American kid growing up in the 1950's and 1960's. I went to school and played Little League baseball. I had a few girlfriends and a couple of paper routes. I sometimes worked after school washing dishes in a local restaurant for twenty-five cents an hour.

The only thing atypical might be that I tested above average on the IQ scale. This was probably because of my mother's high IQ, as reflected in her and my father's parental overlay SRO, which resulted in me. Evidently, I was within my parents' IM range.

During my junior high and high school days, I went to class, played ball, threw papers and worked with my dad on several unsuccessful backyard-type entrepreneur startups. I graduated from high school with barely a 'B' average, but scored 1440 on my SAT, and studied chemical engineering during my first two years of college.

I got drafted and served in the military during the Viet Nam era. I played ball in the Army league, and got an unofficial offer to play minor league baseball. Even though it had been a dream of mine ever since I was a little kid to play professional ball, I rejected the offer to finish college. I also rejected it because it was only the minors. Had it been the majors, I'm sure it would have been a different story. Something like, "College what?"

Of course that didn't happen, so after being honorably discharged from the Army, I went back to college and graduated from a medium-size school with a degree in business. At the beginning of my business career, I was gung-ho in pursuit of the American Dream. I worked for corporate America, large and small, in sales, sales management and executive positions.

As I progressed in my career development, I pursued a number of my own entrepreneurial startups as president and CEO, some successful, some not. I published a couple of small circulation magazines, and have written several screenplays, none produced as of yet.

I got married once, for about a year. It was one of those wrong place, wrong time, wrong reason kind of deals. I almost got married a couple of other times, but to no avail. I may have had those ICT events in past LifeCycles, and may have them again in future LCs, just not this time.

I realize I have made some pretty significant tradeoffs in pursuit of my entrepreneurial and writing careers. I missed out on lifelong true love, marriage and family, and the ICT impact those things have on an LC, both positively and negatively. I missed those things this trip.

However because of the road I took with this LifeCycle, I have also been exposed to many ICT events that others may not experience. As I dealt with capitalism in my entrepreneurial ventures (which were like my babies), I experienced relationships similar to, and in place of, love and family, intermittent throughout my career.

I have faced fiscal and operational do-or-die decisions in business that tested my integrity to the max. Doing the right thing in business, as in life, is sometimes more difficult than it should be. Fortunately, and sometimes even unfortunately, I always tried to do the right thing. Did I always do the right thing? Looking back in retrospect, maybe not, but I always tried.

Do I have regrets? Certainly, I have my share. I don't think you can go through an LCs LiveTime without doing or saying things that you later regret. But by definition, if you have a regret about something, it means it has already happened. It is in the past, and unchangeable, so don't worry about it. Learn from it.

We can always play the what-if games in an attempt to second-guess the outcome of ICT events, postmortem. "What if I had done this?" "What if I had done that?" "What if I had said this or that?" It doesn't matter. Whatever it is, it's already happened and you can't change the past. If it's a regretful event, learn from it and move on.

Anyone who says they have no regrets in their life is either not being truthful with themselves, or is someone who never really tried to do anything with their life. And if the latter is really the case, that person should regret not having anything to regret.

The bottom line is this. We all make mistakes in our LCs. The most important thing is to learn from them. And by doing so, we will improve our ICTs and consequently reduce the chances that we will repeat the same mistakes in future LCs. And as a result, we indirectly improve our prospects for future LifeCycles.

All we can do is to try to do what we think is right. If what we think is right, turns out to be wrong, then regret it, experience genuine remorse, learn from it, and move on. Next.

Movie Quote: "Maid in Manhattan", 2002, Jennifer Lopez, Ralph Fiennes. Lopez' son posed a hypothetical question to Fiennes the politician, indirectly asking for a second chance for his mom. "It's the sign of character to give someone a second chance. Even if he lies, shouldn't they be given a second chance? I mean nobody's perfect. I mean, if we didn't, we'd never have any congressmen or presidents."

This LC has had its ups and downs, like most of us I suspect. But overall I'd have to say it's been fun. I think I've learned a lot, even though my accomplishments, ICT and IM growth may be miniscule in comparison to what the future holds.

Evolution of *The ILC Theory*

In the mid 1980's, my curiosity got the best of me, and on a dare, I underwent my regression session. Prior to that time, I hadn't given any thought at all to past lives or reincarnation. I was too busy living my life, like most people I would imagine.

My regression session was very peaceful. I reclined on a sofa, and was put into a semi-hypnotic state, eyes closed, very calm and stress-free. It lasted for about forty-five minutes. We recorded it on an audio cassette tape.

The technique my regressor used was to get me to a mental state of mind that was thought-free and removed from any external stimuli. Once that was accomplished, she then asked me to rise up, above my body. "Slowly rise up..., rise up..., rise up. Now slowly come down..., come down..., come down. What do you see?"

When there seemed to be a connection to a previous life, other questions were asked. "What are you doing?" "What are you thinking?" If there was no response from me, she repeated the previous exercise of going up and coming down, presumably in different times, and started again with "What do you see?"

The regression session ended indicating I had lived fourteen times before. We talked about some highlights. I thought it was interesting and somewhat amusing. My real eye opener came, when I listened to the tape at home later that night. It was truly phenomenal to the point that it became believable. My inquisitive mind went to work. *Alright, if this is true,* I surmised, *and I've lived fourteen times before, how does that work?*

That's when *The ILC Theory* began to formulate itself, as I started asking questions. How is reincarnation possible? And if it is possible, why don't I have any memory of those lives? And if I've lived before, how does that work? What happens in between lives? How do I get back to Earth for another life? My questions were many.

Guess what? There weren't any answers. I couldn't find any theory that even remotely attempted to explain any details about how reincarnation or any of its variations actually functioned. Nor could I find any theory that referenced how, why, when and where intelligent life existed in the universe.

Some life-after-death and reincarnation beliefs I found were based on pure faith with zero details. Some were even based on magic, but none attempted to explain how it actually worked.

My questions remained with no apparent answers, so I dismissed it to pursue my career goals. I didn't think much about it until years later, as the world awaited Y2K (Year2000) and the flagrant predictions of a global data meltdown. Of course, Y2K came and went without much fanfare. Then predictions of a 2012 Apocalypse began to surface. So I began again searching for answers to my earlier questions of life-after-death and reincarnation, to no avail.

In 2011, I began development of *"The Intelligent LifeCycle Theory"* in earnest. To accommodate the rapidly evolving scope of the project, *The Theory,* out of necessity, quickly expanded its coverage to include the development, continuity and perpetuation of all Intelligent Life in the Universe.

As you can see, the *The ILC Theory* ended up requiring nearly five hundred pages to comprehensively describe all of its functionality and how its inherent ramifications affect our daily lives. It may be a long story, but it is a good one. I hope you enjoy the read.

Analysis of My LifeCycles

As you look at your own LifeCycle and those of others, it is important to keep in mind that every LC is unique to every Sapien, every time, all the time. As for me, this is evidently my fifteenth LifeCycle. Here are some highlights of a few of my LCs.

My first LifeCycle as an L1.0 was as a prehistoric caveman around 1,000,000 BC. I was a sheepherder around 1000 AD. I was also a fourteenth century gypsy wanderer in the 1300s. My latest LC, prior to this one, was as a relatively unknown lounge singer in Los Angeles in the 1930s and 1940s.

During my audio-taped regression session, I was asked, as a caveman around 1,000,000 BC, at the approximate age of 20, "What do you see?" I immediately responded, "Food!" I was then asked, "What are you doing?" I once again repeated, "Food!" It was obvious, my sole concern was food gathering. At that L1 Sapien level, I was operating from pure survival instincts, adapting to my environment and learning.

Then, I was told to go forward five years, and asked, "What did I see?" There was a silence. I didn't respond. I was then asked, "Are you still alive?" I reluctantly murmured, "No." I was then asked, "What did you learn from this lifetime?" I replied regretfully, "Don't try to kill anything bigger'n you." In those days and times, that was probably a pretty significant lesson I evidently learned the hard way.

Considering my current and previous LifeCycles, I guess I can say I was an average person in most lives, sometimes on the fringe, but relatively normal and in line with the different eras and times of my LCs. Evidently I have led regular, average lives to no great acclaim, like most of us I suspect. Of course, as an eternal optimist, I view my current and past lives as being rich in ICT development, which may be a by-product of being poor, or maybe not.

It will be interesting to see, after my current LifeCycle, how close my personal Sapien *ISAT* scores are to reality. Considering the ICT parameters we use in our *ISAT*, I feel fairly comfortable with my own assessment of my modest Sapien level. However, I won't know for sure until I return to the MilkyWay subHalo, after my current LifeCycle is complete, and I experience *The Theory* first hand.

Whether or not I fulfilled my destiny in this life, or more accurately fulfilled my potential with this life, only time will tell. I only hope I have the opportunity to enjoy many more LiveTimes in the future. I am sure I can do it better next time.

Movie Quote: "Secretariat", 2010, Diane Lane, John Malkovich. After her mother's death and since her father had dementia, Lane had to take over her parents racehorse farm. Lane remembered some advice her father gave her when she was a little girl. He softly told her, "It's not whether *they* think we've won, darlin', it's whether *we* think we've won. Ya just gotta run your own race."

If you're lucky, your LiveTime, this time, will be long enough for some solid ICT development. Even though it may be a bumpy road at times, just hang in there, the ride is definitely worth it, and have some fun while you're at it. May all of your LiveTimes be long times.

15. Appendix

ICT Lists	401
IQ and The Intelligence Module	407
ISAT's ICT Sets	417
Large Number Naming Conventions	429
Other Theories About Life	435
Parental Overlay Module	441
Regression and Hypnosis	445
Reindexing the Brain	451
Research References	459
Ten Commandments	463
Ten Rules of Intelligent Life	465
ILC Theory Terminology	469

The Intelligent LifeCycle Theory

The Intelligent LifeCycle Theory

ICT Lists

POSITIVE ICTs
(Individual Character Traits)

Accepting	Calm	Controllable
Adoring	Candid	Cordial
Adventurous	Capable	Courageous
Affable	Careful	Courteous
Affectionate	Caring	Creative
Agreeable	Cautious	
Aggressive	Celibate	Daring
Alert	Charitable	Dauntless
Altruistic	Chaste	Decent
Ambitious	Cheerful	Decisive
Amenable	Civil	Deferential
Amiable	Clever	Deliberate
Amicable	Comforting	Demonstrative
Analytical	Comical	Demure
Assertive	Commendable	Dependable
Assured	Compassionate	Desirable
Attentive	Competent	Determined
Audacious	Composed	Devoted
	Confident	Devout
Belief-in-God	Concerned	Dignified
Believer	Conciliatory	Diligent
Benevolent	Congenial	Diplomatic
Benign	Conscientious	Discerning
Bold	Conservative	Disciplined
Brainy	Considerate	Discreet
Brave	Content	Discriminant
Broad-minded	Cooperative	Dreamer
	Conservative	Driven

401

Eager
Earnest
Economical
Effective
Efficient
Emotional
Empathetic
Engaged
Enterprising
Ethical
Euphoric
Exacting
Experienced
Extroverted

Faithful
Fastidious
Fearless
Felicitous
Focused
Freewill
Friendly
Frugal
Fun
Funny

Genial
Genteel
Gentle
Good
Goodness

Gracious
Gregarious
Gung Ho

Happy
Heroic
Homogeneous
Honest
Honorable
Hopeful
Horny
Hospitable
Humane
Humble
Humility
Humorous

Idealistic
Immersed
Incisive
Inconspicuous
Incorruptible
Independent
Infuriating
Innocent
Innocuous
Initiative
Intimate
Intrepid

Jovial

Kindhearted
Kindness

Leader
Liberated
Likable
Love
Loving
Loyal

Magnanimous
Manageable
Mannerly
Mature
Methodical
Meticulous
Modesty
Moral

Objective
Observant
Open-minded
Optimistic
Organized
Overt

Passive
Patient
Passionate
Peaceable
Peaceful
Penny-pincher

Permissive	Sacredness	Thrifty
Playful	Sapient	Tolerant
Pleasant	Satisfied	Tranquil
Pleasing	Scrupulous	Truthful
Polite	Self-assured	Trusting
Practical	Selfless	Trustworthy
Pragmatist	Self-reliant	
Precise	Sensible	Unabashed
Prideful	Sensitive	Unbiased
Principled	Sentimental	Understanding
Productive	Serene	Unimpeachable
Proficient	Sexual-normalcy	
Proud	Shameless	Valiant
Prudent	Sharp	Versatile
Prudish	Shrewd	Virtuous
Purposeful	Sociable	Visionary
	Sophisticated	
Quiet	Spirited	Warmhearted
	Stalwart	Warmblooded
Realistic	Straightforward	Watchful
Reliable	Strong	Well-rounded
Religious	Structured	Wholesome
Reserved	Sultry	Willful
Resistible	Sweet	Willing
Resolute	Sympathetic	Wise
Resourceful		Witty
Respectful	Tactful	
Responsive	Temperate	Zealous
Restrained	Tempered	
Risk-taker	Tenacious	
Romantic	Thorough	
	Thoughtful	

ICT Lists *continued*

Negative ICTs
(Individual Character Traits)

Abomination	Caustic	Deferential
Absentminded	Celibate	Defiant
Abstinence	Cheapskate	Demeaning
Abstract	Close-minded	Dependent
Abusive	Cocky	Depressed
Addictive	Coldblooded	Destructive
Argumentative	Coldhearted	Detached
Aloof	Combative	Detrimental
Angry	Complacent	Diffident
Anguish	Complaining	Disagreeable
Antagonistic	Compulsive	Disgraceful
Antisocial	Conceited	Dishonorable
Apathetic	Confined	Dishonest
Apprehensive	Conflicted	Disinterested
Arrogant	Confrontational	Disorganized
	Corrupt	Dispassionate
Barbaric	Contentious	Disrespectful
Belligerent	Cowardly	Distracted
Biased	Creative	Distrustful
Bland	Criminal	Dominating
Boisterous	Crude	Doubtful
Boring	Cruel	Dreamer
Brainless	Cursed	Dry
Brash	Cynical	Dull
Brutality		Dumb
	Daydreaming	
Carefree	Decadent	Egotistical
Careless	Deceitful	Enraged

The Intelligent LifeCycle Theory

Envious
Evil
Exasperating
Extravagant

Fainthearted
Faithless
Fatalistic
Fearful
Flirtatious
Follower
Foolish
Fraudulent
Frigid
Frownful

Genuine
Godlessness
Gutless

Halfhearted
Haphazard
Hapless
Hateful
Hesitant
Hostile
Hypocritical

Imaginative
Imitative
Immature
Immoral

Impatient
Impersonal
Impetuous
Impotent
Impractical
Imprecise
Imprudent
Impulsive
Inadequate
Incompetent
Inconsiderate
Inconspicuous
Indecisive
Indifferent
Indignant
Indiscreet
Indiscriminant
Ineffective
Inefficient
Inept
Inexperienced
Infatuated
Inhospitable
Innovative
Insecure
Insensitive
Intimidated
Introverted
Irreverent
Irritable

Jealous

Lackadaisical
Lascivious
Lavish
Lax
Lazy
Lewd
Lewdness
Liberal
Loathing

Malevolent
Malicious
Mischievous
Miserly
Misleading
Moody

Narrow-minded
Neglectful
Negligent
Neurotic
Non-believer
Nuisance
Nymphomania

Obedient
Oblivious
Objectionable
Obnoxious
Obsessive
Obstinate

The Intelligent LifeCycle Theory

Offensive	Sinful	Undisciplined
	Slow-witted	Undiscriminating
Pacific	Sly	Unemotional
Pathos	Sneaky	Unethical
Pessimistic	Sober	Unfriendly
Petty	Sorrowful	Unheroic
Pompous	Spendthrift	Unimaginative
Possessive	Spineless	Uninspired
Pragmatist	Spiteful	Unkind
Preoccupied	Stingy	Unmanageable
Pretentious	Subdued	Unmotivated
Promethean	Submissive	Unperceptive
Promiscuous	Subordinated	Unpleasant
Pugnacious	Subservient	Unrealistic
	Superiority	Unreliable
Quarrelsome	Surrendering	Unresponsive
		Unromantic
Reclusive	Tacky	Unruly
Reserved	Tactless	Unscrupulous
Reticent	Temper	Unskilled
Rowdy	Thoughtless	Untrustworthy
Rude	Timid	
	Tired	Vacillating
Sad	Tormented	Vague
Sarcastic	Traitorous	Violent
Secretive		Virginal
Secular	Uncivil	Vulgar
Self-centered	Unconscionable	
Selfish	Undemanding	Wary
Shallow	Undersexed	Weak
Shameful	Undesirable	Witless
Shy	Undiplomatic	

IQ and The Intelligence Module (IM)

Intelligence is part reality and part relative, depending upon your perspective. The knowledge component, which is most visible and most often misconstrued as intelligence, is seen as the reality part. The ability of a Sapien to apply credible abstract thoughts to his or her environment is relative and dependent upon the situation.

Deductive and analytical skills are often referred to as the mind. Someone who has these skills is known to have a keen mind. Actually, these attributes are resident in the Intelligence Module (IM), not to be mistaken for the brain, which is the physical organ that carries out Sapien Core instructions. The IM is a vital subset of the Core.

The brain is a physical attribute of the host body, both of which are inherited from the parents. The Intelligence Module, which operates the brain, is the mental component of the Sapien. IM development is primarily affected by a Sapien's LiveTime experiences, even though IMs of the parents do have an impact, during a Sapien's growth years.

Generally, a higher IM equates to more LifeCycles in a Sapien's past, as does a higher SQ, but not necessarily in direct correlation to the other. A Sapien with a high IM does not necessarily have a high SQ. And a low IM does not necessarily mean a low SQ.

The intellect that is inherent in the IM is to be cherished and nurtured, as it is one of the primary contributors to improved living conditions on a planet during Sapien LifeCycles. Intelligence is vital to the development of a Sapien's overall entity. The Intelligence Module accounts for 20 percent of the overall Sapien IEF and SQ Scores.

The IM's intellect component is partially influenced by the parental overlay in that the parents' SRO stipulates a relatively narrow range for IM compliance in the requested Sapien. Occasionally however, an IM mismatch may occur.

Example: Parents with relatively high IQs give birth to a healthy baby boy. When he gets old enough, he is tested. He achieves an extremely below average IQ rating, but his ICTs seem normal. This is a result of an unavoidable mismatch during the Sapien selection process between the subHalo and SRO parental overlay requirements.

Chances are it was a mismatched IM during SRO fulfillment and is no reflection on the parents. The good news is that this couple has the opportunity to help develop this Sapien's ICTs and IM during his new LC, which will indirectly help the parents with their own ICT development as well.

Prominent psychologists have concluded that extreme geniuses and mentally retarded people have similar attributes and constraints. It is also concluded that people have a tendency to underestimate a child with mentally deficient tendencies and overestimate children considered to have superior intellect.

Scientific testing for nearly a hundred years has also concluded that men and women (male/female Sapiens) as groups are equal in their intelligence levels. *The ILC Theory* agrees with this premise, of course. The intelligence component of the Sapien is strictly gender neutral, even though the Sapien itself is gender specific.

IQ Rating Scale

Intelligence Quotient (IQ) ratings are based on mentally-challenging tests developed by mathematicians and psychologists. They are administered by a wide variety of commercial interests. An IQ test measures a person's mental age as a percentage of the person's chronological age and is then multiplied by 100 for standardization. IQ scores range from 20 to 200+. I think you get 20 points for spelling your name correctly.

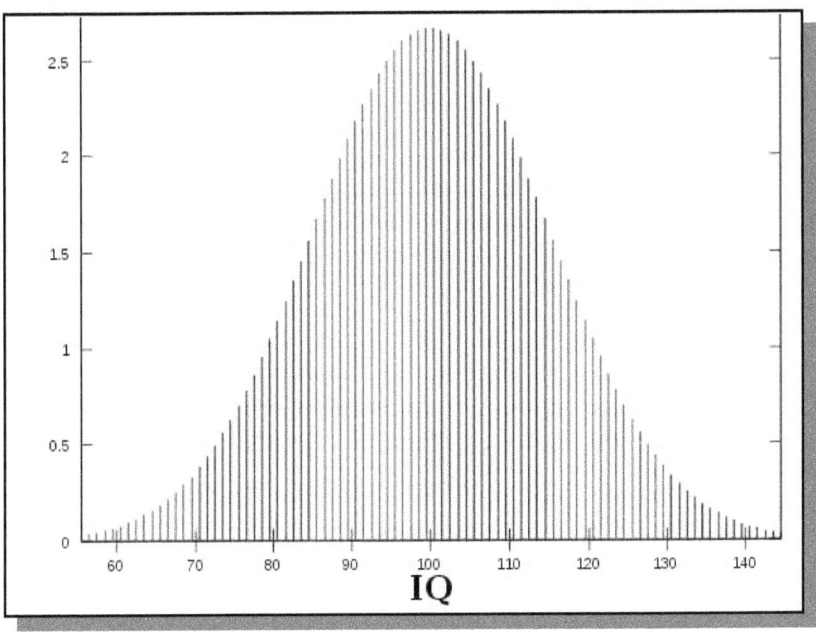

As the above graph illustrates, the IQs of a large enough population are calculated so that they conform to a normal distribution. And that normal distribution equates to 100 as shown. All scores deviating from the norm, above or below, are relative to the base of 100.

Whether or not IQ tests are an accurate measure of intelligence is open to debate. It is difficult to define exactly what constitutes intelligence. It may be the case that an IQ score represents a very specific type of intelligence, even though it is thought to be comprehensive in scope.

A high IQ is generally thought to have positive effects on the development of many Sapien ICTs during an LC. However, a high IQ rating by itself does not provide an accurate picture of the overall Sapien. The SQ does that by including not only the IM, but also the Sapien's ICTs, its true character.

Given the right combination of ICT development or lack thereof, a high IQ can just as easily be used by an evil Sapien. This is evidenced by serial killers, such as Jeffrey Dahmer and Charles Manson, who obviously had significant deficiencies in their sanctity of life ICTs and high propensities for violence, but high IQs.

Mr. Lewis Terman coined the term IQ and designed the original IQ rating scale in 1916. IQ rating scales have been revised over the years, with further clarifications to the highs and lows of the IQ norm.

High IQ Ratings Distribution	
115 to 124	Above average
125 to 134	Gifted
135 to 144	Highly gifted
145 to 154	Low genius
155 to 164	Middle genius
165 to 179	High genius
180 to 200	Highest genius
Above 200	Immeasurable genius

It has been said that the intelligence quotient is rather ambiguous in relation to the power and ability of the brain. *The ILC Theory* agrees with this premise. However, the IQ rating of a Sapien does directly correlate to its level of IM development.

If your IQ score is not as high as you would like, that is okay, because you probably have offsetting ICTs that are developed enough to raise your Sapien score. Remember, the IM is only 20 percent of the Sapien score.

Your IQ is not necessarily good nor bad. A high IQ is good. A not-so high IQ is good too. An extremely low IQ as shown below could mean the Sapien has only had a small number of LCs, so far.

Low IQ Ratings Distribution

50 to 70	Mild mental retardation
35 to 50	Moderate Mental retardation
20 to 35	Severe mental retardation
10 to 20	Profound mental retardation

An estimated 85% of Low IQ Ratings fall in the 50 to 70 category.

The following conversion chart gives you guidance in determining your own IM by comparison to your actual IQ score. This IQ to IM Rating scale has been tailored for *The ILC Theory*, as a new revision to Mr. Terman's work.

The table below shows the conversion from a person's IQ to an equivalent IM rating from 1 to 10. When a Sapien reaches an IQ of 140 and above, the IM ratings are incrementally smaller than at the lower levels, which also means improvements are less frequent.

IQ to IM Conversion Chart

IQ Score	Intelligence Level	IM Rating
Under 60	Mild to Profound Retardation	1.00 – 1.99
60 to 69	Borderline Deficient	2.00 – 2.99
70 to 79	Dullness	3.00 – 3.99
80 to 89	Attentive	4.00 – 4.99
90 to 99	Below Average	5.00 – 5.99
100 to 109	Normal/Average	6.00 – 6.99
110 to 119	Above Average	7.00 – 7.99
120 to 129	Gifted	8.00 – 8.99
130 to 139	Highly Gifted	9.00 – 9.89
140 to 150	Low Genius	9.90 – 9.91
150 to 159	Middle Genius	9.92 – 9.93
160 to 169	High Genius	9.94 – 9.95
170 to 179	Higher Genius	9.96 – 9.97
180 to 200	Highest Genius	9.98 – 9.99
Above 200	Immeasurable Genius	10.00

Example: A person with an IQ of 200+ equates to an IM of 10.00, but that same Sapien may have some ICTs that are severely deficient. So in this example, a super genius could have a lower Sapien score than a person of average intelligence. It all depends on the ICT development percentages.

As with all rating systems intended to measure a Sapien's intelligence, we must look at distribution curves with highs and lows. Most of us fall in the middle and aggregately comprise the norm. The two extremes of these scales are generally treated separately with additional explanations. The IM rating system is no different.

Wisdom and Stupidity

Regardless of IQ and IM ratings, wisdom (L8 status) comes from developing all ICTs in conjunction with the IM. ILC requirements for a Sapien to progress to an L8 include a minimum ICT development level of 8.00 for *all* ICTs (not an average but every ICT), with an IM of 9.90 or higher.

Such a combination of intelligence and character traits provides the Sapien with a well-rounded and balanced energy field that does not require any additional LiveTimes. Once wisdom is achieved, a Sapien becomes a permanent, functioning member of the Halo.

L9 Sapiens are considered near perfect in the development of their IM and ICT sets. A Sapien progresses to the L9 status after developing *all* ICTs over 9.00 with an IM of 9.95 or higher. And of course, an L10 Sapien is perfect, scoring 10.00 in *all* ICTs with a 10.00 IM.

At the other end of the Intelligence spectrum is stupidity. Because of the normal evolution of intelligent life in the universe, stupid Sapiens will always be with us. There is no way around it. New L1.0s are constantly being infused into the subHalo systems for a perpetually evolving new crop of Sapiens with deficient intellects until they grow and develop.

Several names that describe this type of Sapien are recognizable. They include Sapiens that are referred to as a numbskull, dumbsh*t, and/or dumb*ss (DA). The latter seems to capture the image best, so we will call Sapiens blessed with stupidity IM levels, DA Sapiens.

DAs are certainly among us, making it more difficult sometimes for average Sapiens around them to function smoothly. Oftentimes however, DAs provide some semblance of comic relief in our LCs. The good news is they will grow out of it, theoretically. It may take a number of LCs, but they will eventually grow out of it.

Unlike wise Sapiens, it is a little harder to quantify DAs pertaining to minimums or maximums of intellectual performance. Stupidity is more easily described with humorous stories.

Movie Quote: "*Lone Star State of Mind*", 2002, Joshua Jackson, Jaime King. Discussing their intelligence, one turns to the other and declares, "You're so stupid, they had to burn down the school, to get you out of the third grade."

Not to poke fun at stupid people, certainly not, that is just where they are in their IM development cycle. Stupidity seems to require a certain perspective on life and is best understood with humor and acceptance.

One of the most popular quotes describing a low intelligence level Sapien is "doing the same thing over and over, and expecting a different result". True, but at a certain point, the stupidity runs out and the Sapien learns from his or her actions. Chances are very good that if you are reading this book, you are not stupid, so don't worry about it.

Example: This is the story of a true Dumb*ss Sapien, in Nevada. This guy goes into a Bank of America branch and writes "Give me all your money" on the back of one of their deposit slips, and hands it to a teller. The teller says she can't do it without his ID, and hands it back to him. The DA doesn't have his ID. So he leaves with his note, goes back to his car, gets his ID and goes across the street to a Wells Fargo

The Intelligent LifeCycle Theory

branch. He presents the "Give me all your money" note and his ID to another teller. She says she can't do it, because it's on a deposit slip from Bank of America across the street. By this time, the DA is obviously frustrated. He leaves his ID on the counter, runs out the door and takes off. He was caught shortly thereafter... the dumb*ss.

Intelligence Modules are somewhat affected by the technological advancements of a society during each LC. Sapiens do achieve some improvement in their Intelligence Modules through technology and education. However the real IM improvements, those that are permanent and transportable across the universe, come from actual ICT events during LiveTime LifeCycles.

We as a society on Earth measure everything and have determined that intelligence, although seemingly infinite in nature, is in fact finite and measurable. Intelligence is certainly measurable throughout the universe, across all time dimensions. *The ILC Theory* establishes the upper limit of intelligence as an L10 with a 1000 SQ.

The Intelligent LifeCycle Theory

The Intelligent LifeCycle Theory

ISAT ICT Sets

Key ICT Sets

Negative (1.0) ⟶ **Positive (10.0)**

Set 01: Sanctity of Life I
- Antisocial — Sociable
- Brutal — Humane
- Violent — Passive
- Cruel — Kindhearted
- Disrespectful — Respectful

Set 02: Sanctity of Life II
- Evil — Goodhearted
- Sinful — Virtuous
- Immoral — Moral
- Insensitive — Compassionate
- Selfish — Selfless

Set 03: Freedom I
- Witless — Wise
- Confined — Freewill
- Cowardly — Courageous
- Fearful — Assertive
- Tired — Spirited

Set 04: Freedom II
- Fainthearted — Adventurous
- Intimidated — Dauntless
- Undeserving — Proud
- Subordinated — Independent
- Timid — Intrepid

Negative (1.0) ━━━▶ **Positive (10.0)**

Set 05: Gender Relations I
- Aloof — Affectionate
- Indifferent — Caring
- Demeaning — Deferential
- Detached — Adoring
- Manipulative — Loving

Set 06: Gender Relations II
- Frigidity — Sexual-normalcy
- Promiscuous — Faithful
- Dominating — Accepting
- Jealous — Trusting
- Lewdness — Prudish

Set 07: Efficacy I
- Dependent — Risk-taker
- Disorganized — Organized
- Follower — Leader
- Lazy — Ambitious
- Reserved — Enterprising

Set 08: Efficacy II
- Ineffective — Effective
- Incompetent — Competent
- Indecisive — Decisive
- Unimaginative — Resourceful
- Insecure — Confident

The Intelligent LifeCycle Theory

Negative (1.0) ⟶ **Positive (10.0)**

Set 09: Spiritual I
- Non-believer — Believer
- Secular — Religious
- Faithless — Devout
- Godlessness — Belief in God
- Irreverent — Sacredness

Set 10: Spiritual II
- Deceitful — Trustworthy
- Dishonest — Honest
- Immoral — Moral
- Hateful — Loving
- Malevolent — Benevolent

Supporting ICT Sets

Set 11
- Caustic — Amiable
- Inhospitable — Hospitable
- Introverted — Extroverted

Set 12
- Objectionable — Agreeable
- Obnoxious — Affable
- Offensive — Likable

Set 13
- Reclusive — Gregarious
- Sad — Happy
- Unfriendly — Friendly

The Intelligent LifeCycle Theory

Negative (1.0) ⟶ **Positive (10.0)**

	Negative	Positive
Set 14	Absentminded Daydreaming Distracted	Engaged Immersed Attentive
Set 15	Neglectful Oblivious Preoccupied	Focused Observant Alert
Set 16	Complacent Hapless Obstinate	Aggressive Tenacious Assertive
Set 17	Hesitant Conflicted Reticent	Eager Hopeful Willing
Set 18	Barbaric Combative Confrontational	Kindhearted Passive Patient
Set 19	Destructive Hostile Fatalistic	Tolerant Peaceful Idealistic
Set 20	Pugnacious Contentious Argumentative	Conciliatory Pacific Peaceable
Set 21	Boring Dull Fearful	Adventurous Visionary Fearless

The Intelligent LifeCycle Theory

Negative (1.0) ⟶ **Positive (10.0)**

Set 22	Shy	Audacious
	Timid	Bold
	Uninspired	Innovative
Set 23	Disagreeable	Agreeable
	Distrustful	Trusting
	Envious	Altruistic
Set 24	Careless	Careful
	Impetuous	Diligent
	Impulsive	Meticulous
Set 25	Negligent	Watchful
	Reckless	Cautious
	Oblivious	Observant
Set 26	Inconsiderate	Considerate
	Insensitive	Sensitive
	Rude	Polite
Set 27	Tacky	Dignified
	Tactless	Tactful
	Thoughtless	Thoughtful
Set 28	Unkind	Sweet
	Vulgar	Genteel
	Quarrelsome	Cordial
Set 29	Crude	Sophisticated
	Foolish	Shrewd
	Imprudent	Prudent

The Intelligent LifeCycle Theory

	Negative (1.0) ⟶	**Positive (10.0)**
Set 30	Indiscreet	Discreet
	Indiscriminant	Discriminant
	Undiplomatic	Diplomatic
Set 31	Dumb	Sapient
	Unperceptive	Clever
	Brainless	Brainy
Set 32	Bland	Creative
	Dull	Keen
	Unproductive	Imaginative
Set 33	Fraudulent	Genuine
	Imitative	Promethean
	Misleading	Truthful
Set 34	Petty	Charitable
	Liberal	Conservative
	Narrow-minded	Broad-minded
Set 35	Abstract	Precise
	Vacillating	Purposeful
	Doubtful	Exacting
Set 36	Apprehensive	Deliberate
	Lackadaisical	Incisive
	Vague	Thorough
Set 37	Impatient	Accepting
	Insatiable	Satisfied
	Irritable	Genial

The Intelligent LifeCycle Theory

	Negative (1.0) ⟶	**Positive (10.0)**
Set 38	Corrupt Criminal Decadent	Incorruptible Unimpeachable Principled
Set 39	Deceitful Disgraceful Dishonest	Truthful Commendable Honest
Set 40	Dishonorable Immoral Sinful	Honorable Moral Virtuous
Set 41	Sly Sneaky Shameless	Straightforward Candid Decent
Set 42	Unconscionable Unethical Unscrupulous	Conscionable Ethical Scrupulous
Set 43	Belligerent Complaining Confrontational	Serene Tolerant Amicable
Set 44	Corrupt Cowardly Weak	Incorruptible Heroic Brave
Set 45	Fainthearted Gutless Inconspicuous	Bold Courageous Audacious

The Intelligent LifeCycle Theory

	Negative (1.0) ⟶	**Positive (10.0)**
Set 46	Untrustworthy Traitorous Unreliable	Trustworthy Loyal Reliable
Set 47	Dry Frownful Pathos	Witty Comical Humorous
Set 48	Anguish Tormented Cursed	Cheerful Jovial Joyous
Set 49	Sarcastic Sober Sorrowful	Funny Playful Fun
Set 50	Arrogant Brash Conceited	Humble Quiet Humility
Set 51	Egotistic Pompous Pretentious	Demure Temperate Modesty
Set 52	Submissive Subservient Undisciplined	Independent Initiative Disciplined
Set 53	Anger Attitude Enraged	Tranquil Cheerful Tempered

The Intelligent LifeCycle Theory

Negative (1.0) ⟶ **Positive (10.0)**

	Negative	Positive
Set 54	Mischievous Rowdy Uncivil	Composed Dignified Civil
Set 55	Abomination Coldhearted Cruel	Love Warmhearted Gentle
Set 56	Cynical Pessimistic Defeatist	Sentimental Optimistic Transcendent
Set 57	Flirtatious Infatuated Promiscuous	Innocent Adoring Faithful
Set 58	Spiteful Insensitive Hateful	Caring Compassionate Loving
Set 59	Frigid Abstinence Nuisance	Sultry Intimate Passionate
Set 60	Unromantic Indifferent Weary	Romantic Devoted Spirited
Set 61	Obscene Abusive Loathing	Mannerly Innocuous Pleasing

The Intelligent LifeCycle Theory

	Negative (1.0) ➞	**Positive (10.0)**
Set 62	Lascivious Lewd Nymphomania	Wholesome Decent Celibate
Set 63	Promiscuous Undersexed Undesirable	Chaste Horny Desirable
Set 64	Self-centered Shallow Shy	Self-assured Analytical Assertive
Set 65	Spendthrift Extravagant Lavish	Economical Prudent Wise
Set 66	Miserly Cheapskate Stingy	Thrifty Sensible Frugal
Set 67	Addictive Compulsive Obsessive	Controllable Resistible Freewill
Set 68	Follower Insecure Obedient	Leader Confident Self-reliant
Set 69	Incompetent Ineffective Inefficient	Competent Proficient Efficient

The Intelligent LifeCycle Theory

	Negative (1.0) ⟶	**Positive (10.0)**
Set 70	Inept Shallow Slow-witted	Capable Well-rounded Sharp
Set 71	Cynic Diffident Fearful	Visionary Extroverted Risk-taker
Set 72	Carefree Disorganized Haphazard	Methodical Organized Structured
Set 73	Apathetic Coldblooded Detrimental	Caring Warmblooded Benign
Set 74	Disinterested Dispassionate Halfhearted	Zealous Passionate Gung Ho
Set 75	Anger Antagonistic Apathetic	Gentleness Cooperative Understanding
Set 76	Unmotivated Undiscriminating Undemanding	Driven Meticulous Fastidious
Set 77	Impersonal Unemotional Lax	Demonstrative Emotional Discerning

The Intelligent LifeCycle Theory

	Negative (1.0) ⟶	**Positive (10.0)**
Set 78	Petty Narrow-minded Biased	Objective Open-minded Unbiased
Set 79	Impractical Dreamer Unrealistic	Practical Pragmatist Realistic
Set 80	Unmanageable Unruly Immature	Disciplined Composed Mature
Set 81	Indignant Moody Neurotic	Genial Serene Sensible
Set 82	Temper Unpleasant Depressed	Restrained Pleasant Euphoric
Set 83	Boisterous Cocky Defiant	Restrained Prideful Cooperative
Set 84	Disrespectful Offensive Ungrateful	Respectful Deferential Gracious
Set 85	Jealous Suspicious Insecure	Trusting Understanding Confident

The Intelligent LifeCycle Theory

Large Number Naming Conventions

Textual names in numerology attempt to reflect the number of digits a number has represented by zeros. The ***power of ten*** is used as a standard numerical designation to match the text name. This becomes important when you are dealing with spatial distances and infinity.

This type of naming convention makes it easier to understand. It also takes up less space when using large numbers in text. The following table shows the textual name attached to the numerical one.

LARGE NUMBER NAMES

Million	10^6	Tredecillion	10^{42}
Billion	10^9	Quattuordecillion	10^{45}
Trillion	10^{12}	Quindecillion	10^{48}
Quadrillion	10^{15}	Sexdecillion	10^{51}
Quintillion	10^{18}	Septendecillion	10^{54}
Sextillion	10^{21}	Octodecillion	10^{57}
Septillion	10^{24}	Novemdecillion	10^{60}
Octillion	10^{27}	Vigintillion	10^{63}
Nonillion	10^{30}	Centillion	10^{303}
Decillion	10^{33}	Googol	10^{100}
Undecillion	10^{36}	Googolplex	10^{Googol}
Duodecillion	10^{39}		

The above names are generally agreed upon as the official list for use in current numerology naming conventions. Apart from *million*, the words in this list ending with *-illion* are all derived by adding prefixes (*bi-*, *tri-*, etc.) to the stem *-illion*.

The Intelligent LifeCycle Theory

Centillion, with 303 zeros, appears to be the highest name ending in *-illion* that appears in most technical references. Centillion sounds like it should refer to one hundred zeros. *Trigintillion*, often cited as a word in discussions of large numbers, is not included in any list, nor are any names that can be created by extending the *'illion'* naming pattern (*unvigintillion, duovigintillion, duoquinquagintillion*, etc.).

To get the full effect of how big these numbers really are, it is useful to use numerical comparisons that are more familiar. As of 2011, there were 168 countries in the world with over one billion dollars in annual Gross Domestic Product (GDP) and 15 countries with over one trillion dollars in GDP. That would be 15 trillion 168 billion dollars in global GDP, or 15.168×10^{12} as represented with the power of ten.

Such mundane numbers as the global GDP may not seem very interesting, but they are still incomprehensible. If you have ever thought about counting a billion of anything, much less a trillion, forget it. You cannot count that high, and here is why.

Example: If you counted one number every second, twenty-four hours a day, it would take 31.7 years just to count to 1 billion. Say you only counted 12 hours a day, and used the other 12 hours a day to eat, drink and sleep, it would take 63.4 years to finish counting to 1 billion. If you began this mental and verbal exercise when you were 12 and did nothing else with your life, you would be 75 years old before you counted to 1 billion.

Alright, let's assume no one has ever spent his or her entire life doing nothing but counting. Therefore, one billion is such a large number that nobody in history has ever counted that high, ever.

The Intelligent LifeCycle Theory

And for the record, using the same logic of counting one number every second, twenty-four hours a day, seven days a week, it would take you 31,700 years to count to one trillion. That should add new meaning and appreciation to the USA deficit of sixteen trillion dollars.

Googol and googolplex are the two biggest numbers, obviously too large to ever consider counting. Most dictionaries do include *googol* and *googolplex*, which are not to be confused with the Internet giant, which is spelled differently. Large number naming conventions existed way before the Internet.

A googol, represented by 1×10^{100}, is basically the digit 1 followed by one hundred zeros: 10,000,000,000,000,000,000,000,000,000,-000,000, 000, 000,000,000,000,000,000,000,000,000,000,000,000,-000,000, 000,000,000,000,000,000.

Using textual names with which we are familiar, a googol equates to ten thousand trillion trillion trillion trillion trillion trillion trillion. Of course, that is assuming twelve zeros per trillion.

According to Wikipedia, the term googol was coined in 1938 by nine year old Milton Sirotta, nephew of American mathematician Edward Kasner. In 1940, Kasner popularized the concept in his book entitled *"Mathematics and the Imagination"*.

As shown previously, the largest non-conventional number is googolplex, represented by 1×10^{Googol}. Upon exhaustive research into the number googolplex, it became clear that we have invented a number that is so large, it cannot even be succinctly described, much less counted or even written.

By defining a googolplex with the above exponential designation, it inherently implies it is quantifiable, with a finite number of zeros. Well..., yes and no.

However, if you tried to write one Googolplex in standard numeric format, such as 1,000,000,000....., it would be physically impossible to do so. To write the number of one googolplex, it would require more physical space than our known universe encompasses. Really.

Example: Consider printing the zeros of a googolplex in unreadable, one-point font. It would take about 3.5×10^{96} meters to write a googolplex. The observable universe is estimated to be 8.80×10^{26} meters, or ninety-three billion light-years, in diameter, which is way short of a Googolplex of zeros.

Example: The time it would take to write a Googolplex is also extremely prohibitive. If you were to write two digits per second, twenty-four hours a day, it would take about 1.51×10^{92} years to write a googolplex. Therefore, it would take you almost a googol of years to write a googolplex number.

In particle physics, an elementary particle does not have substructure, meaning it is the smallest particle known to science so far. If an elementary particle has no substructure, it is considered to be the basic building block of the universe, from which all other things evolve.

Example: There are about 2.5×10^{89} elementary particles in the observable universe. If you used one elementary particle to represent one zero in a googolplex, you would run out of particles in the universe long before reaching one googolplex.

Therefore, one googolplex, 1×10^{Googol}, is a number so large, it cannot be equated to anything in this universe, nothing, zip, nada. It is highly doubtful that a googolplex is even a useful number in the superverse. A googolplex is literally a googol of numbers. It's not exactly infinity, but it's close.

Back to the real world, other large number names come in handy when discussing the speeds and feeds of the universe. When comparing LightSpeed to StarSpeed, such large numbers can be represented in various ways, as shown below.

Light-Speed (miles/yr)	StarSpeed via UENet (miles/yr)
5,900,000,000,000	5,900,000,000,000,000,000,000,000
5,900 billion	5.9 trillion trillion
5.9 trillion	5.9 Septillion
(5.9×10^{12})	(5.9×10^{24})

The size of the universe has been estimated using the 10^{11} Rule, which represents one hundred billion. Scientists estimate there are 10^{11} galaxies in the universe, and 10^{11} stars per galaxy. This equates to 10^{22} stars in the universe, or ten Sextillion stars.

Even though not directly related to *The ILC Theory*, hexadecimal representation is another way of describing numbers, used in mathematics and computer science. Hex is prevalent in the computer and technology industries.

Numerical	Hex
One hundred billion (10^{11})	174876e800
One trillion (10^{12})	8d4a51000

Here are some interesting alpha/numeric conversions to hex. Although these examples are not exactly related to *The Theory*, it was an amusing exercise during research for the book, so I left them in.

Alpha/Numeric	Hex
StarSpeed (59×10^{23})	e15fa410ec46c (e+20)
SAPIEN (upper case)	53415049454e
Sapien (upper/lower case)	53617069656e
ILC Theory	494c43205448454f5259

Large numbers can oftentimes be very difficult to calculate, write and verbalize. Some are so big, you just cannot count that high in your lifetime. That is why we have developed the number naming conventions as shown. And if that's not enough, here's another method of counting large numbers.

Final Large Number Example: **Q:** How do you count to a trillion? **A:** Ohhhh......, One......, comma, …. zero zero zero comma, zero zero zero comma, zero zero zero comma, zero zero zero. Ha!

So you see, after all those explanations, counting to a trillion isn't so bad. Now that you know how, you can actually count the United States deficit, thought to be impossible before. Just repeat the above example sixteen times.

Other Theories about Life (3+1)

Prior to *The Intelligent LifeCycle Theory*, there were three theories that attempted to explain the evolution of mankind. All three treat the physical body and the soul as one entity. *Determinism, Randomness and Free Will* have different followings in the medical, scientific, and philosophical communities.

The ILC Theory is not intended to be the fourth theory of the evolution of mankind. It is more of a comprehensive theory, defining the evolution, continuity and perpetuation of intelligent life in the universe. It deals with the metaphysical, separate from the physical. If *The Theory* needs a formal theory-type name, it could be called *Intergyism* (intelligent energy-*ism*), as in the Intelligent Energy Field (IEF).

Determinism: This philosophy promotes the idea that everything that happens is pre-determined. Conditions are such that the outcome of an event is determined by the outcomes of previous events, related and/or unrelated. Thus, the outcome of the event is the only possible outcome and is therefore pre-determined. In physics, this interdependency of events is also known as the cause-and-effect relationship between people, things, actions and events, sometimes related, sometimes disparate.

There are a number of interpretations involving Determinism. In each case, the deterministic slant relies on presupposed connections and dependencies between people, things, actions and events. And the primary factor controlling the event, in each sub-theory case, is based on assertions that are incontrovertible, without exception.

Everything is predisposed to, and by definition must adhere to, predetermined outcomes of any and all experiential events during a lifetime, without exception. It has been suggested that such theories have evolved from different historical perspectives. And these type of theories should be considered with reference to their historical significance.

Determinism is most often used in context with the cause-and-effect analogy. Another physics theory that might apply with this thought process would be the concept that "every action has an equal and opposite reaction" affecting other actions and events. And thus, all actions are interrelated with outcomes that are unequivocally pre-determined.

Opinions on Determinism vary as to the scope of their pre-determined assumptions. Some say determinism only relates to Earth. Others say that the universe itself is a single pre-determined system. Determinism works well with the evolution of the physical realm, but not so much in the evolution of the metaphysical component of life.

Randomness: This theory is somewhat of an oxymoron. It espouses the lack of predictability, which in itself makes it predictable. It is often used to represent well-defined statistical properties of an event, sometimes referred to as a lack of bias. This concept, which relies on random input, is prevalent in computer technology today.

The process of random selection is highly predictable. When items are randomly selected from a finite group, the probability of selecting an item will be exactly proportional to its percentage of the overall population of the group. No more, no less.

Example: If you randomly selected ping-pong balls, numbered from 1 to 10, each number would be drawn exactly 10 percent of the time, over the course of thousands of selections. This is the theory that precipitates the payout percentages in Lotto, slot machines and most casino games. Randomness is highly predictable. If it were not infinitely predictable, casino gaming as an industry would have to close their doors.

Randomness implies that things happen on a whim, without regard to purpose or direction. All events occur purely at random, with no cause-and-effect, no conscious choice. This concept proffers a non-order to things, involving an incoherent pattern of events.

Random occurrences of events in life do exist and affect a Sapien's LiveTime. Sometimes a random event positively shapes a Sapien's LifeCycle. Oftentimes however, the outcome of a random event may be negative, which *The Theory* refers to as the SH Factor. As long as there is a question about the certainty of the outcome of an event, randomness will play a part.

In theory, a random event, based on unpredictable variables, does not and will not adhere to any deterministic pattern of behavior. Most LCs are affected to some degree by random events. A Sapien's ICTs will be affected, positively and/or negatively, from random events. The ICT impact, more often than not, will be proportionate to the amount of impact the random event has on the Sapien's LiveTime. An average Sapien's growth curve is generally influenced to a small degree by Randomness.

Free Will: This concept was not considered a viable theory until recent history. Free Will provides choices, allows decision-making and enhances the Sapien's ability to have some semblance of control over its own destiny during an LC. Even though, most Sapiens' actions generally conform to existing societal standards, which allows for maximum development within certain accepted constraints.

Free Will is at odds with both Determinism and Randomness. If Free Will exists, then Determinism cannot. And if Free Will exists, then Randomness has very little impact. Consequently, if Determinism and/or Randomness exist, then Free Will is no longer viable.

The principle of Free Will has certain intrinsic ramifications in terms of science, religion and society. In the scientific world, Free Will can only exist if it conforms to a myriad of scientific precepts. In religion, Free Will presupposes that an individual's will, including freedom of choice, can only coexist with divine intervention. In society, Free Will implies individual actions, for which the Sapien should be held accountable.

Staunch Free Will advocates are at odds with ardent Determinism followers, calling it the Incompatibilism precept. Both groups believe that their position is logically incompatible with the other. And the Randomness folks believe the other two are incompatible with them. Who's right? Well, they all are right to some degree, if you consider *The ILC Theory* and Intergyism.

However in a pre-Intergyism world, Determinism, Randomness and Free Will are mutually exclusive. Why is it all or nothing, when discussing evolutionary theories? Free Will can't exist if everything is random, so Free Will has no impact. Determinism has no place for Free Will, since everything is pre-determined.

Intergyism: As it turns out, *The Intelligent LifeCycle Theory* does incorporate attributes from all three popularized concepts and makes sense of it all. *Intergyism* (intelligent energy-ism) is *The ILC Theory* term for a more comprehensive approach to evolution. It is an advanced doctrine of life that allows for a more dynamic and fluid environment, in which Sapiens can develop throughout eternity.

Theoretically, LifeCycle journeys are pre-determined exclusive of a Sapien's input. A Sapien has no direct influence over LC assignments. So Determinism exists. Randomness is included, because of the SH Factor, which is always with us. And Free Will allows a Sapien the ability to develop ICTs and learn from LiveTimes, thereby enhancing prospects for future LCs.

The Theory expands the scope of intelligent life beyond Earth. Its assumptions, specifically character traits, are expected to be similar to those of other intelligent worlds throughout the universe and possibly across other universes as well.

As you contemplate the origin of intelligence in the universe, you must seriously consider infinity. When, where, how and why did intelligent life begin, trillions and trillions of years ago? Why does Determinism, Randomness and Free Will play the roles they play in the intrinsic evolution of intelligent life in the universe? I suspect this is how it's always been done, since infinity, and will probably continue to infinity.

The Intelligent LifeCycle Theory

Parental Overlay Module

The Parental Overlay Module (POM) is a critical component of the Sapien core. It includes key ICT and IM ratings of both current LC parents, which was the basis for the Sapien selection during any given LC. This accounts for 20 percent of a Sapien's overall SQ.

Beginning with birth, regardless of the method of conception, whether it be from good old fashion sexual procreation, artificial insemination or in vitro fertilization, the parental overlay is pivotal to the Sapien selection process. Once the fetus successfully grows its Sapien-BrainBridge, the POM in the fetus' temporary energy field, generates its Sapien Request Order (SRO). The parental overlay's SRO specifies certain ICT and IM minimum levels via the UENet.

Once the SRO is received by the appropriate subHalo, Sapien selection begins with comparisons of POM requirements to those of current Sapiens in RestTime. Fortunately, the subHalo Sapien selection process accurately matches ICT/IM requests, within certain margins and within required time frames. And the vast majority of the time, the end result is a Sapien with very similar traits to those of the parents.

To conform to SRO specifications, Sapiens selected generally meet the minimum parental overlay requirements with matches or near-matches. The child Sapien grows up exhibiting traits similar to those of its parents. That is why there are so many similarities between child and parent, both physically and mentally. Occasionally however, the timing may not allow the luxury of waiting for a near match between the child and the parents.

Here's a what if. What happens when an ICT/IM mismatch occurs, sending a high ICT/IM Sapien to parents with low ICT/IMs? Does that reduce a Sapien's SQ during this LC, since its parental overlay contributes 20 percent to the Sapien's score? Yes and no.

It can go either way. It depends on the Sapien. If the Sapien is timid and acquiesces, allowing the lower-level parental overlay to affect its words and actions, then yes, it could negatively affect a Sapien's current growth rate and SQ rating.

However, if a Sapien is developed enough in certain ICTs such as confidence, compassion and understanding, then the above average Sapien with below average parents may actually benefit from the disparity in such a unique symbiotic relationship. The Sapien may be exposed to ICT events he or she may not have been exposed to under normal circumstances. This could result in the Sapien enhancing ICTs that might not be addressed otherwise.

Even with mismatches, the parents are of course ultimately responsible for raising and maturing their little Sapiens, as they evolve and adapt to the inherent growth cycles of their host bodies. During this growth period, the Sapien's ICTs are adjusting to his or her new LifeCycle constraints, and adapting accordingly, as the body develops and begins to mature. Needless to say, parents can have a special impact on their little Sapien's growth, hopefully more positive than negative.

If Sapien selection is considered the first phase of a Sapien's new LC, then parenting should be considered the second phase of a Sapien's development during an LC. It is a critical function in *The ILC Theory*.

Depending on the methods used, or lack thereof, parents can help their little Sapiens, just as they were helped by their parents, when they too were once little Sapiens themselves. Remember, your little Sapiens will generally have similar ICTs and IMs to yours, but they still need the fermentation process you can provide during their growth years, as they adapt to their new surroundings in their new LifeCycles.

The parental overlay includes ICT and IM traits from the parents. But most parental characteristics that are passed on to the child are physical. In reference to heritage and family bloodlines, the Sapien is not affected to any great degree by its parental overlay's previous LCs. Lineage from a family tree in the physical world has little impact on a Sapien's recurring LifeCycles.

Say you traced your heritage back seven hundred years to the 1300s. That is great. It may be good for a few *ooohs and ahhhs* at cocktail parties, but in reality, it is relatively meaningless. In the long run and the short run, family heritage has little if any effect on any aspect of a Sapien's LiveTimes. It is just the way the physical gene evolves. Each LC is different and unique, and each LC has its own family tree. You will have a new family tree next time.

If you are adopted, or if you have foster parents or no parents, you may feel like you are missing out on something that others sometimes take for granted, the extended family. It is certainly easier to say than do, but don't worry about it, just make your LC work for you.

Even though your parents were not there to guide you when you were young, your Sapien is still the same as it was when you were born, maybe even better now that you have many ICT events under your belt. Your parental units provided their service by bringing you into the world. But do not feel alone because you have no biological parents to lean on. There is not much room in a LifeCycle for an identity crisis. You are your own Sapien.

Think of the positive ICT events that you had in orphanages and/or foster homes that helped shape your ICTs. Seriously. In fact, that seemingly disconnected environment may have directly and indirectly offered more character-building events than other Sapiens' LCs.

The parental overlay component of a Sapien's core is always present in each LC, as a natural result of the humanoid reproduction process. When an LC terminates, the Sapien retains its parental overlay until rejuvenation and prepping in the subHalo, just before the next LC. Before the Sapien transfers to the new LC, its Parental Overlay Module is reset to zero to accommodate the new parental overlay in the new LC prior to birth.

Regression & Hypnosis

Past-life regression sessions, as therapy, have been developed since the 1950s by psychologists, psychiatrists and mediums. Some were and are credentialed, many are not.

Past-life regressions are used with various levels of hypnosis to produce a semi-hypnotic or hypnotic state in a subject to recall what are thought to be memories of past lives or previous incarnations. Techniques used during past-life regression involve the subject, while in a semi-hypnotic state, answering a series of questions that may reveal identities and events of past lives

Regressions can accomplish a number of positive results for the regressee. Traditionally, regressions were used in a spiritual setting. They have also been used in psychotherapy. Past-life regressions by definition imply that reincarnation exists.

Inferences to past-life regressions can be found as early as 200 BC in the Hindu religion in India. Hindus thought the soul was under real pressure that was created by the aggregate effect of past-life images on a person's karma.

Regression memories contain just enough fact to accurately describe a previous life, but with enough fiction to make it interesting. There are some who regard such things as fantasies or delusions.

ILC Logic: Sapiens who consider regressions as fantasy may not have had enough LifeCycles yet to fully understand the possibilities and ramifications of such memories, but that is alright. That is just where they are in their own LifeCycle development. They will grow out of it, maybe not in this LC, but they will evolve.

Past-life memories might be construed as a form of extra sensory perception (ESP), mental telepathy or some other type of unexplained mystery. Past-life regression studies are considered a pseudoscience by skeptics on a good day. The beliefs of many regression supporters can best be described as reincarnation-lite. They believe reincarnation exists, but have no thoughts as to how, why, when or where it occurs.

Stories of past-life regressions are sometimes unintentionally distorted by either the regressee or the regressor. Past-life recollections that get media attention are those where the subject claims to have been a famous person in a previous life, such as the woman, who believes she was Cleopatra. Not sure, but I think there have been several women claiming the Cleopatra heritage. Now that is not to imply the woman was not Cleopatra. Someone alive today may have been Cleopatra in a previous life. Maybe it was her, maybe not.

At this point in our acceptance of recurring lives as a society, or should I say our lack of acceptance, the chances for some regular Joe to have been Napoleon in a past life are relatively small. Nothing negative about Joe, but if he believed in reincarnation and past lives, he would be in the minority of Sapiens alive today. Add to that possibility, the remote chance that Joe actually located that specific past life in a regression session, and he actually was Napoleon in his LC Registry.

For that combination to be present in the same person in today's socioeconomic climate, out of the billions of combinations possible, would be a stretch. However, anything is possible in *The Intelligent*

LifeCycle. And after all just like Cleopatra, someone alive today may have been Napoleon.

The phrase *may have been* is used, because the Sapiens who actually were Cleopatra and Napoleon may still be in the MilkyWay subHalo during an extended RestTime. Or they may be on another intelligent planet in another galaxy by now, even though that is a much lower probability, since most LCs usually re-occur on the same planet.

The fact is the vast majority of our previous LifeCycles were average lives, without much fanfare or documentation to prove our previous existences. Even so, it is still extremely interesting to find out about our previous LCs. After all they are a part of our past, and they have undeniably shaped our individual futures.

Past life information is located in the Sapien's LifeCycle registry, deep inside the Sapien's core, and is not easily accessible by the Sapien. In order for a Sapien to access these files and remember previous LCs, he or she must undergo a regression session through some form of hypnosis.

To have access to the Sapien's LC registry, the Sapien must shut down all other programs and applications running in its brain. With all sensory perceptions and subconscious routines quieted during the regression, all energies can then be focused entirely on retrieving previous LifeCycle data files. Some of the LC files may also include what we call today an audio/video attachment, representative of the Sapien's LC.

During regression, after establishing the identity of the Sapien in a specific LifeCycle, gained from the subconscious LC registry, the question and answer period begins. At this point, the Sapien can recall whatever stored information is available about the LC, but probably not as much detail as sometimes is embellished during the session.

Only important ICT events that encapsulate the essence of an LC are stored, primarily because of storage capacity limitations within the Sapien's core. Detailed descriptions, beyond the stored data, are a result of the person embellishing a scene or incident through personal experience, media influence and/or regressor influence.

The odds are significantly against being able to recall insignificant details of previous LCs. Memory retention is the first consideration. The Sapien does not have the memory available to recall very much detail about one previous life, much less multiple previous lives.

Even though the brain may have storage capacities needed for this, that particular brain was not present in any of the previous lives. And just as important, previous life details might conflict with current life realities and cause confusion and conflicting ICT inferences during this LC, if they were remembered. Sorry, but that's the reality of life.

As the regression continues, questions about activities, sights and sounds help define a Sapien's LC and his or her perceptions of it. The final question following each LifeCycle in many regression sessions is, "What did you learn from this life?" By asking this question, it implies there has been an improvement in an ICT, as a result of the LC. Sound familiar?

However brief it may be, the information available in the LifeCycle registry is in fact a permanent record of our LCs. However, embellishment of that information does sometimes occur for the reasons mentioned, resulting in more detail than is recorded in the registry. It may make for good entertainment though.

It has been shown is a few studies that participants able to recall any detail at all about previous lives are those that already believe in reincarnation. That may be true, in certain cases, because those who are open to the concept of reincarnation may be more willing to allow access to their LC Registry. Reincarnation research is a recognized form of parapsychology.

The Intelligent LifeCycle Theory

Re-Indexing The Brain

The human brain is probably the most sophisticated technology known to man. And despite the many years of man's attempts to replicate its functionality and capability with today's modern computers, we have yet to even come close to replicating the brain's true power and innate storage capacities.

The brain controls all of the human body's functions with electrical impulses that activate its organs, limbs, bodily functions and of course, multi-media memory. The memory portion of the brain is perhaps the largest single storage device ever conceived, with virtually unlimited capacity, certainly in the trillions of terabytes of data.

All our memories are stored across multiple brain modules, or nodes. Everything we've ever done, said or experienced during our body's time on earth, from womb to tomb, is saved in our brain's memory.

All of our lifetime experiences are stored, from eating ice cream at the neighborhood drug store at the age of eight, to driving vehicles at high rates of speed as a young adult, to cramming for a physics final in college, to all of the average mundane things we do every day. All of these memories are stored in the brain for recall in vivid color, complex data calculations and streaming audio/video-like files.

Everything is stored there, and I mean *everything*, as evidenced when one day you suddenly remember something that happened perhaps decades before, and it is just as real as if it happened the day before. The memory portion of the brain (both short and long term memory) and the recall process are analogous to a massive database available to the user, the Sapien occupant of the body.

The storage cells that contain all this information are not necessarily contiguous in the storage/memory area. As new experiences occur daily, the new multi-media information is stored in the next available space, and therein lies the problem.

As in any database, there are pointers that guide the user to particular pieces of information, when a request/query is made. And as with any database, the storage of data becomes convoluted and more difficult to retrieve/recall as new data is continually stored requiring more pointers to handle searches to locate and retrieve it.

Think of it as a Table of Contents (TOC) or index in a book, with information possibly organized by chronological dates, type of activity, people, places, things, sensory delineations, and many more categories, or any combination thereof. In the case of the human brain's memory database, it is definitely a perpetual work in progress (as long as you're alive). It must accommodate a myriad of new memory entries on a daily basis, thus continually corrupting the normal hierarchy of storage.

When a computer database begins to experience a degradation in performance, the time required to complete a query increases. The database must be reindexed or reorganized to its original hierarchy as much as possible to restore and regain its performance.

By reindexing the database, all data is reorganized in more effective groups, thus eliminating much of the older pointers and improving the search results. Databases today may be reindexed periodically on a regularly scheduled basis to maintain performance. The larger the database, the more frequent reindexing is required. Today, we have database systems that continually reindex in real time.

With the brain's memory when you attempt data retrieval of a certain memory, you are directed to go to a certain cell in memory, as a page in the book's TOC analogy. Correlations with the Internet may even be more applicable.

When you get to the page you requested, you may be sent to subsequent pages for more information on the topic that has been stored, since the original TOC was designed. Then you might be directed to other pages for more entries relevant to the same topic that were stored even later than that. Think in terms of searching a term on *Wikipedia* and all those additional links to follow for more information on the term. It's like that.

In this scenario, the brain follows the pointers until the desired data is found. For example, you might wish to remember a person's name from years ago. In the TOC, your brain might first look under the people category and follow the pointer to the page listing men and women, page 83 for example. If it's a man's name, your brain may give you another pointer leading to an expanded list of males you have met, known, or heard of, say page 192.

When you get to page 192, you may get another pointer that tells you to go to page 2,276 for names of American men you have met. Then page 2,276 may provide another pointer leading you to another page with a list of men you have met organized by decade. And finally you find the correct entry.

When your brain is at its peak during early adulthood, this whole process may only take a few seconds. It is done with speeds far surpassing current data transmission rates as we know them, probably more closely approximating the speed of light or even beyond.

However the older a person gets, the more data has to be searched and the more pointers are required to find the desired name, probably exponentially. The older your brain is in biological years, the longer it takes to navigate through all the pointers that have been added over the years. An older brain may finally remember the man's name, when pointed to page 2,895,521. This could easily attribute to the lengthy time required to remember things. It may take an hour, a day or even a week or longer.

When the desired data is finally located and retrieved, it may suddenly pop into your current memory, interrupting all other functions of the brain, when you verbally exclaim, "That's it, that's him, John Jones." Of course, other people around you may not have a clue as to your sudden burst of knowledge.

The older a person gets, the more demand is placed on the memory database for information retrieval, as a result of the voluminous amounts of data that is absorbed (input) into RAM, RAM-X and permanent storage. The more data that accumulates daily on top of all the existing data from past experiences (during current LC only), the more difficult it is to recall specific memories. Because of the increased number of pointers required to lead the brain to retrieve specific pieces of an image or experience, it will naturally take longer to successfully retrieve the memory.

The older a person gets, the longer it takes to remember things, to the point that one day, you may legitimately say, "I think I'm beginning to lose my memory." I know it will feel like you are actually losing your memory, but not so. All your memories are still there intact, you are just losing your ability to retrieve them. Unless, we can develop a method to *Reindex the Brain*.

Think of your brain as the computer that runs your physical body. Your Sapien is analogous to your computer's operating system, which runs the brain's memory database in background, 24/7. The memory function of the brain resembles a highly sophisticated database management system, let's call it the Memory Management System (MMS) with the following components:

> **Memory Management System: MMS**
> *Component, Activity and IT Device Equivalency:*
>
> ***Current Memory:*** RAM (Random Access Memory, chip storage, multiple terabytes) records and stores everything you see, hear and do, 24/7. During the day, this storage function copies everything to RAM-X. When you sleep, it finishes that day's memory transfers, clears memory and shuts down. When you awake, current memory is clear and ready to start recording a new day.
>
> ***Short-Term Memory:*** RAM-X (Expanded Current Memory, dedicated online disk storage, multi-terabytes) stores memory data for a short period of time, one week, maybe one month depending on the actual configuration and capacity of the physical brain modules.
>
> ***Long-Term Memory:*** As memories reach their shelf life in short-term memory, data is transferred to a larger disk array with less bandwidth, but readily available upon memory recall.
>
> ***Archiving Data:*** Data is constantly being transferred and archived to and from RAM and RAM-X to permanent offline storage. In older technologies, this function would be equivalent to offline magnetic tape storage.
>
> ***Data Retrieval:*** The MMS interfaces with the Sapien's Intelligence Module (IM), which enhances or diminishes the speed and accuracy of memory retrieval.

Over time a massive database, such as the brain, will out of necessity add increasing numbers of pointers to index massive amounts of new data as required. Most computer database systems must be reindexed periodically to eliminate excessive amounts of pointers and thereby improving performance. The brain as we know it does not do this.

There is also a physical component that could be repaired to improve the memory function. In some cases, the connection between RAM, RAM-X and permanent storage may get damaged (wires get cut). This seems to be the area most commonly being studied, since there may be a surgical solution. When this disconnect occurs, memory database pointers become less than manageable between RAM and disk storage. Older memories are still available, but maybe not as accessible. As RAM fills up and can no longer be transferred/archived, short term memory loss can occur.

Since the brain's database cannot be reindexed with today's technology, the disconnect between RAM, RAM-X and long-term storage may become permanent. When short term memory gets full and can no longer transfer to permanent storage, short term memory will suffer. When this occurs, the brain no longer spends time searching in Current and Short Term Memory, but instead searches in older, long-term memory areas. This could account for a person being able to remember things easily from years before, but not something that happened just yesterday.

I suspect this is one of the main issues facing scientists and medical researchers as they continue their efforts to find a cure for a variety of mental disorders. Re-indexing the brain could possibly eliminate memory loss, dementia and Alzheimer's, or at least enhance the prospects of memory recall.

As a layman, a non-scientist, I can only speculate on possible methods required to physically reindex the brain. Possibly some form of tetroshock therapy (way more advanced than electroshock) could be utilized to reindex the brain, and/or mend broken circuits between RAM, RAM-X and permanent storage. And as in any application using such therapy, safeguards would need to be used to minimize any impact on the Sapien itself. Keep in mind, all of a person's experiences are still stored in the brain's memory cells, but may not be accessible without reindexing or surgery.

As we increase our technological gains and apply new discoveries to the repair and/or replacement of physical body parts and organs, someday we may live for hundreds of years. We've already made significant progress on this front with heart and kidney transplants, artificial limbs, enhanced internal medicine gains and other medical procedures.

This, along with our nutritional learning curve, has already increased our average life expectancy on Earth from the mid fifties in the early twentieth century to today's average of seventy plus years. Since the Sapien is a perpetual entity, it can survive in LiveTime as long as the body can support life. To make Re-Indexing the Brain a reality, the probability is that Earth will need to make the advancement to at least a C5 or C6 IP.

The Intelligent LifeCycle Theory

Research References

The ILC project relied on many information sources during research for this book. They all were, and are, highly useful. The following sources were used during *ILC Theory* research. Thank you.

http://ahdictionary.com/   http://www.merriam-webster.com/

http://www.collinslanguage.com/english-dictionaries-thesauruses/

http://thesaurus.com/

http://www.thefreedictionary.com/

http://www.google.com/

http://education.yahoo.com/

http://www.google.com/earth/

http://www.snopes.com/

http://en.wikipedia.org/wiki/Main_Page

http://en.wikipedia.org/wiki/Wikimedia_Commons

Wikipedia and Wikimedia Commons are freely licensed document and media file repositories, primarily public domain items. They are 100 percent non-profit, and would appreciate any and all donations.

The Intelligent LifeCycle Theory

The Intelligent LifeCycle Theory

The Ten Commandments

The biblical chronology of the Ten Commandments dates back to the days of Moses, around 1527 BC, Exodus 20:1-17. The following is one of the versions we found that seems to directly state the commandments intent.

Ten Commandments

I. You shall have no other gods before me.

II. You shall not make any carved image or likeness of another, and you shall not bow down to them nor serve them. For I, the Lord your God, am a jealous God, showing mercy to those who love Me and keep My commandments.

III. You shall not take the name of the Lord your God in vain, for the Lord will not hold him guiltless who takes His name in vain.

IV. Remember the Sabbath day, to keep it holy. Six days you shall labor and do all your work, but the seventh day is the Sabbath of the Lord your God. For in six days, the Lord made the heavens and the earth, the sea, and all that is in them, and rested the seventh day. The Lord blessed the Sabbath day and hallowed it.

V. Honor your father and your mother, that your days may be long upon the land which the Lord your God is giving you.

VI. You shall not kill, except for reasons of self-defense, capital punishment and war against aggressors attempting to take away your god-given rights to freedom.

VII. You shall not commit adultery.

VIII. You shall not steal.

IX. You shall not bear false witness against your neighbor.

X. You shall not covet your neighbor's house; you shall not covet your neighbor's wife, nor his manservant, nor his maidservant, nor his ox, nor his donkey, nor anything that is your neighbor's.

The Intelligent LifeCycle Theory

The Ten Rules Of Intelligent Life

The Ten Rules of Intelligent Life are fairly self-explanatory. You may wish to interpret them from your own perspective, but I feel confident that anyone with an L4.0 Sapien Rating or higher knows exactly what they mean. And there are a number of parallels between our Ten Rules of Intelligent Life and the Ten Commandments.

Doing the right thing isn't always easy, to say the least. However, if you recognize the value of *The Rules*, and you strive to adhere to them during your life, your LiveTime will be that much more rewarding. And it should enhance prospects for your next LC. These are common rules of behavior that most Sapiens follow instinctively.

ONE
Never intentionally terminate a Sapien's LifeCycle

Explanation: Basically, do not kill anybody, and do not kill yourself. It is a Natural Law of the universe, also espoused by most religions and probably Agnostics and Atheists too, who may not believe in a supreme being, but believe in the sanctity of life.

Prematurely terminating a Sapien's LC (murder or suicide) is not acceptable, a mistake that may take lifetimes to correct. If the goal of intelligent life is to preserve its own evolutionary process, which means allowing all Sapiens sufficient LiveTime to develop, then murder or suicide disrupts the normal process of that goal. Not good.

Disclaimer: Unless early LC termination is done for self-survival under the threat of death, crime prevention, or in wars to protect the freedoms of a race or species.

TWO
Oppose those who attempt to infringe on your inalienable right to freedom

Explanation: Every living thing wants to be free, intelligent beings even more so. This is also a Natural Law of the universe.

Example: They say a flower grown indoors will lean toward the window to get closer to the light for nourishment, but what it is really doing is just trying to get out, to be free.

Disclaimer: Your right to freedom is only an inalienable one, if you work hard to protect it

THREE
Do not lie, cheat or steal

Explanation: Anytime you lie, cheat or steal, you are negatively affecting a number of ICTs of other Sapiens, in addition to your own. Do not do to others that which you would not wish done to you. Bottom line, don't do that.

FOUR
Honor and love your mother and father

Explanation: After all, they gave you this life. They are your Parental Overlay and responsible for your current LifeCycle and are now a part of you and your LC lineage.

FIVE
Treat others with respect

Explanation: Treat others with respect, the way you wish to be treated. It is not always easy, but try.

Disclaimer: Unless they are violators of the first three Rules, in which case, Rule No.5 may be optional.

SIX
Enjoy each day as the special time that it is

<u>Explanation</u>: Since you do not know when this LC will terminate, and you do not know when the next LC will begin, it is up to you to make the most of the LiveTime you get during this life. Your next LC may reoccur within a few years, or may not happen for a hundred years, you just do not know. However, as Earth's birth rate continues, there is a good chance your next LC may reoccur sooner than later.

SEVEN
Always try to do the right thing,

<u>Explanation</u>:   Unless your conscience module is switched off, you know the difference between right and wrong. Always try, and that should apply to everyone. Soyaseetimmy, if you always did the right thing in reality, you'd already be an L9. It is right, to try to do right.

EIGHT
Help other Sapiens, who may be less fortunate, when possible.

<u>Explanation</u>: By helping others, you are giving them a better chance to develop their own ICT set during this LC.

<u>Disclaimer</u>: Donating money to non-profit, top-heavy management organizations may not actually help those in need, proportionate to your contribution. But it may be, as they say, the thought that counts.

NINE
Try to forgive those who negatively transgress on your LC journey

<u>Explanation</u>: Forgiveness is a very positive ICT. As you encounter transgressors, just remember, they are trying to live their LCs too, and

are probably having just as many problems with life as you.

Disclaimer: Unforgiving feelings may seem warranted, if the transgressor destroyed someone or something you loved, but try.

TEN
Always attempt to enhance and positively develop your ICT set

Explanation: Every Sapien during every LC has certain Individual Character Traits that need attention and could use improvement. As you positively enhance your ICTs, it not only helps you in this LC, but it will also hold you in good stead for your next LC, a better life.

Observations

It is interesting to see how many of these rules are being damaged or at least bent on a daily basis by many, who may not know the value of improving their Sapien's ICT levels. These Rules cover a broad spectrum of ICTs innate in each of us. They are good, moral rules that benefit all Sapiens. And don't take it so seriously, have some fun.

There are good Sapiens and evil Sapiens. Fortunately, the majority of Sapiens are relatively positive. Even so, sometimes good people get caught up in life during their current LC, and do things detrimental to the ICT development of themselves and others. Try not to do that.

Movie Quote: "The A-Team", 2010, Liam Neeson, Bradley Cooper. The beautiful female department of defense agent accuses a CIA agent of not following the rules, or better yet, not having any rules. The agent responds, "CIA's got rules. They're just cooler than yours."

ILC Theory Terminology

ILC Term	**Definition**
ADP	Attention Deficit Personality
Advanced Sapiens	L8s, L9s and L10s
C4 Stretch	Period in a C4-IP LifeCycle, when an IP has a high net Sapien growth rate as births far exceed deaths. Sapien growth augmented by Sapien transfers from less developed IPs.
CNCC	Central NanoCell Control Module
CORE	Concentric Octahedral Residual Energy
Dark tetra matter	One trillionth the mass of dark matter
DA Sapien	Dumb*ss Sapien, stupidity level
HALO	Holistically Assured Lifecycle Oasis, home base for all L8s to L10s, one per universe
HIT	Halo Intervention Transfer for L8/L9 LCs
ICT	Individual Character Trait
ICT Event	Live, experiential situation during LC
IEF	Intelligent Energy Field (Sapien/soul)
IEF L Rating	Sapien developmental levels, L1.0 to L10.0
ILC	Intelligent LifeCycle
ILC Theory	Evolution and perpetuation of intelligent life in the universe, infinity on steroids
IM	Intelligence Module (IQ equivalent)

The Intelligent LifeCycle Theory

Intergy	Intelligent Energy
IPs	Intelligent Planets (not Internet Protocol)
IP Index	IP Rating, average IP Sapien level times 100
ISAT	Individual Sapien Analysis Testing
L10 Sapien	Extremely rare Sapien, god status
L9 Sapien	Very rare Sapiens, angel status
L9IC	L9 Sapien in charge of subHalo
L8 Sapiens	Rare Sapiens, wisdom status
L1 to L7 Sapiens	Sapiens under development
LC1	Sapien's first LifeCycle, activated from L0.0 status to L1.0, generally on C1 to C2 IPs
LCs	LifeCycles, Sapien LiveTimes or Cycles
LELE	Life Extinction Level Event, death of a planet as a life-supporting planetary host
LiveTime	Sapien time in a host body during an LC
NanoCell	One billionth of a cell
Nfinitoid	Holistic entity encompassing all intelligent life in the universe with no beginning and no end, but with a definitive scope
OCP	Obsessive Compulsive Personality
OSD	One Shot Deal, traditional religious belief
PLC	Planetary Life Cycle
POM	Parental Overlay Module
Quantifiable Infinity	The ability to measure an Nfinitoid

The Intelligent LifeCycle Theory

Relative Subjectivity	Decisions based on LiveTime experiences
Rejuvied	Sapien rejuvenation before each LC
Rest Time	Sapien time spent in subHalo between LCs
Rotating Ls	L8s and L9s rotating in and out of Halo and subHalo administrative assignments
Roving Ls	L8s and L9s available for HITs, generally within the constraints of specific galaxies
SAP	Sapien Abrogation Pit, subHalo section equivalent to hell, for Sapiens with many LCs but who remain extremely low in SQ
SAPIEN	Standard Astrologically Perpetuating Intelligent Energy Nucleoid (Sapien/Soul)
Sapien-BrainBridge	SBB, the Bridge is the tetrical interface between Sapien and brain, transceiving ICT/IM data
Sapien Grab	Sapiens absorbed in a subHalo en masse, following a LELE
Sapien Index	An IP's average IEF level times 100
SER	Sapien Exit Request
SH Factor	Sh*t Happens component to randomness
SQ	Sapien Quotient, ISAT score times 100
SRO	Sapien Request Order (non-oxymoronic)
StarSpeed	One trillion times the speed of light
subHalo	Regional/Galactic Halos
subUENet	UENet nodes servicing individual galaxies

Superverse	Universe of universes (10^{11} universes)
TDW	Time Dimension Warp between 2 universes
TetraCell	One trillionth of a cell
Tetrazyme	One trillionth of an enzyme
Tetrical Ionic Charge	One trillion times an electrical charge
Tetricity	One trillion times the capacity of electricity
Tetronic Charge	Tetrical ionic charge unique to each Sapien
Tetroshock Therapy	Way past electroshock therapy
UEF	Universal Energy Field (Halo)
UENet	Universal Energy Network

www.ingramcontent.com/pod-product-compliance
Lightning Source LLC
Chambersburg PA
CBHW071655170426
43195CB00039B/2199